PRENTICE HALL
HISTORY OF MUSIC SERIES
H. WILEY HITCHCOCK, editor

MUSIC IN MEDIEVAL EUROPE, *Jeremy Yudkin*
MUSIC IN THE RENAISSANCE, *Howard M. Brown*
BAROQUE MUSIC, 3RD ED., *Claude V. Palisca*
MUSIC IN THE CLASSIC PERIOD, 3RD ED., *Reinhard G. Pauly*
NINETEENTH-CENTURY ROMANTICISM IN MUSIC, 3RD ED., *Rey M. Longyear*
TWENTIETH-CENTURY MUSIC: AN INTRODUCTION, 3RD ED., *Eric Salzman*
FOLK AND TRADITIONAL MUSIC OF THE WESTERN CONTINENTS, 3RD ED., *Bruno Nettl*
MUSIC CULTURES OF THE PACIFIC, THE NEAR EAST, AND ASIA, 3RD ED., *William P. Malm*
MUSIC IN THE UNITED STATES: A HISTORICAL INTRODUCTION, 3RD ED., *H. Wiley Hitchcock*

third edition

MUSIC CULTURES OF THE PACIFIC, THE NEAR EAST, AND ASIA

William P. Malm

Prentice Hall, Upper Saddle River, New Jersey 07458

Malm, William P.
Music cultures of the Pacific, the Near East, and Asia / William P. Malm.— 3rd ed.
p. cm.—(Prentice-Hall history of music series)
Includes bibliographical references, discographies, and index.
ISBN 0-13-182387-6
1. Music—Asia—History and criticism. 2. Music—Oceania—History and criticism. I. Title. II. Series.
ML330.M3 1996
780'.95—dc20

94-48578
CIP
MN

Editorial/production supervision: *Harriet Tellem/Margaret Antonini*
Acquisitions editor: *Bud Therien*
Buyer: *Robert Anderson*

Simon & Schuster/A Viacom Company
Upper Saddle River, New Jersey 07458

Printed in the United States of America
10 9 8 7 6 5 4 3 2 1

ISBN 0-13-182387-6

Prentice-Hall International (UK) Limited, *London*
Prentice-Hall of Australia Pty. Limited, *Sydney*
Prentice-Hall Canada Inc., *Toronto*
Prentice-Hall Hispanoamericana, S.A., *Mexico*
Prentice-Hall of India Private Limited, *New Delhi*
Prentice-Hall of Japan, Inc., *Tokyo*
Simon & Schuster Asia Pte. Ltd., *Singapore*
Editora Prentice-Hall do Brasil, Ltda., *Rio de Janeiro*

CONTENTS

FOREWORD

Students and informed amateurs of the history of music have long needed a series of books that are comprehensive, authoritative, and engagingly written. They have needed books written by specialists—but specialists interested in communicating vividly. The Prentice Hall History of Music Series aims at filling these needs.

Six books in the series present a panoramic view of the history of Western music, divided among the major historical periods—Medieval, Renaissance, Baroque, Classic, Romantic, and Contemporary. The musical culture of the United States, viewed historically as an independent development within the larger Western tradition, is discussed in a separate book. The rich folk and traditional music of the Western hemisphere and the rest of the world are treated in two volumes, and the nine volumes of the series are a distinctive and, we hope, distinguished contribution to the history of the music of the world's peoples. Each volume, moreover, may be read singly as a substantial account of the music of its period or area.

The authors of the series are scholars of national and international repute—musicologists, critics, and teachers of acknowledged stature in their respective fields of specialization. In their contributions to the Prentice Hall History of Music Series their goal has been to present works of solid scholarship that are eminently readable, with significant insights into music as a part of the general intellectual and cultural life of human societies.

H. WILEY HITCHCOCK, *Editor*

PREFACE

The purpose of this book is to survey the basic kinds of music and musical instruments found in the major Oriental civilizations and in the island cultures of the Eastern Hemisphere. It also is intended as an introduction to the basic attitudes, techniques, and nomenclature of the discipline of ethnomusicology. These two goals are commingled, so that reading a given chapter provides preliminary information about the musical ways of one part of the world, whereas reading the entire book gives one an overview of the continuities and uniqueness in non-Western music, as well as a basic vocabulary with which to discuss music from any part of the world. Those general concepts not discussed in this book appear in Bruno Nettl's companion volume, *Folk and Traditional Music of the Western Continents,* in this series.

Many musics from dozens of cultures and countries have been crowded into the following seven chapters. The chapters themselves are based primarily on geographic areas, but cultural cross-references are found both in the text and the index. The updated selected list of audiovisual materials at the end of each chapter provides the reader with a channel to some of the sounds of the sonic events discussed, but it must be remembered that only a small part of the total musical effect can be ascertained by listening to the recordings of music in the book, other recordings, or even video tapes. Where possible, background information has been provided and vocal examples include both the romanization and the meaning of the text. It should be noted that the field of ethnomusicology has grown so rapidly since the second edition of this book (1977) that even these brief area surveys and materials lists have had to be done over almost completely. The book map continues to help the reader locate unfamiliar places mentioned in the text. The geographic and cultural regions surveyed in this book represent a majority of the world, so not every genre and music-related word in the myriad languages and dialects of our areas can be discussed. I apologize to all the performers of music or musical instruments that are not mentioned. The topic and term selections are based on my pedagogical goal: to provide basic methods and materials for world music studies with examples from areas found in the title of this book.

I use four basic approaches here: the anthropological, historical, organological, and musical. The anthropologist or behavioral musicologist looks at the place of music in culture, at the values a society attaches to it, and at the people who practice it. Historical musicology will be applied most often in literate societies such as those of India and China where historical periods and theoretical constructs were well established long before the monkish scholars of Europe "invented" the bases of Western art music. Archaeology will also help us in the reconstruction of historical data from destroyed civilizations as well as nonliterate societies. However, although the legends of the ancient and tribal worlds have some use to musicology, potsherds and burial mounds do not give the historical musicologist much to work with. They may prove useful, nevertheless, to the organologist, the student of the history and development of musical instruments.

Organology is important to this book, for many times the only information available in an area is a description of its instruments. Such details tell us only a little about the actual music. When coupled with similar information from other areas, however, they can prove useful for studying possible diffusions of musics throughout the world. They also prepare readers for what they should expect should they visit a given area in search of traditional music. The excellent line drawings throughout the book are of great help in furthering these organological goals.

The first-edition drawings were done by Masakazu Kuwata (Figures 2, 5, 7, 9–15, 18, 22, 24–25, 27–32, 34, 36, 39–44, 46–47, 49–51, 53, 55–56, 59–77) and new drawings for the second edition were by Elizabeth McGregor (Figures 1, 8, 16, 17, 45, 69, 70, 71, and 78) were done Elizabeth McGregor. Special thanks are due to Robin Wilt, who enriches the third edition with eighteen fine new illustrations (Figures 3, 4, 6, 19, 20, 21, 23, 26, 33, 35, 37–40, 48, 54, 57, and 58). Ms. Wilt met technically challenging assignments with skill and imagination. Her additions make it possible to discuss many cultural and organological points that mere description cannot provide. Human figures have been added whenever possible not only to illustrate crucial playing positions but also to give a sense of instrument sizes. General measurements have been added to the titles of all instrument pictures that do not have a human in them. These measurements are based on research and on examples from the Stearns Collection of Musical Instruments of the University of Michigan. Most instruments cited in this book come in several sizes, but the use of measurements or performers plus sincere attempts to balance proportions of figures in each plate are meant to alleviate the chronic problem of illustrating the vast world of musical instruments with single pictures.

Whenever and wherever possible, we have been product musicologists; that is, we have looked directly at the musical sounds and tried to find out where they come from, how they make sense, and how one can learn to appreciate them. It is axiomatic that all musics do make sense, for they always consist of the disciplining of tones according to the aesthetic criteria of their particular time and culture. An understanding of such musical logics is the basic goal of this book.

Two major problems in preparing this book were transliteration and transcription. Most of the indigenous terms and instrument names mentioned are derived from languages that have more than one form of romanization. In general I adopt choices of *The New Grove Dictionary of Musical Instruments*, ed. Stanley Sadie (New York: Macmillan Press, 1984) or opinions of regional experts when available. I do not claim any linguistic consistency. Common alternate spellings and other names are shown in parentheses. A new approach to this old problem is the sonic glossary/index that has been included in the book cassette. On this are found all non-western terms, spoken by a native or qualified speaker in the dialect form known to that person. This long overdue teaching and reading aid is made possible primarily by the kind participation of the international community at the University of Michigan. Special thanks to James Bixler who recorded and edited over seven hundred words in some thirty different languages.

Transcriptions of non-Western music in Western-style notation always create some form of distortion. To aid the reader in evoking the proper non-Western sounds I have, whenever possible, provided a cassette of the examples transcribed or discussed in the text. Complete pieces can usually be heard on the commercial recordings from which the example was derived. Complete citations are given in the caption of each example. Thanks to those record companies and field collectors who have so kindly cooperated, readers may use the transcriptions as guidelines and correct their inadequacies by ear. Unless otherwise noted, the transcriptions are the author's own.

Special notational symbols are as follows: (↑) a pitch higher than notated; (↓) a pitch lower than notated; (◡) a time slightly shorter than notated; (⁄) or (╲) a sliding entrance to or exit from a note; and (♫) a series of pitches, with a slide from one to another. A note in parentheses is one that is barely heard. If the transcription is transposed, the approximate original pitch is shown at the beginning in parentheses. Any special symbols beyond these are explained in the examples using them. The examples are meant not only to illustrate specific points in the text but also to provide a variety of types for further analysis or discussion. In this context the third edition has added an etic/emic comparison (Example 1–2) and an Ainu canon (Example 7–13).

This book surveys music from a majority of the world's population and non-Western cultures and languages. No one person can be an expert in such a topic. Thus, I have depended on the writings and opinions of professional friends and critics. Previous editions credit many colleagues, some now gone, who made my initial efforts possible. I have credited additional help for this edition in the footnotes. The editorial staff of Prentice Hall deserves special thanks for their work with a complex and error-ridden manuscript.

Finally, I thank those scholars who were willing to give advice but preferred not to have their names connected with a book in which one author attempts to cover such a vast musical topic in such a few pages. The information and judgments of this book are the author's own responsibility and do not necessarily reflect those of advisors, assistants, or supporting institutions named or unnamed. My hope is that the reader may find in this book a means to a broader understanding of music as a beautiful but often very different worldwide phenomenon.

W.P.M.

LIST OF PLATES

LIST OF MUSICAL EXAMPLES AND CASSETTE CONTENTS

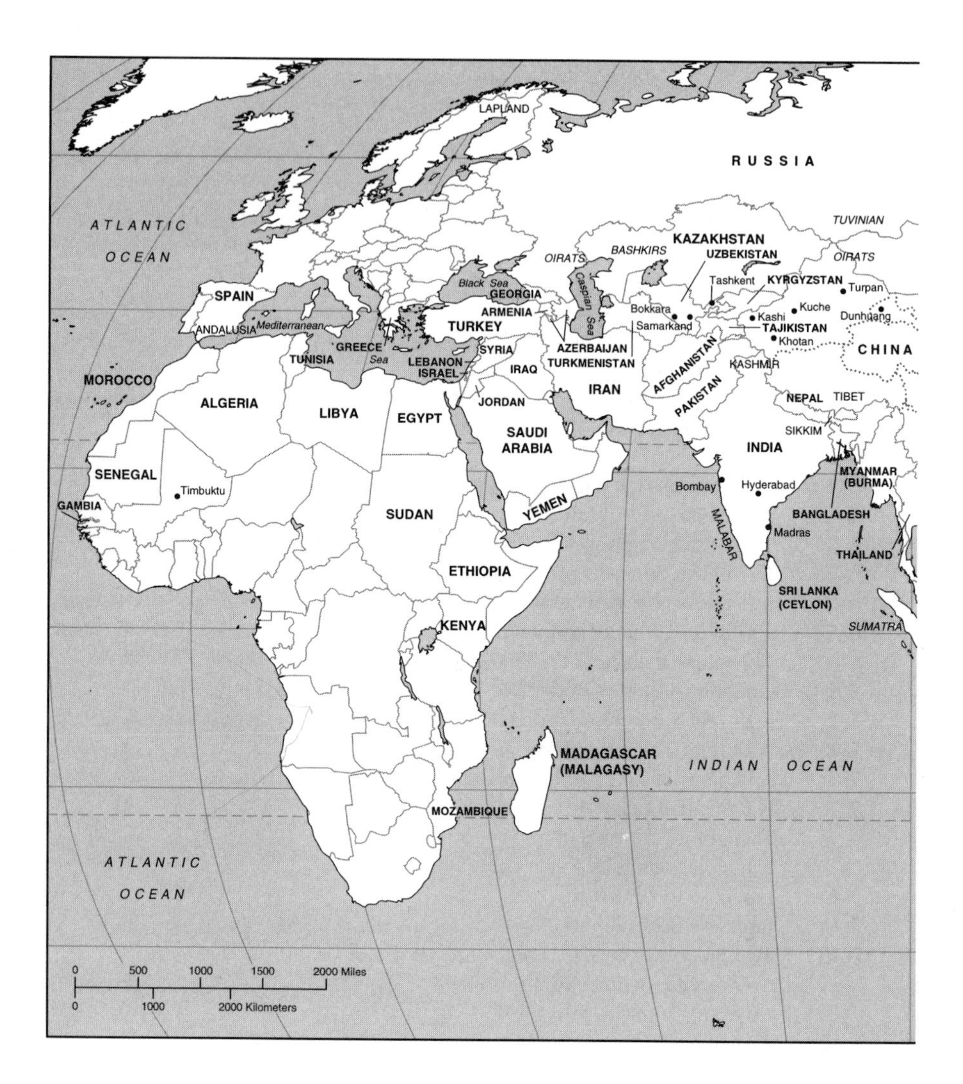
LAPLAND
RUSSIA
ATLANTIC OCEAN
TUVINIAN
KAZAKHSTAN
BASHKIRS
OIRATS
UZBEKISTAN
OIRATS
Caspian Sea
Tashkent
KYRGYZSTAN
Turpan
Black Sea
GEORGIA
SPAIN
Bokkara
Kuche
ARMENIA
Samarkand
Kashi
Dunhuang
ANDALUSIA
Mediterranean
TURKEY
TAJIKISTAN
Khotan
GREECE
AZERBAIJAN
CHINA
TUNISIA
Sea
LEBANON
SYRIA
TURKMENISTAN
KASHMIR
ISRAEL
IRAQ
AFGHANISTAN
MOROCCO
IRAN
PAKISTAN
JORDAN
NEPAL
TIBET
ALGERIA
LIBYA
EGYPT
SAUDI ARABIA
SIKKIM
INDIA
SENEGAL
MYANMAR (BURMA)
Timbuktu
Bombay
Hyderabad
GAMBIA
YEMEN
SUDAN
MALABAR
BANGLADESH
Madras
THAILAND
ETHIOPIA
SRI LANKA (CEYLON)
KENYA
SUMATRA
MADAGASCAR (MALAGASY)
INDIAN OCEAN
MOZAMBIQUE
ATLANTIC OCEAN
0
500
1000
1500
2000 Miles
0
1000
2000 Kilometers

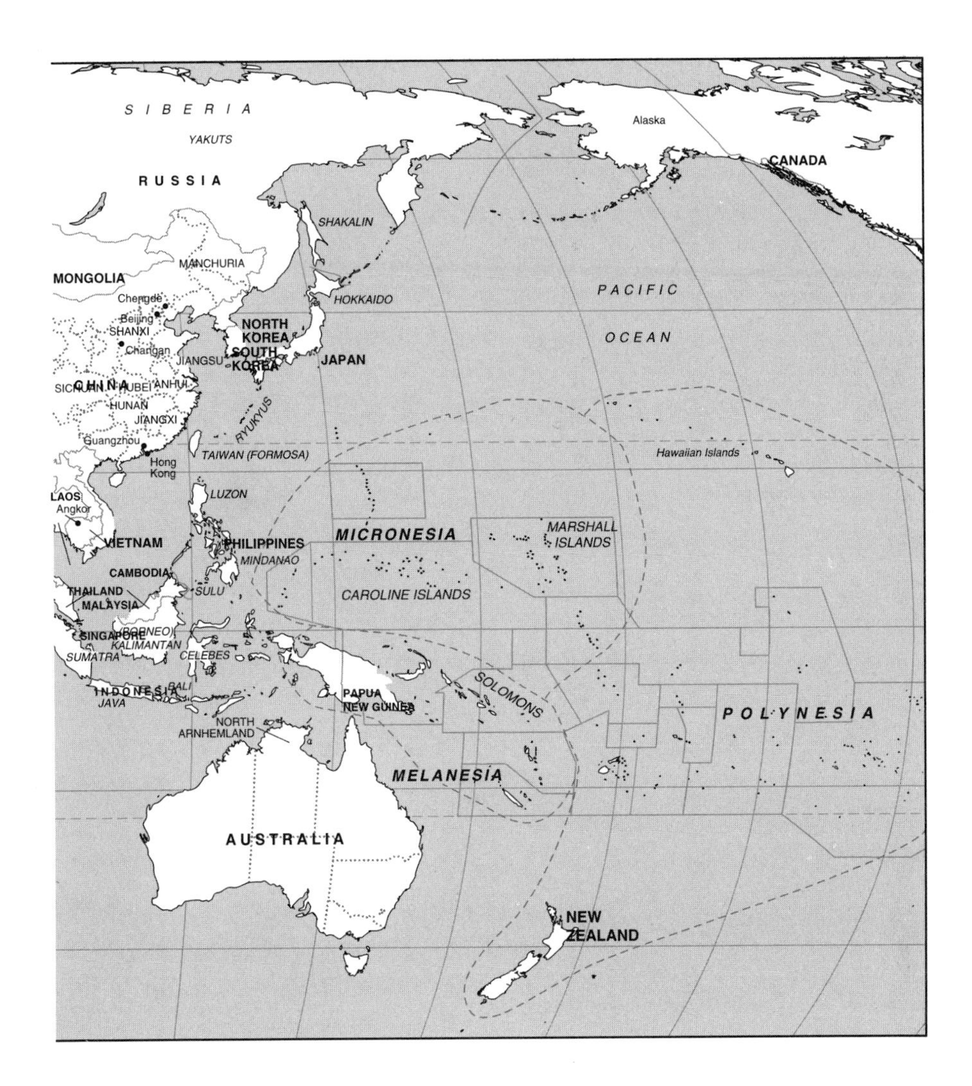
SIBERIA
YAKUTS
RUSSIA
Alaska
CANADA
SHAKALIN
MANCHURIA
MONGOLIA
Chengde
Beijing
SHANXI
Changan
NORTH KOREA
SOUTH KOREA
HOKKAIDO
JAPAN
JIANGSU
CHINA
SICHUAN
HUBEI
ANHUI
HUNAN
JIANGXI
Guangzhou
Hong Kong
RYUKYUS
TAIWAN (FORMOSA)
PACIFIC
OCEAN
Hawaiian Islands
LAOS
Angkor
LUZON
VIETNAM
PHILIPPINES
MINDANAO
MICRONESIA
MARSHALL ISLANDS
CAMBODIA
CAROLINE ISLANDS
THAILAND
MALAYSIA
SULU
SINGAPORE
(BORNEO)
KALIMANTAN
SUMATRA
CELEBES
INDONESIA
BALI
JAVA
PAPUA NEW GUINEA
SOLOMONS
POLYNESIA
NORTH ARNHEMLAND
MELANESIA
AUSTRALIA
NEW ZEALAND

ONE
OCEANIA

Oceania is a collective term for all the islands and cultures of the Pacific Ocean. As shown on the map in the front of the book, Oceania is usually divided into four sections: Australia, Melanesia, Polynesia, and Micronesia. Although the Ryukyu Islands are technically part of Micronesia, and the Malay archipelago from Indonesia to the Philippines is also sometimes considered a section of Oceania, we discuss the music of these areas in later chapters. This chapter surveys the music from the four traditional areas of Oceania in the order just listed. At the same time we introduce certain basic concepts and terminologies that have been found useful in the study of music worldwide.

AUSTRALIA

A musical field trip to the towns and farms of Australia would soon uncover there a rich crop of old ballads and dances that were brought to the continent by Anglo-European settlers. Thus the music is filled with Scottish and Irish tunes as well as new pieces in their style, although the social events may be called bush dances and aboriginals may be playing concertinas or fiddles in the band.[1] There are also a host of traditional and new folk and music hall pieces that deal with the history of Australia from the resettlement of convicts through gold rushes, hunting, and herding to service in Commonwealth armies.[2] As with every urban culture we discuss in this book, traditional European and new concert genres exist in Australia.[3] The international and indigenous styles of the flourishing popular music industry are yet other aspects of all world musics.[4] As we enter our first culture area, Australia, it is important to realize that, in an electronic and high-speed world, very few world musics exist in isolation. Still, we can note that Australia, like the United States and Canada, does have many enclaves of European and Asian musics (Greek, Italian, Indian) that tend to preserve "old" styles which no longer are used in the country of their origins. This so-called *marginal survival* is one of the topics being studied at Australian government and scholarly research centers. However, their major concerns tend to be the traditions of the aboriginal tribes that first possessed this continent.

The music of these Australian aboriginals is an excellent and impressive base for an introduction to the study of the structure and meaning of music in world cultures. Imagine, for example, a group of short dark men painted with sacred markings of ostrich down and blood; they dance in a circle, holding each others' thighs, and leap like kangaroos while uttering animalistic shouts. What descriptive words come to mind? Stone Age, primitive, savage? All have been applied to the peoples of the Arnhem Land Aboriginal Reserve, which is located on the northern tip of Australia between the city of Darwin and the Gulf of Carpentaria. Among the most archaic cultures still in existence, they are organized in bands, the simplest political units. Their society reflects a dual structure; that is, every creature must belong to one or the other of two basic groups called moieties. Aboriginal material culture seems minimal, for these peoples survive today primarily on government-subsidized reservations or through forms of hunting, fishing, and food gathering that often involve moving with the wandering game. "Common sense" would lead us to expect that their music would be rather pallid, yet field workers are unanimous in their praise of aboriginal songs. What is there to admire?

[1] For examples see Dobe Newton & Jan Wositzky, *The Bushwackers Band Dance Book* (Collingwood, Victoria: Greenhouse Publications, 1980).

[2] See Bill Scott, *The Second Penguin Australian Songbook* (Ringwood, Victoria: Penguin Books Australia, 1980); Hugh Anderson, *The Story of Australian Folksong* (New York: Oak Publications, 1970); Ron Edwards, *Tune Origins for Australian Folk Songs* (Holloways Beach, Queensland: Rams Skull Press, 1973); and John Meredith, R. Covell, and P. Brown, *Folk Songs of Australia and the Men and Women Who Sang Them* (Kensington, NSW: The New South Wales University Press, Vol. 1, 1967; Vol. 2, 1987).

[3] See Roger Covell. *Australia's Music Themes of a New Society* (Melbourne: Sunbook, 1967), or Deborah Crisp, *Bibliography of Australian Music* (Armidale, NSW: Australian Music Studies Project, 1982).

[4] See Peter Manuel's *Popular Musics of the Non-Western World* (New York: Oxford Press, 1988) or the periodical *Popular Music*.

One of the first notable aspects of Arnhem Land music is its meaningfulness to the culture. Music is used throughout an aboriginal man's life to teach him what he must know about his culture, about his place in it, and about its place in the world of nature and supernature.[5] As a baby he is encouraged to dance and sing about everyday tasks. At puberty he learns his first lineage songs—about the totemic plants and animals of his clan and the history and mythology of the group—which belong to his lineage and have specific melodic formulas and modes that distinguish them from other groups' songs. In the bachelors' camp he learns more lighthearted songs that are the basic entertainment media for the band. When he marries and enters further into group responsibilities, however, it is the clan songs that are the central part of his education and his source of strength in times of trouble. His maturation can be measured in the esoteric knowledge he has acquired through song, and as an old man he knows his honor is based partly on his mastery of the secret sacred songs of the band.

The music of nonliterate peoples in general shares this direct functionality with that of the Australian aboriginals. Literate civilizations, by contrast, tend to increase the separation of music from life. For example, Western college students must learn to "understand" a Beethoven symphony. Aboriginals understand their music naturally. Westerners can understand aboriginal music also, if they are willing to learn its language and laws and listen to it in terms of itself. It cannot be compared with a Beethoven symphony because it has nothing to do with it.[6] Both, however, can be enjoyed once we know what to listen for in each. Thus our first indigenous cultural example demonstrates clearly the primary rule motivating and directing the structure of this book: Music is *not* an international language. It consists of a whole series of equally logical but different systems.

As we look briefly at selected examples of such systems in Oceania and Asia, we will be able to see only a few of the ethnological or musical factors that comprise their basic units. Even such brief views, however, will display some of the wondrous results of humans' combinations of culture and sonic events and will help us realize the ingenuity and potential artistry of the human mind. We have already implied some of the cultural functions of music in Australian aboriginal societies. Let us see next what their members can do with an ant-eaten tree branch.

One of the very few—if also best known—Australian aboriginal musical instruments is the *dijeridu (dijeriduu, dijeridoo, digeridoo),* seen in Plate I, Figure 1. This hollow eucalyptus branch is blown so that, by nasal breathing and back pressure in the pipe, constant tone is maintained. The pipe end may

[5] This tradition in the context of Western education is found in Catherine J. Ellis, *Aboriginal Music, Education for Living* (St. Lucia: University of Queensland Press, 1985).

[6] The author acknowledges inspiration for these thoughts from the last chapter, "Progress?" of the posthumous book of Curt Sachs, *The Wellsprings of Music* (The Hague: Nijhoff, 1962).

PLATE I. Australian aboriginal instruments

FIGURE 1. Rhythm sticks and a *dijeridu*.

be placed in a large shell or can to aid the back pressure and the resonance. The instrument is stored in a stream or in mud to keep it moist and soft-toned. Some nine different tone qualities can be produced by a skilled player.[7] The actual pitches played are usually two, a tenth apart. By alternating the tone qualities and pitches, the drone player produces a varied rhythmic and coloristic background for a singer, who often works his melodic line against the drone in a manner reminiscent of Indian classical music. Some *dijeridu* today are made from modern materials such as cans or plastic tubes. Good tones can still be produced from these instruments.

A skilled drone player is highly respected and may travel with a professional songman to enhance trade meetings or other interband assemblies. In all but a few compositions, the songman himself or some other performer plays rhythm sticks like those shown in Figure 1. In almost all compositions the songman or another person either maintains with such "time sticks" an accurate beat or creates a rhythmic ostinato characteristic of the style of the kind of piece being performed. There are several different regional styles within Arnhem Land itself as well as among the peoples in other parts of Australia, as in the York peninsula and on the distant western coast. Handclaps instead of rhythm sticks are preferred by some groups, whereas clashing boomerangs or sticks beaten on the ground are characteristic of many of the central desert tribes far south of Arnhem Land.[8] Beating on log drums or on the side of the drone pipe is found among some northern coastal groups, perhaps reflecting their comparative proximity to New Guinea. Notched wooden scrapers appear in some northwest and western tribes, and the so-called bull-roarer can be found in a few northeastern cultures and in one from the central desert. The bull-roarer is an oblong wooden board that is spun overhead on the end of a string. Strictly speaking, it is not necessarily a musical instrument, for its sounds in secret rituals are not considered as independent sonic events but rather are thought to be the sounds of the supernatural itself. Women are forbidden to approach the ceremonial area when the whirl of the bull-roarer is heard.

If the sound of the bull-roarer is not technically music, a logical but somewhat disconcerting general question arises: What is music? In the context of world music two answers are possible. One is purely intracultural and the other is potentially universal. The first is that a sonic event can be called music only if the knowledgeable carriers of the culture in which it appears call it music themselves. This definition depends on the opinion of the people actually living in the culture and ignores what an outside listener may feel about the sounds. The second definition is that any sonic event may be considered and

[7] The basic tones, patterns, and sonic pleasures of the instrument are found in Trevor Jones's *The Art of the Dijeridoo* (Wattle Ethnic Series, no. 3).

[8] An excellent map of the distribution of musical instruments in aboriginal culture is found in Alice Moyle's booklet (p. 73) accompanying the recording *Songs from the Northern Territory* (Canberra: Australian Institute of Aboriginal Studies, 1967), cat. no. I.A.S. M-001/5. This booklet also summarizes regional styles.

studied as though it were music if it combines the elements of pitch, rhythm, and dynamics so as to communicate emotionally, aesthetically, or functionally in a manner that either transcends or is unrelated to speech communication. Under this definition, one could "analyze" bull-roarer sounds to find their "musical" characteristics without considering how the native performer or listener may view or react to them.

To our earlier remarks about the functionality of music in many societies we must add that the study of music in world cultures may choose to ignore the sonic events altogether, or at least to link them primarily with their reasons for existence within a culture. Such a broad, flexible approach to the study of music is found in the discipline called *ethnomusicology,* which may be defined as the scientific study of music in any world culture or subculture in terms of its actual sounds and performance practice, in its relation to the specific culture, or in comparison with other cultures.[9]

We have spoken briefly of the power of Australian aboriginal music in some of its cultural contexts and in its instrumental performance practice. Let us turn now to the actual music. Australian aboriginal music is sometimes classified in three categories: secular, sacred, and secret. These categories are generally more functional than musical. Most secret pieces are also sacred, but a sacred song may appear in a secular situation (like hymns at the Grand Old Opry in the United States), and specific songs may have a variety of sacred or secular texts (like, in the United States, "John Brown's Body," "Mine Eyes Have Seen the Glory," and "Little Peter Rabbit"). There are many sacred songs (such as Example 1–1A) that have solemnity and texts of great meaning. Quite often such a melody may be turned into a secret piece by the place where it is performed or by an "inside" meaning of the text that only the initiated can understand correctly. The texts of secular songs are often topical, with references to events or people of significance to the groups at the time.

Examples 1–1A and 1–1B are Western notations of a Madayin (Maraian) sacred song and a Yirrkala "Djatpangarri" comic dance, both from Arhem Land. The first example is from an all-night series of chants that call up spirits of people, ghosts, mythic heroes, and natural species. The text here is about a large barramundi fish that may be part of a myth or the symbolic creature of a clan. The title and much of the text of the second example are vocables, although the singer may call the names of groups led in and out of the dance and control their movements with beats of the two rhythm sticks and short interjec-

[9] This definition is the author's; see also Bruno Nettl's *Folk and Traditional Music of the Western Continents,* 3rd ed. (Englewood Cliffs, N.J.: Prentice Hall, 1990), 27–31.

EXAMPLE 1–1. Two Australian aboriginal songs transcribed from the recording *Tribal Music of Australia* (Smithsonian/Folkways 4439, side 2, track 6 and side 1, track 2 [second entrance]; book tracks 1 and 2). Transcription and sound used by permission.

EXAMPLE 1–1A

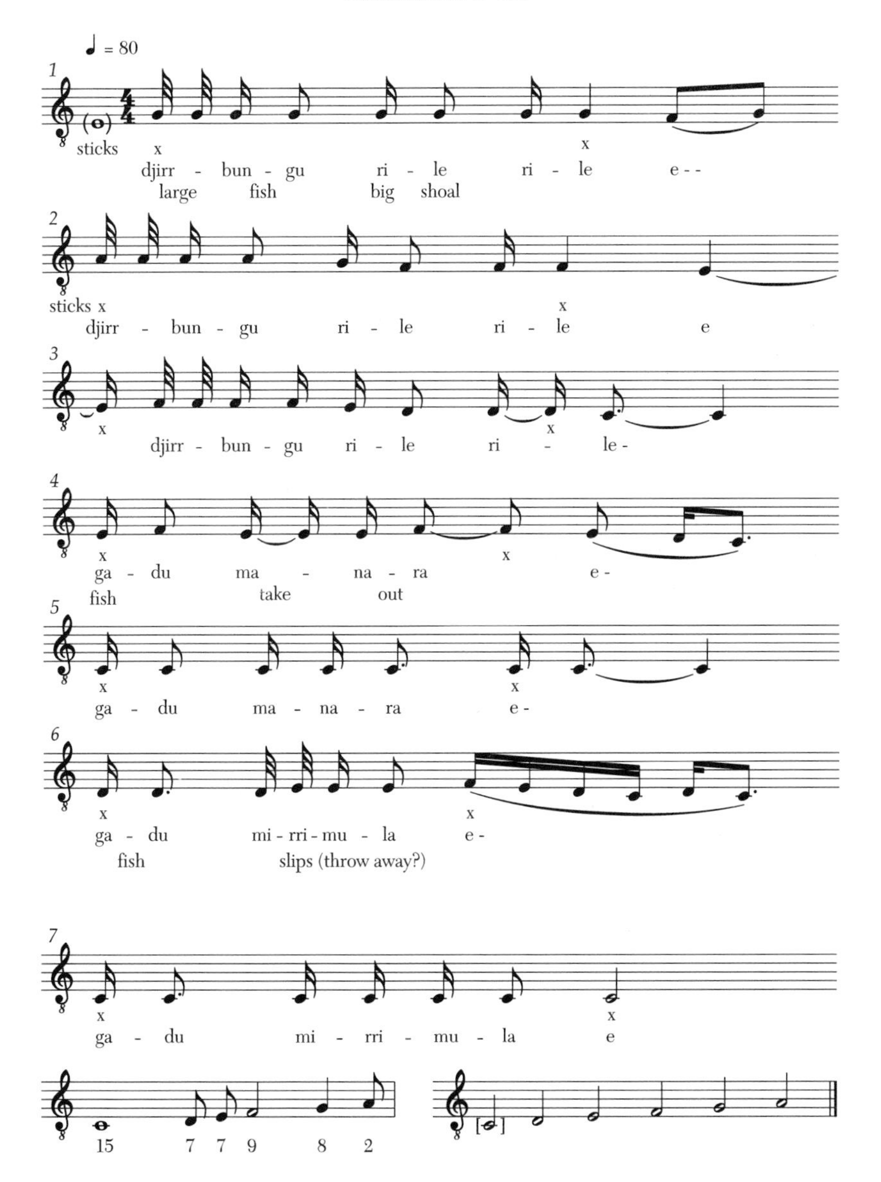

EXAMPLE 1–1B

= 164

3

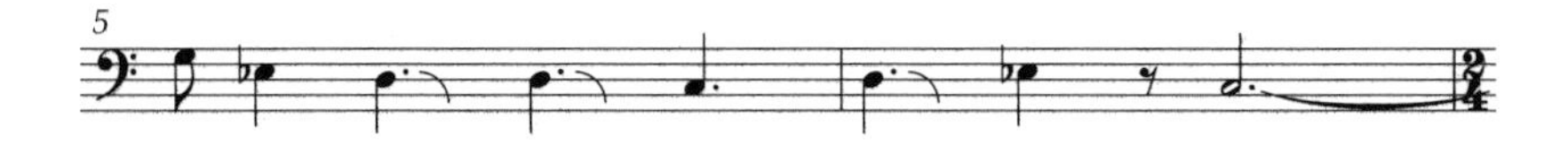
5

7

9

11

15 17 5 21 15 1 22 1
range

tions (measures 7–12).[10] The basic rhythm and tonality are maintained by the *didjeridu*. Such dances are popular in social *corroboree* meetings.[11]

So far, the information we have presented about Australian aboriginals could been acquired without recordings or notation. Ethnological field work and interpretation certainly are the core of this "ethno" side of ethnomusicology. They help us understand *who* makes music and *why, who* listens and *why, where* and *when* it occurs, and *how it functions* in society. However, equally interesting things are found in studying *what* the sonic event is and *how is it structured*. For that we turn to the "music" side of ethnomusicology.

RUDIMENTS OF ETHNOMUSICOLOGICAL MUSIC NOTATION AND ANALYSIS

As with the data of most sciences ("ologies"), the recordings, transcriptions, and analyses of sonic events in ethnomusicology may or may not be of concern to the indigenous performers from whom the material was acquired. That is not the music researchers' immediate concern. They want to know the characteristics of the sound elements and forms in the music from a given culture. The use of conventional sonic abstractions like Western notation and pitch names help us compare research results with other world sonic events transcribed in similar formats.[12] Such research data is not meant to be "right" in an indigenous context, but is used to help us understand and explain to each other the marvel of so many equally logical but different music systems in the world. Fortunately, this book's cassette provides the original data.

Western Notation Conventions for Ethnomusicology

Example 1–1A is written in the *vocal music* format, since a sung text is included. Eighth notes or shorter notes are written with *flags*[13] if each note is

[10] This section of the music is believed to be inspired by observations of Australian army drill practice. The genre seems to have originated during World War II when troops were stationed in the area. One aboriginal noted it was essentially a mission-related phenomenon because it allowed the airing of risqué gossip without the missionaries' knowledge. The author thanks Steven Knopoff of the University of Pittsburgh for information about these two examples.

[11] It is generally believed that terms like *corroboree* and *didjeridu* are English distortions of indigenous terms, although they are commonly used today. The word *didjeridu* is thought to be an onomatopoeic memory aid (a mnemonic) that represents some of the mouth movements one makes to produce the correct sounds. The Yolngu of northeast Arnhem Land call the instrument a *yidaki*.

[12] The original name of the field was comparative musicology *(vergleichende Musikwissenschaft)*. The "correct" notation for transcriptions is an ongoing debate in the discipline. See Kay K. Shelemay, ed., *Garland Library of Readings in Ethnomusicology*. Vol. 4, *Musical Transcriptions* (New York: Garland, 1990).

[13] The four basic parts of Western pitch notations are a head ○, a stem |, a flag ⎾, and a beam ⊓. For explanation of other notational conventions used in this book (such as the arrows and slides of Example 1–1) see Preface, page xiii.

on a separate syllable (the first three beats of measure 1). *Beams* are used if the notes are on the same syllable (the last beat of measure 1). Example 1–1A also uses the convention of writing the music an octave higher than it sounds. This is often done to ease comparisons with other examples written in the treble clef. Example 1–1B is notated in the *instrumental music* style, for a text is absent. Eighth notes or smaller time units on the same beat tend to be joined by beams. It is written in the bass clef to accommodate the area of the actual sound. The note in parentheses before the time signature indicates the recording began on that pitch[14] and has been transposed in the transcription for research reasons. Example 1–2 shows one line of a *descriptive (etic)* transcription that attempts to notate exactly what was performed. This is followed by a *prescriptive (emic)* notation that is a generalized version based on the study of the entire performance. The latter is especially useful when doing comparative studies. Note also that the "key signature" is etic; it is not meant to imply a Western key but only to show what pitches were used.

Performance Practice

A first observation found in the notation or recording concerns *performance practice.* Example 1–1A is for songman and rhythm sticks only; 1–1B adds a *didjeridu* drone (notated for the first two bars only). Both examples use a solo singer who also plays the rhythm sticks.

Time

Besides showing *tempo* in metronome marks (the number of beats per minute) and notating the rhythm of the sticks and its relation to the vocal part, one can note *meter*—that is, a scheme of time in music that allows one to perceive the basic pulse *(tact)* as being organized in units with implied "first" beats and perhaps other accented beats. Such units are called *measures;* their implied beats need not be those of the accents of the music itself. The apparent caution of this ethnomusicological definition of meter and measure reflects the fact that a major part of the world's music is oral, and thus one's interpretation of the metric structure of a music is often rather subjective and based on one's own cultural rhythmic experience. This is true for Example 1–1 because the performance is totally oral. Example 1–2 shows a notation of oral music based on text and form; barlines are not used at all.

If time units are notated in measures of the same length, as in Example 1–1A, a piece can be described as being *isometric.* If the units are of equal

[14] The actual pitch of recorded performances is problematic. Sometimes an A 440 appears before a field tape but not on a commercial copy. The speeds of copying machines vary as do the machines used to play a tape. The transcriptions of the first edition of this book were a half step lower than here because an American copy of the examples was transcribed while in Japan where the current is different. So much for perfect pitch in our electronic age!

lengths, but not each a multiple of two or three (such as 5/4 or 11/4 as opposed to 3/4 or 4/4), the music is sometimes described as being in an *asymmetrical isometer.* We should note, however, that this convenient term is somewhat ethnocentric, since a measure that may seem asymmetrical to a Central European or American is quite even to someone in the native population of a culture in which such meters are common (as in East European dance music). The term *asymmetrical* is used here as part of common professional parlance; it implies no specific interpretation by a given listener. If the internal beat units are evenly subdivided (as in 4/4 or 12/8), a meter can be called *divisive.* If the internal subdivisions are uneven (such as $\frac{2+3}{4}$), a meter can be called *additive.* If the length of the notated measure units keeps changing (as in Example 1–1B), the piece may be described as *heterometric.*[15] If different parts are using different meters at the same time one could call the event *polymeter.* If the *dijeridu* part of Example 1–1B had been shown in measure 7 as being 12/8 under the 2/4 and 4/4 of the vocal line it could be called polymetric.

Rhythm is not the same as meter. It consists of a distribution of long and short time units and accents. If this distribution is repeated it is called an *isorhythm.* The first few measures of both pieces in Example 1–1 seem to repeat such rhythmic patters. Isorhythm is common to all musics, for most sonic events are usually not read from scores but heard. Whether the event is a symphony, a popular tune, or an aboriginal sacred chant, to the listener it is aural. Repetitions are memory aids, thus the logical necessity of redundancy in orality or aurality. In vocal music, the individual word structure or poetic form may influence rhythm. In this context, note the rhythm in Example 1–1A when the words change (measure 4).

Our two Australian examples illustrate *tempo giusto,* a steady *metronomic* beat. If a piece of music has no sense of an even pulse, it may be said to be in *free rhythm.* Example 3–1 (p. 73) is in *parlando-rubato* style, for its rhythms tend to follow freely those of speech.

The increase or decrease in the number of events in a music reflects *rhythmic density.* Example 1–1A is denser than 1–1B although the tempo is slower. The effect of emphasis created by a change in the length of notes is called an *agogic* accent. You can see it in the shift from short to long units at the end (the cadence) of Example 1–1B. Changes are common at the endings of most world musics (including the West) for what makes a *cadence* a cadence is that *something different* happens, be it rhythm, harmony, or pitch.

Pitch and Tone Systems

Among the characteristics of a melody derived from pitch data are (1) *scale,* (2) *pitch center,* (3) *range,* (4) *frequency* of pitches, (5) *cadence patterns,*

[15] In this example the choice is primarily to illustrate heterometer although it only represents one way an outside listener could transcribe the vocal line. The performers no doubt felt a steady isometer based on the *dijeridu* line.

(6) *melodic formulas,* (7) prevalent *intervals,* and (8) *contour.* Note again that these characteristics may be more meaningful to a researcher than to a performer. The first four observations can be made quickly by writing at the end of a transcription a *weighted scale* (see Example 1–1A). Using an eighth note as a value of 1, the frequency of each pitch is shown. If there are octave duplications they are included (Example 1–1B). The most frequent pitch is given the largest time value and the rest are graded shorter according to the frequency of their use. The use of frequency as the way to determine the pitch center for an unknown tone system is problematic, for a piece may use a *reciting tone* more than a *finalis* (the tonic).[16] Example 1–1B illustrates this problem. Is C or F the pitch center? The final high F's are shouts and may not really belong to an abstraction of the tone system. The researcher's opinion is made clearer in the second .rendering of the scale in Example 1–1B. Octave duplications are left out and a bracket is put around the transcriber's pitch center choice. Scales are often described by Greek-derived terms: Thus Example 1–1 is *hexatonic* (six-toned) and 1–1 is *pentatonic* (five-toned).

We spoke earlier of cadence patterns. The repeated C's of Example 1–1A (measures 5 and 7) are static tonal implications of cadence; 1–1B uses longer durations to create something different, that is, a cadence. Note also that the C's of Example 1–1A imply a tonic; in 1–1B they do not. There is not enough material here to speak of melodic formula in the tradition, but the isorhythmic phrases in both examples could be data for such a study. The frequency of intervals is sometimes used for such searches.[17] Those of Examples 1–1A and B would be listed as follows:

	Major 2nd	Minor 2nd	Maj. 3rd	Min. 3rd	4th	5th
Ex. 1–1A	15	9	1	0	0	0
Ex. 1–1B	6	4	1	2	0	0

Contour can be described as ascending, descending, pendulous, or terraced, or it may be shown by graphic lines. The contours of Example 1–1A and the first half of Example 1–1B are basically descending. They also might be called terraced, that is, they stay on one plane and then move to another. Examples 1–5 (p. 30) and 4–2 (p. 116) may be said to be *static* because their melodic movements and intervals are quite limited. If a melody moves primarily in seconds, as in Example 1–1A, it is *conjunct;* if it uses larger intervals between notes, it is *disjunct* (Examples 3–1, p. 73, and 6–2, p. 172).

[16] See Jeremy Yudkin, *Music in Medieval Europe* (Englewood Cliffs, N.J.: Prentice Hall, 1989).

[17] Both interval counts and weighted scales were popular research devices in the early twentieth century when comparative studies were in vogue. Although less in use now, they remain potentially valuable tools.

Form cannot be analyzed in Example 1–1A because it is not a complete piece. The excerpt in 1–1B could be described as an AB form as far as it goes. The form of Example 1–2 is shown in the transcription. Here are some useful terms for describing other relatively short, repetitive pieces. *Iterative* describes the form of a piece in which one small melodic formula tends to be repeated throughout (as in the Anglo-American children's chant, "Rain, rain, go away"). If a piece returns to its first phrase after a digression, the form is *reverting* or *closed* ("Swanee River" is an example, and most pop music uses the form AABA). If in either of these forms the same large formal unit is used for next text, the form can also be called *strophic* or *stanza* (like "Oh! Susanna" or "Clementine"). If a piece continues to add new melodic material, it is called *progressive* or *through composed.*

In vocal music, another important characteristic is the relation of music to text. When one note is used for each syllable of the text, the style is *syllabic* (Example 4–1, p. 111). If one syllable is used with many notes, the style is *melismatic* (Example 3–6, p. 94). If a few notes are used occasionally for one syllable the style is *neumatic*[18] (Example 7–5, p. 218).

The study of text also offers opportunities for finding relations between language accents and music accents as well as musical reactions to important or colorful words in the poem.

Although there is much more that one can do with music analysis,[19] these basic tools will help the researcher or the musically curious layperson to understand a given music in terms of itself. We must add that only an innate musicality and an enthusiasm for finding beauty in sound will turn this knowledge into positive music appreciation.

Looking once again at the pieces in Example 1–1, we can see that analysis reveals their similarities and differences. They share an isorhythmic tendency, a descending contour, a similar range (a sixth), and a conjunct melodic style. Example 1–1A is notated isometrically and 1–1B heterometrically. The examples differ in performance practice, tempo, scale, and cadences. Although the text of Example 1–1B is not shown, from the recording one can hear it is syllabic; 1–1A is syllabic in the first half of each measure, neumatic in the last half of measures 1 and 4, and slightly melismatic in the last of measure 6. Space does not permit such lengthy analyses of each example in this book, but the format we use here should prove useful in your own efforts at analysis.

[18] The term comes from a European medieval notation symbol *(neume)* used to represent a group of notes.

[19] See more examples in Nettl, *Folk and Traditional Music of the Western Continents,* and Vol. 5 of *The Garland Library of Readings in Ethnomusicology,* ed. Kay K. Shelemay (New York: Garland, 1990).

MELANESIA

Northeast of Arnhem Land is Papua New Guinea, the largest island in the world. The great varieties of peoples who inhabit its mountains, jungle, and coastal plains range from Negroid Melanesians to Papuans and small-statured Negritos. Its musical cartography has yet to be drawn, but already the music has revealed a vast and colorful range of styles.

One common performance practice in Papua New Guinea is group singing in unison or octaves; such music is called *monophonic,* a term describing solo line music. Sometimes one performer will sing a line that is answered by another singer or a group using the same or a different melody. This is *call-and-response* or *responsorial* style, and it too is common in Papua New Guinea. It can be seen and heard in Example 1–2 (book cassette, track 3). If one group sings the call and another group sings the response, the performance practice is

EXAMPLE 1–2. A garden rite song from Kaagu, Papua New Guinea, recorded by Vida S. Chenoweth in November 1965 (now in her Archive no. 12, tape 3, side 1; book cassette, track 3). The transcription is from her book *The Usarufas and Their Music* (Dallas: S.I.L. Museum of Anthropology, 1979), 203. Tape and music used by permission of the author and elders of Kaagu village.[20]

[20] The text states that a ritual using a specific leaf will make the new garden grow. Chenoweth could not release the tape without permission of the performer because the example was a rite. Contact with the village found the performer dead and the rite no longer performed. The elders asked for it to be included so the tradition could be recalled if needed. This is an example of the problems of ethnics in the use of indigenous materials.

called *antiphonal.* Regardless of the number of people involved, if only one melody is heard at a time the music is monophonic.

When many people are involved in a performance, the possibility is great that various pitches will appear at the same time. Whether this is deliberate or accidental, the resulting texture is *multipart* music. There seem to be three basic types of multipart music in the world: homophony, polyphony, and heterophony. By definition they all must have more than one part[21] and use different pitches. The terms *same* and *different* are helpful in distinguishing the three types of multipart music as shown here:

HOMOPHONY

IN HOMOPHONY	DIFFERENT	PARTS ARE PERFORMING
	DIFFERENT	PITCHES IN BASICALLY THE
	SAME	RHYTHM PATTERNS AT THE
	SAME	TIME (e.g., a chorale-type hymn)

POLYPHONY[22]

IN POLYPHONY	DIFFERENT	PARTS ARE PERFORMING
	DIFFERENT	PITCHES IN
	DIFFERENT	RHYTHMIC PATTERNS
	OR IN THE SAME	RHYTHMIC PATTERNS THAT
	BEGIN AT DIFFERENT	TIMES (e.g., a canon)

HETEROPHONY

IN HETEROPHONY	DIFFERENT	PARTS ARE PERFORMING THE
	SAME	MELODY AT THE
	SAME	TIME BUT WITH
	DIFFERENT	VERSIONS
		(e.g., simultaneous variations)

Homophonic texture is seen in Example 5–4 (p. 154). It is more common in Western music, where tunes are often built on chords (harmonies) that move in progressions. Indeed, this harmonic orientation is one of the major differences between Western and much non-Western music. Traditional Western music may be said to operate on a *polarity system:* There is a tune on top, polarized against a bass line below, with the middle filled in by chords. By contrast, most of the music discussed in this book may be called *linear.* Of course Western music has lines, but as our tunes flow forward we tend to look down (listen) to make sure we are on the right chord. The linearity of aharmonic[23] music more

[21] In all these definitions the word *part* is used rather than *voice,* since it may be applied to any music, instrumental or vocal.

[22] In an attempt to find a culturally neutral term, the author invented the Latin-Greek word *disphony* ("separate sounds") and Fredric Lieberman once suggested in correspondence the term *paraphony* ("parallel sounds"). Neither term entered common usage so the ambiguous, culture-loaded term *polyphony* remains our present option.

[23] That is, harmony has nothing to do with the music except as occasional texture.

often concentrates on melodic and rhythmic subtleties and tensions. This will become evident as our study progresses.

Polyphony can be heard on track 5. If the melodies of the various parts are quite similar, the style may be called *imitational* polyphony. If they are basically the same tune but are begun at different times, as in tracks 4 and 38 (Example 7–13), the polyphony may also be called *canonic.* As seen in heterophonic Example 3–1, p. 73, the different parts are performing the same tune at the same time, but each part is making its own melodic or rhythmic variant.

Putting the whole sonic texture vocabulary together, we have the following: (1) monophony—unison or octave sounds; and (2) multipart—two or more sounds, with their rhythmic relationships differentiated as homophonic, polyphonic, or heterophonic. These terms are useful in talking about world musics as long as one "stays loose." Textures change and cannot always be clearly differentiated.

Applying some analytical methods to Example 1–2, general Melanesian melodic tendencies in the music of the areas recorded and studied so far can be noted. The example is rather typical in its disjunct melodic use of thirds and fourths. The scale is pentatonic but contains a half step (C to D flat), unlike the standard anhemitonic (no half step) pentatonic seen in Example 1–3. Note that the "key signature" of Example 1–2 places the three flats where they occur without any reference to Western tone systems. Example 1–2 shows other common Melanesian melodic styles: narrow ranges and static contours with little change. Melanesian melodies may also descend in the terraced contour we noted earlier in Example 1–1 from Australia.

In general, Melanesian music seems less word oriented than that of Polynesia and Micronesia. Some texts are sung in archaic languages unknown to the performers. This may be because of a heavier emphasis on function and ritual in Melanesia. *Vocables*—syllables without meaning—may be used to turn the voice into an instrument rather than a vehicle for text. Still, vocal music predominates, as does monophony.

It should be evident by now that melodic style may sometimes be a valid, if only partial, aid in the search for larger views of various cultures. As we implied earlier, the theory and symbolism of the music of a nonliterate culture are also part of the general "worldview" *(Weltanschauung)* of that (or any

EXAMPLE 1–3. The basic tonal vocabularies of a *gisalo* song from the Kaluli of Papua New Guinea. Book cassette, track 4, is from the *Music of Oceania* series recording *Kaluli Weeping and Song* (Musicaphon BM 30 SL 2702, side 1, band 1). Used by permission of the Institut für Musikwissenschaft der Universitat Basel, Switzerland.

other) culture and thus are best approached from an anthropological as well as a musicological point of view. For example, in order to study the cultural "meaning" of the slit-gongs *(garamut)*[24] found all over Papua New Guinea, one must take into consideration the manner in which the large logs are hollowed out and slotted on one side so the sound can come out in the right "spirit," as well as the particular meaning of the various patterns played on them. Similarly, one must know the significance of the figures carved on a gong, especially when one end of it is stuck in the ground and the carved head on the other end becomes a totem, the sound of the instrument representing the very voice of a god. Many large horizontal slit-gongs are placed in special houses; the uses of these houses as well as the situations in which the gongs are used may reveal much about the people as well as about their music. Thus an ethnomusicologist should be a person of many viewpoints in order to appreciate fully the meaning of music in a given culture.

Such symbolism in music and musical instruments is common to most nonliterate cultures and is found in the music of many literate civilizations as well. (The so-called masculine and feminine cadences of Western art music are an example.) In Papua New Guinea, the masculine–feminine idea is used to explain, among other things, the double rows of tubes found on some panpipes. Such an explanation is not merely fancy; it is a native form of music theory. Natives have constructed their theory in analogies because, like classroom teachers, they have found them to be an effective way of presenting abstract material orally. Of course, such analogies also lock music into meaningful relationships with the things they value in their culture.

For example, the Kaluli people of the tropical rain forest in Papua New Guinea have expressed a theory of vocal music with metaphors that join the concept of sound with that of water.[25] The drop of a minor third is a *sa,* a word that can mean waterfall, and the generic term for a waterfall sound, *sa-gu,* is used in music to mean a pitch center. The onomatopoeic term for continual waterfall flow, *sa-gulu,* is used when a melody stays on a pitch center for a long time. The word *gulu* alone applies as well to the "flow" of an even meter; *kubu,* "water splashing sounds," can mean a choppy melody, and *golo,* "waterpool swirls," describes music that slows down and then returns to tempo. Example 1–3 shows the common interval (not pitch) vocabulary for Kaluli genre called a *gisalo* song heard in book cassette, track 4. The descending major second (D to C) is called a *gese,* a prefix for verbs of speaking, singing, whistling, or weeping that implies a descending, plaintive sound. The combination of the major second and minor third or fourth (D C A, D C G, or A G E) is found in the call of

[24] Given the plethora of languages and dialects in Papua New Guinea, the most common pidgin terms are used here based on the opinions of regional experts. The best survey of area instruments and their local names is Vida Chenoweth, ed., *Musical Instruments of Papua New Guinea* (Ukarumpa, PNG: Summer Institute of Linguistics, 1976).

[25] See Steven Feld, "Flow Like a Waterfall: The Metaphors of Kaluli Musical Theory," in *Yearbook for Traditional Music,* 13 (1981), 22–47.

a regional bird.[26] Bird calls are considered sounds from dead children, so singing in a weeping style should employ a similar vocabulary. Kaluli myth and theory transform what we might call "nature" into "culture" by endowing nature's sonic patterns with human associations, meanings, and symbolism. In so doing the music of nature and the nature of music come to have an equally "natural" feeling—tacit, conventional, and unconscious.[27]

Book cassette, track 5, is a different type of song from the same region. It is being used during woodcutting. One hears the same canonlike call-and-response and tonal vocabulary, but note that the pitch center is the lowest notes whereas the *gisalo* song it was a minor third higher (see Example 1–3). From this we learn that there is not only a tonal vocabulary system in Papua New Guinea but genre-related modes as well. The Western major and minor mode system is obviously not the only method of mood and music. Note also that the imitations in tracks 4 and 5 are not clearly separated as in Western canons. This "lift over" style is consistent with the layers of overlapping sounds that emanate from the jungle night and day; it is particularly evident in track 5 where one hears the birds and the singing of the workers mixing as the woodcutting raises to a climax. Such an environmental sonic event may remind you of some contemporary Western music. The major difference is function. One is communally created to enhance work; the other is composed by one person for eventual use in a concert hall. Both functions are valid, but what a different context!

Obviously, the lack of textbooks in a tribal society does not mean its music is without a systematic base. It is, in fact, one task of the ethnomusicologist to look for the logic underlying each culture's music. Comparative musicological theories are derived from searches in the data of such musics, often inspired by the trends in science at the time. For example, acoustical mathematics and Darwinian evolution theory contributed to the work of Eric von Hornbostel (1877–1935). He combined interval measurements of Oceanic and Latin American panpipes with ancient Chinese music writings to support the theory of overblown fifths *(Blasquinten)*.[28] This, in turn, was used to explain why a unit of the first three or last three pitches of Example 1–3 are found so often in hex and children's songs (C C A D C A, "Johnny Is a Sissy").[29] Linguis-

[26] Birds and music are handsomely described in Steven Feld, *Sound and Sentiment* (Philadelphia: University of Pennsylvania Press, 1982).

[27] The last two sentences derive from a letter of Steven Feld to the author, June 20, 1991.

[28] See Jaap Kunst, *Around von Hornbostel's Theory of the Cycle of Blown Fifths* (Amsterdam: Royal Institute for the Indies, Mededeeling no. 76, Afdeeling Volkekunde no. 27, 1948), reprinted in Vol. 2 of *The Garland Library of Readings in Ethnomusicology*, ed. Kay K. Shelemay (New York: Garland, 1990). For Hornbostel's writings in German with English translations see *Hornbostel Opera Omnia* (The Hague: Nijhoff, 1975).

[29] See Lajos Bardos, "Natural Tonal Systems" in *Studia Memoriae Belae Bartok Sacra* (London: Boosey & Hawkes, 1958) and Mark Liberman, *The Intonational System of English* in Outstanding Dissertations in Linguistics Series (New York: Garland, 1979). A hex song invokes magic power to protect or to curse. An ubiquitous Western example mentioned earlier is "Rain, rain go away."

tics, semiotics, and computer, social, and environmental sciences have been applied at some time in twentieth-century music studies (recall the emic and etic transcriptions and the Kaluli music theory). Research trends of a generation continue to change our perspectives on music, but the topic remains intriguing.

The first musical impression visitors receive in Papua New Guinea is usually the sight and sound of hourglass-shaped drums such as the one shown in Plate II, Figure 2. These drums *(kundu)* are single-headed and 90 cm or more long. The open end of the drum may be zoomorphic. It is shaped like the mouth of a bird, crocodile, or fish, and the sounds of the drum are sometimes described by natives as imitations of the calls of regional birds.

The hourglass drum and the songs it accompanies play a central role in the ceremonial life of Papua New Guinea. For example, in the long religious Hevehe drama of Papua, constant musical accompaniment is required for every stage of the cycle, including the making of special houses, masks, and costumes beforehand as well as the actual ceremonial events.[30] When this ceremony still flourished, it often took years to complete one Hevehe, for the entire cycle might stop for six months if a death occurred in the tribe and the resulting taboo on drumming was not lifted by one of the deceased's relatives. The drum was the symbol of the Hevehe dancer's power. It was relinquished by the dancers only at a final ceremony in which they were symbolically (though not actually) killed and their magnificent giant masks destroyed.

Example 1–2 was such a functional piece. It was only used in a ceremony meant to guarantee the success of a new garden. The garden borders were brushed by the leaves of a specific plant named in the text. Now that the garden owner is dead, the song and its text no longer exist in the village; their function had ended. This practical approach to music in Melanesia, as opposed to art for art's sake, can even be found in the establishment of relations of individuals to their social matrix. For example, in a family or tribe there is often a pair of flutes (like the one shown in Plate III, Figure 4) that represents the tutelary spirits. An essential part of any boy's initiation ceremony is his introduction to the family flutes and the manner in which they should be played. Such flutes have no finger holes, so music is created by cooperation between at least two players. The flutes and their music are thus concrete symbols of the nebulous but important concepts of lineage and familial continuity.

Bamboo is the basic material of Melanesian flutes and trumpets, although conch shells and other woods may be used for larger trumpets. Papua New Guinea trumpets are used to frighten the enemy during battles, to signal success, and to enhance ceremonies. Not all Melanesian flutes and trumpets are end-blown. Sometimes only one end of the instrument is open and a mouth hole is cut on the side. As shown in Figure 4, fingers can be placed on the sides of the hole to form a flexible mouthpiece. Melanesian flutes' pitches are

[30] F.F. Williams, *The Drama of Orokolo* (Oxford: Clarendon Press, 1940), discusses the Papuan drama cycle in anthropological detail.

PLATE II. Papua New Guinean instruments

FIGURE 2. Papua New Guinean *kundu* drum. (75–100 cm long)

FIGURE 3. Papua New Guinean jew's harp.

PLATE III. Oceanic flutes

FIGURE 4. Papua New Guinean side-blown flute.

FIGURE 5. Oceania nose flute.

derived from fundamental pitches and overtones. On some instruments these may be changed by opening and closing the end of the pipe with a hand or finger. The sonic limitations of the instruments are overcome by making sets of them in different lengths (thus different fundamentals) and playing them in groups.[31] This togetherness in music is as interesting sociologically as it is pleasing sonically.

Ensemble recordings from the Solomon Islands[32] reveal an impressive variety in multipart textures and compositional sections. The name of the composer and the topic of each piece are known. This is, in fact, rather common in Melanesia, for compositions or dances are often "owned" by an individual or group, and "copyright clearance" or purchase is necessary for other persons to perform them. Thus, although we dealt earlier with the high functionality of music in nonliterate cultures, it is equally important to know that the cult of the composer and the building of multisectional forms, well known in the West, do not necessarily require the trappings of notation or a literate society. As we mentioned earlier, there is a logical necessity for redundancy in musical illiteracy, for the repetition of some fundamental parts makes possible the building of more complicated strata. However, when one hears the changes of texture, tempos, and tunes in music of such so-called primitive ensembles as the panpipes of the Solomons, it is obvious that individual compositional talent and group rehearsal and skill are as much a part of the Melanesian islanders' music as they are of European chamber music.

While noting the technical skills of Papua New Guinean instrument makers, we have emphasized the functionality of their products. Among the instruments used primarily for self-amusement is the jew's harp or jaws harp (Plate II, Figure 3). In Papua New Guinea such an instrument *(susap)* is made of a short piece of bamboo in which a tongue (in technical terms, a *lamella*) is cut. The jaws harp is placed across the player's mouth. The tongue of the instrument is made to vibrate by either plucking the end of the body with the thumb or, as seen in Figure 3, by activating the instrument with a string attached at the end. The player then creates a melody by changing the size of the mouth cavity, Jew's harp players obviously have an intuitive understanding of the basic acoustics of music. This type of instrument is found all over the world and is as much at home in its metallic form in the United States, Europe, and Siberia as it is in its bamboo form in Oceania.

The need to make musical instruments seems irresistible. Melanesians use a host of regional materials such as gourds, seed pods, coconut fronds, crayfish shells, and animal parts plus wood, cane, and bamboo.[33] Perhaps the most striking sonic ingenuity is the use of a beetle held before the mouth so the beat-

[31] For details and sounds see Gordon Spearitt's recordings in *Music of Oceania* (Musicaphon BM 30 SL 2700, 2701).

[32] *Aré Aré*, Vols. 1 and 2. Collection Musée de l'Homme LDM 30104 and 30105. See also the book by Daniel de Coppet and Hugo Zemp, *Aré Aré* (Paris: Editions du Seuil, 1978).

[33] An impressive list is found in Vida Chenoweth, ed., *Musical Instruments of Papua New Guinea* (Ukarumpa, Papua New Guinea: Summer Institute of Linguistics, 1976).

ing of its wings can be turned into different pitches like those of a jaws harp. Out of this environmental treasure come not only the winds and percussion but also strings. Strips are cut along a bamboo or sago palm tube in such a way that they are free from the tube along their lengths but still are attached at both ends. As seen in Plate IV, Figure 6, these ends are wrapped so they will not break off when wooden bridges are jammed under the strip. In Figure 6 only one bridge is used in the center so two pitches are possible. The strip becomes tight and plucking or striking it produces a musical tone.[34] If the tube is small and the sound weak, a gourd or one's mouth may be used as a resonator (see Figure 6). A tube zither from distant Madagascar is shown in Plate IV, Figure 7, for it follows the same principle although the number of strings is greater. They now may be attached and made of metal rather than being cut out of the body itself. Still, both examples reflect the power of ecology.[35]

The more one studies music in a world context, the more one becomes sensitive to and impressed by the delicate balance that continually exists between music and the sociological, psychological, religious, and physical conditions in which a society lives. Waves of international synthetics inundate most of the world. There are new popular music styles along the coasts of every Melanesian island, and portable tape machines and radios seem to penetrate the deepest jungles. Nevertheless, the power of regional traditions shows remarkable and heartening durability. They have become, for many, the most effective way to identify a people in an ever-shrinking world.[36]

Our introduction to Melanesian music has revealed a full complement of instrument types and textures from static monophony to complex polyphony. To find the musical styles of the more famous Polynesian culture of Oceania, we must move farther out into the Pacific.

POLYNESIA

The islands of the Pacific are scattered over such a wide area that one would expect to find a highly varied series of isolated cultures. A combination of amazing navigational skills and migrational incentives, however, has bound the Pacific cultures together in many ways. We will point out common characteristics while drawing our examples from special regional forms.

Although a common picture of Oceania today is one of tropical islands filled with lovely people and easy living, the history of Polynesian societies is generally one of war and oppression. Strict caste systems have predominated,

[34] Construction of such instruments can be seen on the *JVC Video Anthology of World Music and Dance* no. 29 as well as the flutes and jaws harps mentioned earlier.

[35] See Theodore Grame's "Music and Bamboo," *Ethnomusicology*, 6/1 (1962), reprinted in *Readings in Ethnomusicology* (New York: Johnson Reprint Corp., 1971).

[36] A powerful example in Latin America is found in Anthony Seeger's *Why Suya Sing* (New York: Cambridge University Press, 1987).

PLATE IV. Island tube zithers

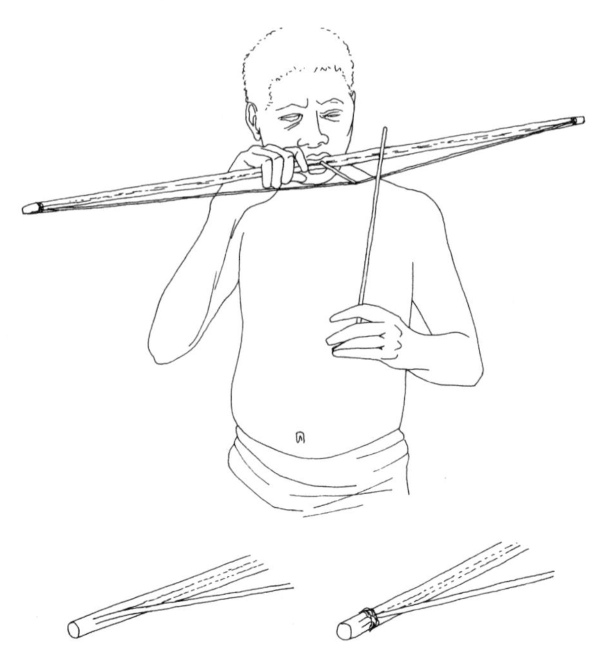

FIGURE 6. Melanesian tube zither.

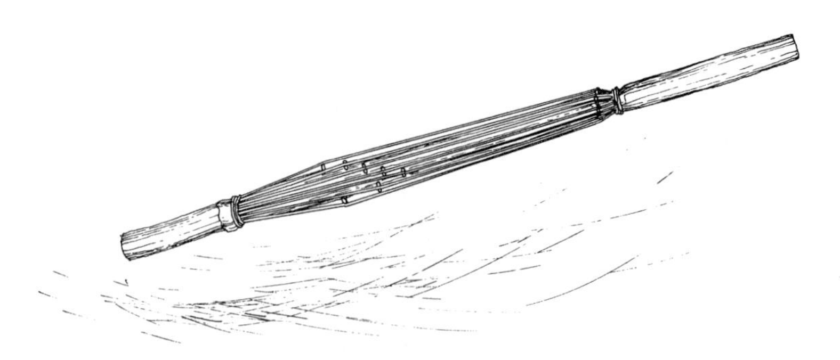

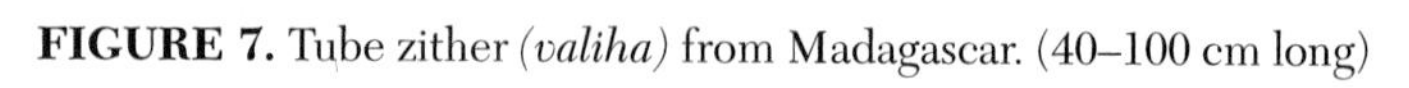

FIGURE 7. Tube zither *(valiha)* from Madagascar. (40–100 cm long)

with the aristocracy surrounded by the greatest supernatural power (*mana*) and the most *tabu* (or taboo).

Before the entrance of European diseases, the Polynesians' greatest problem was overpopulation. The consequent needs for territorial expansion brought about extensive warfare. This warfare is reflected in some of the energetic posturing dances still done today throughout Oceania. The *haka* of the Maori of New Zealand is an example, although it can be danced by both men and women and used for entertainment as well as battle. Example 1–4 was used for both, for it is said to have been sung as entertainment designed to lead to a revenge killing.[37] The music for these dances is sung in a declamatory reciting style called *heightened speech*. The notation of such music is difficult, and some form of graph, like that of Example 1–4, is preferable to the Western five-line staff.[38] The example shows typical *haka* performance practice in which the pitch rises as the leader calls out the main words before a chorus responds. This process is known in English as *lining out* and is common to many oral traditions from Euro/American rural churches and Africa to Oceania. In Maorian *haka* vocal sounds and various body percussions such as stamping feet, clapping hands, and slapping thighs help to keep the rhythm.[39] Such performance practice is common to both Polynesia and Micronesia. In general, the music and dance of these areas of Oceania can be considered extensions of poetry, thus they contrast in function and style from most of the Melanesian traditions we discussed earlier.

Because text is important in Maori music, one finds that strict rhythm and a proper vocal unison are of equal concern. Such an interest is not merely a matter of aesthetics. For the Maori to break the continuity of a song is to invite death or disaster. This is true for the more melodic *waiate* songs, whether they be death laments or love songs, and the melodically static *paatere* chants. Although the latter may seem at first to be slanderous gossip, they contain important tribal or personal genealogies. Chants concerning such matters appear throughout Oceania, for the individual's place in the social and political structure of society is largely determined by one's family tree. In the preliterate period, genealogical chants were the best way of keeping track of such complicated information. Thus insistence on accuracy in the rendition of chants and the seriousness of musical training were, and to some extent still

[37] For the story, see Mervyn McLean and Margaret Orbell, *Traditional Songs of the Maori* (Auckland, NZ: Auckland University Press, 1975), 138. The text says "Everyday Te Aea. We meet at everyday, Te Aea," Te Aea being the place of the killings. Today, New Zealand rugby fans all know a *haka* that is part of the opening ritual of a Maori team. Foreign competing teams are often compromised.

[38] See various approaches in Vol. 4 of *The Garland Library of Readings in Ethnomusicology*.

[39] A colleague once suggested that such sonic instruments should be called *corpophones*. Musical instruments are usually defined as being things beyond the human body. See "Instruments" in *The New Harvard Dictionary of Music*, ed. Don Randel (Cambridge, Mass.: Harvard University Press, 1986). Drawings of dance movements are seen in Alan Armstrong and Reupena Ngata, *Maori Action Songs* (Wellington: A.H. & A.W. Reed, 1973).

EXAMPLE 1–4. A Maori *haka* dance song transcribed from the recording *Maori Songs of New Zealand* (Smithsonian/Folkways 4433, side 1, band 6; book cassette, track 6). Sound and transcription used by permission.

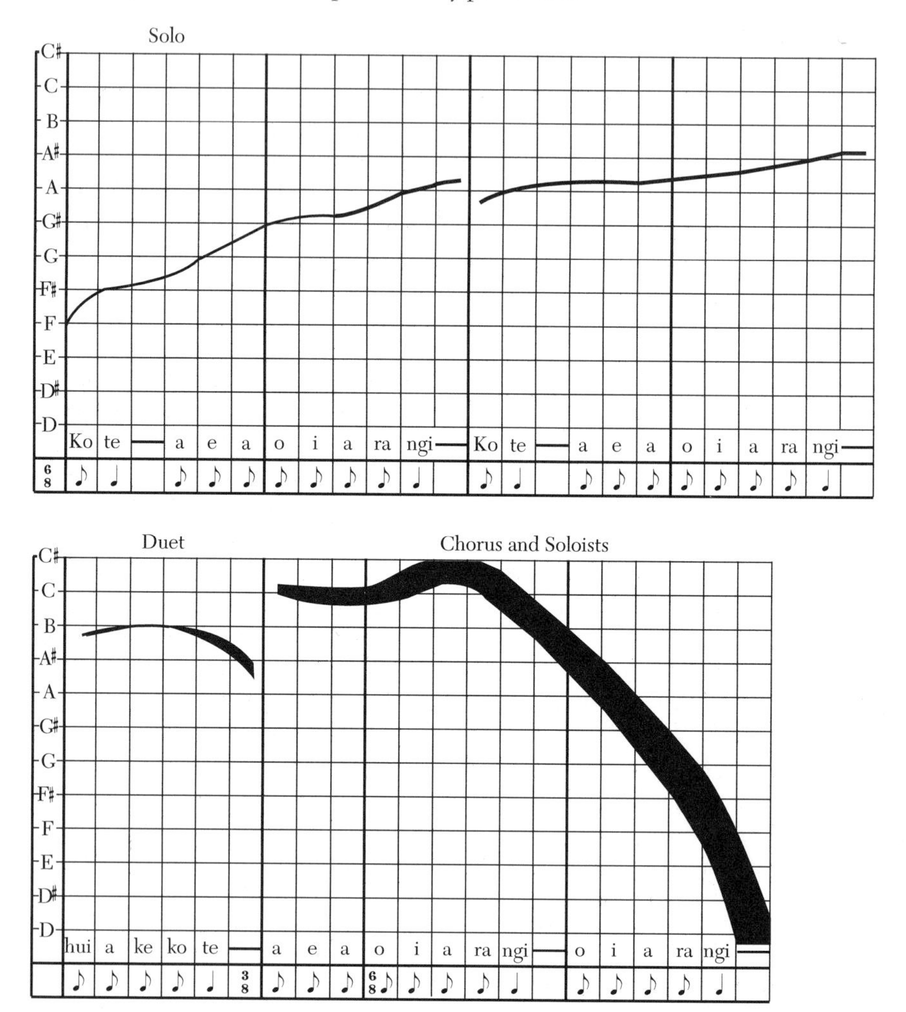

are, important. They help identify the social position of a performer as well as provide protection from potential supernatural (or sociological) harm. Under such conditions, musical style tends to remain conservative and to resist the influence of other musical cultures. Such is the case in some Polynesian and Micronesian groups.

Maori songs concentrate on a reciting tone called the *oro.* In the genealogical chants and similar forms of tribal historical chants, this tone is surrounded by tones of indeterminate pitch so no specific scale system emerges. A study of *waiata* songs has shown that seemingly meaningless ornamented solos by the lead singer are actually "cueing" devices that help distinguish the formal divisions of the piece.[40] But even the more melodic Maori pieces that use specific, accurately sung notes may employ only three or four tones and use an iterative or progressive form. Such limited melodies serve primarily as memory aids in presenting the words; the songs are listened to for the information they contain more than for a musically satisfying effect. Because of the strong word orientation of such music, many songs are without meter or are heterometric, shifting accent to keep in step with the text.

In analyzing the tonal systems of Maori chants, one often finds tones that do not fit within the tempered twelve tones of the Western scale. These "notes between the notes" are not mistakes. They are reflections of a different cultural concept of standard pitches. When one tries to notate these so-called *microtones* in Western five-line staff notation, there is obviously a problem. This is sometimes solved by placing plus (+) or minus (–) signs or arrows (↑ or ↓) above the notes that lie outside the Western tempered scale. Unfortunately, this system does not tell the reader how much higher or lower a given pitch may be. This problem was solved by Alexander Ellis (1814–1890) when he devised the *cents system.* He divided the octave into 1,200 equal parts. One hundred of these divisions represent the standard Western tempered half-step. If, therefore, an interval is 76 cents, its relation to the 100-cent half step or any other size of interval calculated in cents is easily seen.[41] Thus the cents system is an accurate comparative method for measuring intervals that in turn can be used to describe scales. Measurement of an individual pitch, however, is indicated by the number of vibrations per second, for the cents system measures only intervals. Originally both cents and vibration measurements were made by ear with the aid of a device called a calibrated monochord. This consists of a single string stretched over a board on which either cents or vibration figures are marked. The pitch of the string can be changed by moving a bridge along the calibrated board. The ethnomusicologist then tries to match the sound of the monochord with that of the musical tone in question. Today electronic equipment can be used instead, with much greater accuracy.

Not all Oceanic melodies are difficult to notate and describe tonally. There are many lyrical tunes. There are also various forms of indigenous as well as Western-influenced harmonies. They appear in the form of drones, triads, and (occasionally) fourths and fifths. The most common indigenous vocal polyphony of Oceania is a drone that is often sung in the same rhythm as the melody or in a repeating pattern (an ostinato). Much of the polyphonic music in Oceania today, however, reflects the influence of four-part Christian hymns or

[40] See Mervyn McLean, "Cueing as a Formal Device in Maori Chant," *Ethnomusicology,* 12/1 (1968).

[41] Most measurements are now done by electronic and computer systems. To see the logarithmic methods, read the original Alexander Ellis article (1885) reprinted in *The Garland Library of Readings in Ethnomusicology,* Vol. 7; see Jaap Kunst's *Ethnomusicology* (The Hague: Nijhoff, 1959), 2–9; or see Kathryn Vaughn on pitch measurement in *Ethnomusicology an Introduction,* ed. Helen Myers (London: Macmillan, 1992), 462–68.

two-part pieces that had been specially designed for missionary work by using pentatonic tunes and often a call-and-response performance practice. An example of a mixture of traditions is the Tahitian *himene* (elsewhere *himeni, imene*). Its style of polyphony combines Western-derived counterpoint with an indigenous drone. Although the name is obviously based on the word *hymn,* the texts of such music are sometimes secular. When such foreign and native elements are combined, the process is called *acculturation.* This is the basic process shaping Oceanic music today.

A good Oceanic example of acculturation in a musical instrument is the Hawaiian *ukulele.* It is a native version of the Portuguese mandolin or guitar *(bragha),* which was imported to Hawaii in the late 1870s. Today its name is Hawaiian, the chords it plays are Western, and the tunes sung to its accompaniment are a mixture of both. The Hawaiian manner of playing "slack-key" guitar with different tunings and of stopping the strings with a metal bar or a bottle is yet another aspect of modern Hawaiian music. Electric amplifiers contribute to its sliding, twangy sound. It may have begun when Latin American herdsmen arrived with the first cattle, but it is very Hawaiian now.

The ukulele also has a Hawaiian ancestor called the *ukeke.* This instrument is a stick of wood to which are attached two strings that are raised from the wood by a bridge at each end. One end is placed on the player's mouth to give the instrument a resonance chamber. It was played primarily for evening serenading, and missionaries forbade its use.

We showed in our Melanesian survey that there are indigenous classifications of instruments. Hawaiians traditionally used some eighteen categories of instruments based on their use or the material from which they are made (*pahu hula,* "dance drum"; *kala au,* "strike wood"; or *ili ili,* "pebbles"). All these fine systems present a problem when trying to speak about world music. In the early twentieth century Hornbostel and Curt Sachs (1881–1959) proposed a method of describing and classifying musical instruments in as neutral a scientific manner as possible.[42] The system is based on the materials whose vibrations create what we perceive as sound; in this system there are five classes—*idiophones, aerophones, membranophones, chordophones,* and *electrophones.* In describing indigenous Hawaiian instruments we also will illustrate terminology from *organology,* the science of musical instrument research.

The *ukeke* and the ukulele are classified as chordophones because their sound is produced by the vibration of a string. Actually, there are four kinds of chordophones. The *ukeke,* for example, is a *zither* because its strings are the

[42] See Erich von Hornbostel and Curt Sachs, "Classification of Musical Instruments," translated from the original German by Anthony Baines and Klaus P. Wachsman in *Galpin Society Journal,* 14 (1961), 3–29, reprinted in *The Garland Library of Ethnomusicology Readings,* Vol. 6, and reproduced in *Ethnomusicology an Introduction,* ed. Helen Myers (London: Macmillan, 1992), 444–61. A shorter version is found in Curt Sachs, *The History of Musical Instruments* (New York: Norton, 1940), 454–67.

same length as its soundboard.[43] The ukulele, however, is a plucked *lute* because its strings are parallel to its soundboard and extend beyond it along a neck or fingerboard. (The Western violin is an example of a bowed lute.) The other two types of chordophone are not found in indigenous Polynesian music. They are the *harp,* with its strings at right angles to the soundboard, and the *lyre,* whose strings are suspended from the crossbar of a yoke and are parallel to the soundboard. A Southeast Asian example of a harp is shown in Plate XXII, Figure 54 (p. 155); an Ethiopian lyre is shown in Plate VII, Figure 17 (p. 69).

Another instrument indigenous to Hawaii is the *puili,* a set of split bamboo beaters played in pairs. This is classified as an idiophone, an instrument whose sound is produced without stretching the basic material of which it is made. The gourd rattle *uliuli,* topped with feathers, is another Hawaiian idiophone; so is the *ili ili,* a double pair of smooth lava pebbles that are clicked like castanets. The double calabash *(ipu),* which is hit on the sides and thumped on the ground is also idiophonic. The *pahu* skin-head drum, however, is a membranophone, because its tone is generated by a vibrating membrane. Unlike the hourglass-shaped drum of New Guinea and its environs, the *pahu* drum is cylindrical. The sides of the cylinder are often carved into open latticework at the bottom so the lower half of the body is a stand for the drum rather than a resonating part of the instrument. This form of drum and the hourglass type are the two typical forms found in Oceania.

A common form of wind instrument in Oceania is the nose flute (Plate III, Figure 5), which in Hawaii is called the *ohe hano ihu.* It is classified as an aerophone, since its sound is caused by the vibration of a column of air. The conch-shell trumpet of Hawaii is also an aerophone, although the method of setting the air column in vibration differs. These differences are noted in the subclasses of aerophones. If the sound results from blowing across a hole, the instrument is a *flute* (end-blown or side-blown, depending on the position of the tube). If the air column is directed to a thin edge someplace below the point of mouth contact, as in a recorder or tonette, the instrument is a *block flute* or fipple flute. *Reed* aerophones use either single or double reeds that can be *free* (not touched directly by the lips) or *controlled* by lip pressure. If buzzing lips create the sound, the instrument is a trumpet or horn. All forms of aerophone appear in Oceania. In Hawaii, however, only the flute and trumpet types are found. The former is played for self-amusement and the latter for signaling and for ceremonial effect.

The main use of Hawaiian idiophones and membranophones is to accompany the *hula,* the characteristic dance of Hawaii. Musically the *hula* is a *mele* chanted poem. The gestures of the dance interpret such texts. Occasionally, instruments are used during *oli,* the nondance declamatory chants. As shown in Examples 1–5A and B, Hawaiian *oli* and *mele* music reflect typical

[43] The tube zither in Plate IV, Figure 6, could be called an *idiochord* because the string, as shown in the drawing, is actually still an attached part of the bark of the tube.

EXAMPLE 1–5. *Oli* and *mele hula* chants from *Hawaiian Chant, Hula, and Music* (Smithsonian/Folkways 8750, side 1, tracks 1 and 2; book cassette, tracks 7 and 8). Transcription and recording used by permission of the Smithsonian.[44]

EXAMPLE 1–5A

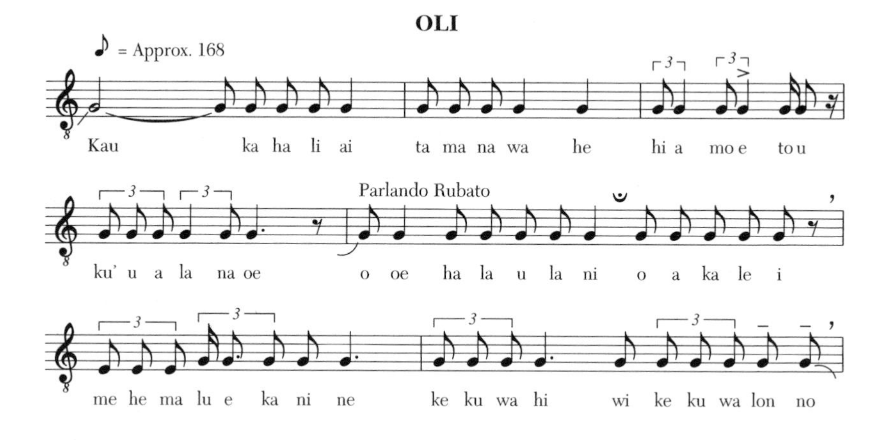

styles of Oceania. The *oli* transcribed is practically a monotone and completely word oriented in rhythm. The *mele hula,* by contrast, uses a three-tone (tritonic) scale, and the words are fitted into an isometric accompaniment on two drums. Note that even in such a restricted music the singer creates great variety by using ten different rhythmic versions of the first two beats of each measure while maintaining continuity with the same rhythm for the last two beats in every measurement except measure 16. Such ingenuity is easier to see in notation than to produce in performance. (The art of the *hula* is by no means restricted to the gracefully symbolic and occasionally erotic movements of the dancers.) Once again we see how the native musician displays the human talent for shaping musical materials in an interesting fashion.

The qualities we have seen in Hawaiian music are found in the myriad other island cultures that are part of Polynesia. Poetic vocal music predominates; chant, songs, or dance accompaniment and indigenous multipart music blend with the missionary traditions. Studies of the music and dance of Tonga, Samoa, and Tahiti bring new terms and musical or choreographic subtleties to please us, but in our extensive musical/intellectual journey we cannot stop at

[44] Example 1–5A is a prayer to Laka, goddess of the hula. The text of seven of its eleven lines says: (1) At the time of my sleep, (2) a memory appears, (3) Awaken, (4) O Halua-lani, (5) O Hoakalei, (6) The bird is singing, (7) on the mountain. In Example 1–5B the opening word relates to a legendary place in Tahitia (Kahikilaulani) or a place from which gods are thought to have come to Hawaii. The complete text has never been translated. This footnote information is courtesy of Dr. Elizabeth Tatar of the Bishop Museum, Honolulu.

EXAMPLE 1–5B

HULA

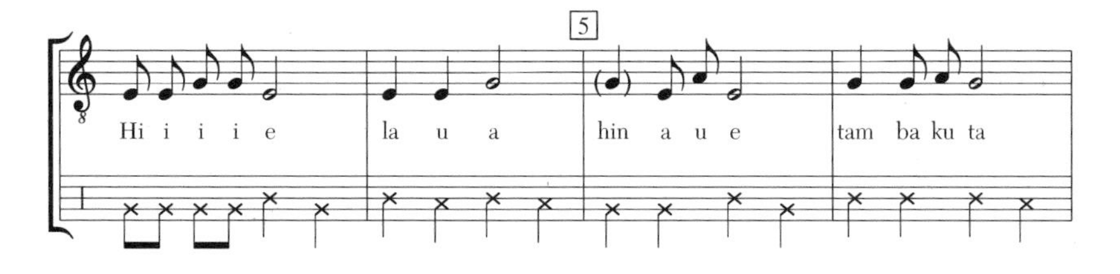

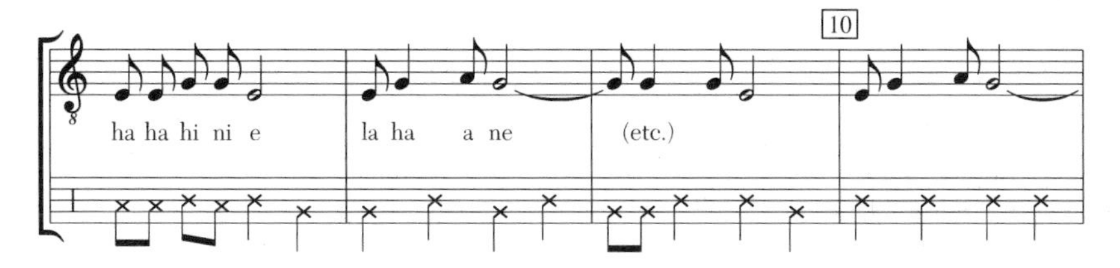

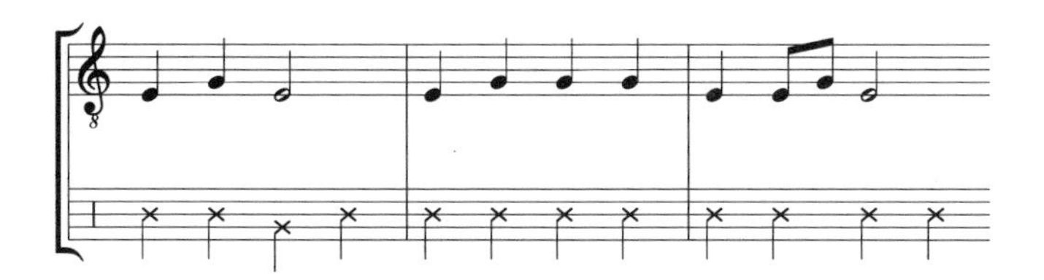

every inviting port.[45] The island cultures themselves have frequently visited one another and exchanged styles of dance and music. Tourism has played an important role in both the retention and change of Oceanic arts.[46] "Pan-Pacific pop" provides several mixed styles to tempt our sonic palette; the many immigrant Asian populations that now reside in Oceania present yet another musical challenge. Given the long journey ahead, our intellectual boat must sail on to the Northwest indigenous ocean traditions.

MICRONESIA

Many of our general statements in the previous section referred to both Polynesia and Micronesia because, although naturally there are differences that must arise between cultures on atolls and islands so distant from each other, our generalities about poetry orientation and the resultant emphasis on vocal music and dance hold basically true throughout these two areas of Oceania. The first studies of Micronesian music itself resulted from a few early twentieth-century German expeditions in the Caroline Islands plus isolated German, American, and Japanese efforts before and after World War II. These studies reveal a predominantly vocal tradition emphasizing heightened speech or a static melodic style, like that heard in the West when a litany is chanted. Homophony, when it appears, is based on any interval, although parallel fourths seem most common, along with the use of drones. The integration of singing with gesture is perhaps the most impressive aspect of Micronesian music culture: Line dances or sitting dances are abundant, and movement is as much a part of a lament as it is of an invocation or a serenade.

The musical instruments of Micronesia are few. The shell trumpet and nose flute (like that in Plate III, Figure 5) are the most common, although standard flutes and jaws harps are found. Occasionally one even finds a single-reed aerophone made of cane or bamboo. A common idiophone in Micronesia is a stick carried by men in certain dances; the performers strike one another's sticks in the course of the choreography. Indigenous stringed instruments are rare, although one can find local imitations of ukuleles and guitars. Membranophones, likewise, are not common, although the hourglass single-headed drum found in New Guinea is also used as far north as the Marshall Islands. In keeping with the ecology of atoll life, the skins of these drums are made of

[45] For fine armchair visits read Richard Moyle, *Tongan Music* (Auckland, NZ: Auckland University Press, 1987), and *Traditional Samoan Music* (Auckland, NZ: Auckland University Press, 1988). For dance see Andrea Kaeppler, "Polynesian Music and Dance," in Elizabeth May, ed., *Music of Many Cultures* (Berkeley: University of California Press, 1980), 134–53, and Jane Moulin, *The Dance of Tahiti* (Papeete, Tahiti: C. Gleizal, 1979).

[46] See George Lewis, "Beyond the Reef: Role Conflict and the Professional Musician in Hawaii," *Popular Music*, 5 (1985), 189–98, or Elizabeth Tatar, *Strains of Culture, The Impact of Tourism on Hawaiian Music*, Bishop Museum Special Publications 78 (Honolulu: Bishop Museum Press, 1987).

shark's belly or parts of the stingray, rather than of lizard or snake skin. There are many atolls without any indigenous musical instruments.

The diffuse cultural history of these scattered islands is partly the result of the variety of colonial powers that have ruled, administered, and even moved indigenous populations. Although late twentieth-century political efforts have placed many Oceanic island groups into the so-called third world or developing nation arena, one could also say that many belong to the disenfranchised or fourth world: people without countries of their own, usually minorities without regional power. All Oceanic arts share the conflict of cultural identification and the economic needs for tourist art.[47] The value of either type of music is relative to the position of the evaluator. Hotel musicians and older tourists fight for local "Hawaiian" sounds. In contrast radio stations and young tourists or natives concentrate on hits from charts of the international pop music industry. Regional youth may also support Pan-Pacific pop as a form of sonic independence. At the same time, for Micronesian men and women at a funeral who sing a repetitive lament filled with sliding indistinct pitches, there is great effect in the music, just as there is great release in singing a dance song even if it only uses three notes. The story a song tells or the poetry it supports may be ample reason for its existence[48] even without the accompanying dance. Music in Micronesian culture today does not loom large in a world survey, but it serves important functions for the people who use it in daily life. One can only wonder what this music might have been like in the days of the great Pacific migrations. Fortunately, centers for Oceanic music studies were established in the 1970s at the University of Hawaii and at the University of Auckland in New Zealand. Through their efforts and those of the new nationalist movements of the late twentieth century, we may find there is much more to learn, hear, and enjoy in this music that still floats on the tides of the Pacific Ocean.

BIBLIOGRAPHICAL AND AUDIOVISUAL NOTES

General Ethnomusicology Sources

Reliable short articles on ethnomusicological terms and world music cultures along with bibliographies are found in *The New Grove Dictionary of Music and Musicians,* 20 vols.; ed. Stanley Sadie (London: Macmillan Press, 1980). A historical view of the discipline is found in the seven volumes of *The Garland Library of Readings in Ethnomusicology,* ed. Kay Kaufman Shelemay (New York: Garland, 1990), and contemporary views in Bruno Nettl's *The Study of Ethnomusicology: Twenty-Nine Issues and Concepts* (Urbana: University of Illinois Press, 1983). See also Nettl's *The Western Impact on World Music* (New York: Schirmer, 1985). Helen Myers edited two volumes in *The New Grove Handbooks in Music*

[47] See Nelson H.H. Graburn, *Ethnic and Tourist Arts: Cultural Expression from the Fourth World* (Berkeley: University of California Press, 1976).

[48] For a fine sense of atoll poetry and music, see Edwin Burrows, *Flower in My Ear* (Seattle: University of Washington Press, 1963).

series: *Ethnomusicology An Introduction* (London: Macmillan, 1992) and *Ethnomusicology Historical and Regional Studies* (New York: Norton, 1993).

In an ever-expanding field, the abstracts in *RILM Abstracts* and the bibliographies of every issue of *Ethnomusicology* are most useful. Articles and reviews in the latter and in the *Yearbook for Traditional Music* and *The World of Music* are equally important. Three ten-year indexes of *Ethnomusicology* exist; *The World of Music* equivalent is in 20/1 (1988). A topic index of Vols. 1–21 of *Asian Music* is found in 21/2 (1990). Musical observations in ethnological monographs are found in the Human Relations Area File (HRAF) by using area code letters (like O for Oceania, OJ for Papua New Guinea) and the numbers 355 or 354 for music or musical instruments. Non-English sources are translated. The HRAF is found only in major libraries.

The Western classifications of musical instruments with fine drawings is seen in *Musical Instruments of the World* (London: Paddington Press, 1979). A study of Western and indigenous systems is Margaret J. Kartomi's *On Concepts and Classifications of Musical Instruments* (Chicago: University of Chicago Press, 1990). A source for public school lessons is *Multicultural Perspectives in Music Education*, eds. William Anderson and Patricia Shehan Campbell (Reston, Va.: MENC, 1989). Peter Manuel's *Popular Musics of the Non-Western World* (New York: Oxford Press, 1988) includes Pacific, Chinese, Middle Eastern, and Southeast Asian materials, as does the research in the periodicals *Popular Music* and *Popular Music and Society*.

General Audiovisual Materials

The *UNESCO Collection of Traditional Music* series (IMC UNESCO, 1 rue Miollis, 75732 Paris) is the most complete set of documented non-Western music. Examples quoted in this book are listed as UNESCO Series. Le Chant du Monde produces documented recordings such as the *Collection C.N.R.S.* edited by Gilbert Rouget from the Musée de l'Homme. Smithsonian/Folkways Records is rich in earlier ethnology recordings. The *JVC Video Anthology of World Music and Dance* (National Museum of Ethnology, Osaka, Japan) contains 30 volumes of 500 sequences of mixed value from 100 countries. Examples noted in this book are listed as *JVC Video*. They are reviewed in *Asian Music*, 24/2 (1993).

Oceania Studies

Bibliographies and Regional Special Issues

Historical and modern sources are found in the following sources:

Andersen, Johannes C. *Maori Music with Its Polynesian Background*, Memoir no. 10, supplement to the *Journal of the Polynesian Society*, 1934 (contains many old sources).

Crisp, Deborah. *Bibliography of Australian Music: An Index of Monographs, Journal Articles, and Theses* (Armidale, NSW: Australian Music Studies Project, 1982).

Feld, Steven. *Sound and Sentiment: Birds, Weeping, Poetics and Song in Kaluli Expression* (Philadelphia: University of Pennsylvania Press, 1982).

Fischer, Hans. *Sound-Producing Instruments of Oceania* (Port Moresby: Institute of Papua New Guinea Studies, 1983), translated from the 1958 German edition.

Gourlay, K.A. *A Bibliography of Traditional Music in Papua New Guinea* [1876–1972] (Port Moresby: Institute of Papua New Guinea Studies, n.d.).

McLean, Mervyn. *An Annotated Bibliography of Oceanic Music and Dance* [1777–1979] (Wellington: The Polynesian Society, 1977); *Supplement* (Auckland: The Polynesia Society, 1981).

Moyle, Alice. "Source Materials: Aboriginal Music of Australia and New Guinea," *Ethnomusicology,* 15/1 (1971).

Niles, Don, comp. *Commercial Recordings of Papua New Guinea Music 1949–1983* (Boroko: Institute of Papua New Guinea Studies, 1984), reprint 1985 (New York: Greenwood Press, 1986).

Stoneburner, Bryan. *Hawaiian Music: An Annotated Bibliography* [1831–1980].

Ethnomusicology, 25/3 (1981), Pacific Issue, Adrienne Kaeppler, ed.

The World of Music, 32/1 (1990), Oceania issue, Richard Moyle, ed.

Books and Articles

On library computers, the following author searches will produce rich Australian finds: A. P. Elkin, Catherine J. Ellis, Alice M. Moyle, Richard J. Moyle, and Stephen Wild. Fine general studies are found by R.M. and/or C.H. Berndt such as their *The World of the First Australians,* rev. ed. (Sydney & New York: Lansdowne, 1981). See also R.J. Sheridan, "Music," in *Encyclopedia of Papua and New Guinea,* Peter Ryan, ed. (Melbourne: Melbourne University, 1972), Vol. 2, and the Dieter Christensen and Adrienne Kaeppler article on performing arts under "Oceanic Peoples, Arts of" in *Encyclopedia Britannica,* 15th ed. (1974), 13, 456–61. In the *Bernice P. Bishop Museum Bulletins* see no. 34, E.S. Handy, *Polynesian Religion;* nos. 162 and 185 by Laura Thompson; *Southern Lau, Fiji* and *The Marianas.* E.G. Burrows wrote *Songs of Uvea,* no. 183, and *Native Music of the Tuamotus and Futuna,* no. 109. Helen Robert's no. 29, *Ancient Hawaiian Music,* remains a classic. Oceanic articles in *Ethnomusicology* are Richard Moyle (18/1, 1974); Vida Chenoweth (10/3, 1966); Steven Feld (28/3, 1984); Adrienne Kaeppler (14/2, 1970; 15/2, 1971; 16/2, 1972); Mervyn McLean (12/1, 1969); Hugo Zemp (23/1, 3, 1979); and Steven Wild (28/2, 1984). See also Special Issues.

Song Collections

Beamer, Nova, ed. *Na Mele Hula, A Collection of Hawaiian Hula Chants* (Hawaii: Institute for Polynesian Studies, Brigham Young University, 1987), with cassette.

McLean, M., and M. Orbell. *Traditional Songs of the Maori* (Wellington, 1975).

Moyle, Richard. *Songs of the Pintupi* (Canberra: Australian Institute of Aboriginal Studies, 1979).

Tongan Music (Auckland: Auckland University Press, 1987).

Traditional Samoan Music (Auckland: Auckland University Press, 1988).

Ross, M., T. Donaldson, S. Wild, eds. *Songs of Aboriginal Australia* (Sydney: University of Sydney, 1987).

Rossen, Jane Mink. *Songs of Bellona Island* (Copenhagen: Forlaget Kragen, 1987), 2 vols.

Audiovisual Materials

The Australian Institute of Aboriginal Studies (PGO 553 Canberra ACT 2601, Australia) is a basic source for films, records, and studies. *JVC Video* Vols. 29–30 have Oceanic examples from staged performances at the Fourth Festival of Pacific Arts held in Tahiti in June 1985. Some regional materials from Australia and Melanesia are included. Among Australian records are UNESCO, *Aboriginal Music from Australia* (6586 034) and Smithsonian/Folkways *Australian Folksongs and Ballads* (8718), *Tribal Music of Australia* (4439), and *Songs of Aboriginal Australia and Torres Strait* (4102). For Oceania there are UNESCO *Fataleka and Baegu Music; Malaita, Solomon Islands* (6586 018), and Smithsonian/Folkways. *Polynesian Dance of Bellona (Mungik) Solomon Islands,* Jane Mink Rossen, ed. (4274), and *Polynesian Songs and Games from Bellona* (4273). Record stores are filled with Pacific pop music. Remember to check the record reviews in the journals listed here.

A SONIC GLOSSARY INDEX FOR CHAPTER 1

(Speaker: Vida Chenoweth, Oceanic linguist)

*not on language cassette

TWO
ISLAND SOUTHEAST ASIA FROM THE PHILIPPINES TO INDONESIA

The chain of islands that extends from Sumatra through the Malay Archipelago to the Philippines contains a variety of cultural-historical influences as well as many indigenous developments. In this survey we start at the northeast end of the chain and point out some of the ways in which indigenous and foreign styles have interacted to produce a rich variety of musics and musical instruments.

THE PHILIPPINES

If we look first at the remote tribes of the northern and central Philippine Islands we find that they share many traits with the peoples of Oceania. For example, Philippine tribes have a large repertoire of orally transmitted histories and mythologies which, like those of many Oceanic and Southeast peoples, are often sung in litany style with much use of sliding pitches. In addition, these three areas share instrument types like jaws harps, end-blown and nose flutes, and tube zithers, with frequent use of bamboo. Some mountain peoples of Luzon, however, use flat bronze gongs *(gangsa)*, which imply an earlier Chinese contact. These gongs in the Philippines are used in ensembles or carried by dancers and are struck by a beater or played with hands like a drum. Each performer plays a specific rhythmic pattern on one different-pitched gong. A tune created by such interlocking of different tones or short melodic fragments is known as a *resultant* or *composite* melody. We observed them in Oceanic flute ensembles (see p. 22), but the use of tuned gongs played like drums seems unique to the northern Philippines.

The dominant foreign cultural forces in the Philippines were Spanish and, in the south, Muslim. The Spanish tradition has spread deep into the interior of the Philippines where, for example, one can find a small four-stringed plucked native lute called the *kitara,* a word obviously related to "guitar." Spanish influence becomes ever stronger as one moves toward Philippine urban culture. For example, it is possible to see in a Philippine village a Moro-Moro folk drama about the conflicts between Christian and Muslim knights in ancient Spain. The preservation of this tradition in the Philippines is an example of the principle of *marginal survival,* noted in Chapter 1, which holds that the oldest forms of many traditions are not found at the centers of cultures but rather on their more distant fringes. The most common Spanish tradition in the villages and urban districts of the Philippines is the *rondalla* band and its music. The traditional *rondalla* band contains mandolin-type instruments *(bandurría, laud,* and *octavina),* guitars, a double bass *(bajo)* with a fretted fingerboard, and often an accordion. The band's repertoire includes Spanish, Latin American, and vintage American dance forms (waltz, jota, tango, foxtrot) plus arrangements of Philippine folk songs and *kundiman* sentimental ballads. Some of the dances reflect older Spanish styles, whereas others, such as the Tagalog *kumintang* pantomime dances, seem to mix prehispanic and colonial traditions.[1] Even the famous Philippine *tingkling* dance, in which dancers maneuver between clashing poles, shows a mixture of cultural styles: The basic step is said to come from the movements of a native bird; the arm positions and the musical accompaniment seem to be Spanish.[2]

The dominant style of urban and rural music in the northern and central Philippine Islands is based on the social dances and popular music of nineteenth-century Spain, with some influence also of local *zarzuela* (light operas) and Catholic religious music. However, prehispanic music traditions are still strong in the mountain tribes of the north as well as in the jungles of many of the southern islands. Islam, in addition, is a strong influence in the south, partly because of post–fifteenth-century Indonesian contacts. Musically, the parallels between Indonesia and the Philippines are seen most easily in the many non-Oceanic instruments found among the Moros and other southern peoples. For example, xylophones *(gabbang),* often used to accompany story-

[1] A similar kind of compromise can be noted in the urban and rural music of South America, particularly in its western and northern coastal areas.

[2] The study of the relationship of this dance to similar forms in Southeast Asia belongs to the discipline called ethnic dance or ethnochoreology. See "Foundations for the Analysis of the Structure and Form of Folk Dance: A Syllabus," *Yearbook of the International Folk Music Council,* 6 (1974). The publication is now called the *Yearbook for Traditional Music.* See also the publications of CORD (Committee on Research in Dance).

tellers, Muslim religious songs, or musical flirtation contests, are found in the Sulu Archipelago.

Whereas flat gongs in the North imply Chinese influence, knobbed (bossed) gongs reflect influences from the island cultures southwest of the southern Philippines (see map). The best known examples are the *kulintang*[3] ensembles. They are found in various combinations east from Kalimantan. The ensemble of the Magindanao people of Mindanao, Philippines, consists of a held gong *(badendil* or *tunggalan)* struck with a hard stick, a single-headed goblet-shaped drum *(dadabuan),* or two double-headed drums *(gendang* or *gandang),* plus hanging gongs with deep sides *(agung)* or short *(gandingan)* and a set of eight to eleven knobbed pot gongs *(kulintang)* that are placed on a rack (somewhat like one row of those in the *bonang* shown in Plate VI, Figure 15).[4]

The instruments enter one at a time in special rhythmic patterns to create a stratification of sounds somewhat similar to that of Indonesian orchestras. The major difference in a *kulintang* performance is that each piece is based on a so-called rhythmic mode rather than on a melodic theme. As we see later in our Indonesian study, however, this emphasis on rhythm and on contour rather than on melody may be a crucial factor in most non-Christian musics found along the chain of cultures from the southern Philippines to Sumatra.

Another instrumental clue concerning the cultural inheritances of the southern Philippines is the *gitgit,* a small bowed lute with three strings that is often played by young men as they go courting. It is a diminutive version of the ubiquitous Muslim spike fiddle, known most commonly as the *rebab.* The *rebab,* in its original Near Eastern form, is believed to be not only the distant ancestor of the Philippine *gitgit* (via the Indonesian *rebab;* see Plate VI, Figure 12), but also the predecessor of the bowed lutes of Europe, from the medieval *rebec* to the modern violin.[5] A belief in such a widespread relation of instruments is held by adherents of the *theory of diffusion,* which claims that every basic instrument type was invented only once and then spread about the world in variant forms. An opposing *theory of polygenesis* holds that each instrument was invented in several different places at different times; the variants of such separate inventions may or may not have overlapped as each form spread about. So far, neither theory seems to offer the exclusive answer to the questions of relationships between musical instruments around the world; one can find examples that seem to support each argument. The relation of the *gitgit* to the *rebab,* however, certainly fits best within the concept of diffusion.

Another instrument of the southern Philippines and Sulu that seems closely connected to Indonesia is an end-blown notched flute around the top of

[3] For various spellings and names of the *kulintang* and its instruments see *The New Grove Dictionary of Musical Instruments,* Vol. 2, ed. Stanley Sadie (London: Macmillan, 1984), p. 481.

[4] Drawings of these instruments and variants are seen in *The New Grove Dictionary of Musical Instruments,* p. 480.

[5] Examples of such variants are seen in *The New Grove Dictionary of Musical Instruments,* p. 480. Violins are often *biola* in Southeast Asia.

which is tied a rattan band that helps direct the stream of air. Its construction and playing method are those of the Indonesian *suling*. A more complex relation between cultures is demonstrated by the Philippine *kudyapi* (Plate V, Figure 8). This term is sometimes used generically for native-made plucked lutes, including a diminutive version of the guitar. The *kudyapi* important to this discussion, sometimes called a boat lute because of its shape, is a two-stringed plucked lute with five rather high frets. Some claim that its most distant ancestor may be an ancient Indian chordophone called the *kechapi vina*, but it has many more immediate Southeast Asian relatives, such as the three-stringed crocodile zither (*mi gyaung*, Plate V, Figure 9) of the Mon in Burma, the more abstractly shaped Thailand *chakay* zither (Plate XXII, Figure 55), the multi-stringed Sundanese *kacapi* zither with movable bridges (from western Java; Plate V, Figure 10), and the *kachapi, kasapi,* or *sapeh* from Kalimantan, (Plate V, Figure 11) which is a plucked lute with one to three strings that are played in the banjo position rather than horizontally like the other instruments mentioned. The Philippine *kudyapi* is similar to the Mon and Thailand instruments in its physical characteristics and less like the Sundanese and Kalimantanese instruments; regarding its name, however, the reverse is true. This confusion of names and physical features illustrates the principle of *floating terms*, in which a word is transferred from one concept or instrumental type to a very different form as it moves from culture to culture or even within one culture over a period of time. It is important to note this phenomenon early in our study, because floating terms are so frequent that we cannot presume the same term will mean the same thing when it is found in a new cultural context.

Despite our discussion of influences and borrowings in Philippine music, you must not think this is basically a secondhand music tradition. The creative aspects of acculturation have been at work for centuries, and the modern ethnomusicological field worker as well as the nationalistic composers have found and are continuing to find rich stores of native music that reflect the many sides of the musical culture of the Philippines.[6]

BORNEO[7]

By the late twentieth century East Indonesia included the western half of Papua New Guinea (Irian Jaya), the island groups of Molucca and Sunda, Suluwesi (Celebes), and Kalimantan, the southern two thirds of Borneo. The northern coast of Borneo contains East Malaysia (Sarawak and Sabah) and the sultanate of Brunei. Most of these areas have Indonesian-related knobbed gongs, gong orchestras, and end-blown flutes. However, each island also has its

[6] For modern composers see Harrison Ryker, *New Music in the Orient* (Buren, The Netherlands: Knuf, 1991), Chapter 7.

[7] The colonial-period geographic term *Borneo* is used because late twentieth-century political boundaries names make any overall discussion difficult for general readers.

PLATE V. Diffusion examples from Southeast Asia

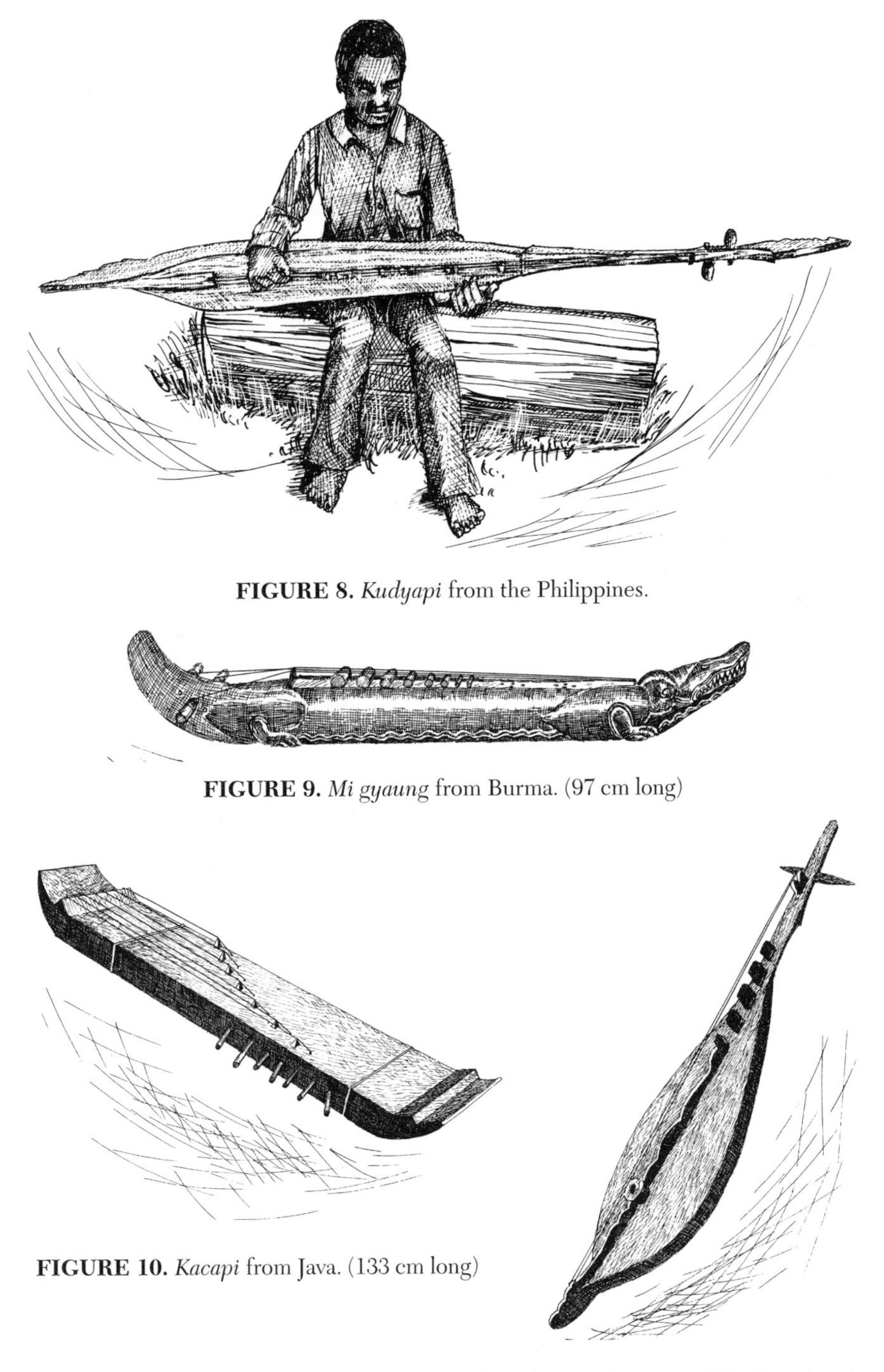

FIGURE 8. *Kudyapi* from the Philippines.

FIGURE 9. *Mi gyaung* from Burma. (97 cm long)

FIGURE 10. *Kacapi* from Java. (133 cm long)

FIGURE 11. *Kachapi* from Kalimantan. (25–30 cm long)

own, quite different kinds of music. We use the large island of Borneo as an example.

The Muruts of North Borneo (Sawarak) sing in an indigenous drone-based harmony unknown in Central Indonesia. We spoke of similar harmonies in Oceania and Papua New Guinea; they also exist among isolated groups in Taiwan and Southeast Asia, but no connection has been established as yet between these various systems.

Most of Borneo's melody and harmony is not based on Javanese scales but uses a five-tone scale without half steps, the so-called *anhemitonic* pentatonic (see Example 6–3 p. 177). Although this scale is popular throughout East Asia, its use is so widespread even in other parts of the world that it cannot be said to prove connections between cultures. However, one instrument in Borneo indicates a fairly clear link with the Asian mainland. This is an aerophone consisting of a gourd windchest holding several pipes, each of which contains a free reed. When holes on the pipes are closed, either chords or melodies can be played. Such instruments are believed to be the oldest harmonic instruments in the world. They seem to have originated in Southeast Asia, probably Laos, and spread throughout East Asia. Thus this tribal instrument of Borneo belongs to a chain of instruments that runs from the folksy *khaen* of Southeast Asia and China (Plate XXI, Figure 53) to the aristocratic *sheng* (Plate XXIV, Figure 61) of ancient China and the *sho* of the present-day Japanese court orchestra. Its most recent relatives are nineteenth-century European derivatives called the harmonica and the accordion.

These non-Indonesian examples from Borneo show that even in a seemingly isolated area a complex of influences can be absorbed into the current native style. Change is as much a part of a nonliterate culture as it is of the Western art-music world. Pure native or classical style reflects at best only a single point in a cultural time continuum, albeit a lovely one.

As areas "develop," whole villages are moved to make way for dams, roads, and industry. Ethnomusicologists attempt to dash before the machines to preserve cultures in audio or visual archives, but living traditions are changing traditions.[8] The sound and function of an ensemble of *sape (sapeh, sambe)* lute players from Sawarak performing onstage in Tokyo is not the same as that of headhunters chanting heterophonically over a *sapeh* ostinato together with the steady beating of a drum and a knobbed gong.[9] A gentler change is heard when a Murut tribe sings the English words "bye bye" in indigenous-style harmony based on the pentatonic scale.[10] All three of these examples are "native"

[8] For Dayak song texts see Carol Rubenstein, *The Honey Tree Song* (Athens: Ohio University Press, 1985), and *The Nightbird Songs* (Dumfriesshire, Scotland: Tynron Press, 1990).

[9] For the former see *Asian Musics in an Asian Perspective*, ed. Fumio Koizumi and others (Tokyo: The Japan Foundation, 1977), 38–47, and its recording. For the latter listen to band 1, side 1 of *Borneo* (Contrepoint MC 20.112). Studies on the instrument and its music are found in *The New Grove Dictionary of Musical Instruments*, p. 44–47, 100–12, 214–16.

[10] Listen to track 4, side 2, of *Murut Music of North Borneo* (Smithsonian/Folkways 4459).

to the particular groups involved and for the particular time in which they were performed.

Field workers often feel Western music has a pernicious influence on non-Western traditions, but if the non-Western culture carriers adapt it to their music, then the new musical resultant *is* the native style. When we turn to the main islands of Indonesia we can still find native traditions that have not yet succumbed to Western influence.

INDONESIA

The northern and eastern political boundaries of twentieth-century Indonesia have been mentioned. Sumatra, Java, and Bali are the three major islands that form the western end of the approximately 3,000 miles of the Indonesia chain. It is from there that the most research on Indonesia's musical arts has been done. We know something of its early culture from many stone and metal artifacts as well as from commentaries written by the Chinese, who were in contact with Indonesia from at least the third century B.C. Indian influence and Brahman Hinduism entered Java in the first and second centuries A.D. Buddhism appeared in the fifth century and was particularly influential during the powerful eighth-century Sailendra Dynasty. Brahmanism remained in parts of the empire and eventually returned to the central courts, where it merged with Buddhist and indigenous cult traditions. Trade and conflict brought various Indonesian empires in contact with the Chinese, Mongol, and Arab worlds. Islam was present in Indonesia by at least the thirteenth century and was quite prevalent by the fifteenth century. Portuguese, Dutch, English, and other Western influences have increased steadily since the sixteenth century. This long line of cultural contacts has helped create the rich mixture of musical styles found in Indonesia today, and, as we pointed out, possible relations may be found between the musics of the ancient high civilizations of Java and those of other native cultures along the Southeast Asian chain.

The Gamelan

In Indonesian, *gamelan* is a generic term for a musical ensemble. It may vary in size from a few instruments to over seventy-five. Such variety can be found not only from island to island in the vast Indonesian archipelago but also within each district of one island. Let us begin with a description of the basic instruments found in a *gamelan* of Central Java.

Although gongs and drums are the core of *gamelan* music, singing is frequently an important part of Central Javanese composition. A female soloist (*pesindhen*), a male unison chorus (*gerong*), or a mixed chorus (*gerong bedayan*) may be used, and subtle hand-clap beats can be heard in sections of many modern performances. The delicate ornamented music of the chorus is said to relate to the melody of the two-stringed *rebab,* a bowed lute (Plate VI, Figure 12), whereas the female soloist part is more analogous to that of the end-blown *suling,* a flute. The *suling* has sometimes been called a ribbon flute because, like the Philippine models, its air is directed toward the blowing edge by a piece of rattan tied around the circumference of the flute. The metal strings of the Indonesian *rebab* are tuned in fifths and fingered without pressing the strings against the pole. The tension of its animal-hair bow is maintained by hand, as is done in the European gamba tradition. In some *gamelan* compositions another stringed instrument is used, the *celempung* (*tjelempung*),[11] a zither called by some a *siter.* It has twenty-six metal strings tuned in double courses, that is, adjacent pairs of strings are tuned to the same pitch, giving a total of thirteen tones.

The bronze metallophones of a *gamelan* fall into two basic types, those with slabs or keys and those with knobbed gongs. The *saron* shown in Plate VI, Figure 13, has keys set over a box resonator. It is played with a wooden or sometimes bone mallet (*tabu*). As each new note in a melody is played, the previous one is dampened with the thumb and forefinger of the left hand. In this way the melody emerges clearly.

The *saron* comes in three sizes. The highest and smallest is called the *saron panerus* or *peking,* the middle the *saron barung,* and the lowest is the *saron demung.* In *gamelan* instrument families, there is generally a direct relation between the size of an instrument and the density of its music, the smaller and higher pitched instruments playing more notes than their larger and lower-pitched relatives.

The wooden-keyed *gambang kayu* xylophone uses a box resonator like the *saron* but is played with padded disks attached to two long thin sticks. Padded disks on short hand-held sticks are also used to play the *gender,* a series of thin bronze keys of fine alloy suspended by strings over individual tube resonators. Plate VI, Figure 14, shows the largest form, the *gender panembung* or *slentem.* It is played like the *saron* with only one stick, but the higher pitched *gender barung* and its upper-octave companion, the *gender panerus,* are played with two. The combination of key, resonator, and padded beaters produces a mellow, nonpercussive sound. Stopping this resonant tone is a problem in the higher *gender* because the two hands often play separate elaborating parts. This is solved by a supple wrist action that allows players to stop the last note played with their finger or the side of their hands while playing the next note.

A prominent member of the knobbed gong family is the *bonang* shown in Plate VI, Figure 15. Its bronze knobbed gongs are placed on ropes laced in a wooden frame and are played with two padded sticks. Like the *saron* and *gender,* it comes in three sizes. Although *bonang* music can be quite elaborate and melodic, the instrument belongs to that class of knobbed gongs whose

[11] The first spelling of Indonesian terms throughout this book conforms to the official national system. Common earlier romanization may also be shown.

PLATE VI. Java

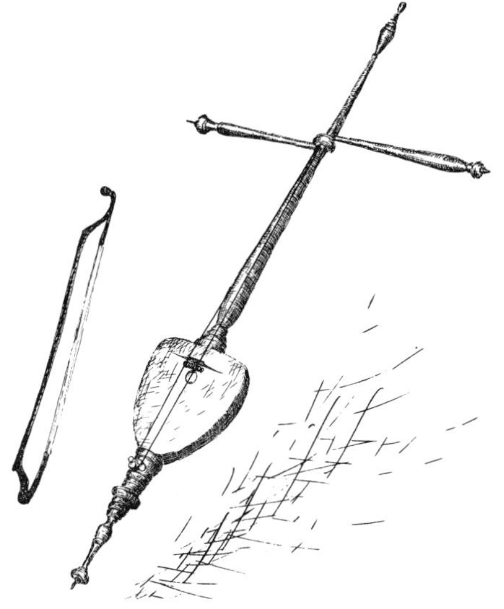

FIGURE 12. *Rebab.* (110–112 cm high; bow 60–70 cm long)

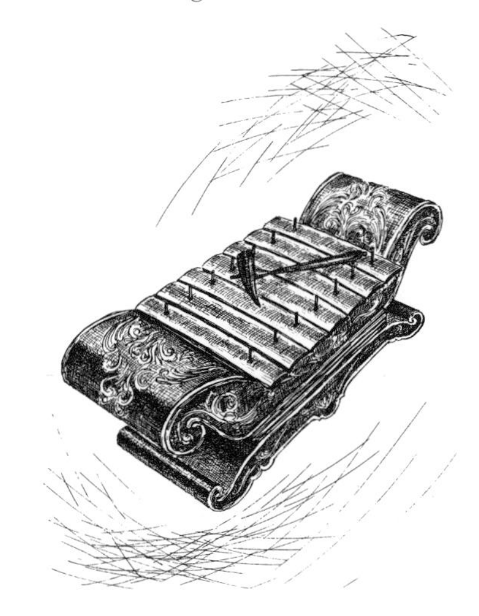

FIGURE 13. *Saron.* (60–100 cm wide)

FIGURE 14. *Gender.* (90–100 cm wide)

FIGURE 15. *Bonang.* (130–170 cm wide)

fundamental function is to mark the time. Thus the *bonang* holds a vital position in the joining of the mosaic of many layers of sound into one coherent musical event. The time-marking function of knobbed gongs becomes clearer when we observe the actions of four other instruments with the onomatopoeic names of *kethuk, kenong, kempul,* and *gong.* The *kethuk* is usually a small single horizontal knobbed gong set on ropes in a wooden frame and struck with a padded stick to produce a sharp, deadened "kethuk" sound. The *kenong* consists of a set of larger knobbed gongs placed in similar wooden frames. The *kempul* is a set of hanging knobbed gongs; the *gong agung* or *gong siyem,* which hangs impressively at the back of the orchestra, produces the deepest sound of the four.

In Java there are two basic kinds of *gamelan* playing: the loud style, with an emphasis on the bronze instruments, and the soft style, in which the flute and the stringed instruments may appear.[12] In the soft style, the *rebab* player is the leader, whereas in loud playing the leader uses *kendhang* (*gendang*) barrel drums with two lashed heads. There are also more intimate chamber music ensembles, such as a trio in Sunda (western Java) that consists of a singer, a *suling* flute player, and a *kacapi* (*kachapi*) zither player (Plate V, Figure 10). In keeping with the floating-term tradition we discussed earlier, there are several different kinds of Javanese zithers called *kacapi.* Those of the type shown in Figure 10 have from six to eighteen strings that are tuned with terminal pegs and movable bridges.

Throughout Indonesia we find an endless variety of *gamelan,* including some whose instruments are made of iron or bamboo. Ensembles of the bamboo instrument called the *angklung* have gained in popularity, perhaps under the influence of Western music education bands. Each *angklung* consists of two or more bamboo tubes tuned in octaves and hung from a frame above a slotted resonator tube in which the ends of the tuned tubes are suspended. When shaken, each *angklung* produces one pitch at as many octave intervals as it has hanging tubes. In order to play a melody it is necessary to have as many players as there are tones in the scale of the tune (unless some players use two *angklung* on different pitches). Each player shakes his or her *angklung* in a different rhythm in order to produce the melody, in a more complicated version of the composite melody technique sometimes used by Western bell ringers and by the Philippine gong beaters mentioned earlier.

In addition to the many different kinds of ensembles in Indonesia there are, of course, a variety of musical styles, extending from trance rituals to popular music. The *kroncong* popular songs are of historical interest because they

[12] Compare this with the two styles of orchestra in Southeast Asia discussed in Chapter 5, pp. 148–54.

were first derived from sixteenth-century Portuguese sailors' music. All Indonesian pop music is not from such old sources, nor is it all from the international music industry products. In the late twentieth century the *dangdut* genre speaks to Indonesian youth not only of love (as all pop music genres must) but also of unemployment and the power of born-again Islam.[13] The most powerful influences on the many styles of Indonesian music as well as literature, however, are the tales of the hero Pandji and the local versions of the Hindu *Ramayana* and *Mahabharata*. These stories have been preserved primarily through the oral traditions of the theater and solo songs as well as in orchestral and dance pieces. Of particular interest is the *wayang kulit* shadow puppet theater. The puppet operator *(dalang)* recites entire dialogues and comments to the accompaniment of an instrumental ensemble. Audiences may watch from either side of the shadow screen while the moral truths and conflicts of Indonesian thought are brought to life in epic performances that may last from sunset to dawn. The agrarian king-centered culture from which such Indonesian art forms developed may prove to show deeply rooted influences on the very structure of traditional musics as both culture and music are studied more thoroughly.[14] During Indonesia's struggle toward modernization, attempts have been made by traditional artists to relate to a changing society and lifestyle.[15] Music conservatories, notation, shorter performances, and new compositions are reflections of this concern. At this point we have clear information only about the traditional manner in which Indonesian music is put together.

Javanese Music Theory and Practice[16]

The most general Javanese term for composition is *gendhing*. Although a composition may consist of several sections or movements, the fundamental unit is the *gongan*, consisting of all the events that occur between one stroke of the largest gong and the next. Example 2–1 shows the many layers of polyphonic stratification typical of *gamelan* music that occur during one *gongan* of

[13] See Margot Cohen, "The Whole Archipelago's Doing the Dangdut," *Wall Street Journal*, July 18, 1991, A9.

[14] See Judith Becker's "Earth, Fire, Sakti, and Javanese Gamelan," *Ethnomusicology*, 32/3 (1988). Becker notes that the earth-derived metals, heat of metallurgy, and power of the spirit from which these ingredients are taken influence not only the importance of the *gamelan* to rulers but also the possible value of timbre in older *gamelan*.

[15] Essays concerning Javanese traditional worldviews can be found in the writings of Clifford Geertz, such as his *The Religion of Java* (New York: The Free Press, 1960). Part of the musical struggle for modernity is discussed in Judith Becker's *Traditional Music in Modern Java* (Honolulu: University of Hawaii Press, 1976).

[16] The author thanks Judith Becker, University of Michigan, and her graduates for much of the following explanation, although responsibility for the interpretation is mine.

EXAMPLE 2–1. One version of a *gongan* in *ketawang* form and *slendro manyura* mode from the Javanese *gemelan* piece "Puspawarna." Book cassette, track 9, recorded by Marc Benamou and used with his permission.[17]

[17] Dr. Susan Walton informs me that this is a standard "signature" opening piece for concerts held at the *mangkunegara* court in Surakata. The opening section heard on the tape uses one *(Continued)*

[EX]AMPLE 2–1 (con't)

[sin]gers to be part of a performance and seldom relates to the mood of the piece. The male vocable [inte]rjections are called *alok* or *sanggakan*. Commercial recordings of the same piece are heard on [Java]nese Court Gamelan (Nonesuch H 72044) and a Solonese version on Vol. 2 (H 72074).

EXAMPLE 2–1 (con't)

of the traditional classical four-line opening poems. The word *tresna* is the last word c
and means "love." Puspawarna means "nine kinds of flowers." The text consists of nine
ing with flowers, implying the nine *rasa* (moods) of Javanese aesthetics. The section r
"This is a medicinal flower (for the body) that makes the body's movement beautiful,
gracious, and draws the hearts of others to the person using it." The poetry is primari

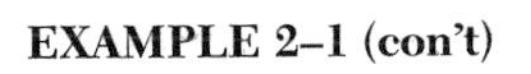

EXAMPLE 2–1 (con't)

the piece "Puspawarna."[18] Beneath the *saron* parts is shown the modern Javanese cipher notation (*kepatihan*). In this notation one can see a series of the smallest melodic units in Javanese theory; these are called *gatra* and are sets of four sonic events, including silences if they occur. Thus in Example 2–1 there are four *gatra:* .3.2, .3.1, .3.5, 6.3.[19]

Because (apart from the *kepatihan*) Example 2–1 is in linear Western notation and is furthermore only a small portion of the whole piece "Puspawarna," it is difficult to visualize the strong cyclic underpinning of the entire musical structure. The insightful Dutch musician and scholar Jaap Kunst (1891–1960) first sought to describe this phenomenon by inventing the term *colotomic structure,* by which he meant a system that marks off music into temporal units according to the entrance of specific instruments in a specific order at specific times. In recent years, studies by both indigenous and Western scholars have suggested a different approach to the structure of Javanese music and to its possible relation with other aspects of Indonesian life.[20] This view considers music as fundamentally a linking together of temporal cycles that continually subdivide in two. Example 2–2 diagrams the kinds of binary cycles that exist among the time-marking instruments in a Javanese composition set in the temporal form *ketawang* as used in the one *gongan* transcribed in Example 2–1. The *ketawang* cycle is played at double speed in the first *gongan* of this composition, but thereafter, as in most Javanese music, it is repeated at normal speed in each of the *gongan* that follow. In Example 2–2 the entrance of the gong is shown at the top of the circle. The eight sounds of the time markers are shown with letters outside the circle (T = *kethuk,* P = *kempul,* and N = *kenong*). Each time marker's divisions are built on those of its immediate successor. Therefore the *kenong* divides the gong cycle in half with its two sounds. The *kempul* divides the *kenong* part in half with its two sounds that interlock with the *kenong* divisions to divide the cycle into four parts. The *kethuk's* four sounds slice the total cycle further into eight parts. The first entrance of the *kempul* (P) is shown in parentheses because in some Central Javanese traditions it may be omitted (as it is in Example 2–1). This absence of a time marker is called a *wela,* an empty place, something that is missing from its assigned

[18] This notation is a composite of several sources: transcriptions from the recording by Francesca Cassara and Richard Wallis and reconstructions for those lines not clearly audible derived from known performance practice and from part books. Additional help was given by Wayne Forrest, the Javanese musician Sumarsam, and the director of the original performance group, Ki Wasitodipuro. A *celempung* zither, the drums, and an additional time marking *kempyang* part have not been included. The actual pitch of tone 6 is nearer Western B flat than A, and the pitch of note 5 may be closer to F sharp than to G. The placement of barlines is conjectural; they appear here (along with staff notation) for the convenience of Western readers. The actual tonal meaning of the music, outside the limitations and conventions of Western notation, can only be corrected by listening to the actual recording and adjusting one's concept for each pitch.

[19] See the *saron barung demung* line from measure 2.

[20] See Judith Becker, "Time and Tune in Java," in *The Imagination of Reality,* ed. A.L. Becker and A.A. Yengoyan (Norwood, NJ: Ablex, 1979), and Judith and Alton Becker, "A Musical Icon: Power and Meaning in Javanese Gamelan Music," in *The Sign in Music and Literature,* ed. Wendy Steiner (Austin: University of Texas Press, 1981).

EXAMPLE 2–2. The *ketawang* temporal cycle.

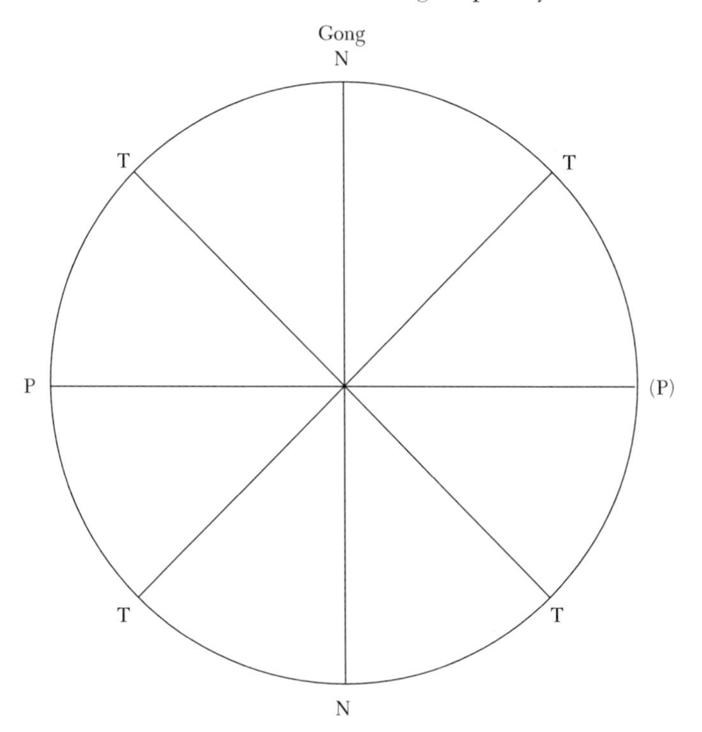

position and thus creating a silence, which is, however, still felt as part of a cycle. Listening to the recording from which Example 2–1 is derived will also reveal that entrances of some time markers such as the *kenong* in measure 3 may be slightly delayed to add extra subtlety to the overall cycle. Final gongs in a composition are often delayed in this manner. The introduction (*buka*) to a piece is often quite free rhythmically, in order not to impose the cyclicity too suddenly on the listener; and the final gong may be followed by an equally free postlude (*pathetan*) for soft instruments like the *gender, suling,* and *rebab.* Thus what appears in print to be a rather rigid system is, in performance practice, often woven in a delicate filigree manner.

A study of the *saron peking* part in Example 2–1 shows that the binary temporal divisions continue as one moves on to the various denser melodic layers of the stratifications. The *gender panerus* part reveals an additional binary division. Such binary expansions or contractions are part of a concept known as *irama.* The *irama* idea has been described as analogous to horizontal lines of dots painted on a balloon. As you blow up the balloon the distance between the dots expands, leaving room for more events to appear between each dot, whereas deflating the balloon brings the dots closer together, leaving little room for more elaborate designs between each dot. In Javanese music, the time markers' placement remains untouched, but the application of the so-called first, second, or third *irama* to the music expands the distance between notes in other melodic parts like that of the *saron* or, more centrally, the *bonang*. This leaves room for denser lines such as are seen in Example 2–1 in the *gender panerus* part.

It is not possible to explain Javanese rhythmic theory and practice fully in a short survey. Perhaps even these very preliminary examples, however, show the great sense of interdependence that is basic to *gamelan* music. This characteristic is one reason why such a complex multilayered music can be performed and maintained without reliance on detailed linear notation. Another unifying factor in this music is its tone system.

There are two basic scales in Java, the five-tone *slendro* and the seven-tone *pelog*. A study of the fixed tunings of the keys from the *saron* and *gender* of many *gamelan* throughout the island indicates there is great variety in the actual pitches of, and intervals between, the notes of these scales, although they are very accurately matched within the instruments of one *gamelan*.[21] The *slendro* scale is particularly varied. The difference between the two scales in one *gamelan* is such that a separate set of melodic instruments must be tuned to each in order to have a complete ensemble. Such a pitch difference may be seen in Example 2–3, which shows a typical (note: *not* a standard) *pelog* and *slendro* tuning, with intervals marked in cents,[22] compared with an idealized Western tempered scale of 100 cents to the half step. The word appearing with each pitch is its name in modern Javanese practice; the arabic numbers are those that would appear in present-day Javanese cipher notation. (Both these names and numbers differ from several previous court traditions; since earlier pitch names are found in many studies of Javanese music, the major ones are included in parentheses in their proper positions.)

In Central Java each scale has three modes called *pathet* (*patet*). These are shown in the upper and lower portions of Example 2–3. On the basis of material available at the time, earlier researchers felt that specific pitches tended to be used melodically in each *pathet* at moments when the time-marking *kenong*, *kempul*, or *gong* appeared. Perhaps influenced by the Hornbostel overblown fifths theory mentioned earlier (p. 18), they found in each *pathet* three so-called gong tones, located fifths apart. Recent research has cast doubts on the indigenous validity of this convenient system. For instance, the large white circles in the *pathet* sections of Example 2–3 indicate those pitches which, on the basis of recent statistics,[23] are used the most frequently in a melody when the gong is struck. The smaller white circle represents the next

[21] See Roger Vetter, "A Retrospect on a Century of Gamelan Tone Measurements," *Ethnomusicology*, 33/2 (1989). In some old *gamelan* in-tuneness is less important than timbre. Their function is to invoke the gods of earth and fire from which their metallurgical power came, and nature is not in tune either. See Becker, "Earth," footnote 14 here.

[22] The specific intervals chosen are derived from measurements for *gamelan* number 5 in Appendices 61 and 62 of Jaap Kunst, *Music in Java* (The Hague: Nijhoff, 1949).

[23] The data for pitch evaluations are derived from Appendix IV in Judith Becker, *Traditional Music in Modern Java* (Honolulu: University of Hawaii Press, 1992).

EXAMPLE 2–3. A Javanese tone system.

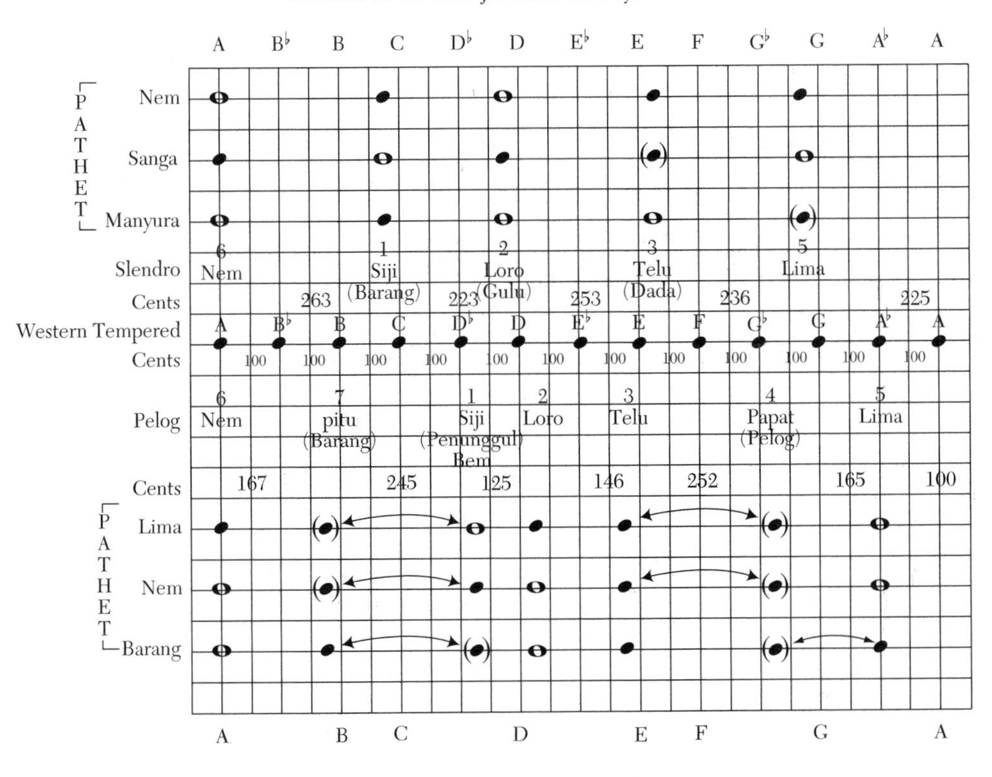

most frequently used pitch for that position. A pitch in parentheses is one that is avoided both as a gong tone and at other places during a melody in the *pathet* indicated. In the *slendro pathet nem,* pitches 6 and 2 occur with about equal frequency. As you can see in their Western note equivalents in Example 2–3, the distance between 6 and 2 is nearly a perfect fourth (A–D), which could be converted into a fifth by placing note 6 an octave higher (D–A). (This logical Western inversion method, unfortunately, is quite outside of the Javanese approach to melody, for the Indonesian musicians think of intervals primarily in terms of the number of slabs between two pitches on a keyed instrument within one octave.)

The predominant pitches of the *sanga* mode in Example 2–3 seem equivalent to a fifth, although it is too big to be a standard Western fifth (712 cents instead of the Western 702). If one searches for fifths between other predominant pitches in other *pathet,* none of the distances in cents between them will match the acoustical 702, nor will they resemble each other (in *pathet lima,* pitches 1 to 5 = 688; in *manyura* 2 to 6 = 714 and 6 to 3 = 739). Thus the Western cycle-of-fifths theory, from both a practical and a scientific point of view, does not seem to be connected directly with Javanese music.

In the *pelog* system, the "avoided" pitches (in parentheses) are used as substitutions *(sorogan)* for their adjacent tones, as shown by the arrows. The use of pitches 4 and 7 or 1 as such alternate tones in the *pelog* modes helps explain why these three pitches are missing on some keyed instruments (such as a *gender*) in the *pelog* section of a *gamelan.* This absence may cause tonal clashes when a five-tone *gender* and a seven-tone *saron* are playing together in a *pelog*-mode piece; it also relates to an important characteristic of *pathet* recognition, and therefore to the entire Javanese concept of melody, for it would appear that pitches and intervals are often not as important in modes as are the contours of certain melodic patterns *(gatra)* and cadences used. This concept of mode and melody as contour more than as interval structure may be a factor as well in the variety of tunings noted earlier between different *gamelan.*

Another factor in mode recognition is melodic register. Instrumentalists often describe a mode primarily in terms of the general range within which its music falls on their instrument. The *slendro pathet nem* is the mode most easily distinguished this way, for its *rebab* and *gender* parts exploit the lowest ranges of these instruments.

Further evidence of the ambiguity of modal functions is the fact that in some music, the mode of the "soft" instruments (voice, *rebab, suling*) may differ from that of the bronze instruments.[24] Still, each *pathet,* like other modes in the world, is felt to be best suited to a given mood, function, or time of the day. Together with the few other preliminary facts and theories discussed earlier, the Javanese tone system is impressive evidence of the logical but different system that continually operates in the equally beautiful tradition of Javanese music.

Balinese Music

Among the many different kinds of *gamelan* in Indonesia besides those of Java, the most famous are on the island of Bali. The boisterous brilliance of the Balinese orchestral sound is completely at variance with the generally sedate quality of Javanese music.[25] In Bali, instruments similar to those of the Javanese *gamelan* are found performing analogous functions. However, the Balinese *gender* and *gangsa* (the latter being the equivalent of the Javanese *saron*) are built in pairs or quartets in each octave size. Although all the instruments in a set are in the same scale, half are "female" instruments, which are tuned slightly lower than their "male" companions. When the two groups are played together they create a shimmering throb because of the beats caused by their tuning differences. This lovely sound is characteristic of the Balinese ensemble. Hard wooden mallets add further brightness to the Balinese sound.

[24] Susan Walton, *Mode in Javanese Music* (Athens: Ohio University Press, 1987).
[25] Compare book cassette tracks 9 and 10.

The softer *rebab* and flute sounds are used and the sounds of several 52-cm-long *suling gambuh* flutes create a strong lyricism in the old *gamelan gambuh* theatrical genre.

Time-marking instruments, like those of Java, underpin all Balinese *gamelan* genres but small double sets of cymbals (*rinchik; ceng-ceng*) add their clash (*ceng*). Two drummers further increase the rhythmic action of the music. Under the aesthetic circumstances, one should not be surprised to find a distinctive style in Balinese elaborating parts. For example, *trompong* two-octave set of knobbed gongs is placed in one row rather than the two-row form of the Javanese *bonang* (Plate VI, Figure 15). In this way a single performer can play it with flourishing movements that come close to or actually are dance.[26] A *reyong* set of twelve knobbed gongs is similarly placed in a row but is played on by four performers.

The principle of interlocking parts is very important in Balinese music. The two drummers play complementary rhythms that result in one very complex line. The *gender,* and sometimes the *gangsa,* also exploit this technique. Example 2–4 shows two short *gender* excerpts and a *reyong* pattern, and their resultants. Those who know Western music history will recognize this as a more sophisticated version of the old European hocketing technique. The creation and perfection of these resultant melodies is one of the delights of Balinese performers.

In Bali, performers are also in a sense composers because, although one musician may create the nuclear theme, he or she will receive suggestions from the players as they are taught by rote their various elaborating parts. This group composition method points up the communal aspect of the *gamelan.* Most Balinese *gamelan* are clubs organized within a ward or village. Part of their vitality stems from their democratic base as well as their thorough integration into the social and ritual life of the community.

Many of the special appeals of Balinese music are heard on track 10 of our book cassette examples.[27] After the stately Javanese ambiance of track 9 one seems to enter chaos. The evil witch *rangda* yells ferociously over the sound of chattering villagers, a dog, and children. The sound reflects constant motion around the temple compound where the mythical drama is being performed. Time markers, cymbals, choreographic signals, and interlocking parts accelerate and slow down as the soldiers and witch drive each other back and forth over the dusty road that is the stage. One senses the élan of really skilled community music and drama.

Another reason for the *gamelan's* survival in the modern world is the fact that its musicians have remained creative. In both Java and Bali, new

[26] A dancer demonstrates this in *JVC Video* no. 9, item 3.

[27] The sound is derived from a 1971 field videotape recorded by Judith Becker in Kuta Beach, Bali, during a village (not tourist) festival. The materials are used with her permission.

EXAMPLE 2–4. Balinese resultant melodies derived from Colin McPhee, "The Five-Tone Gamelan of Bali," *The Musical Quarterly,* 35/2 (April 1949), examples 19 and 21, pp. 274, 275. Used by permission.

pieces and new styles of playing are constantly being developed. In Bali, an individual piece remains only relatively unchanged once it is set. It does not become a fixed, sacrosanct "classic." Some pieces may disappear as new ideas come to the musicians, new dances are created, or the people simply get tired of the piece. Thus the Balinese music and dance world offers a refreshing mixture of traditional and indigenously new art forms.

Music in Sumatra

The historical dominance of Java and the increased migration of Javanese to Sumatra are paralleled by established *gamelan* traditions. However, a look at our map shows how close Sumatra is to continental Southeast Asia. We can divide Sumatran traditions into those of the mountainous interior and those of the coast. *Batak* is a generic term for many of the former groups and the most studied of the latter are the Minangkabau on the shores of West Sumatra across the straits from Malaysia. The widespread buffalo horn motifs, buffalo contests, tiger hunts, magic chants, agricultural ceremonies, and the *randai* drama reflect pre-Islamic life. The *talempong* ensemble of a few knobbed gongs and drums is its *gamelan* base. It has many ceremonial and dance uses and may play to open a *randai* performance of the Minangkabau. The dialogues of the dramas are interspersed with short drum outbursts and sudden self-defense dance movements that seem quite different from other Indonesian traditions, although they share these and their Islamic genres with Malaysia.[28] The *indang* genre uses a line of seated singers/drummers who move or respond in unison song to the religious texts of a leader.[29] Pan-Islamic *rabana* (*rebano*) frame drums (as in Plate IX, Figure 23) are the common instrument. It is the movement and the quatrain form (*pantun*) of the text that seems most indigenous. There are several genres in which men read religious text with frame-drum accompaniment. When two singers or groups are used, the performance can turn into a contest in which questions and answers of regional or secular character as well as religious topics may appear. The same tune repeats endlessly into the night, for audiences follow the text games, not the music. They may even submit personal questions in poetic form for the performers to answer in the manner of shamans who seem always present in Southeast Asia folk traditions. Islamic Sufism is one of the sources of the *dabus* genre in which men sing in Arabic, go into a trance, and perform tests of fire and physical pain. For all the religious restrictions of the arts, pre-Islamic trance dancers are found throughout Indonesia such as the glass-eating Javanese hobbyhorse dancers (*kuda kedang*) and the fighters in Balinese magic animal or witch battles who often turn their knives (*kris*) on themselves.

Conclusion

For all the official and religious restrictions, Western mass communication invasions, and new musical experiments, Indonesian music and theater arts remain numerous and viable. Such musics are pleasing to the ear, and the theoretical systems that govern their structure are fascinating to the intellect. These admirable features are all the more impressive when we remember that the high level of artistic ensemble playing needed to perform such music is maintained by rural as well as urban populations.

If we look back over the entire string of cultures surveyed in this chapter, it should be evident that between the village gong ensembles of the Philippines and the court orchestras of Java there is truly a host of wonderful musics available to the listener who seeks them out. The roots and variations of this knobbed-gong culture are found in continental Southeast Asia (see Chapter 5). To complete its historical background we travel first due west to possible East African connections and the sources of Islam.

[28] Compare the data that follows with Malyasia materials on page 158. See also Mohd. Anis Mo Nor, *Randai Dance* (Kuala Lumpuer: University of Malaya, 1986).

[29] See Margaret J. Kartomi, "Muslim Music in West Sumatran Culture," *The World of Music*, 28/3 (1986).

BIBLIOGRAPHICAL AND AUDIOVISUAL NOTES

Materials for the Philippines and Borneo

An early summary of Philippine music is Norberto Romualdez's "Filipino Musical Instruments and Airs of Long Ago," *Encyclopedia of the Philippines,* Vol. 4 (Manila, 1934), 86–128, and summaries of music and theater are found in the *Encyclopedia Britannica,* 15th ed. (1974), 17, 241, 249, and *The New Grove Dictionary of Music and Musicians,* 632 ff. An introductory book is William Pfeiffer, *Filipino Music* (Dumaguete City, Philippines: Silliman Music Foundation, 1976). Modern research was begun by Jose Maceda in his study *The Music of Magindanao in the Philippines* (Ann Arbor: University Microfilms, 1964) and its Smithsonian/Folkways record, *Music of the Magindanao* (4536). Maceda's study of Kalinga music is in *Asian Musics in an Asian Perspective* (Tokyo: The Japan Foundation, 1977). Maceda and Ricardo Trimillos wrote on Philippine music in *Traditional Drama and Music of Southeast Asia,* ed. Mohd. Taib Osman (Kuala Lumpur, Malaysia: Dewan Bahasa dan Pustaka, 1974). Trimillos's Tausig study is in the *Yearbook for Traditional Music,* 19 (1987). Studies in Muranao music include Steven W. Otto, *The Muranao Kakolitang* (Iligan City, Philippines: University Research Center, 1985), and Usopay H. Cady's articles in *Ethnomusicology,* 17/2 (1973), and in *Selected Reports in Ethnomusicology* (UCLA, Dept. of Music), 2/2 (1975). Smithsonian/Folkways recordings include *Folk Songs of the Philippines* (8791) and *Murut Music of North Borneo* (4459). The *JVC Video* no. 8 contains staged Philippine materials. Lyrichord has two records of Philippine gong music (LLCT 7322 and 7326).

Books and Articles for Indonesia

Music in Java (The Hague: Nijhoff, 1949) in two volumes is the classic work of the inventor of the word *ethnomusicology,* Jaap Kunst (1891–1960). His student, Mantle Hood, supported Kunst's theory of mode in his 1954 thesis *The Nuclear Theme as a Determinant of Patet in Javanese Music* (reprint New York: Da Capo Press, 1977). He continues to do so in *The Evolution of Javanese Gamelan* (Wilhelmshaven: Florian Noetzel Verlag, 3 vols., 1980, 1984, 1988), which also contains personal field notes and conjectures on history in a short story form. Judith Becker's *Traditional Music in Modern Java* (Honolulu: University of Hawaii Press, 1976) brought new approaches to *gamelan* music as does her *Gamelan Stories: Tantric Islam and Aesthetics in Java* (Tempe: Arizona State University Press, 1992). Works of her students include Susan Pratt Walton, *Mode in Javanese Music* (Athens: Ohio University Center for International Studies, 1987), and Andrew Sutton, *Traditions of Gamelan Music in Java: Musical Pluralism and Regional Identity* (Cambridge: Cambridge University Press, 1991). Semiotics and the theories of Clifford Geertz are found in Becker's "A Musical Icon: Power and Meaning in Javanese Gamelan Music," in *The Sign in Music and Literature,* ed. Wendy Steiner (Austin: University of Texas Press, 1981), written in conjunction with Alton L. Becker. Among Judith Becker's many other studies are "Time and

Tune," in *The Imagination of Reality: Essays in Southeast Asian Coherence Systems,* ed. A.L. Becker and A. Yengoyan (Norwood, NJ: Ablex, 1979), reprinted in Kay Kaufman Shelemay, ed. *The Garland Library of Readings in Ethnomusicology,* Vol. 3 (New York: Garland, 1990). In *Ethnomusicology* Judith Becker wrote "Earth, Fire, Sakti, and the Javanese Gamelan," 32/3 (1988) and "A Southeast Asian Musical Process: Thai Thaw and Javanese Irama," 24/3 (1980). Important indigenous research by Javanese musicians between 1930 and 1975 is translated in *Karawitan. Source Readings in Javanese Gamelan and Vocal Music,* ed. Judith Becker (Center for South and Southeast Asian Studies of the University of Michigan, Vol. 1, 1984; Vol. 2, 1987; Vol. 3, 1988). Other writings are found in Ernst Heins, *Music in Java: Current Bibliography 1973–1989* (Amsterdam: Universiteit van Amsterdam Ethnomusicologisch Centrum Jaap Kunst, 1989). Margaret J. Kartomi has opened new areas with her *Matjapat Songs in Central and West Java.* Oriental Monograph Series no. 13 (Canberra: Monash University and Australian National University Press, 1973), and "Music Strata in Sumatra, Java, and Bali" in *Music in Many Cultures,* ed. Elizabeth May (Berkeley: University of California Press, 1980). A useful view of ensembles East of Bali is *The Music of Lombok* by Tilman Seebass and others (Bern: Francke, 1976). The classic Balinese references are Colin McPhee, *Music in Bali* (New Haven: Yale University Press, 1966), his *House in Bali* (New York: John Day, 1946), and Walter Spies's *Dance and Drama in Bali* (London: Faber & Faber, 1938). A handsome addition with color photographs is Michael Tenzer's *Balinese Music* (Seattle: University of Washington Press, 1991). *Ethnomusicology* articles include Vincent McDermott and Sumarsan, "Central Javanese Music: The Patet of Laras Slendro and the Gender Barung," 19/2 (1975); William Van Zanten, "The Tone Material of the Kacapi in Tembang Sunda in West Java," 30/1 (1986), R. Anderson Sutton, "Musical Pluralism in Java," 29/1 (1985); and Rene T.A. Lysloff, "Non-Puppets and Non-gamelan: Wayang Parody in Banyumas," 34/1 (1990). *Asian Music* articles include Peter Manuel and Randal Baier, "Jaipongan: Indigenous Popular Music of West Java," 18/1 (1986); Sean William, "Current Developments in Sundanese Popular Music," 21/1 (1990); and Benjamin Brinner on *suling* playing, 24/2 (1993). A study of contemporary compositions for all Asia is Harrison Ryker, *New Music in the Orient* (Buren, The Netherlands: Knuf, 1991).

Audiovisual Materials

The UNESCO record series includes *Music of the Kenyah and Modang in East Kalimantan* (5056); *Vocal Art from Java* (6586 042); *Java: Historic Gamelan Orchestras* (6586 004); *Bali: Court Music and Banjar Music* (6586 008); and *Balinese Theatre and Dance Music* (6586 013). Nonesuch Explorer series includes *Tonggeret* (18987); *The Jasmine Isle* (72031); and *Javanese Court Gamelan* (72044, 72074, 72083). Their records for Bali are 72015, 72037, and 72046. The Lyrichord *Gamelan Music of Bali* is 7179. CDs from Indonesia include King Records World Music Library (KICC 5127-28 and KICC 5129-31) and Harmonia Mundi (D 8003 and 8014).

A SONIC GLOSSARY INDEX FOR CHAPTER 2

Philippine (P[F]ilipino)
(Speaker: Adelwisa Agas Weller)

agung. See Indonesian
badendil (gong), 39
bajo (bass viol), 38
bandurria (plucked chordophone), 38
biola (a term for violin), 39 (fn. 5)
dababuan (drum), 39
dandai. See Indonesian-randai
gabbang (Sulu xylophone), 38
gandingan (gong), 39
gangsa* (flat gong), 37
gendang, gandang*, See Indonesian *gendang*
gitgit (bowed lute), 39
kachapi*. See kudyapi
kitara* (plucked lute), 38
kudyapi (chordophone), 40, 41 (Fig. 8, Fig. 11), 154
kulintang (gong set), 39
kumintang (Tagalog pantomime dance), 38
kundiman (ballad), 39
laud (lute), 38
octavina (mandolin), 38
rondalla (band), 38
tingkling* (folk dance), 38
tunggalan (Mingindanao gong), 39
zarzuella* (light opera), 38

Indonesian
(Speaker: Magaretha Sudaisih)

agung (gong), 39
alok (vocable interjections), 48 (fn. 17)
angklung (bamboo idiophones), 46
barang (a pitch or mode), 55 (Ex. 2–3)
barung (mid-sized gamelan instrument), 44
bonang (knobbed gong set), 39, 44, 45 (Fig. 15), 46, 48 (Ex. 2–1), 54, 57, 58
buka (introductory section in gamelan music), 53
celempung (Indonesian zither), 44
ceng-ceng (Balinese cymbals), 57
dabus (song form), 59
dalang (puppeteer), 47
dandut (Indonesian pop music), 47
demung (large gamelan instrument size), 44
gambang kayu (gamelan wooden xylophone), 44, 48 (Ex. 2–1)
gambuh* (Balinese ensemble), 57
gamelan (generic term for ensemble), 43–51, 54, 55, 57, 65, 145, 148, 196
gandang. See *gendang*
gangsa (Balinese idiophone), 56, 57
gatra (Javanese small melodic unit), 52
gendang (drum), 39, 46, 152, 160
gender (gamelan instrument), 44, 45 (Fig. 14), 48 (Ex. 2–1), 53, 54, 56, 57, 148, 151
gendhing (generic term for composition), 47
gerong (male chorus in gamelan), 43, 48 (Ex. 2–1)
gerong bedayan (mixed chorus, Java), 43

*not on language cassette

*not on language cassette

THREE
MUSLIM AFRICA, ETHIOPIA, AND THE NEAR EAST

The ancient and modern cultures of the Near East[1] and Africa contain many rich musical traditions. Our survey refers to some of the Hebrew, the Christian, and the ancient musics of this vast area, but it concentrates on the more characteristic tradition of the overall region: Islamic music. In Chapter 2 we already noted an influence of Islamic music eastward as far as Indonesia and the Philippines, and in Chapters 4 and 5 we mention its effects on Central, South, and Southeast Asia. The major topics of this chapter are the music of an area called the Near East (or Southwest Asia) as well as the music of North Africa. The chapter is also concerned with Muslim music from the traditional trade routes along the east coast and the upper half of the west coast of Africa as well as the southern edges of the Sahara desert. Ethiopia is treated separately because of its basically non-Islamic tradition. Let us begin at the most southern point of the cultural chain and move gradually toward the better known meccas of music in the Near East.

[1] If we relate this area to the rest of Asia it could be called West Asia or Southwest Asia and North Africa. Viewing it from the European perspective of previous centuries the terms *Middle East* or *Near East* are more common. The latter is used here because, at present, most related materials are found under that term.

MUSLIM AND BLACK AFRICA

The largest island off the southeast coast of Africa is Madagascar. It is the home of the Malagasy Republic, which is named after a regional culture with a language belonging to the Malayo-Polynesian family and closely related to the speech of South Central Borneo, although it contains borrowings from Arabic, African Bantu, and some French. Thus the music of this area should reflect a related mixture of styles. Bowed chordophones from the Muslim *rebab* and Western violin family are both to be found in Madagascar, along with French military drums, flutes, trumpets, and clarinets. Such instruments may be combined in many ways to accompany the open-air *hira-gasy* theatricals. These performances consist of music and dance plus long moral songs or proverbial speeches. In some parts of the island, Western drums and flutes have become essential parts of otherwise purely native funeral ceremonies.

Perhaps the most controversial aspect of music on Madagascar is its hypothetical relation to that of Indonesia and Southeast Asia. At least two Malagasy instruments seem reminiscent of traditions found in areas on the opposite side of the Indian Ocean: the *valiha* tube zither (see Chapter 1, Plate IV, Figure 7), with 12 to 18 strings, and the *jejo vaotavo* stick zither, with 4 to 12 strings. The latter looks much like the Southeast Asian model shown in Plate XXII, Figure 56 (p. 155). Both these instruments are used by secular bards. The *valiha* is also found in French-African popular music ensembles, often combined with a guitar and bass. This tube zither is commonly made to sound louder by placing one end of it on an empty gasoline can. Unlike its Asian counterparts, the *valiha* also exists in a boat-shaped zither form. In either form, the *valiha's* use of diatonic scales and parallel (organal) harmony in thirds is derived from Africa, not Indonesia. Indonesia, however, has sometimes been considered to be the inspiration of the Madagascan xylophones, consisting of sticks of wood placed upon the legs of the seated player.

The Chopi tribesmen of Mozambique, on the coast of Africa west of Madagascar, provide richer materials for potential Indonesian-African comparisons. They play extended dance suites (*ngodo*) with large orchestras made up of many-sized xylophones called *timbila.* These instruments have wooden keys and gourd resonators which, like other resonated African xylophones, have a sound hole thinly covered with a membrane to produce a characteristic African buzzing sound. The poems used in the Chopi suites are topical, not classical as in Java; nevertheless, the *gamelan* concept seems to hover in the background. There have been attempts to show even further relationships with Indonesia through the study of xylophone tunings among the Chopi and in more distant parts of Africa.[2] However, the most common shared traits of these two areas are found in the musical legacies of Islam, for Africa and Indonesia are at two

[2] The best known and most controversial is A. M. Jones, *Africa and Indonesia: The Evidence of the Xylophone and Other Music and Cultural Factors* (Leiden: E. J. Brill, 1971).

ends of an Islamic cultural stream. This stream is generated centrally in the Near East rather than flowing directly from east to west or vice versa, and it is this Islamic influence on black Africa that offers the most fruitful comparative material.

As we implied earlier, Islam extends in Africa over much of the Hamitic and Negritic areas of the east coast, across the Mediterranean littoral, and down through West Africa to the fringes of the Sahara. Since these areas have different pre-Islamic cultures and worldviews, it is not possible to generalize about the manner in which all respond musically to Islam. In some cases the two traditions seem to have been able to live side by side, whereas in others, particularly those among blacks who moved across the Sahara to North Africa, the Islamic music is colored by indigenous elements. There are some musical changes in black African music, however, that imply Muslim influence (although, at this point, it cannot be proved).[3]

Possible implications of Islamic influence have been found in performances of black singers who ornament their lines with quick microtonal shakes and mordents and use a tense, nasal voice quality. A Muslim influence may be inferred if, when voices and instruments combine, the accompaniment is not the multiple drums or ostinatos on a melodic instrument as found in Central Africa, but rather a single drum (often of kettle, hourglass, or frame-drum form) or two connected kettledrums or a bowed stringed instrument (like the *rebab*) playing heterophonically. In general, it seems the polyrhythms of pagan Africa have given way to single rhythmic lines wherever Islam has become dominant. In addition, the several harmonic and polyphonic traditions of pagan Africa have become less prominent under Muslim culture, for in general Muslim music tends to be monophonic, although heterophony and drones can also be found. Finally, Muslim influence seems responsible for the appearance in Africa of double-reed instruments.

Interesting if ambiguous mixtures or separations of two musical cultures are found at the terminals of the Sahara caravan routes. The Wolofs of Senegal and Gambia, for example, show such a mixture: They use both cylindrical and pot-shaped single-headed drums in groups to produce African polyrhythms for their secular dances, but when their holy man sings Muslim hymns (*qasida*), a small kettledrum called a *tabala* is used, along with an iron beater; together, these produce simple single rhythms much more akin to the music of the rest of the Muslim world.

Wolof society has a class of professional entertainers (*gewel* or *griots*) who, in keeping with both black and Muslim traditions as well as those of many other cultures, are considered to be lazy, boisterous, and low class.[4] Neverthe-

[3] Two discussions of this problem are found in the chapters by Lois Anderson and by Akin Euba in *Music and History in Africa,* ed. Klaus Wachsmann (Evanston: Northwestern University Press, 1971). For a discussion of other black African styles, see Bruno Nettl, *Folk and Traditional Music of the Western Continents,* and H. H. Nketia, *The Music of Africa* (New York: Norton, 1974).

[4] For a discussion of the curiously consistent low position of musicians in world societies, see Alan P. Merriam, *The Anthropology of Music* (Evanston: Northwestern University Press, 1964), Chapter 7.

less, they are well paid, for music is an essential, functional part of many phases of African life, just as it is in Oceania. The performances of these musicians reflect a black and Muslim mixture, for they sing praise songs—a common pagan African genre—with tense North African voices. They also tell stories to the accompaniment of a plucked five-stringed *halam* lute. The narrative traditions they use are as old as the camel caravan routes of Muslim and even pre-Muslim Africa. However, whereas the Muslim caravan narrators used bowed, heterophonic accompaniments to their tales, the Wolofs play plucked, dronelike harmonies. Similar mixtures of styles can be found all along the fringes of the Sahara.

ETHIOPIA

So many peoples have traded or fought in the Sudan, which lies between North Africa and Ethiopia, that its musical culture offers several interpretations. Ethiopia itself, however, has always presented a special cultural image because, despite its basically Islamic environment and occasional Islamic invasion, its fundamental religion has for centuries remained a variant of Coptic Christianity. Ethiopia was also the home of another ancient religious tradition, Falasha Judaism.[5] In many remote areas, particularly in the South, there also are tribes that exhibit polyphonic styles more typical of neighboring parts of black Africa, such as composite flute melodies and canonic singing. Nevertheless, the traditions of Christian Ethiopia remain central to the musical characteristics of the country.

Ethiopian chants (*degwa*) as performed by official church singers (*debteras*) exhibit the melodic restraints and repetitions typical of word-oriented music functioning in a ceremony. Like most such religious music, Ethiopian chant at first sounds highly redundant, but a study of the tradition shows a skillful use of ornamentation, with melodic units and tonal emphases that make it possible for one to distinguish specific modes as well as appropriate ritual melodies. The melodies are preserved in a special, rather complicated notation; however, although singers learn to read it well, their basic lessons are given in the rote method, for, as most musicians know, the ear is a more efficient organ than the eye in learning music, particularly if the music is as melismatic as Ethiopian chant.

Few instrumental sounds emanate from the inner sanctum of the round churches. Outside some rural churches one may find a set of sonorous stone slabs (*dowel*) which are used like church bells; a drum (*kebaro*) may be heard

[5] An excellent study of the Falasha tradition as well as its relation to Ethiopian Christianity is Kay Kaufman Shelemay, *Music, Ritual and Falasha History,* Ethiopian Series Monograph no. 17 (East Lansing: African Studies Center, Michigan State University, 1986). It now survives in Israel.

inside most churches. The jangling sistrum (*tsenatsil*) shown in Plate VII, Figure 16, is a ritual instrument that may also be an example of the marginal survival of an object formerly used in ancient Egyptian, Greek, and Roman traditions.

The large ten-stringed *bagana* lyre is often referred to by Ethiopians as the descendant of David's harp in the Old Testament, but its use is not liturgical. It accompanies classical poetry or songs of religious or philosophical text. The smaller *krar* lyre shown in Plate VII, Figure 17 is an equally interesting instrument and more widely used in Ethiopian secular music, as is the one-stringed *masenqo* bowed lute of more recent Muslim origin. Whatever the "true" origin of any of these instruments, their use in Ethiopia often seems creatively acculturational. A possible example of such a mixture of traditions may be heard on side 2, track 2, of *Folk Music of Ethiopia* (Smithsonian/Folkways 4405). Here a nasal-voiced singer plays a Muslim-like spike fiddle to accompany a black-style praise song in honor of his Christian emperor. (By now you probably realize that the concept of "pure" music is not a very useful one as long as there are frequent cultural contacts in the world and a few good ears attached to imaginative musicians in each culture.)

Although various African groups we mentioned earlier in this chapter show unique variations in their acculturation of musical styles, the general principles stated have given some indications of the directions that black African music may take under Muslim influences. Our look at an Ethiopian example actually led us beyond black Africa to an area of Caucasoid dominance—which in turn leads us to North Africa and to the Near East itself.

THE PAN-ISLAMIC TRADITION

Although we have noted Islamic influence in Africa, the Philippines, and Indonesia (and note it further in Central, South, and Southeast Asia in later chapters), the mainstream of Western Islamic culture can be found in an expanse of territory extending from southern Spain along the African coast of the Mediterranean and up through the Near East, where it splits, first in the direction of Iran and second via Turkey into Eastern Europe. At the terminals of this stream the traditions are quite mixed, particularly in Eastern Europe. But within the non-European confines of this core area—that is, from Morocco to Turkey—there is a unity of culture we call the *pan-Islamic tradition,* realizing that historically and geographically the peoples making up this category include such non-Islamic groups as Near Eastern Christians and Jews as well as pre-Islamic Arabs, and that there is an even greater variety of peoples in other Islamic areas, which we discuss in later chapters. The pan-Islamic core encompasses a variety of peoples, such as the Turks of Central Asian origins, the Aryan Persians, many kinds of Arab and Semitic peoples, and the Hamitic converts of North Africa. One can expect many differences within such a large grouping of

PLATE VII. Ethiopia

FIGURE 16. *Tsenatsil.* (15–18 cm high)

FIGURE 17. *Krar.*

peoples, but the pan-Islamic label is still useful, for the spread of Islam has directly or indirectly brought certain unifying elements to the culture of this vast area.

Our discussion of pan-Islamic music falls into the general categories of folk, art, popular, and religious music, recognizing that extensive interpenetration of styles and instruments has occurred among them. Under these categories, representative examples are chosen from one or both of the subareas within the basic pan-Islamic world. One is the desert and coast of North Africa, the so-called Maghrib (Maghreb), which includes the modern nations of Morocco, Algeria, Tunisia, and Libya, with Egypt as a cultural buffer zone between this area and the next. The other subarea is the Near East proper, which includes Iran, Syria, Iraq, Jordan, Saudi Arabia, Lebanon, Oman, Aden, and Yemen. For most of this survey Turkey is included in this latter area, although its Central Asian background gives it many special traits. Hebraic Palestine (Israel) is treated separately.

Folk Music

The dominant pre-Islamic peoples of North Africa were the Berbers. With the seventh-century rise of Islam and the eleventh-century migrations of Bedouin Arabs, the Berbers were pushed into the mountains or out onto the desert where they, in turn, displaced black groups. Today the Berbers are Muslim, but their present culture often reveals a patchwork of Muslim and indigenous ideas. This can be heard in the music of the Tuaregs, who once controlled caravan routes in the Sahara northeast of Timbuktu but now are basically nomadic peoples along the southern fringe of the desert and into Niger. When women sing, ornaments characteristic of Muslim music in this area are missing, although the standard Arab accompaniment of percussion or hand clapping and female yodeling are common.

The two major Tuareg percussion instruments reflect the ingenuity of a pastoral society that often must follow its flocks. Both instruments are often made from household items and are quite portable. For example, the Tuareg word for drum, *tende* (*tendi*),[6] means "mortar" because its body may be a food-grinding mortar. A skin is attached across the bowl and struck with the hands and kept moist by splashing water on it or from water earlier placed inside the mortar's bowl. Sometimes two long pestles are strung through the ropes holding the goatskin over the mortar (see Plate IX, Figure 21). The head is tightened by placing weights on ropes or leather strips that form "seats" on both

[6] There are at least three regional Tuareg dialects and various European romanizations. The northern dialect spellings are used throughout this discussion with variants in parentheses. The source is Caroline Card Wendt's chapter on Tuareg in the Africa volume, ed. Ruth Stone, of *The Garland Traditional Music Series* (New York: Garland, 1992). We thank Wendt for her aid in Tuareg information. See her "Tende" in *Cross Rhythms*, ed. Kofi Anyidoho and others (Bloomington: Trickster Press, 1983).

ends of the pestles as on a teeter-totter. Women may sit on the two ends of the pestles, so the pitch of the drum can depend on the number or weight of women sitting on each side! When the music is over, the mortar and pestles return to their culinary functions. Similarly, two sizes of bowls are used to create the so-called Tuareg water drum (*assakalabu*). A large bowl is filled with water in which the second bowl is placed upside down. Sticks are used to beat on the overturned bowl. Although called a drum, it is an idiophone (until it returns to its original household use).

Men are known to play the *tende* and also tambourines, but traditionally women are the instrumentalists. However, men do sing, especially at the sensuous *ahal* entertainments. They perform highly ornamented, heroic love songs to the accompaniment (usually by a woman) of a one-stringed fiddle *anzad* (*amzhad, inzad, imzhad;* see Plate VIII, Figure 18).[7] The heterophonic nature of these songs can be seen in the excerpt shown in Example 3–1. From this discussion it seems that Tuareg women's music is more oriented toward some non-Muslim style possibly derived from old Berber culture, black slaves, or the black African environment in which many live. Male music, however, seems Muslim. During the Ramadan holy month the Tuaregs sometimes join with Arabs and Muslim blacks at an oasis for a night of ecstatic dancing. The unique musical mixtures of such nights offer dramatic illustrations of the continuous interchanges of ideas and styles in the desert.

Along the coast and in the mountains of North Africa the pan-Islamic style prevails. There are, however, occasional remnants of the Greco-Roman occupation of the land as well as specific Berber and Jewish songs. The expulsion of the Sephardic Jews and later the Moors from Spain in the fifteenth century had its musical effect on North Africa as well. Earlier, during the heydays of Moorish Spain, the various courts in Morocco, Tunisia, and Algeria learned much about Arab classical music from Hispanic artists. The thirteenth-century Bedouin invasion destroyed this Berber culture and its economy, so that today Berber songs and dances are commonly found only in the remote Atlas mountains of Algeria. But even these remnants exhibit traits common to the entire pan-Islamic tradition. For example, one description of Berber mountain dances notes the typical Arab circling line-dance pattern and the use of tambourine accompaniment.[8]

If one goes north of the mountains and out onto the coastal plains, the Islamic influence becomes even clearer. Professional epic poets appear, and they are often accompanied by an end-blown flute commonly called the *gasba* or *qasaba*. The Near Eastern equivalent of this is called the *nay*. Both instruments have five or six finger holes and tend to be played slanted slightly to the side of the player in a manner reminiscent of both the *sib* of ancient Egypt

[7] See Geoffrey Holiday, "The Tuareg of the Ahaggar," *African Music*, 1/3 (1956).
[8] See *JVC Video* no. 17.

PLATE VIII. Near Eastern folk chordophones

FIGURE 18. A Tuareg *anzad* (*inzad*).

FIGURE 19. A Moroccan folk *rebab* and *guinbri*.

FIGURE 20. An ancient Egyptian plucked lute.

EXAMPLE 3–1. A heterophonic love song from the recordings *Tuareg Music of the Southern Sahara* (Smithsonian/Folkways 4470, side 1, track 3; book cassette, track 11). Transcription and recording used by permission.[9]

[9] The text refers to a young man singing about a man leading a camel. cf. Caroline Card Wendt. "Regional Style in Tuareg Anzad Music," *To the Four Corners,* ed. Ellen Leichtman (Warren, Michigan: Harmonie Park Press. 1994), 81–106.

(Plate X, Figure 26) and the *suling* of modern Indonesia. *Gasba* are made of either cane or metal. Whether such flutes play heterophonic vocal accompaniments or free-rhythmic solos, their florid, breathy, melodies are typically pan-Islamic.

A majority of pan-Islamic folk music is purely vocal. It is either performed as a solo or in call-and-response manner with a unison chorus as shown in Example 3–2. If accompaniment is desired, the most common type is a hand clap on the main accent of a duple meter (Example 3–2).[10] The most popular instrumental addition is illustrated in Plate IX, Figure 23. It comes in several distinct forms and sizes throughout the pan-Islamic world and is called by many names, the most common of which are *duff, daff, taar,* and *bendir.*[11] Its basic form is a circular, single-headed frame drum, either plain or with snares attached beneath the skin. Metal disks may be set in the frame or metal rings attached around the inside of the rim behind the skin. There are also diamond- and square-shaped tambourines. Regardless of its shape or size, the tambourine is a vital element in most lively forms of pan-Islamic music—particularly dances, wedding songs, and other music sung primarily by women.

Wedding songs are a significant part of pan-Islamic female music. These are often performed by professional singers hired for the occasion. Weddings also require another typical pan-Islamic instrument, the double-reed aerophone known in the Maghrib as the *zukra, zamr,* or *gaita* (Plate X, Figure 25). It is more commonly known in the Near East by the Persian term *surnay* or the Turkish *zurna* (*zorna*). This double-reed conical aerophone normally has seven holes in front and one in the back. The stereotyped Western imitations of Near Eastern music are inspired by its nasal, "outdoor" sound. Most players place the reed inside the mouth so no lip pressure is possible. When the instrument is played in this way, the bulging cheeks of the player are, in fact, the bag of a human bagpipe. Actual bagpipes with and without drones are found throughout the Maghrib as well as up the Nile River in the Sudan. A more common pan-Islamic aerophone, however, is the double clarinet shown in Plate X, Figure 24. Standard names for it are the *arghul, mizmar, mijwiz, zamr,* or *zamar.* It is sometimes mislabeled as a double flute or double reed. Properly described, it is a double clarinet, for it consists of two cylindrical pipes, each of which has a single beating reed. These are placed inside the mouth and vibrate freely. Sometimes the reeds are within a wooden cup that the player places against his or her face, thus avoiding the need to "swallow" the reeds. One may play parallel melodies on the two pipes or use one as a drone. Since there are normally

[10] The descriptive transcription of this example shows heterometer in the first chorus. As the performance settles in on book cassette, track 12, the meter becomes purely an isometric duple.

[11] Excellent distribution maps of all major pan-Islamic instruments and their various names are found in the *Cultural Atlas of Islam,* ed. Ismaeil & Lois Al-Faruqi (New York: Macmillan, 1986). Note that the Moroccan version in Figure 23 has a finger hole to help hold the frame. This is not true of all examples.

EXAMPLE 3–2. A Druse song from the recording *Arabic and Druse Music* (Smithsonian/Folkways 4480, side 1, track 6; book cassette, track 12). Transcription and sound used by permission.[12]

five or six finger holes on each pipe and only four fingers available on each hand for playing, you might wonder about the function of the extra holes. They may be plugged to change the pitch level of the melody or drone (note the bottom hole of the right-hand pipe in Figure 24). Since there are no octave holes in the rear of the pipes, *arghul* melodies are restricted to a six- or seven-note range. By using nasal breathing, however, a good player can keep up a lively stream of music so the tone never stops. This instrument comes in all sizes; the largest is found in Egypt, where the drone pipe is over 1 meter long.

Besides the tambourine there are three other characteristic membranophones in the pan-Islamic world. The word *tabl* or some variant of it is used to designate most cylindrical drums as well as several with kettle-shaped

[12] The text is, Soloist: "This party is our party. And this evening gathering is ours [too]–our commandant [chief] and his followers [us]." Chorus:"This is our reward." The translation is courtesy of R.M. Rammuny and the romanization is by Ernest McCarcus, both of the Near Eastern program of the University of Michigan. Concerning the heterometer see footnote 10.

PLATE IX. Near Eastern percussion

FIGURE 21. A Tuareg *tende* drum.

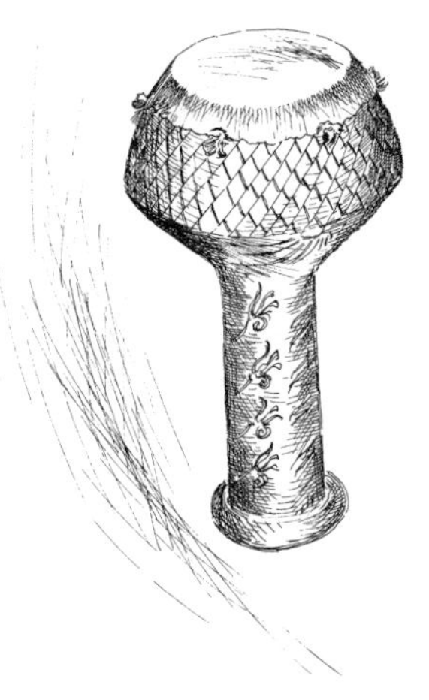

FIGURE 22. A *tombak* or *darbuka*. (35–45 cm high)

FIGURE 23. *Duff*. (25–55 cm diameter)

PLATE X. Near Eastern winds

FIGURE 24. A *mizmar* or *arghul.* (42–52 cm long)

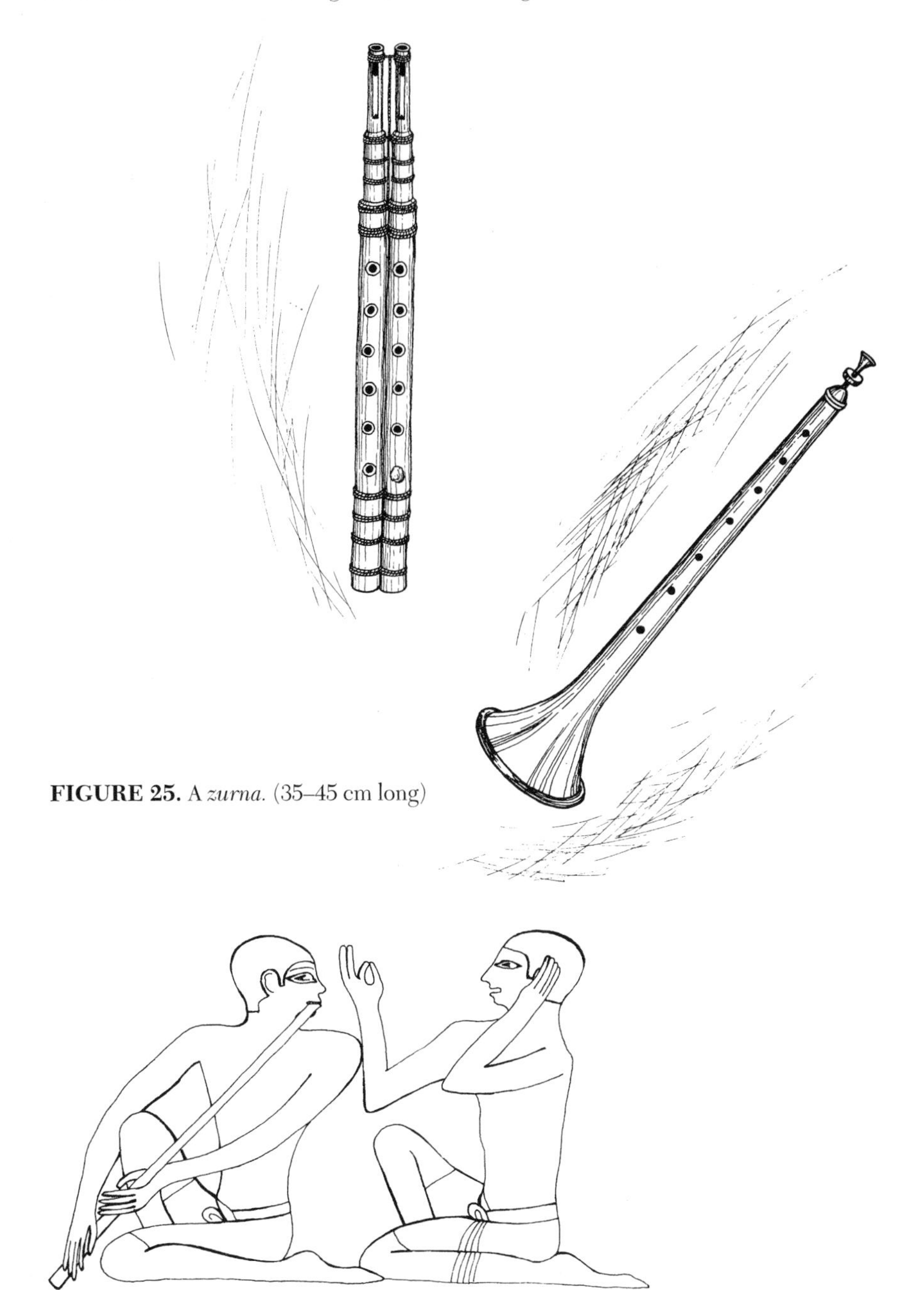

FIGURE 25. A *zurna.* (35–45 cm long)

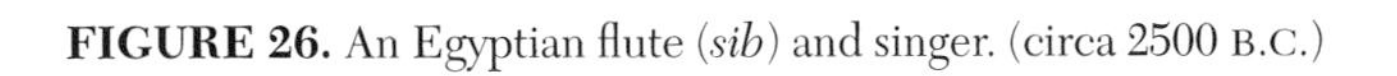

FIGURE 26. An Egyptian flute (*sib*) and singer. (circa 2500 B.C.)

bodies. An inseparable pair of small kettledrums called *naqqara* is found even as far east as Tibet. Indeed, it may be that some instruments such as these *naqqara* came from Central Asia to the Near East with the migrations of the various Turkic peoples. Today this instrument is likely to show up in the café orchestras rather than in folk music. The same may be said for the most popular pan-Islamic drum of all, the single-headed drum with a pottery or metal vase body, called the *darbuka, darabukka, dombak,* or *tombak* (shown in Plate IX, Figure 22). It can be played in any one of three ways: upright, tucked under the left arm, or held upside down and struck from below. In any position it provides a lively beat for Arab music of all kinds.

A few plucked lyres (Figure 17) are found in regional traditions of the Sudan and northeast Africa as well as the Arabian peninsula. More common pan-Islamic stringed instruments are some form of lute. Plate VIII, Figure 19, contains one of many versions of the one- to three-stringed *guinbri* (*gimbri, gunbri*) plucked lute seen in North Africa. It usually has a skin-covered body (the shape varies) and a rounded neck pole. It is often held horizontally at chest level by standing musicians. Plate VIII, Figure 20, shows that both the instrument and playing position may have ancient Egyptian ancestors. The *rebab* bowed lute of Figure 19 is being used by a Moroccan street narrator.[13] It is historically connected with Figures 12 (p. 45), 31 (p. 83), and Figure 18, but note the differences. The Javanese *rebab* is a closer relative of spiked fiddles such as Figure 30 (p. 83). The bows of the other three instruments are the same, but note that each is held in a different manner. The *rebab* player method reminds one of yet other relatives, the ancient rebecs and rebels of Europe.[14] The *anzad* is bowed in the opposite direction of the Moroccan *rebab.* One is tempted to relate the Moroccan bowing style to the narrator's standing position, although it is the same when used in classical music.[15] The pole of Figure 19 is not a fingerboard like those of some other examples. Rather it is merely a holder for a peg that places the thick string out in space to the side of the pole. Here it can easily be fingered on the side by the middle-finger joints rather than by fingernails or tips. Little hand movement is required, as this *rebab* accompaniment consists of interjections of the same short tune between the narrator's similarly short lines. It is the text, not the tune, that tempts passersby to listen. The story is the reason for the music. The public storyteller may be a tradition as ancient as cave dwellers. Our Moroccan example evokes more recent, that is, medieval traditions like *A Thousand and One Nights.*[16]

[13] The image is abstracted primarily from items 1 and 2 of the *JVC Video* no. 17.

[14] See David Munrow, *Instruments of the Middle Ages and the Renaissance* (London Oxford University Press, 1976).

[15] See Alexis Chottin, *Tableau de la musique marocaine* (Paris: Geuthner, 1939), Plate IV opposite p. 48.

[16] Middle Eastern folktales first noted in the ninth century and best known in the West in their 1885 translations by Sir Richard Burton.

In Turkey and parts of the Near East, several different plucked and bowed lutes can be found in folk ensembles. Plate XI, Figure 28, shows a *tanbur, (tambur)*, a popular Near Eastern plucked lute. It has a small pear-shaped wooden body, a long fretted neck, and from two to ten metal strings in double courses. In Turkey and Turkish-influenced Eastern Europe (including Greece and the Mediterranean islands) there is a wide variety of long-necked lutes, particularly in folk and popular music performances. The most frequent names for such instruments are *saz, buzuq* (*bozuq* or *bouzouki*), and *baglama*. The *kemanchay* (*kemanche*), found in Turkey and Persia, is a bowed lute with three or four strings that found its way into Europe through the many *lira* and other bowed lutes of East Europe and Greece. It is also one of the important ancestors of the European *rebec*, which eventually evolved into the Western violin. This cycle was completed in recent centuries when the Western violin was, in turn, used by Muslim musicians as a substitute for the *rebab*, from which it originated.

So far we have noted as typical pan-Islamic folk forms wedding songs, love songs, epic tales, and line dances (the *dabka* or *debka*). Naturally, there are also camel caravan songs (*huda*). To these we must add various religious songs in praise of the saints or in honor of pilgrims returning from Mecca, as well as the special songs of splinter Muslim sects and the ecstatic chants of the dervish groups. Liturgical music as such is very restricted in orthodox Islam. The calls to prayer (*adhan* or *azan*) by the muezzin from a minaret are usually quite ornate; the intoning of prayers and sections from the Koran in a mosque is done to specific restrained chants. Both the calls to prayer and the chants, in fact, are not considered to be music, and therefore are acceptable within the mosque. Another example of such "nonmusic music" in the pan-Islamic world is the recitation of certain classical poetry. Both examples are useful reminders of the fact that different cultures have different definitions of the word *music* (see p. 5).

Theology and Music in Islam

The rise of conservative Islamic theology in the late twentieth century has reinforced the concept that the reading (*qira'ah*) of the holy Qur'an (Koran) is the core of all Muslim sonic events.[17] Some contemporary Islamic writings use the term *sawt*, "sound," to separate religious sounds from secular materials and for the "musical" (*sawti*) aspects of all religious sonic events.[18] The Arabic term *musiqa* (*musiqi, musiki*) is applied to the folk traditions mentioned earlier as well as military band music (of Islamic states). The further a musical genre is from chant, the less "legitimate" it is in the ears of

[17] See Lois Al Faruqi, "Factors of Continuity in the Musical Cultures of the Muslim World," *Progress Reports in Ethnomusicology*, 1/2 (1983–84), and her "The Status of Music in Muslim Nations," *Asian Music*, XII/1 (1981).

[18] See Chapter 23 of the *Atlas of Islamic Culture;* also Hiromi L. Sakata, *Music in the Mind* (Kent, Ohio: Kent State University Press, 1983), Chapters 3 and 4.

PLATE XI. Near Eastern plucked lutes

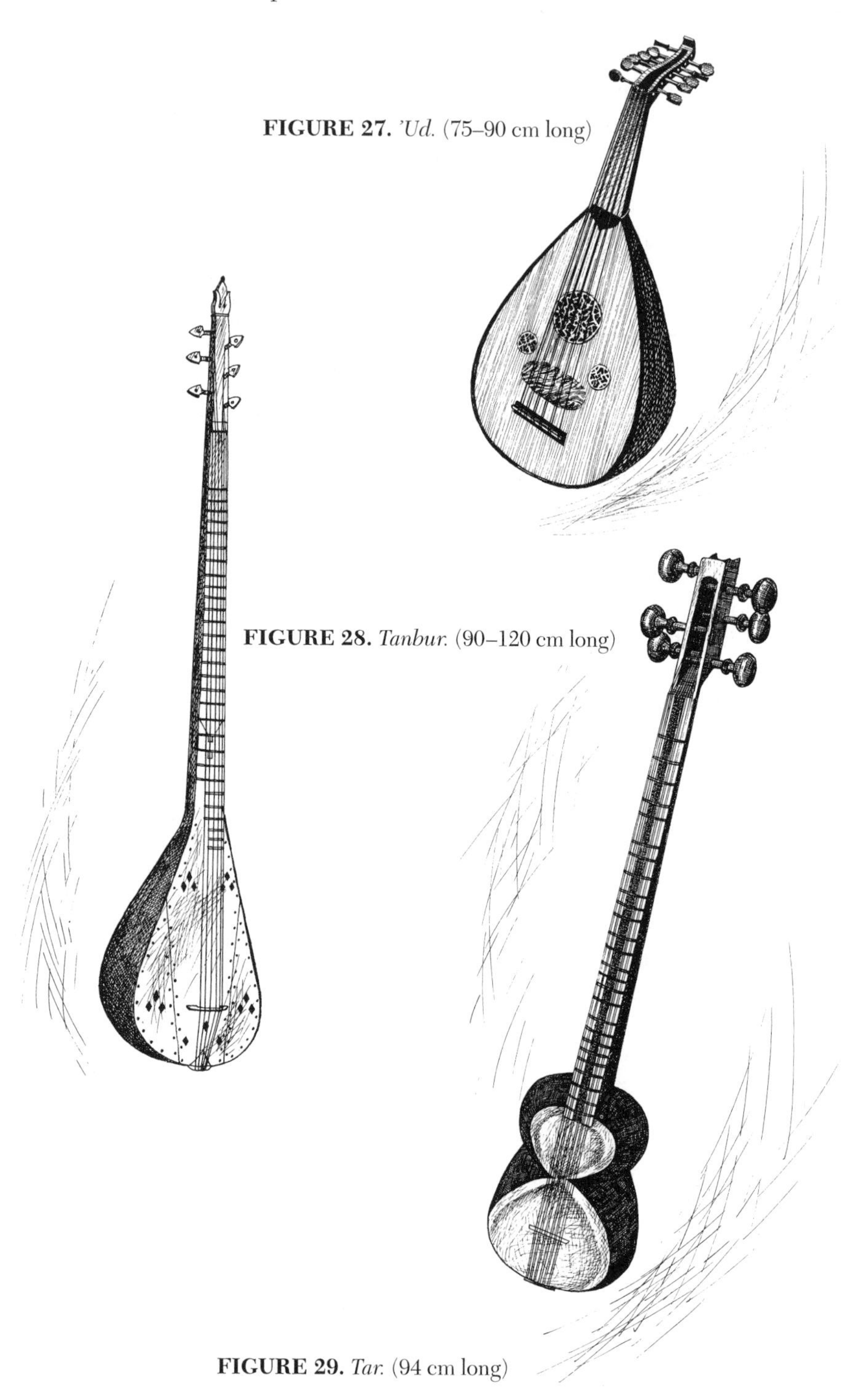

FIGURE 27. *'Ud.* (75–90 cm long)

FIGURE 28. *Tanbur.* (90–120 cm long)

FIGURE 29. *Tar.* (94 cm long)

theologians. Sensual and non-Islamic music are the most illegal. Music often conflicts with theologies. In Islam there are mystical sects that greatly value the functional and spiritual use of music. By the same token, the teachings of the Sufi sect of Islam are often declared to be fundamental to the artistry of both sacred and secular forms of Islamic music. The best known mystical order is the Mevlevi (Mawlawiyah) sect, whose *sama* part of its services involves men who continue to turn to the accompaniment of prayers and sometimes instrumental music.[19] Although officially discouraged since 1925, the Mevlevi still survive in Turkey and a few other eastern parts of the Muslim world, and their dance style may also have been absorbed into some of the trance-dance traditions of Islamic Southeast Asia. In the Near East today, a similar atmosphere in a secular context is found in the ceremonial exercises of special physical culture clubs such as the *zur khaneh* in Iran. These are accompanied by an epic-singing drummer who, like the leader in a Mevlevi service, marks off the divisions of the ceremony with the sounds of a bell.

Additional Islamic ceremonial music outside the mosque is heard at weddings, funerals, and other family events. Such occasions usually require the service of the wailing *zurna* oboes and various drums. During the Ramadan holy month in North Africa the oboes, and even horns (*neffar* or *nafir*), are used for the call to prayers. In addition, one may hear wandering bards playing one-stringed fiddles and singing *qasida*, songs praising the careers of Muhammad (A.D. 570–632) and the saints. Today these itinerant *qasida* tend to deal with more current events, although they may retain an opening line in praise of their prophet. The term *qasida*, however, is better known as part of the classical music that is heard today in the cafés and in private concerts.

Before discussing classical music, we must mention one Muslim ensemble, especially because of its influence on Western music. It is the famous Turkish Janissary military band, which consists of bass drums (*darwul*), trombones (*boru*), cymbals (*zil*), double kettledrums (*nakkare*), and *zurna* oboes. Normally there are nine players on each type of instrument, plus performers who strike the ground with a clanging bell-tree called, in English, a Turkish crescent or Chinese pavilion.[20] Many eighteenth-century pieces *alla turca*, by such composers as Mozart and Beethoven, are imitations of this ensemble; modern variants of it are heard in some Shriners' parades in the United States.

Classical Music

CLASSICAL AND MODERN INSTRUMENTS. Since we have already mentioned so many instruments, it seems logical to continue our organological inventory in a classical context before turning to the complications of the music

[19] See the ceremony in *JVC Video* no. 16.

[20] See a modern group in parade in *JVC Video* no. 16. Their repertory is heard on UNESCO CD *Les Janissaires* (B 6738).

itself. The human voice, of course, is a major vehicle for Muslim classical music, since much of it is related to poetry. The folk-derived *nay* end-blown flute mentioned earlier is used in classical music, as are tambourines and various forms of the *tombak* drum (Figure 22), known in some areas as a *zarb*. The two small *naqqara* kettledrums can be found in some North African and Turkish classical ensembles.

The chordophone families are particularly well represented in Islamic music. The most common term for the classical bowed lute is *kamanja*. It may be a two- to four-stringed spike fiddle held upright like the Persian *kamanchay* (Plate XII, Figure 30) or a Western-style violin held either upright or horizontally from the hip. Both positions are used for the *keman,* which is found particularly in North Africa and Turkey; a Moroccan version in the upright position is shown in Plate XII, Figure 31. Next to it in Plate XII, Figure 32, is the two-stringed Moroccan *rabab*. This small upright bowed lute is unique, for, unlike such instruments as those of Figures 12 and 18, it has a fingerboard that is actually a hollow extension of the body along its short neck to the peg box. The Persian classical *kamanchay (kemanche)* of Figure 30 shows clearly why such an instrument is sometimes called a spike fiddle. The spike allows the player to rotate the instrument in order to accommodate the bowing of its two to four metal strings. On some instruments the spike fits into a metal plate so the player may place the instrument on the calf of the leg. The *kamanchay* has a membrane face of sheepskin and can have a globular or cylindrical body. Note that all the bows being used to play the instruments in Plate XII (as well as those of most of the other bowed lutes mentioned in this book) require the use of fingers to maintain bow tension.

Long-necked plucked lutes such as the *tanbur (tambur)* in Figure 28 float freely among pan-Islamic folk, popular, and art traditions. The word *tar* in the Near East and in Central Asia is used as a final syllable in the names of many such instruments. In Persian classical music an example is the four-stringed *sehtar*. The Iranian *tar* plucked lute shown in Figure 29 is quite different. It has six double courses of metal strings stretched over a membrane-faced figure-eight-shaped body. The gut frets along its neck are movable like those of most pan-Islamic plucked lutes. This is necessary so that the fret positions may be adjusted to the requirements of the various pan-Islamic tone systems (discussed later).

The most famous Muslim plucked lute is the *'ud* (Plate XI, Figure 27); it has a narrower bodied, long-necked variant, the *kwitra* (in Turkey the *lauta*). The *'ud* form shown in Figure 27 has five double courses plus a single high string, but there are many variations in the stringing of the instrument. Although the *'ud* often has movable gut frets like the *tar*, it sometimes is played fretless for more flexibility.

We noted that a few lyres still exist in East Africa and the Arabian peninsula, but harps are no longer used. A harp called *chang* in Persian is found in historical records and in paintings; however, the present-day *vaji* arched harp

PLATE XII. Near Eastern bowed lutes

FIGURE 30. *Kamanchay.*

FIGURE 31. *Keman.* **FIGURE 32.** *Rabab.*

of Nurestan and harps among Central Asian archeological artifacts are the only actual instruments of this type found in this area of the world. They are good examples of the principle of marginal survival, as is the *saung kauk* harp of Burma. Zithers, by contrast, are quite widespread. The Persian *santur* (*santir*) (Plate XIII, Figure 33) dulcimer is of special interest because it is the ancestor of a variety of instruments, from the Western cimbalon and piano to the Chinese *yangqin.* Seventy-two metal strings, in quadruple courses, are stretched across a set of bridges set on a shallow trapezoidal body; the strings are struck with two delicate hammers. The florid sounds of Persian music played on the open strings of a traditional *santur* tend to merge into an exotic mesh of tone color, although there are modern versions of the instrument that have a sound-dampening mechanism like that of a piano and thus are able to separate melodic tones. The stringing method of the *santur* varies: Sometimes the pegs (around which the string ends are wound) are on both sides of the body like those of most American hammered dulcimers; sometimes the pegs run along only one side, as may be seen on the *kanun* (*qanun*) shown in Figure 34. This psaltery is found in Turkish and Arab ensembles. Its 72 gut strings are plucked by small picks (seen in Figure 34) that are normally attached to the player's index fingers. Most Arab models have small levers under the strings at the peg side, making it possible to change the pitch slightly for tunings to different scales.

CLASSICAL MUSIC THEORY. As we intimated earlier, there were many centers of musical culture throughout the Islamic world. The oldest was probably Persia, which contained remnants of ancient Babylonian thought as well as some infusions of Greek ideas. This area was conquered by the Arabs in the seventh century and musical traditions were then mixed. As sultanates proliferated along the ever-extending line of Islamic conquests, Muslim musicians and music theorists found patronage in courts as far distant as Samarkand in Central Asia and Salamanca in Spain. The defeat of Islam in Spain in 1492 forced Iberian scholars to flee to North African courts, so that today there is a school of so-called Andalusian classical music in the Maghrib. The rise of the Ottoman Turkish empire from the thirteenth through the sixteenth century led to other centers of activity, such as Alexandria and Baghdad. Although this last great Muslim empire was politically rather static until its demise in the twentieth century, its musicians remained creative and active through at least the eighteenth.

The historical outline given here is reflected in the contemporary scene, for the modern Muslim classical tradition can be divided into four major schools: the Persian, with its center in Iran; the Arab, which flourishes in Egypt; the Andalusian, as it is practiced in North Africa; and the Turkish. Modern practitioners from the various national schools that lie within these four larger traditions continue to expand the theory and practice of their art, but they all retain certain basic concepts we can label as the ancient pan-Islamic classical music theory.

PLATE XIII. Near Eastern zithers

FIGURE 33. *Santur.*

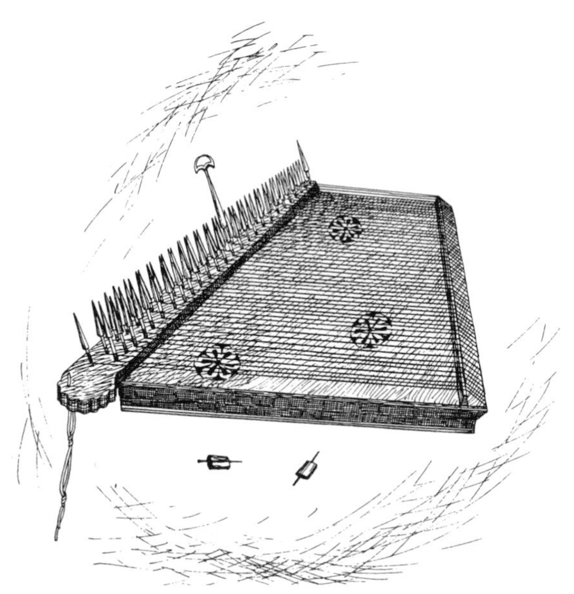

FIGURE 34. *Kanun.* (70–100 cm wide)

Studies in musical theories and practice are usually applied to what is called "classical" or "art" music. We implied in Chapter 1 that such terms might be appropriate functionally to any music culture. Used in connection with large urban literate societies, the terms refer to music traditions that were appreciated and supported by the economic or governmental control groups of those societies. In the Near East, however, such aristocratic musics were already well established on both the courtly and tribal levels before the coming of Islam in the seventh century. In the Bedouin tribal camps, the poet-musician (*shair*) occupied a special place in the culture by virtue of his or her shamanistic powers and commentaries on regional society. In pre-Islamic courts like those of Central Asia and Persia, female dancers (*mughammiyat*) or singers and African musicians were part of a tradition that was happily accepted by subsequent Islamic rulers. They, in turn, increased the import and exchange of all kinds of "exotic" foreign musicians.

Islamic musical scholarship first reached an apogee with the works of such men as Al Kindi (d. circa 870) and Al Farabi (d. 950), who combined Greek, Persian, and Arab concepts into brilliant syntheses. Al Farabi's "Grand Book of Music" (*Kitab al musiqi al kabir*) is one of the monuments of music theory; it was read at the medieval University of Paris as well as in Salamanca and Baghdad.

The lives of other famous Islamic music theorists demonstrate the continuing intercultural exchange of traditions. Ibn Sina (Avicenna, 980–1037) came from Central Asia to Persia, where he wrote on every intellectual topic of the medieval world, including music theory. A ninth-century musician named Ziryab left Baghdad to work in the Muslim court of Cordoba, Spain; from there his style of performance, teaching, and composing spread to other courts. Later important music scholars were the Persian Safi al-Din al-Mummin (d. 1294), who served the Mongol conquerors of Baghdad, and Abd Qadir Ghaibi al Maraghi (d. 1435), who provided the first extensive examples of Persian music in notation while working for the Turkish Ottoman rulers.

From the surviving literature of many musicians' writings, we are able to glean much information about the names of famous musicians and compositions, but most of these works are primarily concerned, like similar medieval European studies, with the science of acoustical music theory.[21] The scholarly tradition has carried on through the nineteenth and twentieth centuries.[22] Our discussion on the theoretical base of Islamic art music concentrates on modern scholarship because it is closer to contemporary performance practice.

[21] An annotated list of basic scholarly writings from the ninth through the thirteenth century is found in the *Cultural Atlas of Islam,* 449–54. See also Henry G. Farmer, *The Sources of Arabian Music* (Leiden: E.J. Brill, 1965).

[22] For examples in Lebanon, Mikhail Mashaqa (1800–1888); in Turkey, Rauf Yekta Bey (1871–1935) and H. Sadettin Arel (1889–1955); and in Iran, Mehdi Barkechlin. A 1932 Cairo conference on Arab music brought together the best of both indigenous and Western scholars.

incomplete graphic representations. Second (and this point relates to the first), even the most traditional classical musician will tend to hold his or her own interpretation of the modal aspects of a *maqam,* so various schools of the same tradition may describe a *maqam* in quite different ways. This is also possible in the pan-Islamic tradition, since professional performers, like many other musicians discussed in this book, are more concerned with skills in performance than accuracy in intellectual abstractions.

The theoretical concepts just outlined are pan-Islamic, and the terminology is often similar in Arabic- or Turkish-speaking countries. We noted the early influence of Persian thinking on this topic so we use its contemporary music theory and words to look in more detail at another equally logical and handsome pan-Islamic system. Since the eighteenth century, Persian music theory has recognized twelve modal structures called *dastgah-ha* (singular, *dastgah*). The term means scheme, "apparatus," or hand position. One interpretation of this system is shown in Example 3–4.[27]

The seven *dastgah-ha* considered basic are marked with Roman numerals. The remaining five, marked with parenthetical arabic numerals, are felt to be auxiliaries (*avaz,* "songs," or *naghmah,* "melodies") to a primary *dastgah,* four to *Shur* and one to *Homayun.* Study of Example 3–4 quickly reveals that one cannot easily distinguish a *dastgah* on the basis of pitch alone; for instance, *Mahur* and *Rast panjgah* appear to be the same scale. Each *dastgah,* like an Arab *maqam* or Turkish *makam,* is better recognized in practice by special melodies (*gusheh-ha,* the plural of *gusheh* or *gushé*). These in turn emphasize specific melodic contours, cadence formulas, and conventional final tones *(ist)* or reciting tones (*shahed*). (*Ist* and *shahed* are indicated in Example 3–4 in their most commonly accepted versions.) The auxiliary or satellite originally may have been melodies that gained nearly equal stature with the primary modes and were referred to in performance by their own name rather than that of their parent *dastgah.* Today their secondary status is noted by the narrower range of their melodies and by the smaller number of compositions based on them in the *radif,* the collection of all the *gusheh-ha* in the Persian art music tradition.

It must be remembered that Muslim musicians do not play scales, they play pieces, and that only in a performance context do the essential characteristics and mood of a *dastgah* emerge. Nevertheless, the tonal abstractions of Example 3–4 give some idea of the rich vocabulary from which such music is constructed. The microtonal arrows in the notation, for example, show that there are obviously more than twelve pitches in the Persian octave. In practice there are an infinite number (although only seven are used at one time), because individual performers, like many jazz musicians, have their own interpretations of the "correct" pitches of a given scale or piece.

[27] For others, see the Farhat and Zonis readings cited in the bibliographical notes of this chapter.

EXAMPLE 3–4. One abstraction of the Persian *dastgah* system.

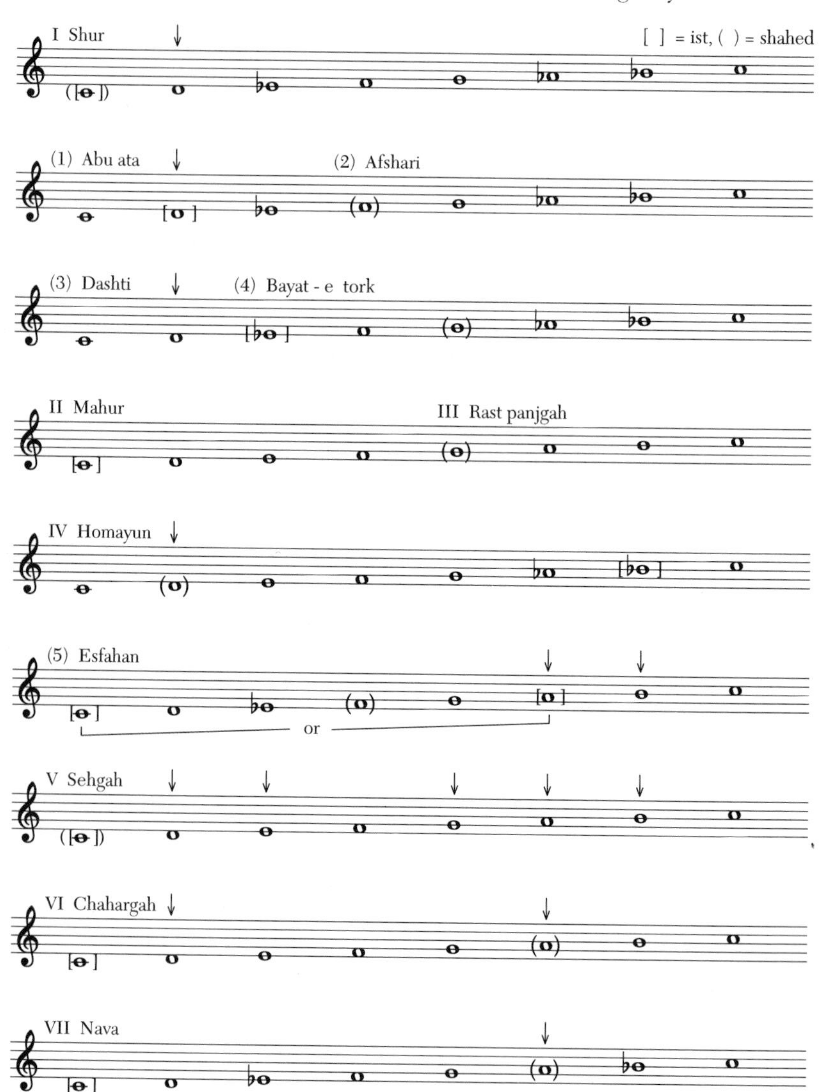

The most common Persian theory continues to view the octave in two tetrachords a whole step apart, each consisting (as in Western scales) of two whole steps and one half step. Some twentieth-century Persian music theorists hold that there are different sizes of seconds: a major second (approximately 200 cents), a minor second (near 100 cents), a neutral second (about 150 cents), and an enlarged second (some 255 cents); the last combined with a minor second can result in a neutral third (355 cents). There is no agreement as to the actual size of these intervals among theorists or among practicing musicians; thus the inaccuracy of our notation in Example 3–4 is appropriate.

The Greek terms *limma* and *comma* mentioned earlier are used in Persian theory as well to create tiny divisions within the octave. However, remember that there actually is no microtonal "chromaticism" in any of the pan-Islamic musics although that term is often used in writings about so-called Oriental music. This descriptive error is usually caused by the "out-of-tune" sound of Near Eastern music. It is, in fact, placed very accurately and artfully with the varied intervals mentioned earlier.

The word *avaz,* besides being used to indicate a satellite scale, is frequently applied to the unmeasured rhythmic style of music that in Iran is most common in classical music. (It is shown in Example 3–6.) In such *avaz* the major rhythmic consideration is that of the classical poetry which so often is part of the performance.[28] Classical pan-Islamic music theory, like that of medieval Europe, included a set of rhythmic modes: short rhythmic units constructed from combinations of poetic feet. While these modes may still be discussed academically, they are not used in the living tradition of Persian classical music. Today there are three basic styles of measured pieces. One is the *chahar mezarb,* which has a fast tempo, an ostinato, often a drone effect, and melodic passages that are of rather wide range. The second is the *kereshmah,* which emphasizes variants on the pattern ♩ 𝅗𝅥 ♩ 𝅗𝅥 ♩ ♩ 𝅗𝅥 ♩ 𝄽. The third is the *zarbi,* a word that simply means "rhythmic"; this style contains many different patterns.

Rhythm plays a more important role in Turco-Arabian classical genres. The meaning of its technical terms varies with writers and areas. One generic term for a rhythmic mode is *iqa'* (plural, *iqa'at*) and its repetitive use is *dawr* in Egyptian, *taqm* in Syria, *usul* in Turkey, and *mazim* in the Maghrib. These repeats could be considered an isorhythm, ostinato, or time cycle depending on the pattern's length. In twentieth-century practice, the units may be from only a few beats to 179. Pan-Islamic rhythmic patterns are generally taught or written in the mnemonics of a drum or tambourine. Drum mnemonics appear below the Turkish version of the rhythmic pattern *remel* in Example 3–5. Two note positions have been used in the staff notation to help you visualize the different sounds on the instrument; they are not intended to suggest absolute pitches. Example 3–5 also includes a modern Arab version of the same-named pattern to show, as in Example 3–3, the variety of interpretations found for the technical terms of pan-Islamic music.

[28] Excellent examples are found in Ella Zonis, *Classical Persian Music* (Cambridge: Harvard University Press, 1973), 129–30.

EXAMPLE 3–5. Two versions of the rhythmic pattern *remel,* after *Encyclopédie de la musique*, ed. A. Lavignac and L. de la Laurencie (Paris: Librairie Delagrave, 1922), pp. 2773 and 3054. Used by permission.

Our few comments on pan-Islamic music theory have implied only indirectly the extensive Muslim studies that exist in the physics of sound and tunings. Further commentary would reveal in Islamic theory a subtle combination of mathematics, aesthetics, and philosophy as well. The real beauty of the system for most people, however, lies in the living art of musical performance.

Classical Music Performance Practice. Modern Islamic classical music tends to be performed in one of two ways. The first consists of improvisatory solos or duets, as we see in the typical Persian *gusheh* of Example 3–6. The second style uses unison instrumental ensembles and choruses that perform accurate reproductions of florid but not freely ornamented traditional melodies. Both styles are heard frequently in Turkey, Egypt, and the Maghrib. Related distinctions in pan-Islamic music are found in how rhythmically free or measured a composition may be and in the degree to which it concentrates on important tonal aspects of the *maqam* in which it was originally set.

Recall that the fundamental identifying elements of a *maqam* are tonal emphasis, melodic formulas, and contours. These elements are best communicated in a monophonic or heterophonic texture. Having noted the emphasis on tetrachords and pentachords in describing the tone system, the composing or improvising of music in small, repeated, conjunct sonic segments is equally logical. When the music is improvised, the intricacy of arabesques, of tension and release around a tonal center, and the gradual rise to new tonal centers and tetrachords become aesthetic goals of great power. One listens not for themes and their developments but rather for ever-expanding insights into the elements of a *maqam*.[29] Thus the seeming melodies of the Persian *radif* collection mentioned earlier are not like themes from a sonata or symphony; the latter are developed by a composer and reproduced in performance as accurately as possible, whereas the melodies of a *radif* are guides for improvisations, no two of which may ever sound the same. Even when there is poetry, the power of the *maqam* dominates. There is no word painting, no musical change for happy or sad words. Rather the two sonic arts enhance each other, a beautiful poem sung in a beautiful way. It is comparable to the Muslim calligraphic ideal in which there often are many repetitions of the same sacred words in a book or the tiles of a building in an infinite variety of highly ornamental designs.[30]

MUSICAL FORMS. There are as many and as varied forms in pan-Islamic classical music as there are in the Euro-American art-music tradition. In this survey we speak of only a few of the better known forms. Vocal forms flourish because of the importance of Arab and Persian poetry in Islamic music, and thus the names of many musical genres are those of poetic forms as well. The classical *qasidah* odes can still be heard sung, along with the shorter strophic *tawshih* songs that grew out of the Moorish-Spanish tradition. Still other songs, the *muwashshah,* are relatively fixed in their rhythm but are felt to be filled with a Sufi spirit of mysticism, a force which, as we mentioned earlier, is often said to inspire much of Muslim music. Arab *layali* songs are freer rhythmically; they are often performed by one musician who plays his or her own accompaniment and improvisations on the *'ud.* The best known Turkish songs are found in the *beste* and *sarki* forms.

Persian musicians generally speak of a *gusheh* without distinguishing between vocal and instrumental pieces. More specific distinctions between, and extended mixtures of, instrumental and vocal forms are found, however, in the classical suites of other Islamic cultures. The term *nawba* or *nuba* for suite is found in Arab sources as early as the sixteenth century and is still used in that meaning in the so-called Andalusian tradition of North Africa, which came

[29] Some genres modulate to other *maqam*, but they return to the original one.

[30] A fine comparative study, hard to find, but excellent, is Lois Al Faruqi's *Islam and Art* (Islamabad, Pakistan: National Hijira Council, 1985).

EXAMPLE 3–6. A Persian *gusheh* from the recording *Iran* (Kassel: Barenreiter-Musicaphon Record BM 30 L 2004), side 1, band 1; book cassette, track 13). Transcription and sound used by permission of International Institute for Traditional Music, Berlin.[31]

[31] This poem by Sa'di (d. 1292) begins, "Friend! Do not listen if people tell you that I have any other friend than you, that night and day I think of any other thing or any one but you." The full poem is seen and heard on the original recording.

from Moorish Spain in the fifteenth century.[32] In the suites of North Africa and Egypt and the *fasil* suites of Turkey, all the principal sections are supposed to be in the same *maqam*. There may be some eight to ten sections within a suite, and one finds modulations to other modes within a section, but in theory the music should return to the original *maqam* at the end of each disgression. Within each movement of a suite there are usually several subsections, called in North Africa the *khana* or *cana*. Both these subsections and the movements themselves may be differentiated by changes of mood or by the particular rhythmic patterns that each employs.

The specific movements played in a given performance of classical music vary. In addition, individual movements may be played separately. For example, both the introductory solo instrumental improvisations (*taqsim* or *taksim*) of Arab or Turkish suites and their vocal equivalents, the *gazel*, are frequently heard in solo recitals. Their original function was to set the basic mode, mood, and melodic phrases of the *maqam* of the suite that would normally follow. (This is also the function of the *daramad* that open Persian classical compositions.) However, if the performer is talented enough and there is sufficient rapport between the musician and the audience, the improvisation in this introductory movement may be sufficient for a complete performance. Even the ensemble-and-chorus movements, such as the North African *abyat* and *barwal*, the Turkish *pesrev* (*bashraf*), and the lighter sounding *semai*, make acceptable concert pieces by themselves because they have within them changes of tempo and mood. When pan-Islamic music is performed in its multimovement form, however, it displays a subtlety of design and an architectonic structure that reveal the true intents of the Muslim artists. A sense of order is established in these suites through the early presentation of melodic and modal ideas that are then permutated throughout the various movements. At the same time, the set order of rhythmic changes gives to the knowledgeable listener a sense of logical progression in time as well as that feeling of anticipation so important to the active participation of any audience in a musical experience. This does not mean a Muslim audience must necessarily listen with the kind of specific intellectual concentration that we attempt to instill into Western listeners. Rather, much like Muslim calligraphy, Muslim classical music presents a large tracery of intersecting lines; one may choose to follow the peregrinations of a given melody or simply relax in the beauty of the general design. This attitude is reflected in the circumstances of performance of Muslim classical music, for, although there are some formal concerts in which the arrangement and deportment of the musicians and audience are strictly regulated (as they are in Western concert halls), this music is frequently heard also in cafés. Listeners may listen, sip, or converse as they see fit. Here also, the classical tradition may be mixed with the new and the popular: A *taqsim* may be followed by a love song or by the

[32] For its marginal survival as a ceremonial form of Muslim music, note the Malaysian *nobat* on page 152.

music of that kind of gyrating female dance for which the Near East is so famous. Classical ideals obviously suffer under such circumstances. Nevertheless, the music of the modern café orchestras of the Near East and the Maghrib is an excellent example of the manner in which musical styles continue to interact throughout the world of music.

Popular Music

There probably has been some kind of topical, easily learned entertainment music in every urbanized culture of the world. One way to characterize popular music is under the acronym TIPEE, which translates as follows:[33] T = timely; I = international; P = pluralistic; E = eclectic; E = evanescent.

While the basic topic of popular music has been and, hopefully, always will be love, songs appear that refer to important issues of the day; they are *Timely*. They are *International* primarily in the sense that every country has some, and many of them travel freely through the international music market. The market is *Pluralistic;* there are genres produced for each generation and class. *Eclectic* refers to the freedom in popular music to mix any idioms, as long as the resulting piece will sell, and *Evanescent* describes the speed with which most recording stars fade behind the light of new rising performers. At first sight the telecommunications industry seemed to have created an additional kind of pan-world popular music by making the latest hits of Europe or America known worldwide instantaneously.

However, the Near East, like the rest of the non-Western world, is not merely a passive receiver of this idiom. In addition to faithful reproductions of Western idioms it has produced it own form of synthesis from a mixture of Western and indigenous elements. Such compromises tend to follow typical lines.

First, Western tempered tuning takes over and those native instruments incapable of performing in that tuning tend to drop out, often to be replaced by some similar Western instruments. The clarinet, for example, is often substituted for the *zurna* oboe. The vocal part becomes less florid and less nasal, and the melodies themselves tend to be phrased in the foursquare manner of Western popular music and to use the reverting rather than the progressive form. If a lead singer is backed by a vocal group, as is common in many Western popular recordings, the group will sing a unison response, an ostinato, or occasionally a drone rather than harmony. Harmony may appear in pan-Islamic popular tunes through the use of a piano or accordion, although sometimes even these instruments will be played in a monophonic manner. One of the most revealing ways to discover the cavalier approach to harmony exhibited in many Arab popular tunes is to follow the bass part. It usually is more concerned with reproducing a standard Near Eastern rhythmic pattern than with establishing a solid

[33] This is derived from the author's "Popular Music under a Tipee," *A Celebration of American Music*, ed. R. Crawford, R. Lott, and C. Oja (Ann Arbor: University of Michigan Press, 1990).

harmonic bass progression. Sometimes this native rhythm pattern will be altered, however, to fit into the rhythm of one of the standard South American dance forms such as the beguine, tango, or rumba.

During the Euro-Asian colonial period (circa 1750 to 1950), pan-Islamic music influenced the West primarily in exotic concert music (particularly in France) plus a few pop tunes like "The Shiek of Araby" (1921) or "Caravan" (1937). The late twentieth-century increase in Islamic work forces in Europe has had a more direct musical and marketing influence on some European popular music industries.[34] As we noted in previous chapters, indigenous recording industries have flourished at the same time. They not only spread Western and local popular idioms but also folk traditions that normally would not have been heard outside a small area.[35] Many Arab generations are served by the rerelease of recordings by the one Egyptian star who never seems to fade, Umm Kulthum (Um Kalthum, 1908–1975).[36] She took her father's lessons in Qur'an reading to the fields of radio, film, and concert music from 1922 until her death. We have said that music styles do not remain static; pan-Islamic popular music is certainly an East-West case in both directions.

A Historical Interlude: The Ancient World of the Near East

Although this book deals primarily with the contemporary scene, we cannot ignore the many evidences of music that come from the very cradle of civilization and give us our earliest clues as to the first uses of music by urbanized people.

The oldest records of the ancient civilizations show that music was already a highly organized activity. In Mesopotamia, for example, the presence of guilds of musicians can be traced back as early as the fourth millennium B.C. Among the endless legal documents that dominate the famous cuneiform clay tablet collections one can find contracts for singers from such guilds, employed to intone the psalms in Sumerian temples.

Documents from Sumerian scribal schools[37] reveal not only the fact that they were taught in temple buildings by lower-ranked priests but also that

[34] An old example (1986) is the record *Dissedenten* subtitled *Life at the Pyramids*, with cuts like "Berlin Beduins," "Sultan Swing," and "Song for Winnie Mandela." The performers are German and Arab; discovered by an Italian promoter; recorded in Casablanca, Tangier, Zimbawe, and Paris; mixed in Tangier, Spain, and Germany; produced by Shanachie [an Irish name] Records (64001), with cover photos from Zurich and distribution from New Jersey.

[35] For details on the Egyptian record industry and its music see Salwa El-Shawan Castelo-Branco, "Some Aspects of the Cassette Industry in Egypt," *The World of Music*, 29/2 (1987), and the excellent articles by Ali Jihad Racy in *Ethnomusicology*, 20/1 (1976) and 26/3 (1982).

[36] See Virginia Danielson, "The Qur'an and the Qasidah aspects of the Popularity of the Repertory Sung by Umm Kulthum," *Asian Music*, 19/1 (1987).

[37] For student life in such schools see Chapter 6 of Samuel N. Kramer's *The Sumerians* (Chicago: University of Chicago Press, 1963) or his *Schooldays* (Philadelphia: University Museum, 1949). See also Cyril J. Gadd, *Teachers and Students in the Oldest Schools* (London: School of Oriental and African Studies, 1956).

the students had to learn to sing cult hymns in an archaic language. Are we talking about Sumer, 1300 B.C. or Paris, 1300 A.D.?[38]

Collections of Babylonian liturgies themselves indicate that large numbers of such singers were used, sometimes accompanied by reed pipes, flutes, drums, or tambourines. The excavations of Ur (twenty-fifth century B.C.) have revealed examples of such instruments as double pipes, clappers, and sistrums, along with an eleven-stringed harp that seems to be the progenitor of harps all along the ancient trade routes of the Orient to the far reaches of China and Japan.

Plate XIV, Figure 35, is from a late seventh-century B.C. bas-relief of a procession of harps (*zakkal*) carved at Susa. Compare it to the eighth-century A.D. harp found in Japan (Plate XIV, Figure 36) and ponder the power of human ideas and of camels' feet.

Large ensembles of double pipes, percussion instruments, and various styles of harps are seen in the bas-reliefs of later Assyrian and Babylonian ruins. At the same time, written records show us that the ancients knew much about the science of music and acoustics and had evolved a complex theory of the relationship between music and other elements in the universe.

In Egypt, the earliest dynastic records also show a highly evolved art of music. Egyptian art from the twenty-sixth century B.C. shows male musicians playing various harps, reed pipes, and long end blown flutes.

As seen in Plate X, Figure 26, this flute (*sib*) of the fifth dynasty (2500 B.C.) was held to the side, as are most *nay* in the Near East today. Figure 26 also shows the singer who joins in this ancient song covering his ear in a tradition that will never end in vocal music.

Continual change in musical taste was as true in the ancient world as it is today. In the New Kingdom (circa 1507 B.C.) foreign female musicians from the Near East became the favorites of the courts (see Figure 20), and with them must have come new, "exotic" music. The walls of many tombs and monuments chronicle in much detail the eras of change in Egyptian music history. Yet the musicians who accompany the solemn rites and joyful dances pictured there are mute; no music remains. Like most Near Easterners today, the ancients seem to have taught their music by rote, and the sound apparently died with the performers. There have been, however, attempts to decipher what may be a rudimentary notation involving hand gestures (chironomy) as seen in several wall paintings.[39] In addition, studies of string lengths, frets, and finger holes in both pictures and artifacts have been used as the basis for inferences about Egyptian scales, and finger positions of harpists in drawings have been used to show the possible existence of harmonies in fourths or fifths.

Most recently, one example of Hurrian cuneiform writing dating from the second millennium B.C. has been transcribed and played on a reproduction

[38] See Nan Cooke Carpenter, *Music in the Medieval and Renaissance Universities* (Norman: University of Oklahoma Press, 1958), 46.

[39] See Hans Hickman, *Musicologie Pharaonique* (Kehl Librairie Hertz, 1956). Look also at the hand gesture of the singer in Figure 30.

PLATE XIV. Ancient harps of West and East Asia

FIGURE 35. A seventh-century B.C. Assyrian harp.

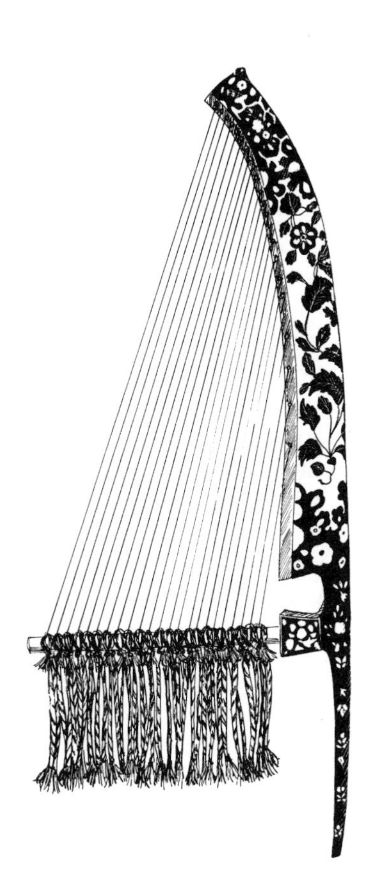

FIGURE 36. An eighth-century A.D. Japanese *kugo* harp. (137.8 cm high)

of an ancient lyre with the claim that it is the "oldest" known melody—although, like a *maqam*, it may be only a framework for an actual melody.[40]

There has been little agreement in the interpretation of these remnants, or regarding the one supposed example of music notation in cuneiform. This does not mean, however, that the musical legacy of the ancient world is completely lost. The Babylonian connection of music with the universe passed on into the Persian tradition. The Egyptians of Plato's time were still possessors of coveted knowledge in both music practice and theory. Thus much that we credit to Pythagoras and other great Greek music theorists may have deeper roots in Alexandria and the Nile Valley. In addition, the legacy of ancient Egypt is found in the shapes, tunings, and playing styles of such folk instruments as the *arghul* double clarinets in Egypt, the *genibri* of North Africa, the many end-blown flutes of the Near East, the *halam* of the Wolofs, and the sistrums of the Ethiopian Copts and the ancient Greeks and Romans.[41]

One of the most famous Egyptian harp songs was a funeral piece that said, "Let music and song be before you. Leave behind all evil and think only of joy until the day comes when we journey to that land that loves silence."[42] This seems a fitting tribute to the vitality that was, and the silence that now is, the condition of music from the ancient world.

Jewish Music in the Near East

Among the several non-Muslim religious groups in the Near East, the Jews are the most numerous and widespread. Their tradition differs from the Muslim world in two ways. First, whereas the Muslim religion was spread by conversion and conquest, the Jewish tradition remained basically esoteric and nonevangelistic. Wandering Jewish groups spread about the world but remained religiously separated from their host cultures. There was a cross influence between Jewish and Gentile music cultures, particularly in secular songs, but much of Jewish religious music held to older forms.

The second difference between the Jewish and Muslim musical worlds came with the creation of the state of Israel in 1948. Instead of a continual extension of cultural influence as in Islam, there was in Israel a sudden compression of co–religionists from widely scattered ethnic groups. This concentration of cultures had made Israel (and, for the same reason, cities like New York,) a rich hunting ground for ethnomusicologists.[43]

[40] A. D. Kilmer, "The Discovery of an Ancient Mesopotamian Theory of Music." *Proceedings of the American Philosophical Society*, Vol. 115 (1971), 131.

[41] For a discussion of the survival of ancient Egyptian instruments, see Hans Hickman, *Catalogue d'enregistrements de musique folklorique égyptienne* (Strasbourg: Heitz, 1958).

[42] See Miriam Lichtheim, "The Song of the Harpers," *Journal of Near Eastern Studies*, 4/1 (1945), 178. My thanks to Carlton Hodge of Indiana University for advice on the paraphrase of the original translation.

[43] American examples are Mark Slobin's *Tenement Songs: The Popular Music of the Jewish Immigrants* (Urbana: University of Illinois Press, 1982) and *Chosen Voices: The Story of American Cantorate* (Urbana: University of Illinois Press, 1989).

Each Jewish community in Israel today offers special musicological opportunities. The Yemenite Jews, for example, have been extensively studied in the belief that their music represents the oldest Near Eastern Jewish style. The Yemenite religious chant shown in Example 3–7 illustrates their tone-centered, ornamented litany style. The Sephardic Jews, by contrast, are studied for the *romanzas* of Spain they have preserved since the time of their expulsion (1492). The ghettos of the German, Slavic, and Balkan states created the Ashkenazi tradition with its interesting cross fertilization of European, Russian, and Yiddish musical styles. Jewish communities from the Near East and even congregations from India, have brought their unique musics to Israel. Once settled there, each group of such people tends to use four or five musical styles interchangeably.

First, there is the fairly unified liturgical style. After the destruction of the second temple by the Romans (70 A.D.), the Jewish liturgy turned from sacrificial rites to an emphasis on prayers and invocations. These have been passed on to every congregation. Thus even groups distant from each other seem to share the melismatic, free-rhythm cantillations of the cantor. Most Jewish cantillations are influenced by the *maqamat*. This is quite evident in the more ecstatic Chasidic and Cabalistic sects.

EXAMPLE 3–7. A Yemenite Jewish chant from the recording *Folk Music of Palestine* (Smithsonian/Folkways 4408, side 2, track 3; book cassette, track 14). Transcription and sound used by permission.[44]

[44]The text is Exodus, chapter 14, verses 30 and 31, beginning. "And the Lord saved on that day Israel from the hands of Egypt; And Israel saw Egypt dead on the shore of the sea." Chapter 15 then contains Moses' song to the Lord in thanks for the sea. Consultation and the romanization of the standard text and the Yemenite dialect were kindly provided by Gene Schramm from the department of Near Eastern Studies at the University of Michigan.

A second style is found in the singing of religious poems (*piyutim*). These show greater variety with many borrowings from Gentile traditions. The Jews, like the Protestant Christians, have used many secular tunes for such religious purposes. These tunes, in turn, have introduced new melodic styles into the Jewish tradition. For the Near Eastern Jew, Muslim and Armenian-Russian folk songs were a great source. In Europe, each country has made its contributions to such music. The songs without words (*nigun*) of the Chasidic sects are excellent examples of this kind of Jewish music.

A third tradition consists of the secular songs of the Israeli Jew's former homeland. Whether these songs are direct borrowings from a Gentile tradition or specific tunes from a ghetto, they reflect most clearly the land of their origin. Thus one can hear the difference between a German Jew singing a thoroughly Teutonic piece or a Yiddish tune and the old homeland songs of a Rumanian or French Jew.

Israeli Jews may pick up as a fourth tradition the pan-Islamic style that exists all around them. When they do so they completely change their vocal style and idiom. Such changes in style are not uniquely Jewish. For example, every American Christian youth uses a voice quality on Saturday night totally different from the one he or she uses on Sunday morning. This fact, unfortunately, cannot be shown in present-day music notation. Nevertheless, such things as voice quality, facial expression, and gesture should be included in the ideal description of a musical style.[45]

The fifth tradition of the Israelite Jew is the music of the modern state. The bond of Israel is religious and political, not ethnic. Therefore, there has been a concentrated effort on the part of Zionist musicians to "create" a new secular folk music. This music is actually a kind of popular music composed by professional songsmiths and deriving its inspiration from the agricultural, economical, and political aspirations of the state and its citizens. The instruments used to accompany such music reflect the acculturation of styles in Israel. Near Eastern tambourines and goblet drums may be combined with a short block flute (*halil*) and European guitars and accordions, sometimes as an accompaniment for the *hora*, a Near Eastern line dance. The modes of the melodies are often Near Eastern, but they are harmonized with European or Russian chords that discourage the use of indigenous nontempered notes.

The harmonic tendencies of secular music have come into the synagogues as well, where choirs sing harmony and electric organs play irrelevant chords behind the cantor's melos. As we said before, the study of any music culture presents only moments in a time continuum, not finalities. The unusual polyethnic quality of Israel has created a striking musical mixture as well as research and compositional opportunities.

[45] Attempts were made to include them in style description. See Alan Lomax, *Folk-Song Style and Culture* (Washington, D.C.: American Association for the Advancement of Science, Publication no. 88).

BIBLIOGRAPHICAL AND AUDIOVISUAL NOTES

Books and Articles

Among studies on the African areas of this survey are Norma McLeod, "The Status of Musical Specialists in Madagascar," *Ethnomusicology*, 8/3 (1964), and Curt Sachs, *Les Instruments de musique de Madagascar* (Paris: Institut d'Ethnologie, 1938). See also Hugh Tracey's *Chopi Musicians* (London: Oxford University Press, 1948). Chopi music is heard in the Smithsonian/Folkways album *Africa South of the Sahara* (4503). For Ethiopia, see A. Kebede and K. Suttner, *Ethiopia—The Music of the Coptic Church* (Berlin: International Institute for Comparative Music Studies, 1969), and Michael Powne, *Ethiopian Music* (London: Oxford University Press, 1968). See also Kay Kaufman Shelemay's *Music, Ritual, and Falasha History* (East Lansing: African Studies Center, Michigan State University, 1986) and her "Zema: A Concept of Sacred Music in Ethiopia," in *The World of Music*, 3 (1982).

The writings of Lois Al Faruqi (1972–1986) are fundamental to Islamic music studies, in particular her *An Annotated Glossary of Arabic Musical Terms* (Westport, Conn.: Greenwood Press, 1981) and Chapter 23 in *Cultural Atlas of Islam* (New York: Macmillan, 1986). *Asian Music,* 19/1 (1987), contains her article on Qur'an chanting and Virginia Danielson's study of its influence on Umm Kulthum. Another Qur'an study is by Krisitina Nelson in *Ethnomusicology,* 22/1 (1981), which also contains Bernard Lortat-Jacob on Berber music and George Sawa on survivals of medieval Arabic performance practices. The journal's studies of modern conditions are in articles by Salwa Al Shawan, 28/2 (1984), and Ali Jihad Racy, 30/3 (1986). *Asian Music*, 22/1 (1991) has articles on Turkish music by Walter Feldman and by Irene Markoff and one on Egypt by Virginia Danielson. *The World of Music*, 3 (1986) deals with music and Islam. Useful short articles on various traditions are found in Robert H. Browning, ed., *Maqam: Music of the Islamic World and Its Influence* (New York: Athens, 1984). A wide view with illustrations is Jean Jenkin and Poul Olsen Rovsing, *Music and Musical Instruments in the World of Islam* (London: World of Islam Festival Publishing, 1976). Near Eastern religious musics are discussed in *Encyclopédie des musiques sacrées,* I (Paris: Labererie, 1968).

In *Music of Many Cultures,* ed. Elizabeth May (Berkeley: University of California Press, 1979) one finds introductions on Arab music by Josef M. Pasholezyk, Iranian classical by Ella Zonis, Ethiopian by Cynthia Tse Kimberlin, and Jewish by Abraham Schwadron. Iranian traditions are the topic in Ella Zonis, *Classical Persian Music: An Introduction* (Cambridge: Harvard University Press, 1973) and Bruno Nettl, *The Radif of Persian Music* (Champaign, Ill.: Elephant & Cat, 1987). Pan–Islamic theory is emphasized in Owen Wright's *The Modal System of Arab and Persian Music* A.D. 1250–1300 (Oxford: Oxford University Press, 1978), Karl L. Signell, *Makam Modal Practice in Turkish Art Music* (New York: DaCapo Press, 1986), and George Sawa, *Music Performance Practice in the Early Abbasid 320 A.H./750–932* A.D. (Toronto: Pontifical Institute of Mediaeval Studies, 1989). Ahabib Hassan Tuoma's *Die Musik der Araber* (Wilhelmshaven: Florian Notzel Verlag, 1988) provides a good introduction, as does his article on the *maqam* phenomenon in *Ethnomusicology*, 15/1 (1971). North African art music is the subject of Mahmoud Guettat's *La musique classique du Maghreb* (Paris: Sinbad, 1980).

The earlier work of Kurt and Ursula Reinhard has been reprinted, *Musik der Turkei* (Wilhemshaven: Heinrichshofen's Verlag, n.d. [circa 1970]). Other older introductions are Rauf Yekya Bey, "La musique turque," and Jules Rounat, "La musique arabe," in *Encyclopédie de la musique . . .*, A. Lavignac, ed. (Paris: Librairie Delagrave, 1922), Part 1, V. A classic reference is Baron Rodolphe D'Erlanger's six-volume *La Musique arabe* (Paris: Geuthner, 1930–49) as is Alexis Chottin's *Tableau de la musique marocaine* (Paris: Geuthner, 1939) and Henry George Farmer, *A History of Arabian Music* (London: Luzac, 1929). Sheherazade Qassim Hassan and Philippe Vigreux have edited the documents and studies of the famous 1932 conference in *Musique Arabe. Le Congrès du Caire de 1932* (Ciro: CEDEJ, 1992).

Jewish Music (New York: Holt, Rinehart and Winston, 1929) is by the founder of Jewish music research, Abraham Zvi Idelsohn (1882–1938). His bibliography and biography are in Volume 5 of *Yuval, Studies of the Jewish Music Research Centre* (Jerusalem: Hebrew University of Jerusalem, 1986). Contributors include such noted scholars as Edith Gerson-Kiwi, Ruth Katz, Israel Adler, and Kay Kaufman Shelemay. The latter's article in *Yuval*, V, opens new paths in both Ethiopian and Oriental Jewish studies. Other volumes of *Yuval* are equally valuable. The Idelsohn 1922–1923 10-vol. *Thesaurus of Hebrew Oriental Melodies* has been reprinted in English (New York: KTAV, 1973). For other transcriptions see Chemjo Vinaver, *Anthology of Hassidic Music* (Jerusalem: The Jewish Music Research Centre, Vol. 2, 1985). Irene Heskes's *The Source Book of Jewish Music* (Westport: Greenwood Press, 1985) is an annotated bibliography. Aron M. Rothmuller, *The Music of the Jews* (Canbury, N.J.: A.S. Barnes, 1967) and Eric Werner, *The Sacred Bridge* (London: Oxford, 1958) are standard references. See also Amnon Shiloah and Erik Cohen, "The Dynamics of Changes in Jewish Oriental Ethnic Music in Israel," *Ethnomusicology*, 27/2 (1983). American cantorial history is found in Mark Slobin's *Chosen Voices* (Urbana: University of Illinois Press, 1989).

For the ancient Near East see *The New Oxford History of Music*, I (London: Oxford University Press, 1957). Hans Hickman, *45 Siècles de musique dans l'Egypte ancienne* (Paris: Richard-Maxse, 1956), was a major ancient Egyptian music scholar. Early surveys of ancient music are found in Francis W. Galpin, *The Music of the Sumerians* (Cambridge: University Press, 1937) and Curt Sachs, *The Rise of Music in the Ancient World, East and West* (New York: Norton, 1943). See also Lise Manniche, *Music and Musicians in Ancient Egypt* (London: British Museum Press, 1991).

Audiovisual Materials

The World of Islam, Images and Echoes: A Critical Guide to Films and Recordings (New York: American Council of Learned Societies, 1980) is a fine start. The *JVC Video* nos. 16, 17, and 18 contain Near Eastern and North African materials. Refer also to Smithsonian/Folkway, *Africa South of the Sahara* (4503) and the

UNESCO Anthology of African Music, *Music of the Ethiopian Coptic Church* (BM 30 L 2304) and *Music of the Cushitic Peoples of South-West Ethiopia* (BM L 2305) and (BM 30 SL 2314). For music of North Africa there are UNESCO or Harmonia Mundi CDs *Morocco* (D 8002), *Algeria* (D 8037), and *Egypt* (D 8038). *UNESCO* earlier LP series included *Tunisia* (BM 30 L 2008). Other West Asian recordings in these series are *Syria* (D 8013, D 8039), *Yemen* (D 8004), *Yemenite Jews* (D 8024), *Kurdish Music* (D 8032), *Oman*(D 8211), and *Turkey* (D 8303, D 8204). UNESCO others include *Zaidi and Shafi'i: Islamic Religious Chanting, N. Yemen* (6586 040), *Iqa'at* (6586 038), *Jewish Yemenite Diwan* (6586 037), *Taqasim and Layadi: Cairo Traditional* (6586 010), *Arabian Music: Maqam* (6586 0060), *Iranian Dastgah* (6586 005), and *Jewish Music* (6586 001). King Records World Music Library includes Turkey, Iran, Iraq, and Azerbaijan in the 51000 CD series. Lyrichord has *Turkish Folk Music* (LLCT 7289) and Rounder has *Masters of Turkish Music* (CD-1051).

A SONIC GLOSSARY INDEX FOR CHAPTER 3

Amharic (Ethiopia)

(Speaker: Teshone G. Wagaw)

bagana (lyre), 68
debteras (Coptic church singer), 67
degwa (chant), 67
dowel (sonic stone slabs), 67
kebaro (Coptic drums), 67
krar (lyre), 68, 69 (Fig. 17)
masenqo (bowed lute), 68
tsenatsil (sistrum), 68, 69 (Fig. 16)

Other African languages

(Speakers: Makha Fall, Farazahiherivolanirina Ramiandrisoa, Caroline Wendt, Benigna Zima)

ahal (Tuareg songs), 71
amzhad, anzad (Tuareg bowed lute), 71, 72 (Fig. 18), 73 (Ex. 3–1), 78
assakalabu (Tuareg water drum), 71
gewel. See *griot*
griot (Wolof entertainer), 66
halam (African lute), 67
hira-gasy (theatrical Madagascar), 65
imzhad, inzad. See *anzad*
jejo vaotavo (stick zither, Madagascar), 65
ngodo (Chopi dance suite), 65
tabala.* See Arabic tabala
tende, tindi (Tuareg drum), 70, 71, 76 (Fig. 21)
timbila (Chopi xylophone), 65
valiha (tube zither, Madagascar), 24 (Fig. 7)

Arabic

(Speaker: Raji. M. Rammuny)

Abd Qadir Ghaibi al Maraghi (fifteenth-century scholar), 86
abyat* (suite movement), 95
adhan (call to prayer), 79

Greek
(Speaker: Dimitri Coucouvanis)

Hebrew
(Speaker: Lili Cahlon)

Persian
(Speaker: Soheila Amirsoleimani)

Turkish
(Speaker: Didar Akar)

*not on language cassette

FOUR

CENTRAL AND SOUTHERN ASIA

Central Asia is an immense landlocked area extending from the Caspian Sea eastward to China and Mongolia, with Siberia to its north and Afghanistan and Iran to its south. Its terrain varies from mountains to grassland steppes and arid deserts. Southern Asia consists of the subcontinent south of the Himalayan mountains and Afghanistan. For centuries the musics of Central Asia and Afghanistan have interchanged their indigenous styles with those of the Near East and South Asia. Thus they are excellent geographic and cultural areas through which to move on our musical journey from the Near East to Southern Asia.

MUSIC OF THE CENTRAL ASIAN REPUBLICS

Although the southern republics of Georgia, Armenia, and Azerbaijan on the west shores of the Caspian Sea are filled with numerous traditions from their many neighbors,[1] we limit our discussion to the Central Asian republics of

[1] Useful surveys of all the republics with bibliographers are found in Volume 19 of *The New Grove Dictionary of Music and Musicians*, ed. Stanley Sadie (London: Macmillan, 1980), 334–424. With the advent of the 1992 Commonwealth Republics, spellings of names and places became fluid. For example, Kirghiz can be Kyrgyz. Traditional Russian romanizations are used here.

Kazakhstan and Turkmenistan on the eastern shore, and Uzbekistan, Tadjikstan, and Kirghizstan still farther to the east. For most Westerners this area is a terra incognita, but historically it has been a land of many civilizations and many visitors. Some of its travelers have been merely observers or merchants—like Marco Polo—but a majority of those who crossed the borders of Central Asia had more militaristic or evangelistic intentions. A list of these visitors includes the feared names of the leaders of every horde that poured out of inner Asia to plunder Europe and the Near East, such as Jenghiz Khan, Kublai Khan, and Tamerlane; it also includes the eastward-moving standard-bearers of Islam as well as the westward-directed advance guards of ancient Chinese armies. In a word, this area, plus Afghanistan to the south, contained the major routes of commerce and conquest for centuries. The results were a series of colorful and generally short-lived cultures as varied as the outside influences that pressed in upon them.

Logical influences on traditional Central Asian music are its contiguous Near Eastern cultures. This is easily seen in the presence of such musical instruments as various double clarinets (like Plate X, Figure 24) and conical oboes (Plate X, Figure 25). A Turkish tradition is heard when the oboes play in pairs, one instrument being a drone. The long end-blown flute (Plate X, Figure 26) seems to follow the flocks of pastoral peoples from the ancient Near East to present-day Central Asia (as well as Eastern Europe). The Near Eastern tambourine (commonly called the *doira* here) and small pairs of kettledrums (*nagora*) are also present. All the chordophones of Persia can be found, particularly in the art-music ensembles of Tadjikstan, Uzbekistan, and Azerbaijan. Such ensembles play suites in the best pan-Islamic tradition. In Tadjikstan and Uzbekistan these suites are known as *makom;* the Azerbaijan suites are sometimes called *dastgah.* These two terms obviously relate to the Near Eastern words, although their meanings are changed. Many other terms, such as mode names and the titles of movements within the suites, relate to the pan-Islamic tradition discussed in Chapter 3, but their uses often reflect specific Central Asian national styles.

We have noted that several centers of Muslim music theory were located in Central Asia. Al Farabi himself is said to have been born in Turkmenistan, and the eleventh-century theorist Ibn Sina (known in the West as Avicenna) was educated in Bokhara. These men were but two of many scholars who contributed to the general progress of Muslim music theory. Of more importance to the Central Asian art-music tradition was the work of Najmuddun Kaubaki (1512–1576). He made a definitive analysis of the *Shashmakom,*[2] the basic collection of *makom* suites on which all modern Tadjik and Uzbek classical performances are based. Another important innovator was Niyazmuhammad Mirzabashi Kamil (1825–1899), who created a tablature called *khorezm* notation, in which the entire *tambur* part of the *Shashmakom* was written.

[2] A translation of the introduction to a twentieth-century edition is found in *Asian Music,* 13/1 (1981).

If we move from the art music of Central Asia to the folk and popular idioms, we find many variations on Near Eastern instruments.[3] Variants on small-bodied, long-necked plucked lutes such as the *tambur* (Plate XI, Figure 28) and *setar* are found in the two-stringed *dutar*, the three-stringed *komuz*, and the two-stringed *dombra*. The last comes in a great variety of shapes, some

EXAMPLE 4–1. A *komuz* song from Kirghizstan (Smithsonian/Folkways record 4535, side 4, track 3; book cassette, track 15). Transcription and sound used by permission.[4]

[3] For pictures of folk instruments from all of the republics, see *Atlas muzykalnykh instrumentov narodov SSSR*, ed. K.A. Vertkov (Moscow: Musyka, 1963).

[4] The text is: "Oh companion of the Kot country, your kinsman my father [played] the komuz as if it were nothing. We will respect the friend (i.e., the komuz) on which our ancestors played." Our thanks to Uli Schamiloglu of the University of Wisconsin for his translation; romanization, and comments. The text is a conventional opening for a narrative song. Since the recording comes from an oral tradition, the transcription may be more pedagogical than actual. Besides organal harmony, it was chosen to illustrate heterometer and certain diacritical markings. The original record notes said the music is in 2/4 time. No one asked the performer. He probably thought text, rather than meter.

of which are influenced by still further variants of the same chordophone (for example, the *balalaika*). Despite the interrelations of the instrumental types, the musics played on these various forms are not necessarily the same.

Compare the syllabic Kirghiz folk song in Example 4–1 with the heterophonic styles of Examples 3–1 and 3–6. The organal harmonic accompaniment in parallel fifths (or fourths) is typical of much Turkish-related folk music, particularly in Central Asia. The slight rush of beats (measure 6) is more common in the latter.

Another important feature of Central Asian music is the presence of long epic narratives. From the traditionally unaccompanied songs of storytellers, many of the famous folk epics of this area have been recovered. Kazakh and Kirghiz musicians often play textless narratives in which the entire story is pictured instrumentally.[5] Competitive songs are also found, in which the contestants vie with each other through improvised verses in a manner quite like that found throughout the Romance-language countries of Europe.

With the absorption of Central Asia into the Russian Empire in the nineteenth century, it joined other non-Western cultures in the conflict of maintaining its own tradition and also accommodating Western idioms. Both Russian and indigenous composers made efforts to combine the two musical worlds with moderate success. During the Soviet communist era of the twentieth century (circa 1918–1991) Central Asia faced a somewhat different challenge. It was subjected to considerable collectivization under the general communist policy of "reconstruction," in which folk art music, by Marxist definition, reflects the social and political conditions of the people.[6] This policy produces several curious results. First, field collectors were instructed to collect only music that falls within these ideological goals and to admonish singers who persist in performing overly religious, sarcastic, or sensual musics. Secondly, the analysis of such music as was collected was made to conform to certain specific state doctrines such as the predominance of the 12-note chromatic scale system in people's music. In Central Asia the latter policy caused much scholarly hedging, since many "wrong notes" show up in the Islamic ornamented styles. Finally, the goal of collecting was not solely the archival preservation of traditional materials (although much valuable work was done in this area); rather, the music collected was primarily raw material for the use of Western-style composers who were to produce new "realistic" music based on national idioms.[7] The music was also frequently arranged for state-supported "folk" orchestras and choruses, which then become the major media through which the music was made available to the people in performances and on records.

[5] See Asiya Mukhambetova, "Philosophical Problems of Being in the Art of the Kazakh Kuyshi," *Yearbook of Traditional Music*, 22 (1990).

[6] An interesting exception is found in Slawomira Zeranska-Kominek's "The Classification of Repertoire in Turkmen Traditional Music," *Asian Music*, 21/2 (1990). As tribes with no elite to destroy, their collectivization was less than elsewhere in Central Asia.

[7] The specific doctrines of Marxist music can be read in Rena Moisenco, *Realist Music* (London: Meridian, 1949).

Many individual folk singers were honored by the state, particularly if they created new socialist-oriented songs. However, the emphasis was on ensemble and choral music; this reflected the basically collectivist nature of the Soviet attitude toward music. Since the original idiom was often soloistic, this musical collectivization was bound to affect such characteristics as ornamentation and tuning. The specific arrangements of reconstructed music reflected a strong orientation toward such ideals of the central conservatory in Moscow as Western harmony and tempered scales. Thus reconstructed Central Asian music often sounds suspiciously like nineteenth-century Russian romanticism. In the 1970s, however, transcriptions and actual recordings of regional styles began to appear, and state support of performance and research in national idioms showed encouraging signs of constructive rather than reconstructive action.[8]

AFGHANISTAN

The twentieth-century country of Afghanistan shares borders with China, India, Pakistan, Iran, and Central Asia. In both ancient and modern times these borders, like those of the Central Asian republics we just discussed, were crossed many times by the routes of commerce or war. One artistic result of this constant flow of cultures can be seen in the amazing statuary found in the ruins of Afghanistan's ancient cities. The physical features of these statues are those of every type within the Indo-Caucasian family plus a liberal sprin kling of the Mongoloid types. Thus Afghanistan is an important link in th chain of cultures binding Europe and Asia together.

Musically, this linkage can be heard by listening to pieces from varic regions of Afghanistan. The western and northern musics of the country dominated by Near Eastern or Central Asian styles, whereas eastern Afg music is heavily Indian-oriented. The former tend to use a slightly n quickly ornamented vocal line; the latter prefers a softer, lower tone qualit artful portamento slides. Although the northern border was closed for time, the traditional wanderings of the many ethnic groups of Central Asi created fairly large pockets of "minorities," many of whom maintain the lier musical traditions. A study of northern Afghan musical life[9] has sho the major sources of most musical events are the local and regional r Their teahouses are filled every market day (usually twice a week) or holiday with men who enjoy gossip and the entertainment of at le player (*damburachi*) and singers who often perform in Uzbek or T The modern administrative or industrial cities rely more on the nat

[8] See Barbara Krader, "Recent Achievements in Soviet Ethnomusicolog on Russian Terminology," *Yearbook of Traditional Music*, 22 (1990).

[9] Mark Slobin, "Music and the Structure of Town Life in Northern Afg *musicology*, 14/3 (1970).

from the capital, Kabul, with its mixture of idioms in a popular style similar to that discussed in Chapter 3. There are, of course, a few regional or big city musicians who maintain traces of the classical traditions of earlier Central Asian courts or who have taken up the Persian tradition.[10] In addition, the Nurestan peoples in the isolated mountain regions of the northeast use an arched harp (*vaji*) that may be a marginal survival of an instrument often found in the archaeological remains of ancient Near Eastern cultures.

The major nomadic (*kuchi*) culture of southern and western Afghanistan is the Pashtun or Pathan. Its fundamental musical style is vocal and normally consists of folk poetry (*lundai*) set to various standard tunes. If songs are accompanied, the long-necked *tambur* or *dambura* lute is used commonly, although other Central or Near Eastern instruments, such as the two-stringed bowed *ghitchak* (*ritchak*) lute, also appear.[11] The *ghitchak* is related to the Near Eastern *rabab* although, like its Central Asian counterpart, its body is often made of a rectangular gasoline can. The term *rabab* also appears in Central Asia and Afghanistan, but there it usually refers to a plucked lute, thus demonstrating the concept of floating terms discussed in Chapter 2. Tambourines, flutes, and jew's harps are found as well, once more reflecting a potential mixture of indigenous and Muslim traditions. In contrast, the two-headed *dhol,* a barrel drum common in eastern Afghanistan, points just as clearly in an Indian direction. If we wandered further out into the Central Asian steppes or studied tribal peoples in Afghanistan who had come from that region, we would encounter traditions related to those of Mongolia or even Siberia, but our present musical trail leads more logically to South Asia.

SOUTH ASIA: A HISTORICAL INTRODUCTION

The Indian peninsula from the Himalayan mountains and Karakorum to the island of Sri Lanka (Ceylon) includes a wide variety of peoples, languages, religions, and political divisions. The history of this wide area began with the Dravidian civilization (2500–1900 B.C.), which was in turn supplanted by an Aryan invasion. The caste system and the Hindu religion were already ancient traditions when Gautama Buddha (563–483 B.C.) appeared. Although the Buddhist religion eventually found its greatest strength outside India, the island of Sri Lanka remained a Buddhist stronghold. On the mainland, Hinduism was the dominant force until the Muslim invasion of the thirteenth century. The resultant Moghul courts of North India produced brilliant new Islamic-Hindu are forms; South India became the center of Hindu tradition. The British occupation of the nine-

[10] Excellent studies of local musicians are found in Hiroimi Lorraine Sakata, *Music in the Mind* (Kent, Ohio: Kent State University Press, 1983), and John Baily, *Music of Afghanistan* (Cambridge: Cambridge University Press, 1988).

[11] Drawings of this and other typical Afghan instruments are found in Sakata, *Music in the Mind.*

teenth and twentieth centuries introduced many Western ways, but the basic cultural patterns of India remained those of the Muslim-Hindu world. The political separation of Pakistan from India in the mid-twentieth century and the creation later of Bangladesh are reflections of this split cultural heritage.

The musical divisions of South Asia are many, but the best known classical traditions are two: *Hindustani music,* the music of Pakistan and North India, where Muslim influence is often strong, and *Karnatak* (*Karnatic*) *music* of the south, which claims to be more indigenous. The Karnatak system prevails in Madras, Mysore, Anghra, and Kerala. Hyderabad may be said to be the dividing line between the Hindustani and Karnatak traditions. Although these two traditions use different instruments and vary in their nomenclature, their basic concepts are the same and have been cultivated in South Asia for centuries.

Ancient Indian Music

The study of Indian art music begins with the *Vedic* hymns, sacred Aryan texts to which other materials have been added over the centuries. The Rig Veda is the earliest form still surviving. Some of its verses were rearranged later into the so-called Yajur Veda. The Sama Veda contains selected verses from the same source as used in liturgies. The Atharva Veda is a set of different texts derived from folk religious magic and incantations. The Rig Veda and Sama Veda in India are somewhat analogous to the Catholic and Orthodox Christian chant tradition of the West for, although both sets are actually performed and known only by special groups, their early texts and theoretical implications are considered to be the foundations of many later styles. The Vedic tradition belonged to the higher caste cultures and, because of its religious nature, was the subject of rigorous essays concerning its correct performance. Metaphysically, the physical vibrations of musical sound (*nada*) were inextricably connected with the spiritual world, so that the validity of a ritual and the stability of the universe itself might be adversely affected by a faulty intonation of sacred texts. The rules of Rig Veda chanting emphasize syllabic singing with attention paid to word accent, as shown in Example 4–2. Other schools of Rig Veda singing, as well as most of the Sama Veda tradition are, by contrast, quite wide-ranged, melismatic, and generally unconcerned with word accent.[12]

Although the entire Vedic tradition is little practiced today, its nomenclature and some of its musical worldviews were carried on through religious and secular epics performed for lower caste Indians. The *Natya-Sastra,* attributed to the sage Bharata (circa 5th century A.D.), is said to have been a kind of manual for productions of theatrical forms of this tradition, which were sometimes also called Veda. The original book is most commonly dated in the fifth century A.D., although some place it as early as the second century B.C.; others feel it is a compilation of the works of many persons done between the fifth and

[12] For notated examples of several different Vedic forms, see Nazir Jairazbhoy's "Legacy of India: Indian Music," in *Cultural History of India* (Oxford: Clarendon Press, 1974).

EXAMPLE 4–2. A Rig Veda hymn from the recording *India* (Kassel: Barenreiter-Musicaphon Record BM 30 L 2006, side 1, track 2; book cassette, track 16). Transcription and sound used by permission of the International Institute for Traditional Music.[13]

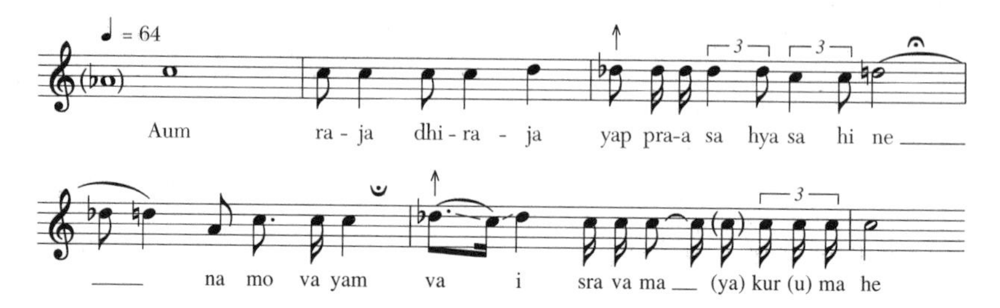

seventh centuries A.D. Whatever its date, it is the traditional link between ancient India and the classical eighteenth- and nineteenth-century musics as they survive today, for music and dance are discussed in it along with various dramatic events. Other important theoretical sources for Indian music are the tenth-century *Brhaddesi* by Matanga, which is the first text to use the term *raga,* and the thirteenth-century *Sangita-Ratnakara* by Sarangadeva, written during the time of pressures from Near Eastern ideas brought in by the Moghul rulers. From the sixteenth through the twentieth century Indian theorists continued to attempt further syntheses and standardizations. In this manner the ancient terms remained, but their meanings began to vary greatly; in some cases the words refer to what they might have meant in ancient music, whereas in others the terms are applied to the musical practices of the time when the book in which they appear was written.[14] In any case, it is obvious that the basic concepts and terminologies derived from the Vedic hymns, as well as the many studies of later centuries, are necessary sources for an intellectual understanding of Indian classical music. They may even apply indirectly to the much larger world of Indian folk and popular styles. Let us turn first to classical Indian theory.

Indian Music Theory

Because word meanings in Indian music have changed so greatly over the centuries, we can deal here only with the more commonly accepted interpretations of musical terms and must leave their subtler and older meanings to the writings of specialists. The very simple outline of basic Indian theory shown

[13] A translation of the opening lines is, "To the king of kings, son of Visravas, whose victories are easily won, we present our respects. May this king of desires, son of Visravas, grant me what I desire—I who am so filled with desires." The record notes continue the translation and show the original text.

[14] For an outline of many such sources, see Nazir Jairazbhoy, *The Rags of North Indian Music* (Middletown: Wesleyan University Press, 1971), 16–26, or Walter Kaufmann, *The Ragas of North India* (Bloomington: Indiana University Press, 1968), 37–58. On page 139 of Volume 14 of *The New Grove Dictionary of Music and Musicians,* Sanscrit sources and their translations are listed.

in Example 4–3 begins with *nada,* the concept of musical sound vibrations with their implied extramusical implications (as mentioned earlier). In ancient India, the smallest interval perceptible to the ear was called a *sruti.* Theoretically there were three different sizes of *sruti*[15] and a total tonal vocabulary of 22 such nonequidistant units within an octave. Like Near Eastern theorists (see p. 90), Indian music theorists did not consider the movement just from one *sruti* to an adjacent one as an interval. Rather, two to four *sruti* were combined to form a *svara,* an actual musical interval or step. In musical practice today the complete tonal vocabulary seems to include only twelve tones, although each has a fairly wide range of tolerance as to actual pitch.[16]

Both ancient and modern practice generally create seven *svara* to arrive at an octave (a *saptaka*). The seven *svara* have special names,[17] but only the first syllable of each name is generally used when writing about these tones. Thus the sounds *sa, ri, ga, ma, pa, dha, ni*—like the Western *do, re, mi*—have become basic terms for discussing or singing Indian music.

In ancient theory, seven *svara* played in order became a *grama,* a scale. Three such scales (the *sadjagrama, madhymagrama,* and *gandharagrama*) are said to be the basic "parent" scales of Indian music, but by the time of the *Natya-Sastra* only the first two are mentioned. (Hence we have parenthesized the third in Example 4–3.) The two surviving scales are normally called by their

EXAMPLE 4–3. The Indian theoretical system in outline.

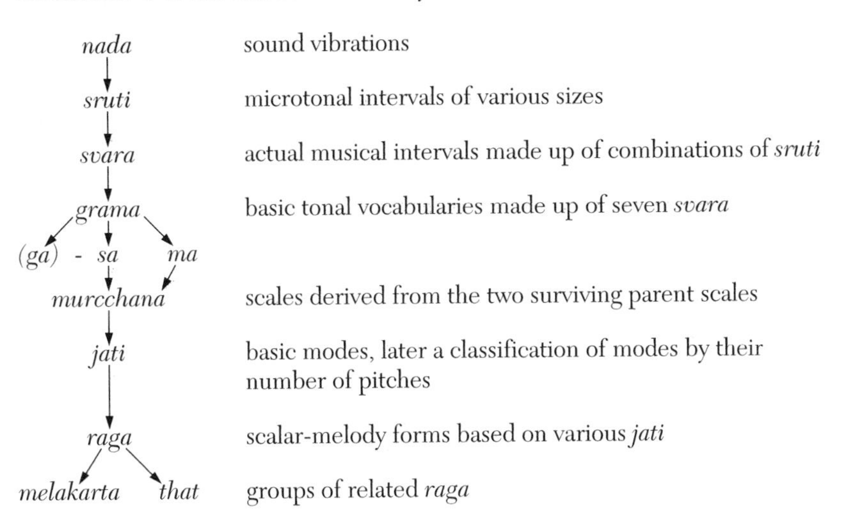

[15] Fox Strangways claims them to be approximately 22, 70, and 90 cents in his *The Music of Hindostan* (London: Oxford University Press, 1914), 115–17.

[16] The variability of actual intonations in the contemporary performance of North Indian *raga* is discussed in Jairazbhoy, *The Rags of North Indian Music,* 164–69. Its relation to ancient *sruti* traditions is questionable. In any discussion of music theory it is important to remember that many excellent performing musicians have no seeming knowledge or interest in the topic.

[17] In North India they are *sadj, risabh, gandha, madyam, pancam, dhaivat,* and *nisad.*

abbreviated names, *sa-grama* and *ma-grama,* and often are listed with their tone names and *sruti* distances as shown in Example 4–4. Very rough analogies with Western notes are shown by letters in the example, for comparison's sake, but the actual pitch of any Indian music, like much Western vocal music, is set by the performer. (Until its association with Western music, Indian music did not concern itself with perfect pitch as opposed to perfect intervals.) The tiny differences in the intervals between the pitches *ma* and *pa,* and between *pa* and *dha,* in the two scales seems very subtle indeed, especially when we remember that modern practice bears little relation to ancient theory. The *grama* are historically important, however, because they were the theoretical parents of five *murcchana* scales, two of which use a raised third (*antara ga;* a pitch equivalent in Example 4–4 would approximate an F sharp) and three of which use both the raised third plus a raised seventh (*kakali ni;* a Western analogy would be C sharp in Example 4–4). By the time of the *Natya-Sastra* the term *jati* appears as well, to imply modes within the two parent scales, the original seven *murcchana* being called "pure" *suddha jati,* and an additional eleven being "modified" *vikrta jati,* some with five or six tones rather than seven (pentatonic *audava,* or hexatonic *shadava,* rather than heptatonic *sampurna*).

EXAMPLE 4–4. The theoretical *sa-* and *ma-grama.*

Sa-grama

pitch name	sa		ri		ga		ma		pa		dha		ni		sa
number of *sruti*		3		2		4		4		3		2		4	
Western analogy	D		E		F		G		A+		B		C		D

Ma-grama

pitch name	sa		ri		ga		ma		pa		dha		ni		sa
number of *sruti*		3		2		4		3		4		2		4	
Western analogy	D		E		F		G		A		B+		C		D

All the terms used so far appear in the *Natya-Sastra,* but the meaning and actual use of such words has changed greatly since then. For example, the word *sruti* today is usually used in the South to mean a basic ground tone of a drone (called *sur* in the North), although Hindustani musicians sometimes call a microtonal ornamentation in performance a *sruti.* Similarly, the term *svara* (often *svar* in the North) may mean either a tone or an interval, just as a Western musician uses, for example, the word "third" to mean both the third note of a scale and an interval of three tones. One early use of the term *jati* was as a means of classifying modes according to the number of notes they contain; to this has been added special melodic characteristics of compositions in a *jati,* as well as extramusical connotations and mood (*rasa*). It is thus through *jati* that we arrive at the better known concept called *raga.*

The term *raga* (the term is *rag* in the North or *ragam* in the Tamil language) can be defined as a scalar-melody form; that is, it is both the basic scale and the basic melodic structure. The term is derived from a Sanskrit root, *ranj,* which means to color with emotion; thus the name implies many features beyond those of actual pitches. Although such extramusical aspects are important to many practitioners of *raga* music,[18] we discuss only a few of the most essential elements found in any *rag* or *raga* from either North or South India.[19]

The actual scale of a *raga* should be shown in both its ascending and descending forms, for they may differ. In addition, the notes may not always proceed in only one direction: Many *raga* change direction, repeating or adding new tones in a quasi-melodic fashion. Also, specific notes within a *raga* sometimes have special ornamentations (commonly called *gamaka*). The so-called ground tone on which the scale of the *raga* begins is called the *sa.* It is the most common note among those comprising the drone that accompanies all contemporary performances of classical music. (It is not known when this practice began.) In Hindustani theory there are two "important" tones (*amsa*) that dominate each *raga:* the *vadi* and the *samvadi.* The *vadi* today is often considered to be the most important pitch melodically in a *raga;* the *samvadi* may be second in importance. The *vadi* is often *not* the ground tone of the *raga.* The *samvadi* is usually a fourth or fifth above the *vadi,* although, like the reciting tones of other musical traditions (such as Christian chant), there are various distributions of fundamental tones. Similar reciting tones (*jiva svara*) appear in Karnatak music, but they are given less theoretical significance. Theoretically, thousands of *raga* may exist. In Indian books there are occasional lists of up to 1,000 *raga* actually named or described. In either Hindustani or Karnatic practice today, however, some 50 *raga* tend to appear most frequently, although individual performers may know a great many more.

Given the large number of possibilities, it is only logical that Indian theorists should organize *raga* into related groups. Perhaps the most controversial arrangements are those attempting to determine the times of the day at which specific *raga* are most suitable.[20] Although not popular today, there was at one time another tradition that arranged tonal materials in terms of *raga* and their *ragini* (wives), each often associated with scenes from romantic or mythological literature or the emotional setting of such scenes. The best known result of this method was not music, but rather the *ragamala* miniatures that have been found in some schools of Rajput-style North Indian painting since the sixteenth century. Traditionally, thirty-six scenes are depicted, each titled only by the name of its proper *raga* or *ragini*. Of more significance musically are the divisions of *raga* into *that* or *mela* (*melakarta*). In the South Indian *Caturdandi-Prakasika* of 1620, Venkatamakhi suggested the grouping of Indian tone

[18] In his *Northern Indian Music* (London: C. Johnson, 1949–54) Alain Danielou lists fifteen essential items.

[19] In Indian musical terms such as *rag* and *raga,* the presence of a final "a" means a Sanskrit spelling is being followed, rather than the Hindi version. This is generally true of South Indian music terms (*svara* rather than *svar, druta* rather than *drut,* etc.) and is used in this survey. North Indian terms often use English plurals (*jati—jatis, bol—bols*) but these are not used here.

[20] See O. C. Gangoly, *Ragas and Raginis* (Bombay, 1958), 90–92, or Kaufmann, *The Ragas of North India,* 14–20.

systems into 72 *melakarta.* These were scales based on connecting six possible tetrachords (four-note groups) within a fourth (for example, C D E F) with another set of six within the next higher fourth (like G A B C). This created thirty-six possible scales (6 x 6 = 36), but the total was doubled by adding another six lower tetrachords, these within an augmented fourth (like C D E F sharp).[21] Although this larger vocabulary was not actually in use at the time, it did serve as an inspiration for the "invention" of new *raga* in following decades. In the 1930s Bhaktkhande organized a framework (*that*) of 32 seven-tone scales to which the many *rag* of the North Indian tradition could be related.[22] Ten of these *that* were considered basic.

We turn now to the Indian theory of musical time. The core of this system is the concept of a cyclic measure of time called *tala.* It can be called a cycle because its basic characteristics continue to appear (like markings around the face of a clock) in repeated sequences as long as there is a steady beat. The actual tempo (*laya*) of Indian music may vary from fast (*druta*) to medium (*madhya*) or slow (*vilambita*). Major factors that contribute to the use and understanding of *tala* remain constant, however. First, there is the Hindustani *matra* and Karnatak *akshara,* or basic beat. Like the Western quarter-note pulse, this beat is capable of small divisions in the context of melodies or details of rhythmic patterns. In the *tala* the *matra* and *akshara* are like the *tact* of a Western meter (p. 10) or the clicks of a metronome. They come to life when they are placed in a *tala* cycle (*vibhaga* or *avarta*), which may total from 3 to 128 beats in length, although 7- to 16-beat cycles are more common. Each *tala* is subdivided into groups of beats. Although these subdivisions are important to both classical traditions, the Karnatak musicians are more prone towards theoretical details and terminology. In the South Indian *tala* the rhythmic groups are known as *anga* and can be categorized as belonging to one of three types: *anudruta,* which consists always of only one beat; *druta,* made up of two beats; and *laghu,* which may have one of five different lengths (of 3, 4, 5, 7, or 9 beats) known as *jati.* Example 4–5 shows *tala* from both of the classical traditions; the two *tala* share the same length (ten beats) but illustrate some of the differences between the northern and southern systems. The Hindustani *jhaptal* is divided in four parts (2 + 3 + 2 + 3), whereas the Karnatak *jhampa* has three *anga* in the categories *laghu, anudruta,* and *druta* (7 + 1 + 2). Both traditions consider the first beat of the entire *tala* (the *sam*) very important, although their approaches to the internal structure of the *tala* may be different. North Indian musicians use the term *tali* to refer to other secondary accents on the first beats of

[21] The clearest explanation of this method, with charts of the *melakarta,* is in Harold Powers, *The Background of the South Indian Raga System* (Ann Arbor: University Microfilms, 1963), I, 17–23.

[22] For a detailed study of the *that* system, see Jairazbhoy, *The Rags of North Indian Music,* or the writings of Bhatkhande listed in Jairazbhoy's bibliography. The *raga* classification system's development is somewhat analogous to that of Gregorian chant, which moved from a multitude of materials to a system of eight medieval modes.

EXAMPLE 4–5. Two Indian *tala* cycles.

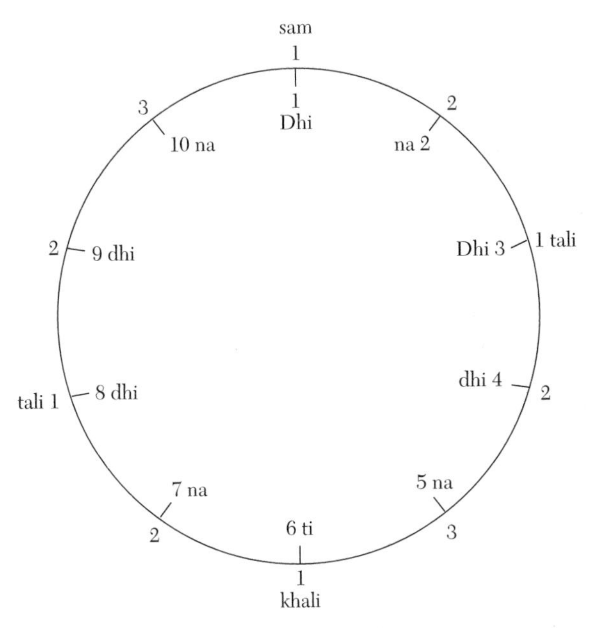

A. The Hindustani *jhaptal tala.*

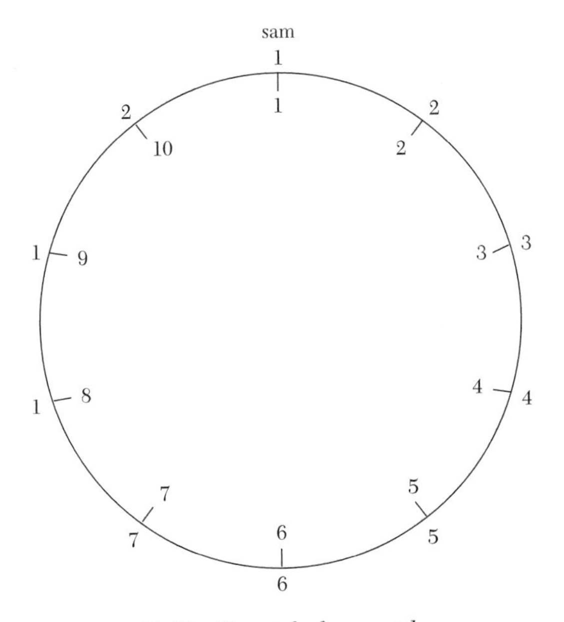

B. The Karnatak *jhampa tala.*

subdivisions. When such first beats are "felt" strongly but seldom actually stressed they are called a *khali* beat. This is seen on the sixth beat of *jhaptal* in Example 4–5, which also contains the other terms just described. Sometimes you can actually see units of the subdivisions enacted visually during a performance, for some musicians as well as listeners keep track of a *tala* by clapping their hands on the *sam* and *talam* beats while waving the right hand sideways on the "silent" *khali.*

The *jhaptal tala* in Example 4–5 includes inside the circle the onomatopoeic mnemonics (*bol*) by which a player learns a specific drum pattern (*theka*) characteristic of the *tala.* This tradition is particularly strong in Hindustani music, and a drummer will remain rather close to the *theka* pattern throughout a composition in order that the melodic performers can move with confidence into extended rhythmic flights. Because both the melodic and rhythmic performers in Karnatak music pay closer attention to the *tala* and its *anga* as such, basic rhythm patterns need not be followed as closely.

Students of European medieval music will recognize the *tala* as a more complex version of the concept of *talea.*[23] However, the combination of rhythmic units of different sizes, common to Indian music, illustrates the *additive* approach to rhythm in contrast to the *divisive* method normally found in the even subdivisions of a measure in Western music.[24] It would seem that the Western fascination with harmonic structures and the South Asian enchantment with melodic and rhythmic systems propelled these two grand traditions in very different directions. Western musicians need to sing solfège and recognize chord progressions by ear in order to feel and understand their past tradition; Indian musicians need to practice their *sa, ri, ga, ma* and be able to beat and wave the divisions of basic *tala* in order to be a true part of their musical world. Whereas the Western professional becomes aware of subtle variations in harmonic structures, the Indian becomes equally sensitive to the rhythms that tend to have become characteristic of each *tala.* Some of this sensitivity will be revealed when we discuss actual performance practice.

Indian Music Practice

Indian musicians must thoroughly absorb some threescore or more *raga* and many *tala* before they can obtain any professional status. This is done first by singing each *raga* and *tala* in an extended series of pedagogical exercises similar to those familiar to Western music students. The Indian's rhythmic training is rather different, however, for in addition to beating and waving the stresses of the *tala,* he or she must also, as we noted earlier, chant the mnemonics (*bol;* in Karnatak, *sollukattu*) that are syllabic vocalizations of the strokes to be played on the drum. The object of Western exercises is primarily instrumen-

[23] See Jeremy Yudkin, *Music in Medieval Europe* (Englewood Cliffs, N.J.: Prentice Hall, 1989).

[24] See Curt Sachs, *Rhythm and Tempo* (New York: Norton, 1953), 24–25.

tal technique plus familiarity with traditional tonal systems; these goals are also sought in Indian pedagogy, but there is also a larger goal, which is so deeply to indoctrinate the student in the possibilities of each *raga* or *tala* that he or she can get to the heart of much Indian music—improvisation.

The art of Indian music has been called guided improvisation, meaning that at all times the musician must be guided simultaneously by the *raga* and the *tala.* In truth, all improvisation that is not merely personal musical rumination must be guided by some rules. Great freedom of improvisation is possible only when there are many rules for guidance. Jazz, for example, with its comparatively simple rules of order, eventually was felt to be too restricted in its improvisational scope, leading progressive jazz musicians to seek new rules, including some Indian concepts, in order to expand their improvisational range. Indian musicians, by contrast, have before them a dazzling array of rhythmic and melodic possibilities, thanks to the thoroughness of the rules that serve as guides to improvisation.

Indian performers are also creators. Like their Western counterparts, they must practice diligently the pedagogical materials of music. Such practice makes it possible for the Western musician to play a given piece time after time without the slightest noticeable variation. There are some compositions in Indian music which require that same precise, nonimprovisatory performance; however, the general aim of Indian practice is for performers to reach the stage where they can play each *raga* in a new way every time without losing its characteristics, which are their guides.

This important distinction in purpose results in a different kind of artist to audience relation. The knowledgeable Western audience listens for a faithful reproduction of the composer's intention and reacts to a combination of the composer's skill, the performer's artistry, and the personal "meaningfulness" of the composition. The Indian audience reacts not to the challenge of reproduction but to the performer's ability to create his or her own music within given bounds. In both cases, the listener must have some foreknowledge in order to appreciate the art of the performance. In the West, this consists of knowledge of the piece, the idiom, or the form. The same kinds of knowledge are useful to the Indian but, in the case of form, the intent is different. Western classical forms of the eighteenth and nineteenth centuries were constructed to introduce the listener to the basic tonalities and themes so their development and return could be followed. Indian classical forms are designed to acquaint the listener with the *raga* (and, sometimes, a basic theme) while still leaving room for the performer to reveal the beauty of the *raga* in terms of his or her own imagination. Because form follows function, we can expect Indian forms to differ from those of the West.

Most Indian forms begin with a rhapsodic, free-rhythmic introduction called the *alapana* or *alap.* Its function is to reveal gradually the notes of the *raga* plus its special melodic characteristics. Even before these notes appear, however, one hears a drone on the "ground tone" (*sa*) of the *raga* plus its fifth.

In *raga* not having a perfect fifth in their scale, the drone uses the fourth or an ostinato figure like *ni, ṡa, ṡa, sa* (in a heptatonic scale, 7, 8, 8, 1). An ostinato-like drone is also found in many performances of other *raga,* particularly if played on a *tambura* drone chordophone. Such patterns differ from the traditional Western ostinato in their general lack of a distinctive rhythmic pattern related to the rhythm or tempo of the composition. Whatever the style of the drone, it is essential in most Indian music today, for it serves as a constant reminder of the music's starting point throughout the performer's peregrinations in the introduction and all the sections that follow.

Since there are at least as many different forms in Indian music as there are in the Western tradition, it is impossible to generalize about what will happen after the close of an *alap.* The most common indicator the *alap* is over and the piece proper has begun, however, is the entrance of the *tala,* usually in the form of a drum part. An informed listener can, in addition, distinguish which type of piece is being played and its Karnatak or Hindustani origin or performance style.

The Karnatak tradition concentrates on forms based on songs, so we might say it has no uniquely instrumental compositions. Quite often the performance involves the actual singing of the song along with "dialogues" between the singer and an instrumentalist, both using the melody of the song. Virtually all of the texts are religious. The best known form is the *kriti* (or *kirtana*), a devotional song which, after the *alap,* consists of three sections: the *pallavi, anupallavi,* and *caranam* (*charanam*). Each section contains or is derived from a setting of religious poetry along with improvisations on the setting's melody, such as the one in the excerpt given in Example 4–6. Although certain artists are able to introduce new ornamental pitches during performances, the basic *raga* is not changed throughout a traditional piece.[25] Different notes or ranges, however, are often emphasized in different sections of a piece so that one feels a sense of tonal progression within the overall one-*raga* composition.

The *dhrupad* of North India is comparable to the strict religious songs of the South; the freer *khyal* is the North's more popular vocal-instrumental form. The *khyal* text itself is shorter than that of the *dhrupad,* and some of it may be left out or sung with ornamentations which make the words incomprehensible in parts of the two sections of the form, the *sthayi* and the *antara.* The Muslim poetic tradition is heard in Persian or Urdu *ghazal* songs. The *thumri* vocal form is more popular perhaps because the words of its romantic texts are clearer and in Hindi.[26] Sufi mysticism is endemic in most North Indian vocal genres. Perhaps the ultimate in purely vocal music forms are the *tarana* of the North and *tillana* of the South, in which there is no text at all but rather sets of meaningless syllables. There also are sections of other pieces in which the Indian *sol-fa* syllables (*sa, ri, ga,* etc.) or drum mnemonics are sung for a

[25] In North India today, one may sometimes hear a so-called *ragamala,* in which a piece does modulate from one *raga* to another and back.

[26] See Peter Manuel, "The Evolution of Modern Thumri," *Ethnomusicology,* 30/3 (1986).

EXAMPLE 4–6. Karnatak flute variations from *Anthologie de la musique classique de l'Inde* (Paris: Ducretet-Thomson Album 320 C 096-8, side 6, band 4; book cassette, track 17). The flutist is Tanjore Viswanathan. Transcription and sound used by permission of EMI.

A. Rama pria - raga

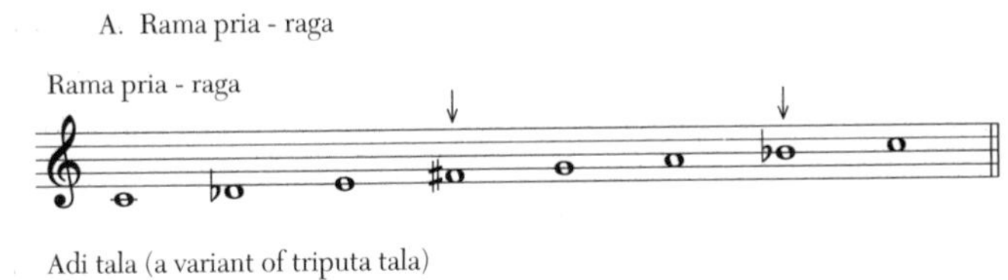

Adi tala (a variant of triputa tala)
1 2 3 4 : 5 6: 7 8

B. "Sandehamunu" by Tyagaraja

considerable time; this is particularly common in dance accompaniments. There are, in addition, lighter vocal genres such as the South Indian *javali,* as well as purely instrumental light forms, the most popular of which is the North Indian *gat.*

The mention here of a few Indian music forms is as lifeless as the word *sonata* unless we imagine each in terms of a live musical event. Let us remember that during the formal progress of a piece the performer may not only be playing on the notes, ornaments, and melodic characteristics of a *raga* and maintaining the rhythmic framework of a given *tala,* but may also be using a well-known melody composed by someone else. This is suggested by Example 4–6, which contains the preliminary lines of the *pallavi* section (after the *alap,* which is not shown but can be heard on the recording) of a performance by a Karnatak flutist based on the song "Sandehamunu" by the composer Tyagaraja (1767–1847). The *raga* and *tala* of the composition are shown in Example 4–6A; the B section of the example starts with one version of the first line of the melody.[27] We can see that the flutist first repeats a florid version of the basic melody. This is followed by the repeat of a so-called *sangati* (fixed variation), which is normally used at the beginning of every performance of this piece before launching into different material or the much more improvisatory variations that will emerge as the performance progresses. The opening beats of the *mrdanga* drum part have been included to illustrate how that instrument enters. Like the opening bars of a symphony, this transcription barely touches the heart of the music but it does suggest some of the artistry of the Indian art-music tradition.

When more than one player is involved in Indian art music, the performance becomes something of a contest. If drums are included, the drummer may try to trip up the other musicians with complicated permutations of the *tala* rhythm. The other players, of course, can play with the *tala* as well. Notice in Example 4–6 how even the composer has set the basic accents and phrasing of his melody in a very subtle relation to the *tala.*

A common North Indian rhythmic device is a *tihai,* in which a pattern, often beginning on the upbeat of an unaccented beat, will be so constructed that three repetitions of it will always end on the first beat (*sam*) of the *tala.* Such a pattern can be extended to such a length that it will be "out of phase" for three complete cycles of a *tala* only to land miraculously on the first beat of the fourth cycle. On such occasions one can hear sighs or see head shakes of satisfaction among the audience. They have experienced in music the kind of thrill one gets from watching a tightrope walker execute a difficult balancing act and end with a graceful leap upright on the wire. For the traditional Indian, however, the experience has been more than a ravishing of the senses. The ethical aspects of Indian music have already been implied. We should note further that

[27] The original tune was transmitted to the author orally by the performer and is therefore open to various interpretations. The text says, "Please clear my doubts." It is a plea to Rama.

most famous composers, such as Tyagaraja (composer of the original on which Example 4–6 is based), are considered saints. This attitude is reflected as well in the concept of the teacher as a guru. Ideally, the teacher's intent is to guide the disciple spiritually through music. As a result, professional musicians may continue to burn incense before the picture of their guru in remembrance of their perpetual debt to their teacher musically and spiritually. Another powerful factor for some Indian musicians is belonging to a professional family (*gharana*) or guild under one teacher.[28]

Basic Indian Instruments

An ancient Indian instrument classification system based on the primary vibrating material helped inspire the contemporary method of the West (see p. 28). Thus chordophones were *tata* ("stretched"); aerophones, *susira* ("tubular"); membranophones, *avanaddha* ("covered"); and idiophones, *ghana* ("solid"). Given the size and cultural diversity of Southern Asia, there is a great variety of regional and nationally known instruments that fit in one or more of these classes. From all that has been said about Indian music theory and practice, we can expect three basic requirements in the construction of instruments suitable for such music. First, there must be a flexibility in pitch production and tuning in order to accommodate the many *raga* and the sliding techniques typical of their melodic ornamentations. This need is reflected in the absence in India of the fixed-pitched metallophones and xylophones found throughout Southeast Asia and Indonesia (although the Western harmonium has become a common part of some North Indian ensembles). A second consideration is the necessity of a constant drone. Because of this, drone strings are common to most Indian chordophones and some instruments are capable of playing only drone pitches. Finally, the importance of rhythm in Indian music necessitates drums as well as rhythmic devices attached to basically melodic instruments. With these three principles in mind we now discuss briefly the major components of India's instrumental treasure house.

Two-headed barrel drums such as those of Plate XV come in many styles from Central Asia to Sri Lanka and many names such as *dhol* (*dholak, khol, tavul, tavil*).[29] As seen in Plate XV, Figure 37, some are played standing, suspended by a strap before the waist as accompaniment for dance or as part of a dancer's accessories.[30] Others are held on or before the lap while sitting cross legged as seen in Plate XV, Figures 38 and 39. Some are played with sticks but most use hands. Figure 38 shows that pieces of doweling are sometimes used to

[28] A sociological and musical geneology is followed in Daniel M. Neuman, *The Life of Music in North India* (Detroit: Wayne State University Press, 1980).

[29] A convenient list of regional names and variants of all classes of instruments is in K.S. Kothari, *Indian Folk Musical Instruments* (New Delhi: Sangeet Natak Akademi, 1968) available at American depository libraries of Public Law 480.

[30] Note the metal bells (*ghanghura*) attached to the dancing drummer's ankles. They are a common idiophonic dance accessory in India.

PLATE XV. Indian membranophones

FIGURE 37. *Dhol.*

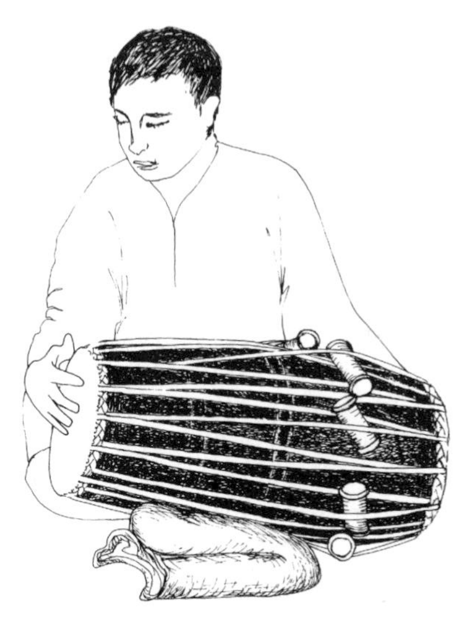

FIGURE 38. *Pakhavj.*

FIGURE 39. *Tabla.* **FIGURE 40.** *Baya.*

tighten the heads and adjust the tuning. This *pakhavaj* (sometimes called the *mrdang*) is used in North India, primarily to accompany sacred *druphad* songs. The *mrdanga* (*mridanga*) of South Indian Kanatak music is similar in shape and playing position but uses paste patches instead of doweling to change pitch and tone quality.[31] The patches may be changed regularly because the drums of Indian music provide both rhythmic and tonal references to the melodic instruments.

Figures 39 and 40 are collectively known as the *tabla* and are well known in the West for their use in Hindustani classical music. Permanent tuning patches are used on both drums. Further tuning is done with the doweling on the *tabla* or, like many Indian drums, the use of a special hammer along its rim or that of the metal bowl-shaped *baya.* Both drums come in several sizes. Traditionally the *tabla* and *baya* are played as a pair by one musician although there also exists a half circle of tuned drums (*tabla tarang*) that can be used melodically like a similar set of bowls called *jalatarang,* which one tunes by filling them with different amounts of water and plays by striking their edges with two thin wooden sticks.[32] One intriguing Karnatak idiophone is the *ghatam,* a spherical clay pot some 50 cm in diameter. It is struck with a variety of hand and finger styles in different parts of the pot, and the mouth of the pot is sometimes placed against the performer's bare stomach to further change its tone and pitch. Some virtuosi even throw the pot in the air and catch it (or let it smash) in time with the beat!

The melodic instrument in Example 4–6 is the unadorned side-blown cane flute (*venu* or *bansri*). In the Indian double-reed family there are many variants of the *shahnai* derived from Near Eastern instruments mentioned in Chapter 3 (see Plate X, Figure 25).[33] South India's most distinctive oboe is the *nagasvaram* (*nagasuram, nayanam*). Its thick, large double-reed is attached to a body some 87 cm long in which there may be more than seven finger holes, the "extra" holes being plugged with wax to regulate the basic pitch of the instrument. It is often accompanied by another conical double-reed instrument, which has few holes because it plays only a drone. The ubiquitous missionary harmonium, with its rigid vocabulary of the Western twelve-tone scale and its harmonic orientation, is inappropriate for South Asian music, but it enjoys popularity among many vocal traditions in North India and Pakistan.

The most famous instrumental creations of South Asia are chordophones. Since instrument making in India is still basically a hand craft, there are many local variations on any given instrument, but the instruments found in

[31] Drums like that in Figure 37 often have tuning patches on the head nearest the doweling and may be played with that head to the right instead of the left as shown.

[32] These instruments may have a Southeast Asian inspiration. See Plate XX, Figure 50, and note the Burmese drum circles mentioned on page 151.

[33] See Nazir Jairazbhoy, "A Preliminary Survey of the Oboe in India." *Ethnomusicology,* 14/3 (1970).

the three plates here show some basic types. On Indian chordophones, three kinds of strings may be found: melodic strings, drone strings, and sympathetic vibrators. This can be seen in the evolution of the *vina*.

It is not clear whether the term *vina* originally referred to an arched harp or a zither such as those seen in Plate XIX.[34] Figure 41 of Plate XVI shows the surviving North Indian *bin*, a tube zither with two large calabash resonators, high frets, four melody strings, and three drone strings, two on one side and one on the other. The high frets make it possible to play the important ornamentations of individual notes by pressing down or pulling the strings to the side. Figure 42 is a *bin sitar*, a little known variant found in Poona; we include it because it helps to illustrate the evolutionary potentials of instrumental design, although it is not necessarily a historical link between the *bin* and later instruments. The two gourd resonators are present, but they are attached to a trough zither body rather than a tube. The number of strings used varies, but the example shown has all three types: five melodic, two drone (on the side), and eight sympathetic vibrators. The frets are quite different from those of the *bin*, for they are metal rods held to the sides of the trough by gut. Such an arrangement makes it easier to adjust the pitches to those of a specific *raga*. This method is probably an adaptation of the movable fret systems we noted earlier on many plucked lutes of the Near East.

The South Indian *vina* in Figure 43 maintains the tradition of melody strings (four) and drone strings (three), Karnatak classicists finding the tone of extra sympathetic vibrating strings distasteful. Note that the drone strings of the *vina* can be used to keep track of the *tala* by stroking them in a proper rhythmic pattern. The *vina* frets are metal rods, although they are set in walls of blackened beeswax rather than tied with gut as are those of the *bin sitar* (Figure 42). The important difference between the Karnatak *vina* and the *bin* and *bin sitar* is that on the *vina* one of the calabash resonators has coalesced with the fingerboard, turning a zither-type instrument into a lute. Also, the upper gourd has become basically decorative rather than sonically functional, although it is used to help balance the instrument when playing. The carved head at the top of the instrument is somewhat functional, as it encloses a storage compartment where a can of coconut oil is kept; this is used to lubricate the performer's fingertips to facilitate their gliding over the metal strings and frets. On this instrument the melodic ornamentations are most often made by pulling the string to one side.

The Hindustani *sitar* (Figure 44) is the Indian chordophone best known in the West. It is a lute developed by Muslim musicians through a combination of Indian principles and those of the Near Eastern *tanbur* family (see Plate XI, Figure 28). The *sitar* often has an upper gourd that, like that of the *vina*, is acoustically nonfunctional. In addition to four, or sometimes only two, melodic

[34] See Louise Wrazen, "The Early History of the *vina* and *bin* in South and Southeast Asia," *Asian Music*, 18/1 (1986).

PLATE XVI. Indian plucked chordophones

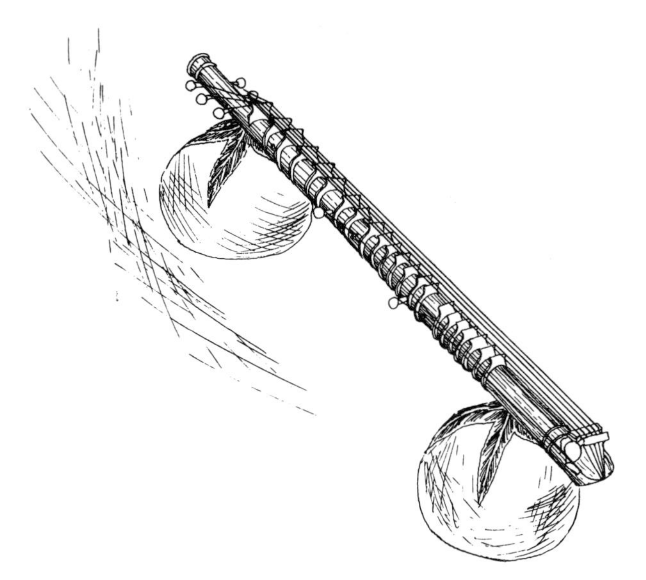

FIGURE 41. *Bin.* (100–122 cm long)

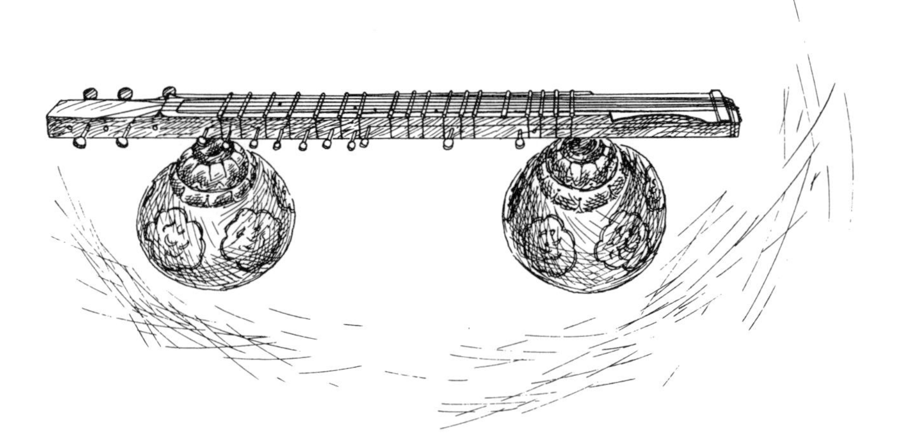

FIGURE 42. *Bin sitar.* (125 cm long)

PLATE XVII. Modern Indian plucked chordophones

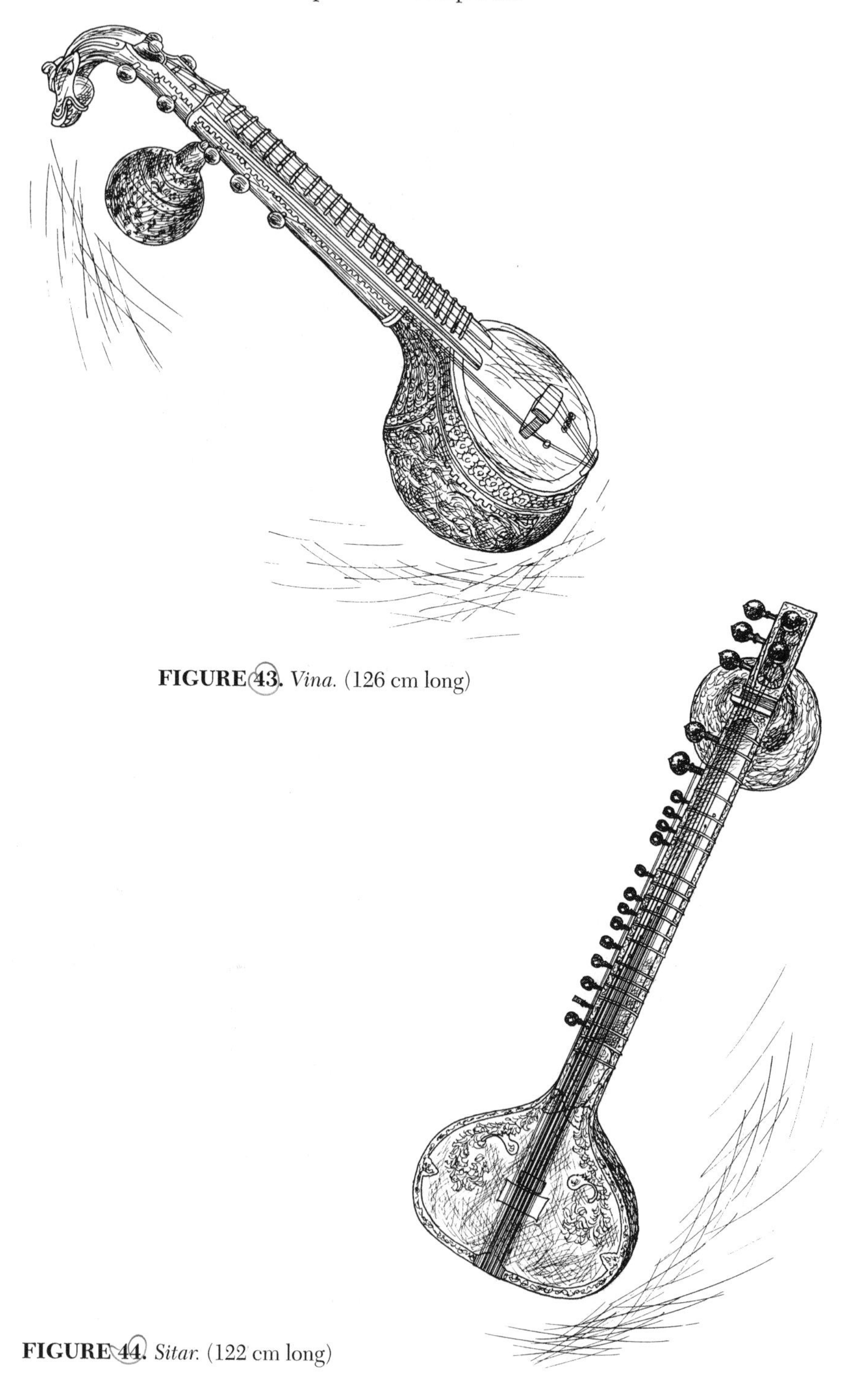

FIGURE 43. *Vina.* (126 cm long)

FIGURE 44. *Sitar.* (122 cm long)

strings and three drones, the *sitar* may have as many as 13 strings whose function is to vibrate sympathetically with notes played on the melody strings. These sympathetic strings give the *sitar* that special hollow sound familiar to devotees of Hindustani music. Room is made beneath the frets for all these strings by having a concave trough along the fingerboard and convex frets tied with gut onto the walls of the trough. These convex frets also make it easier to pull the strings sideways when playing ornaments.

Another well-known but shorter Hindustani lute is the *sarod* (Plate XVIII, Figure 45). Normally, its six melodic and two drone strings are plucked. Several sympathetic strings pass inside the deep body of the *sarod,* which has a parchment soundboard and a metal fingerboard. Perhaps a better known plucked long-necked Indian lute is one that plays no melody at all; this is the *tambura,* whose four (occasionally five or six) metal strings are always played unstopped, in order to produce the vital drone accompaniment for vocal and instrumental performances. The *tambura* is often complemented or replaced by a small one-note hand-pumped reed organ (*sur-petti* or "*sruti* box").

More exotic drones are used by the Bauls religious singers of Bengal. The one string of the *gopiyantro* (*ektara*) is attached to a membrane at the bottom of a gourd or wooden resonator, passing through it to bamboo slats where a peg holds it tight to the drone pitch. The *khamak* likewise attaches one or two strings to a membrane at the bottom of a body that looks like a barrel drum with no upper head. The strings are attached externally to a small pot-shaped drum that is tightened by the left hand which holds it, and is plucked with a small plectrum. Because the hand controls the tension, more than a drone pitch is possible.[35]

The scattered presence of various Near Eastern bowed lutes in South Asia is a reflection of India's extended historical contact with the Near Eastern tradition. Karnatak music reflects the Western experience as well, with its frequent use of the violin, which, however, is braced between the chest and foot rather than held under the chin, and is tuned to the drone tones of tonic and fifth. Its fretless fingerboard is suitable for performing Indian pitches and ornaments properly. Another common bowed lute in India is the *dilruba,* which is a kind of "bowed sitar." Figure 47 shows a *sarangi,* an Indian bowed lute that combines melodic and sympathetic strings, whereas the *sarinda* in Figure 46 has only three melodic strings. Large indentations on the sides of both of these instruments accommodate the movements of the bow as it changes from string to string. Note that only the lower half of the face of the *sarinda* is covered by a membrane; the *sarangi* produces a richer tone, with its face fully covered by a membrane. It is used in the accompaniment of vocal or dance concerts. The *sarinda* is most often found in the hands of street musicians.

[35] See Charles Capwell, *The Music of the Bauls of Bengal* (Kent, Ohio: Kent State University Press, 1986), 89–97. For all their membranes, they are chordophones. The *khamak* is seen in *JTV Video* no. 13. Photos and drawings of both instruments are found in *Musical Voices of Asia* (Tokyo: The Japan Foundation, 1980), 214–19, 223–25.

PLATE XVIII. Indian plucked and bowed chordophones

FIGURE 45. *Sarod.*

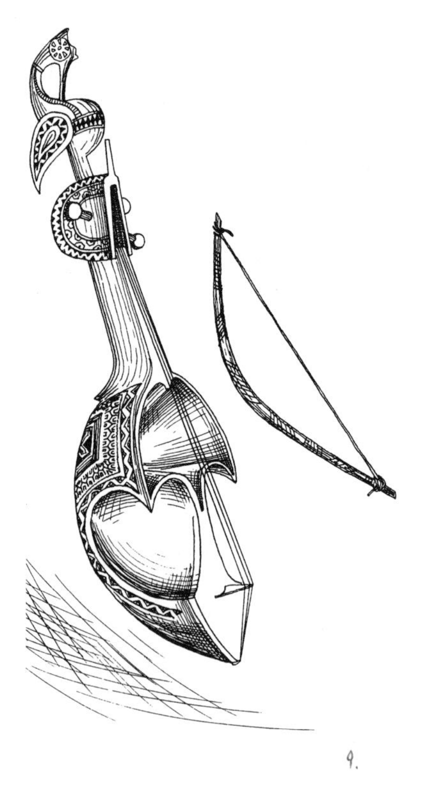

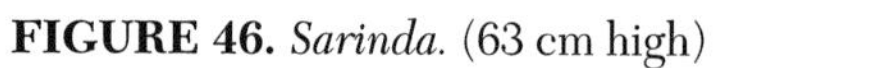

FIGURE 46. *Sarinda.* (63 cm high)

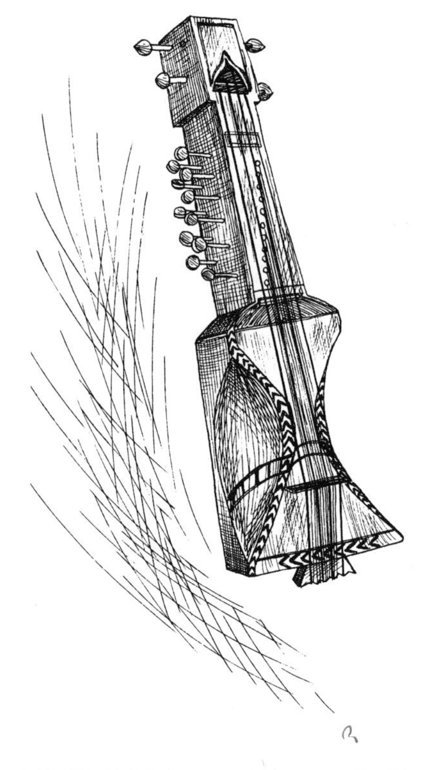

FIGURE 47. *Sarangi.* (60–69 cm high)

The main Indian box zither is the *svaramandala*, which is historically related and physically similar to the *kanun* (Plate XIII, Figure 34). It also shares with some *kanun* the lack of any damping device, and thus it is commonly used to create a wash of sound as a supplement to the drone texture behind the melodic instruments that deal with the tones and embellishments so important in the Indian *raga* system.

Some Indian Folk, Popular, and Theatrical Music Traditions

Perhaps the Indian folk instrument best known in the West is the *pungi*, a double clarinet with free reeds encased in a gourd. Despite all the Western cartoon pictures of oboe-playing fakirs, it is the *pungi* that is the snake charmer's instrument. But the true world of Indian folk music, and much of its art music as well, is found in singing. The fascination of Indian art music has overshadowed folk music as an area of serious study. Even a superficial look at Indian folk music, however, reveals a richness worthy of the lifetime of any field collector. In the central part of India (Nagpur), in the northeastern Naga hills, and on many offshore islands there are collections of tribal peoples whose musics are more reminiscent of Arnhem Land, Borneo, and the jungles of Southeast Asia than they are of Hindu and Muslim South Asia. Antiphonal and responsorial songs, harmonies in fourths and fifths, and even occasional singing in seconds can be found in such regions. At the same time, the lovely boatmen's songs of Bangladesh and the melodies of Kashmir display casually ornamented lines based on *raga* prototypes and sung with soft-toned vocal qualities like those of Indian art music. A treasure of folk songs can be found in each of the hundreds of dialects spoken throughout India. However, the systematic collection of this music has only recently begun; eventually more of it should become available in the West. At present, searches for examples of Indian songs most frequently end up with a collection of popular tunes derived from the enormous number of Indian films produced by the huge native film industry. Such music is a natural part of urbanization and is equally worthy of study, since it is, after all, the primary idiom heard by most Indians. It is not "serious" music, but it often is very creatively Indian. The simpler characteristics of popular music we discussed earlier (see page 96) naturally apply to film-derived music as well, but let us never underestimate the sociological value of this medium and its messages.

Theatrical music of many kinds exists in South Asia: accompaniments on double reeds, drums, and cymbals for religious exercises at the many kinds of temples and shrines; the music for a classical dance or dance-drama form; curved trumpets and massed drum ensembles accompanying a parade of elephants; and accompaniments for a nightclub routine in Bombay. We discuss only the first two types.

Indian theater and dance have traditionally been connected with religious activities. This is easily seen in the Kathakali dance-drama of Malabar, which originally presented its tales from the *Ramayana* and *Mahabharata* in the open-air courts of temples. The accompaniment of these pantomimes and dances consists of drums, cymbals, and narrating singers. Drums form the major part of the accompaniment for the Kandyan dances of Sri Lanka, which relates to the special Buddhist festivals of that island.

The orchestras for the accompaniment of the better known classical dances of South India are more elaborate. These dances, based on the precepts of Bharata's *Natya-Sastra* mentioned earlier, also have religious undertones, for they were originally performed by temple girls (*devadasi*), although today their performers are usually middle- and upper-class women. A standard accompaniment for such dancing is a dance master (who also sings), another singer, a *mrdanga* drum, a *vina* and/or a violin, plus a drone instrument and perhaps a flute or clarinet. The dance master (*nattuvanar*) plays the *talam,* a pair of small hand cymbals that are essential in guiding the rhythmic movements of the dancer. Rhythmic mnemonics and Indian solmizations, in addition to poetic texts, are used by the singers.

The major form of North Indian classical dancing, Kathak, is an indigenous dance style based on the *Natya-Sastra* but influenced by the secular court dances of Persia as introduced by the Moghul rulers in India from the fourteenth century. The accompanying orchestra also shows a mixture, with instruments such as the bowed *sarangi* and the plucked *sarod, sitar,* and *tambura* being combined with the *tabla* and *pakhawaj* drums. A singer is always present.

Although the Kathak and Bharata Natyam dancing are the heart of the Indian classical dance tradition, there are many regional and folk traditions that maintain independent styles.[36] Their accompaniments vary from bagpipes in Northern Pakistan to small bowed lutes with coconut-shell bodies in Manipur. The most common instrument to accompany such dances is a double-headed drum of the *dhol* type (see Plate XV, Figure 37), although many other types can be found. One particularly interesting form is a small hourglass-shaped drum called the *damaru,* which is played by twisting it so that the knotted ends of a cord tied around its waist will strike the skins alternately. This drum is closely connected with the cult of Siva in India; variants of it are found throughout Tibet and East Asia in connection with Buddhist activities.

Nationalist sentiment in South Asia has led to state subsidies for many of the dance and theater forms mentioned here. The real strength of these forms, however, lies in the fact that, despite great efforts at modernization and Westernization, there is still an audience in the Asian subcontinent that follows them, as traditional arts, with interest and pride.

A Theoretical Postscript

As we study the various musics of the world we normally find the traditional idioms on the defensive against Western intrusions. India seems to be an

[36] For details see Balwant Gargi, *Folk Theater of India* (Seattle: University of Washington Press, 1966).

exception. Western art music is hardly taught, and the music of the schools is still almost exclusively Indian. Why? A possible answer may be in the early existence of a thoroughgoing theoretical system with which native musicians could explain themselves when confronted by the analytical Western mind. For most non-Western musicians, the only answer to the question "Why do you play your music in this manner?" is a shrug and a statement like "I play it this way because that's the way it's supposed to go." The same kind of answer can come from many professional Indian or Western musicians. Among them, however, there also exist persons who can analyze their music and show, note by note, where it comes from and "why." Perhaps what is needed in other music traditions of the world are in-depth studies that will make equally explicit the rules of order underlying each system—rules the traditional performers may know only subliminally. Such constructions could be dangerous misinterpretations of the traditional world; however, if correct, they could give traditional artists a vocabulary to explain their music to the outside world. In India, at least, there seems to be evidence that a well-organized music theory and a flourishing performance tradition can absorb the shock of foreign confrontations and react to or imitate them without destroying the special beauty of the indigenous heritage.

BIBLIOGRAPHICAL AND AUDIOVISUAL NOTES

Written Sources

Central Asia

Major studies of Central Asian music are in Russian and are listed in the bibliographies of *The New Grove Dictionary of Music and Musicians,* Volume 19 (articles on the Union of Soviet Socialist Republics). Volume 22 (1990) of the *Yearbook for Traditional Music* contains five articles on Soviet ethnomusicology and Central Asia. Barbara Krader's opening article includes a list of basic studies with translated titles. Victor Beliaev's 1962 survey was translated by Greta and Mark Slobin as *Central Asian Music* (Middletown: Wesleyan University Press, 1975). Mark Slobin also wrote *Kirgiz Instrumental Music* (New York: Society for Asian Music, 1969) and *Music in the Culture of Northern Afghanistan* (Tucson: University of Arizona Press, 1976). Felix Hoerburger's *Volksmusik in Afghanistan* (Regensburg: Gustav Bosse Verlag, 1969) emphasizes the relation of style to Koran chanting; Hiromi L. Sakata, *Music in the Mind* (Kent, Ohio: Kent State University Press, 1983), and John Baily, *Music of Afghanistan* (Cambridge: Cambridge University Press, 1988), combine fine music details with sociological studies of musicians. Baily also wrote "A System of Modes Used in the Urban Music of Afghanistan," *Ethnomusicology,* 25/1 (1981).

South Asia

Studies emphasizing musicians in Indian society are Daniel M. Neuman, *The Life of Music in North India* (Detroit: Wayne State University Press, 1980), and Charles Capwell, *The Music of the Bauls of Bengal* (Kent, Ohio: Kent State

University Press, 1986). Bonnie Wade has provided many useful studies such as "Music in India" in *Music of Many Cultures,* ed. Elizabeth May (Berkeley: University of California Press, 1980), and *Music of India: The Classical Traditions* (New Delhi: Manohar, 1987). She also edited "Performing Arts in India," *Asian Music,* 18/2, (1987), and "India" in *The World of Music,* 32/2 (1990). Her dissertation is *Khyal: Creativity Within North India's Classical Music Tradition* (Cambridge: Cambridge University Press, 1984). The Cambridge series includes Regula B. Qureshi, *Sufi Music of India and Pakistan: Sound, Context and Meaning in Qawwali* (1986). For other studies see Elise B. Barnett, "Special Bibliography: The Art Music of India," *Ethnomusicology,* 14/2 (1970), and Harold Powers's bibliography in *The New Grove Dictionary of Music and Musicians,* Vol. 9, 139–141. Read Powers's "Indian Music and the English Language," *Ethnomusicology,* 14/2 (1970), before approaching the plethora of English studies by Indian scholars. Recommended works are V.N. Bhatkande, *A Short Historical Survey of the Music of Upper India* (Bombay, 1934), P. Sambamoorthy, *South Indian Music,* 6 vols. (Madras: Indian Music Publication House, 1958–69), or O. Gosvami, *The Story of Indian Music* (New York: Asia Publishing House, 1961). Ravi Shankar's *My Music, My Life* (New York: Simon & Schuster, 1968) remains the most readable. See also Manfred Junius, *The Sitar: The Instrument and Its Technique* (Wilhelmshavan: Heinrichskofen Verlag, 1974). Outstanding theses on South Indian music available through University Microfilms (Ann Arbor, Michigan) include Harold Powers, *The Background of the South Indian Raga System* (1963); Robert Brown, *The Mrdanga* (1965); Jon B. Higgins, *The Music of Bharata Natyam* (1973); and T. Viswanathan, *Raga Alapana in South Indian Music* (1975). For Hindustani studies see Nazir Jairazbhoy, *The Rags of North Indian Music* (Middletown: Wesleyan University Press, 1971); Alain Danielou, *Northern Indian Music* (London: C. Johnson, 1949); and Walter Kaufmann, *The Ragas of North India* (Bloomington: Indiana University Press, 1968). An example of regional folk studies is Edward O. Henry, "Jogis and Nirgun Bhajans in Bhojpuri-Speaking India," *Ethnomusicology,* 35/2 (1991). General folk song collections are listed in *The New Grove,* Vol. 9, 158. New traditions are found in Teri Skillman, "The Bombay Hindi Film Song Genre: A Historical Survey," *Yearbook for Traditional Music,* 18 (1986), and Gregory D. Booth, "Brass Bands: Tradition, Change and the Mass Media in Indian Wedding Music," *Ethnomusicology,* 34/2 (1990). Three Indian articles and a South Asian popular music symposium are found in *Asian Music,* 24/2 (1993).

Audiovisual Materials

For Central Asian images see *JVC Video* nos. 3 and 4 and for South Asia nos. 11–13. The UNESCO records include *Azerbaijani tar* (6586 027), *Azerbaidjan* (BM 30 L 2024), *Vina* (6586 023), *North Indian Instrumental Music* (6586 020), *Pakistan* (BM 30 L 2029), and *Afghanistan* (BM 30 L 2003). Under the Harmonia Mundi and UNESCO CD labels are *Pakistan* (D 8028) and *North India* (D 8205, 8017, 8021, 8033). See their catalog for Central and South Asian instrumental or vocal recordings. The King Records CD World Music Library include releases on India (5110-20), Pakistan (5109), and Uzbekistan (5108). The famous Indian performers are found on too many cassette and CD labels to list. A search of the India section of music stores is recommended.

A SONIC GLOSSARY INDEX FOR CHAPTER 4

Central Asia and Afghanistan
(Speaker: Marianne Kamp)

South Asia
(Speaker: Pashaura Singh)

*not on language cassette

FIVE
SOUTHEAST ASIA

The area called Southeast Asia encompasses the countries known in the twentieth century as Burma (Myanmar) mainland (West) Malaysia, Singapore, Thailand, Cambodia (Kampuchea), Laos, and Vietnam. Over the centuries the names and cultural conditions of these various areas have changed often. The magnificent ruins of Angkor Wat (Plate XIX) are monuments to only one of several brilliant kingdoms that flourished in Southeast Asia between approximately the seventh and fifteenth centuries. The Figure 48 drawing is from the northeast wall of the temple Bayon in the giant capital of the thirteenth-century Khmer Empire. It is shown not only for its instruments but for meditation as we approach the world's most active Buddhist area. The other walls of the temple show military triumphs, and here we see a celebration of victory with musicians, acrobats, and dancers. Before the scene could be completed the capital was deserted. Was it disease or someone else's military victory that caused the sculptor to drop his chisel and leave? The dancing figures are incomplete and the tightrope walker to the left is nothing but a body outline, with only a stone block for a head. When the author saw this wall in 1968 it evoked the shadow of a man who was running across a bridge when the atomic bomb hit Nagasaki. In writing a late twentieth-century edition of a book concerning Asian music, little new can be added to this chapter on the Southeast Asian mainland because

PLATE XIX. A wall of Bayon at Angkor Wat from the Thirteenth-Century Khmer Empire, Cambodia.

FIGURE 48. The unfinished festival.

political, military, and religious strife have inhibited music and cultural research except for urban popular genres. Fortunately, the jungles and mountains that surround the ancient and modern urban cultures maintain some tribal traditions despite napalm bombing. Many courtly and tribal refugees of Southeast Asia now exhibit the principle of marginal survival in such distant lands as France, California, Texas, and Minnesota.[1] Colonialism and nationalism, particularly in the nineteenth and twentieth centuries, have made deep inroads into indigenous cultures, but there is still much in continental Southeast Asia that speaks of its ancient and tribal traditions.

The music of Southeast Asia today reflects a mixture of indigenous genius with various combinations of influence from four main external traditions: Indonesia (with its Islam), China, India, and, in more recent times, the West. Hybrid musics have bred further hybrids, so that today it is very difficult to separate the many interminglings and cross influences. Southeast Asian music shows variation not only among all its nations but also between geographical regions within each country. Rather than attempting to discuss subtle cross currents like Sino-Thai and Malayo-Indonesian influences, or regional differences like the Khmer and Champa styles, we begin by discussing Southeast Asian tonal systems in general, then go on to conside the various media and kinds of music based on those systems, in the following order: (1) percussion-dominated ensembles, (2) string-dominated ensembles, (3) wind music, (4) instrumental solo and chamber music, particularly for strings, (5) sacred and secular vocal music, (6) folk and tribal music, and (7) theatrical, rural, and popular music. Although these categories are not mutually exclusive, they serve to illustrate certain cultural continuities as well as some of the variety in Southeast Asian music. For example, all the major genres rely on oral learning rather than notation, and most musics are related to or inspired by some form of theater. Each country, however, has different forms of theatricals and uses different terms for the styles of music and the instruments that relate to the general Southeast Asian tradition. We have picked typical examples in each of the categories just listed and mention some regional variations, without intending to include every nation's terminology or variations.

SOUTHEAST ASIAN TONAL SYSTEMS

The most famous tone system of Southeast Asia is the so-called equidistant seven-tone (heptatonic) scale. In theory these seven tones are 171.4 cents apart, but the manner in which instruments are tuned often alters the actual distance. Example 5–1 shows this equidistant tendency, which in staff notation is indicated by a higher than Western seventh (1026 cents, theoretically). In

[1] Studies of such groups are seen in Amy Catlin, *Selected Reports in Ethnomusicology*, UCLA, 9 (1985).

EXAMPLE 5–1. A Burmese orchestral melody from the recording *Burmese Folk and Traditional Music* (Smithsonian/Folkways 4436, side 1, track 5; book cassette, track 18). Transcription and sound used by permission.

performance these notes give a "neutral" effect (as does the whole-tone hexatonic scale in the West, although its pitches are very different). Some Southeast Asian groups that have had contact with the West tend to adjust these tones to tempered pitches. The origin of the equidistant scale is open to considerable conjecture; at least one theorist has proposed it is the lost *ma-grama* of ancient India.[2] Perhaps rural ensembles may provide information on the more ancient tonal systems since, like the Indonesian *gamelan,* they contain keyed instruments and gongs of rather fixed pitches. One of the most intriguing tone-system arguments of the twentieth century revolves around the tuning of a set of supposedly ancient stone keys found in Vietnam in 1949. Many things can be "proven" according to one's interpretation of the age, tuning, and function of these stones.[3]

Example 5–2 presents yet another of the many scales found in Southeast Asia. This example has an equidistant tendency in the upper three notes, but the resolutions to C of the "neutral" D flat (i.e., a pitch about halfway between a Western D flat and a D natural) and the "gap" between B flat and G create a totally different effect from that found in Example 5–1. This is particularly evident if one listens to the recording (book cassette, track 19). To a Western ear, Example 5–2 sounds suprisingly like the blues; the similarity arises because African Americans have also exploited neutral tones in their traditional music. Example 5–2 however, is a thoroughly indigenous piece.

[2] See Alain Danielou, *La Musique du Cambodge et du Laos* (Pondichery: Institute Français d'Indologie, 1957), 2–3.

[3] A convenient summary of research on these stones is found in Curt Sachs, *The Wellsprings of Music* (The Hague: Nijhoff, 1962),106–8.

EXAMPLE 5–2. A Cambodian wind ensemble piece from the recording *Cambodia* (Kassel: Musicaphon Record BM 30 L 2002, side 1, band 7; book cassette, track 19). Transcription and sound used by permission of the International Institute for Traditional Music, Berlin.

There are seven-tone scales in Southeast Asia that concentrate on a pentatonic "core." The two notes most often deemphasized in such scales are the fourth and the seventh. There are also purely pentatonic pieces (see Example 5–4). A majority of these are of the well-known, no half step (anhemitonic) variety. Even this seemingly simple scale is subject to tonal refinement, for in Southeast Asia it has modal forms, and certain melodies that seem to use a six- or seven-note scale may actually be shifting between one five-note mode and another.[4] These melodic "modulations" are extremely important to the flow of music in such basically nonharmonic traditions as those of Southeast Asia. Here the forward-moving dynamism of the music depends solely on melodic and rhythmic tensions. This flow is further aided in Southeast Asia by the emphasis in each scale on certain "pillar tones"[5] that are melodically consonant; that is, they seem to be at rest and require no further melodic resolution. Other notes in the scale are melodically dissonant or tense and seek resolution into one of the pillar tones. The notes F and C and A might be considered pillar tones in Example 5–1; B flat and F form the pillars for Example 5–2, the remaining tones being melodically tense and in need of further resolution.

Some Southeast Asian tonal traditions have been thought to reflect outside influences. The anhemitonic pentatonic is too widespread and common to imply any such thing, but major-minor pieces usually show hymn, march, or popular music inspirations. Islamic influence is more difficult to pinpoint tonally but does seem to appear in some Malaysian musics (such as Example 5–3).

Attempts have been made to link Southeast Asian tonal systems with those of India by comparing contemporary Indian *ragas* with specific Southeast Asian scales, particularly those used in Hindu-oriented theatrical or religious pieces. The existence of certain beliefs concerning the mood of each scale also implies such a relation. In addition, some Southeast Asian musics use special ornaments on specific notes in each scale, much like those of India. However, some Southeast Asian melodic ornaments involve notes outside the given theoretical scale; this inconvenient fact is mentioned to emphasize that a major problem in musical cultural comparisons is not unlike one found within a single culture: the contrast between theory and practice. On the basis of selected performance practice alone we could compare Indian and Western music if their written theoretical systems did not exist to confound the thesis. When one of the cultures chosen is Southeast Asia, however, the comparison is easier (and potentially more sophistic) because indigenous theoretical writings are rare. Such books that do exist tend to be reflections of Chinese or Indian theory interpreted in terms of local practice. As our knowledge of regional sources in indigenous languages improves, it may be that we discover Southeast Asian theories are as thoroughgoing as those of India, the Near East, East Asia, and the West. Progress in this direction was implied in our discussion of Indonesia but at present we must rely, for mainland Southeast Asian music, on performance practice, sure in the knowledge that the native performer and listener (like similar participants in Western musical events) are subliminally aware

[4] Such a technique has been labeled *metabole* by Trân-Văn-Khê in his *La Musique vietnamienne traditionnelle* (Paris: Presses Universitaires de France, 1962), 225.

[5] The term was first applied to Southeast Asian music by Jaap Kunst in *Music in Java* (The Hague: Nijhoff, 1949), 1, 92, and 94. It is derived from the *Gerusttone* concept of earlier German theorists.

through cultural conditioning of an aggregate of tonal and aesthetic principles that help form their responses to the beauty and logic of the music. A foreign listener does not enjoy this advantage; but a conscious awareness of a few principles, such as those mentioned here concerning Southeast Asian tone systems, may help in learning what to listen for in such music.

INSTRUMENTAL ENSEMBLES

Percussion-dominated Ensembles

One of the core percussive ensembles of mainland Southeast Asia is the Thai *pi phat* band. *Pi phat* ensembles vary from 6 to 14 players. A standard instrumentation includes paired idiophones which, like the sets of three *saron* and *gender* in the Javanese *gamelan,* have different ranges. The 21 wooden keys of the *ranat ek* xylophone (Plate XX, Figure 49) carry the main melodic load, assisted in a lower register by its 17-keyed companion, the *ranat thum.* Their metal-keyed counterparts are the 21-keyed *ranat ek lek* (or sometimes *ranat thong*) and the 17-keyed *ranat thum lek* metallophones.

Circles of knobbed gongs are essential to most of the Southeast Asian percussion ensembles, such as the *pi phat.* In Thailand there are two forms, the lower-pitched 16-gong *khong wong yai* (Plate XX, Figure 50) and the higher-pitched 17- or 18-gong *khong wong lek,* of which the two lowest pitched gongs are nonfunctional. Two kinds of cymbals are also found in a *pi phat.* The smaller ones (*ching*) resemble the small dance orchestra cymbals of India and are seen in Figure 48 in the hands of the player before the harpists and the second musician from the left. The larger set (*chap*) are like the knobbed cymbals found in the Buddhist rituals of Tibet and China. Along with a hanging knobbed gong (*khong mong*) they provide a time cycle structure. Two kinds of drums also assist in this function. One is a large laced-head barrel drum called the *tapone,* both heads of which are played with the hands. The other is a pair of tacked-head barrel drums played with sticks, called the *glong that.* Tuning paste is applied to the heads of both types of drums.

The only instrument that keeps the *pi phat* from being completely percussive is the *pi nai* oboe (in Cambodian, *sralay*) (Plate XXI, Figure 51). This instrument is novel in several ways. Its bulging shape is totally different from that of the standard *surnay-zurna* type found elsewhere in the world or in other ensembles of Southeast Asia (compare Figure 51 with Figure 25). It can be tuned by extending its thick teakwood body with a rim of wax at the lower end. The most novel feature of the *pi nai* is its reed, which is not the standard double, but rather quadruple (Figure 52). Four short rounded reeds made of dried palm leaf are bound to a metal tube inserted in the top of the instrument. These reeds are set in a position vertical to the lips rather than in the Western horizontal position, and the set is "swallowed"; that is, it is placed within the

PLATE XX. Southeast Asian idiophones

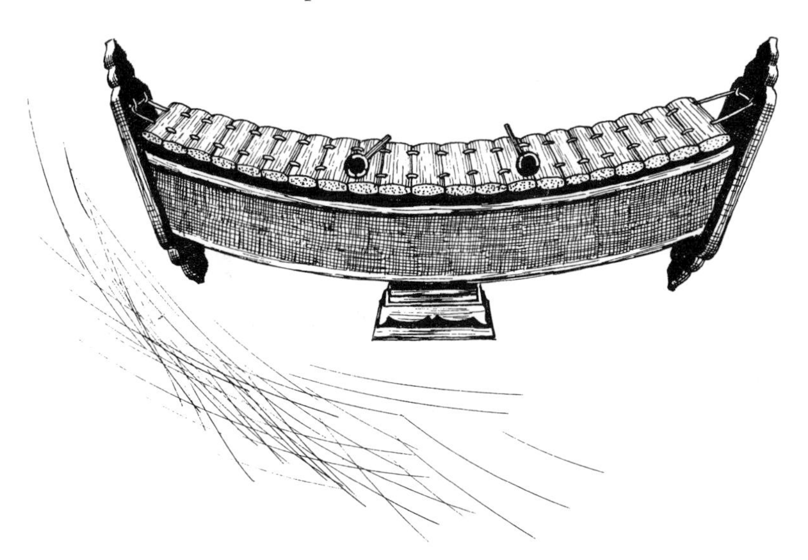

FIGURE 49. *Ranat ek.* (125 cm wide)

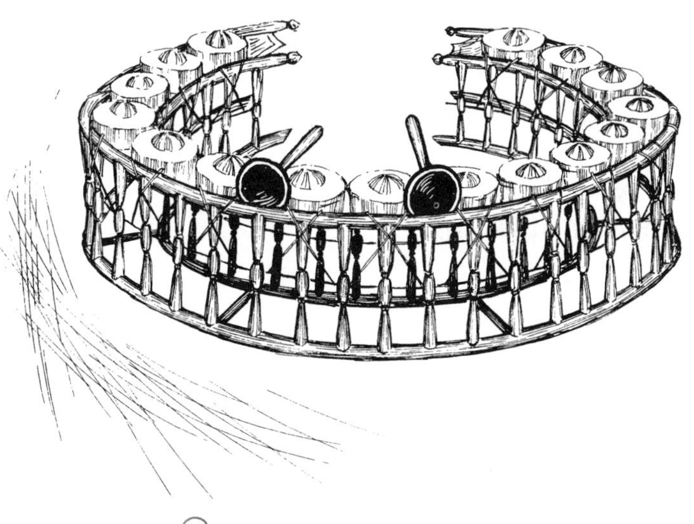

FIGURE 50. *Khong wong yai.* (90 cm frame diameter)

PLATE XXI. Southeast Asian aerophones

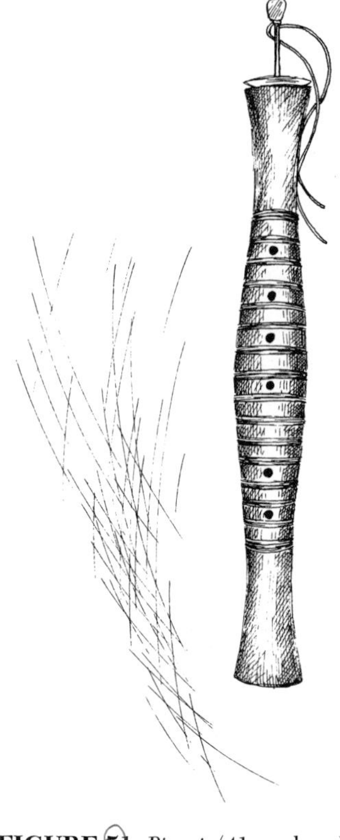

FIGURE 51. *Pi nai.* (41 cm long)

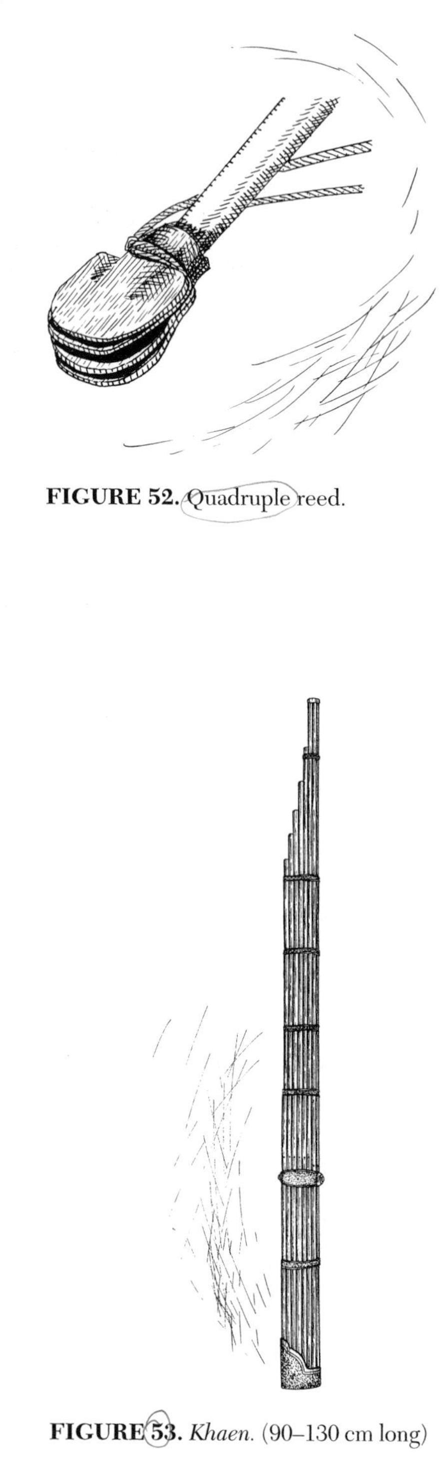

FIGURE 52. Quadruple reed.

FIGURE 53. *Khaen.* (90–130 cm long)

mouth cavity rather than on the lips. The reason for the novel vertical placement is so the player's tongue can touch the edges of some of the vibrating reeds and stop the outer two layers, thus raising the pitch by a fifth (a clarinet does the same with the thumb key). This allows the player to produce different pitches with only six finger holes.

The Cambodian or Laotian *pin peat* ensembles are similar in instrumentation to the Thai group just described. All three were mostly heard in the royal palaces, where they accompanied official ceremonies and classical dramatic presentations. Some private academies of ensemble playing and rural orchestras existed before the late-twentieth-century regional wars. They have survived well in Thailand but such ensembles are unlike Indonesian *gamelan* traditions in that they have little support among the populace other than their use to accompany public theatricals or new national functions. Except for Thailand, the Southeast Asian art musics are found more often among refugees in Europe and the United States where, as we noted earlier, marginal survival may be seen in yet another context.

The Burmese percussion orchestra (*saing waing ah-pwe*) has deeper roots, perhaps because it is more itinerant and travels from village to village in support of the public theater (*pwe*). This orchestra, sometimes called merely a *saing* or *saing waing,* derived its name from its most novel instrument, a set of twenty-one tuned drums (*saing waing*). These are hung on an ornate circular screen which, while partially hiding the performer from view, adds a decorative visual pleasure to the performance. Such an interest in the visual appeal of instruments is characteristic of most Southeast Asian instrumental traditions, and the nonfunctional parts of many instruments are overlaid with traceries and colorings.

The rest of the Burmese ensemble consists of a circle of twenty-one knobbed gongs (*kyi waing*); a large hanging barrel drum (*segi*); large and small cymbals (*ya gwin* and *si*); two long bamboo clappers (*wa let kyong*); and a double-reed aerophone (*hne*) with a conical bore and a very large, loose metal bell. The *hne* reed is unique. Six ply of tender palmyra leaves are bound (three on a side) to create a fan-shaped sextuple reed![6]

The melody for *hne* given in Example 5–1 is an excerpt from a *saing* ensemble performance. Like the other orchestras of Southeast Asia mentioned so far, the melodic instruments in the *saing* ensemble may create together a kind of stratified polyphony. This, and our description in general of various percussion ensembles and their functions in Southeast Asia, brings to mind the Indonesian *gamelan.* Also, the prevalence of melodic idiophones and knobbed gongs, as well as the close connections of the music with dance or drama, are certainly reminiscent of the *gamelan* tradition. Unlike the Indonesian *saron* or

[6] Thanks to James F. Guyat of Baruch College, New York, for bringing this unusual structure to my attention. Compare with the usual four ply seen in Figure 52.

gender, however, few of the continental Southeast Asian melodic idiophones are capable of sustaining long tones, and their melodic style thus tends to be more incisive.

In some Burmese percussion ensembles the major or indeed the only melodic instrument is from the quadruple-reed family just described. Players of such instruments normally use nasal breath in order to maintain a pitch or melody indefinitely, as in the style of Example 5–2. The Burmese *hne* excerpt in Example 5–1 illustrates possible idiophonic influence with its short-breathed lines and sudden changes in melodic direction. Its use of heterometer is atypical of Southeast Asia. The lively, disjointed style of the example relates to the quick puppet-inspired movements of many Burmese dances. Example 5–3 shows a very different florid style from Kedah, in West Malaysia, played on a *serunai* quadruple-reed aerophone in *gendang keling,* an ensemble used for Muslim ceremonial events and processions. The quadruple-reed and portable knobbed gong have Southeast Asian roots, but a Turkish flavor is added by the melismatic tune, "exotic" tonality, and repeated rhythmic patterns played on a pair of two-headed laced barrel drums (*gendang*).[7] A clearer Islamic influence in Malaysia is found in the *nobat* ensemble connected to the courts of regional sultans. Its two barrel drums are called merely *gendang nobat,* but the use of the term *nobat* (see p. 93) and of a small *nenggara* kettledrum, a *nafiri* trumpet, and the *serunai* reveal its relation to similar groups in Muslim India and the Near East. We see the *serunai* in a very different ensemble in our later discussion of theater music.

String-dominated Ensembles

Figure 48 shows harps, zithers with gourd resonators, plus the ubiquitous small hand cymbals in a thirteenth-century Cambodian ensemble. Except for the cymbals, the Thai *mahori* string ensemble differs in instrumention although one wonders, has the music style changed? The main function of *mahori* orchestras is to accompany songs and plays. Like the *pi phat,* they find their main patronage in the capitals, although individual bowed instruments are widespread rurally. Though a *mahori* includes many other instruments, such as xylophones, circle gongs, cymbals, drums, and end-blown flutes, the overall sound is softer than that of *pi phat* groups. The common terms for bowed chordophones are *saw* in Laos and Thailand and *tro* in Cambodia and among the Mons of Burma. There are three basic kinds of bowed lutes in such groups; let us describe primarily their Thai forms. The first type is a three-stringed spike fiddle called the *saw sam sai.* Both its shape and its separate bow relate it to the *rebab* (see Plate VI, Figure 12) and, in fact, the *rebab* itself is used in certain theatrical musics of Malaysia. The second type is the *saw duang* (in Vietnam,

[7] Listening to book cassette, track 20, reveals that both the tonality and the drum patterns become more complex. The entire example is played in one nasal breathing unit! If the gong was not there we might think the example was from Turkey.

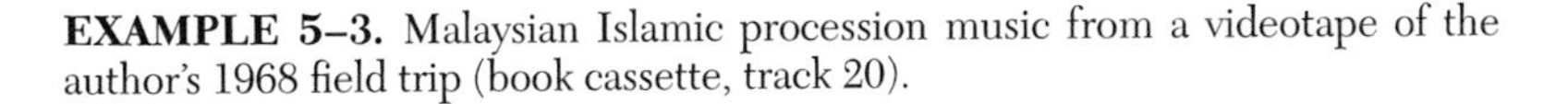

EXAMPLE 5–3. Malaysian Islamic procession music from a videotape of the author's 1968 field trip (book cassette, track 20).

the *cai nhi*). Its two strings lie one above the other, vertical to the body, like those of the Chinese *huqin* (Plate XXV, Figure 62), rather than horizontal to the body, like the strings of a Western violin. The bow passes between the strings like that of the *huqin* rather than over them in the style of the *rebab* or the violin. The body of the *saw duang* is cylindrical and open (like Figure 62). The third type of bowed string instrument, the *saw u,* is like the *saw duang* except the body is usually made of half a coconut shell. Other Chinese-style bowed chordophones with four strings and coconut-shell or cylindrical-shaped bodies also exist in Southeast Asia.

The basic styles of bowed lutes described here are graphic reflections of the confrontation of East and West in Southeast Asia; when the string pegs are inserted from the rear, the influence is clearly that of China, whereas lateral pegs mean a Muslim or Western origin. The term "Western" has been added because the origin of violin-like instruments in Asia is not always clear. A four-stringed violin held horizontally under the chin or at waist level is generally Western-derived when found in South or Southeast Asia. However, the ensembles of the Mon people of Burma use three-stringed fiddles held in a vertical position like the Near Eastern or Indonesian *rebab,* but because of their Western violin-shaped bodies, they look like North African *keman*—except for the special Southeast Asian designs on their scrolls. Organological diffusionism strikes again (along with the imagination of creative indigenous instrument makers)!

Although historically the ancient Mons seem to have used only percussion instruments, their present ensemble includes, besides two of the fascinating violins just mentioned, two small drums, an end-blown flute, and the *chakay* or *mi gyaung* crocodile zither (Plate V, Figure 9), a zoomorphic variant of the ubiquitous Southeast Asian plucked chordophone called in Thai the *chakay* (Plate XXII, Figure 55). The later is already familiar to us from similar instruments noted in Plate V from the Philippines (*kudyapi*), Borneo (*kachapi*), and Java (*kacapi*). India also may play a role in the labyrinthian search for the distribution of such an instrument. The manner in which the three gut strings of the Thailand *chakay* pass over high frets is reminiscent of the *vina*, although the *chakay* sound is less resonant, its playing style is less florid, and it is plucked by a pointed ivory dowel rather than by *vina*-like finger picks.

Another plucked chordophone found in *mahori* bands is the *grajappi* lute. This instrument has four strings in double courses and a long fretted neck whose thin curved line forms a lovely visual image. The Cambodians make great use of this instrument under the name *chapey-thom*. The *dan nguyet* is a Vietnamese variant. Other Vietnamese lutes reflect Chinese origins, such as the four-stringed *dan ty ba*, which looks like the *pipa* (Plate XXIV, Figure 60), and the three-stringed *dan day*, which is a long-necked version of the *yueqin* (Plate XXV, Figure 64). Organological borders are never fixed, and the use of Western guitars and banjos has increased since the mid-twentieth century. One drum of particular interest, is the single-headed pot-shaped *thom* or *thap*, which resembles the Near Eastern *tombak* (Plate IX, Figure 22).

Wind Ensembles and Instruments

The most famous wind ensemble of Southeast Asia consists of a group of *khaen* (*can*, *kaen*, or *khen*). As seen in Plate XXI, Figure 53, the *khaen* is itself a kind of ensemble, since it can play chords and melody at the same time. It consists of from 6 to 16 long bamboo pipes (from 90 to 200 cm) joined in the center or bottom by a single wind chamber. Each pipe contains a single free reed that vibrates when a hole on the side of the pipe is closed. The harmonic, melodic, and drone aspects of *khaen* music can be seen in Example 5–4. Nasal

EXAMPLE 5–4. A Thai *khaen* piece transcribed from the recording *Music of Thailand* (Smithsonian/Folkways 4463, side 1, track 1; book cassette, track 21). Transcription and sound used by permission.

PLATE XXII. Southeast Asian chordophones

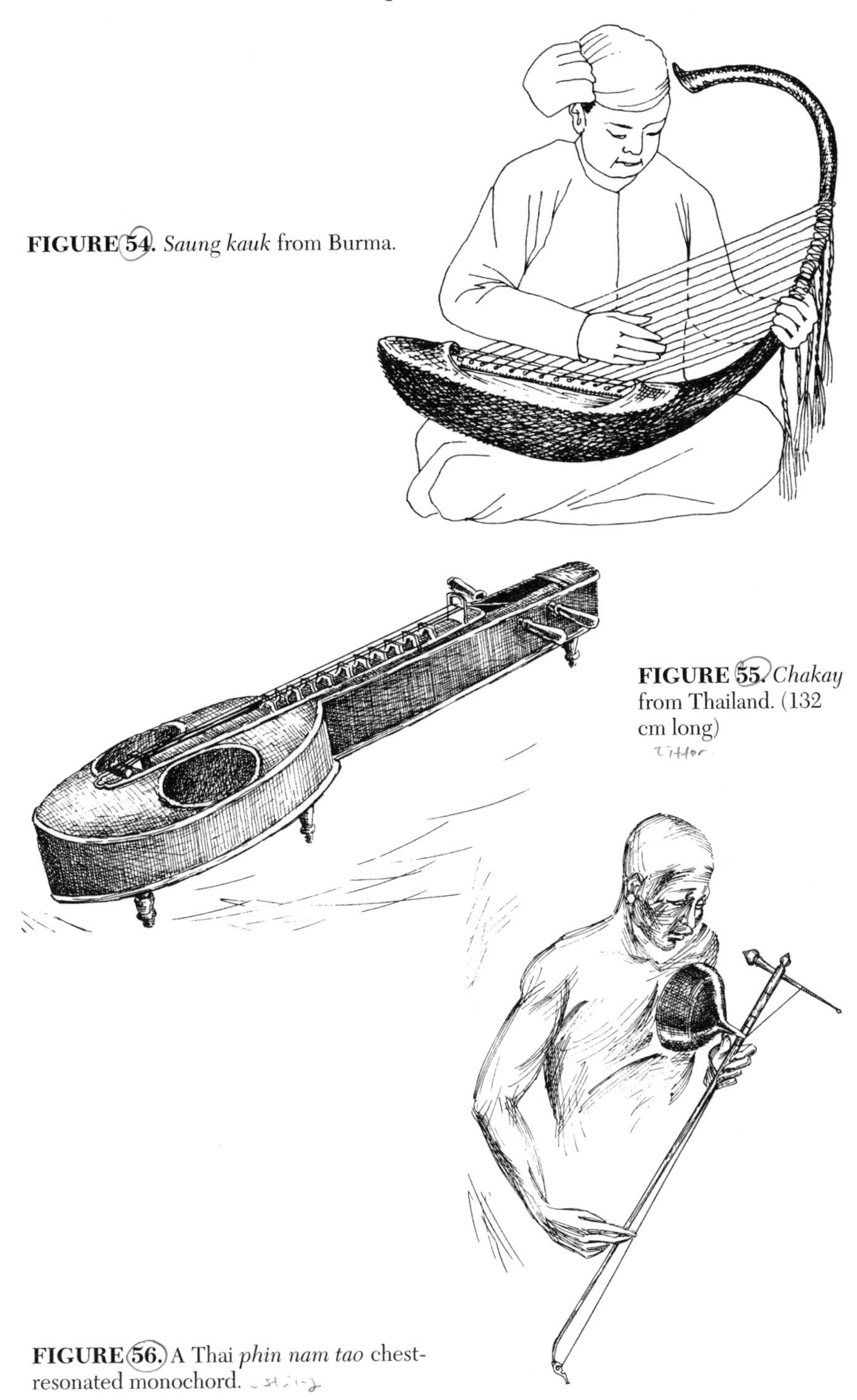

FIGURE 54. *Saung kauk* from Burma.

FIGURE 55. *Chakay* from Thailand. (132 cm long)

FIGURE 56. A Thai *phin nam tao* chest-resonated monochord.

breathing allows the performer to keep the air chamber filled and thus maintain the sound. When *khaen* are played in ensembles, the separate parts are primarily for reinforcement rather than for the addition of new polyphonic lines. It is more often heard as a solo or vocal accompanying instrument. The *khaen* is believed to have originated in Laos, but as we saw in Kalimantan (p. 42) it is widespread throughout South Asia. In addition to being the predecessor of the Chinese *sheng* (Plate XXIV, Figure 61), it may also be a distant precursor of the Western reed organ. In any event, it is one of the more complicated and widespread folk instruments of Southeast Asia. In its folk form, the pipes may stick out of one side (as in the *sheng*) rather than penetrate the gourd.

A variety of both horizontal and end-blown flutes exists in Southeast Asia. The latter include open-end and closed-end notched flutes as well as block flutes. In Thailand they all tend to fall under the term *khlui*. The Thai block flute is perhaps the best known ensemble aerophone, since it appears frequently in *mahori* orchestras. The opening of the block is at the bottom of the instrument rather than at the top (as on the Western recorder). In addition to six finger holes, it has one hole that is covered with a thin membrane to create a soft buzzing sound.

Another important aerophone found in ensembles as well as in solo music is the *pi saw*, also called sometimes a *khlui*. A relative of the *khaen*, it consists of a single free metal reed inserted near the closed end on the side of a long bamboo pipe in which six or seven finger holes have been drilled. The instrument is held sideways (somewhat like a horizontal flute) with the reed portion covered by the mouth. This instrument has a soft clarinet-like tone and produces a pleasant buzzing resonance. It is commonly used for evening serenades in villages. It can be heard on book cassette, track 19. Mention has been made of the quadruple-reed aerophones, which seem to be another distinctive Southeast Asian organological contribution.

STRING MUSIC: SOLO, ACCOMPANIMENTAL, AND CHAMBER

One of the most lovely instrumental solo traditions of Southeast Asia is that of the *saung kauk* harp of Burma (Plate XXII, Figure 54). It is used in classical music to accompany the simple *cho* songs as well as several more esoteric kinds of vocal music, such as the *yodaya*. The *yodaya* are based on a Thai style of song and use of a different tuning, rhythmic mode, and melodic style from those of the *cho* songs. The tuning of the harp is changed by twisting the braids that attach its 14 (formerly 13) strings to the pole. The rhythmic changes in Burmese songs and harp music can best be heard by following the sounds of a pair of small hand bells (*si*) and a clapper (*wa*), which keep the beat much as do the *talam* cymbals of India and, probably, the ancient bell/cymbals seen in Figure 48. Melodic differences in harp music can be found by studying the various principles of modes and modulations discussed earlier in this chapter as they apply to the two Burmese harp song traditions. Extended instrumental interludes in these songs reveal a great interest in melodic variation and extension.

The origins of the Burmese harp have been traced to ancient India, but a living Asiatic tradition of harp music is now unique to Burma.[8] The audiences who sit all night in a Buddhist temple compound to hear it, as well as the rows of young women at the National Music Institute in Rangoon who diligently practice it in ensemble, are perhaps only faintly aware of how rare this music is. If it survives Burma's period of modernization, it will be one of the last classical harp traditions remaining from the ancient world.

Many of the instruments of the classical orchestras of Southeast Asia have a solo literature. The Mon *mi gyaung* and the Thai *chakay* and *grajappi* are good examples. Much of the solo and chamber music of this area, however, is really an arrangement of or accompaniment to vocal music.

One of the most exotic solo string instruments used to accompany the voice is the monochord called in Thailand the *phin nam tao* (Plate XXII, Figure 56). As seen in the drawing, the resonance of the instrument is enhanced by placing the open back of its hemispherical body against the singer's chest.[9] A similar instrument is found in Africa. In Vietnam there is a monochord called the *dan doc huyen* or *dan bau* that uses a standard wooden body as a resonator but stretches its string between the body and a flexible vertical stick. The pitch is varied by pulling the stick sideways to increase or lessen the tension on the string, somewhat like playing tunes on a rubber band. The monochords, plus many of the other strings of Southeast Asia, have their basic repertoire in the courting music and other social music of the villages. They have been joined in recent decades by the guitar and other Western instruments.

Outside the West, the borderline between orchestral and chamber music is very indistinct for, as we have seen, many "orchestral" pieces can be played by rather small ensembles. One can find in Southeast Asia, however, separate repertoires of pieces created specifically for ensembles of two or three people; this can truly be called chamber music, although the relation of parts, as with the music for larger groups, is basically heterophonic. One lovely example is the Vietnamese trio consisting of a two-string pear-shaped guitar (*ty ba*), a flute (*dich*), and a sixteen-string plucked zither (*tranh*). This trio, like much of Vietnam's music, reflects a strong Chinese influence.

[8] In Figure 48, note an ancient Khmer harp similar to Figure 54 but played in the opposite position.

[9] Sensitive writings on the similar four-stringed *phia* instrument blind musicians and Thai drum making are found in the articles of Gerald P. Dyck in *Selected Reports in Ethnomusicology*, UCLA, 2/2 (1975). Note the potential relationships of Figure 56 with instruments in Plate XIX, Figure 48.

SACRED AND SECULAR VOCAL MUSIC

We have already noted that much Southeast Asian instrumental music is used for vocal accompaniment. In addition, there is a rich heritage of narrative musics not directly connected with theatricals. Some are purely vocal, such as the Thai *say pha,* in which performers accompany themselves with four sticks clicked together like castanets. Other narrators use string instruments for ostinato-like backgrounds, and heterophony may also appear; it is found, for example, in survivals of *selampit* narrations in Malaysia, which reflect Muslim influence in their heterophony and their accompaniment by the *rebab* spike fiddle or sometimes the *serunai* oboe. Heterophony can also be found in certain Chinese-based forms, particularly in Vietnam.

Southeast Asian poetry may be recited in a musical fashion, although, as in the Near East, such performances may not be classified as music. We noted in Chapter 3, that "reading" the Koran in Malaysia is not music, although singing *hadrah* or *rodat* poems in praise of the Holy Prophet to the accompaniment of a *rebana* tambourine is a legitimate Malaysian Islamic activity. Unaccompanied praise poems sung by female attendants in Thai or other courts are considered music, as are survivals of earlier court musics such as the North Vietnamese *hat a dao* poems. *Hat a dao* singers remaining today play a rhythmic accompaniment with sticks on a *phach* related to the so-called Chinese wood block while a long-necked three-stringed *dan day* plucked lute supplies a melody to which the singer adds refined ornamentations. In Northern Thailand and Laos several *mawlum* (singing) traditions appear from a solo epic singer or from a male/female team who alternately sing lines while making dance gestures. The most common accompaniment for either style is the *khaen* (*kaen*) mouth organ.[10] Larger *mawlum* groups form light theatrical troupes and may use *pin* plucked lutes and even a Western drum set.

Unison choral singing is heard in some *mahori* pieces and the *zikirbarat* or *dikirbarat* tradition of Malaysia, in which by call and response two groups are led by a soloist in matching the verses or retorts of their competitors. Such song contests are found in many forms in Southeast Asia (for Sumatra, see p. 59). Perhaps the most unusual mass choral sound of the area was that of *mak yong* (*ma'yong*) dance-drama in northern Malaysia. A highly melismatic, heterophonic duet between a singer and a *rebab,* accompanied by interlocking *gendang* drum parts and two gongs was followed by a dance section in which all the performers on stage sing their own melismatic versions of the tune. The resultant massive proliferation of pitches and lines seems to be a unique form of heterophony even in the context of mid-twentieth-century European choral experiments. Southeast Asian singing in large groups is heard more often in reli-

[10] See Terry Miller, *Traditional Music of the Lao: Kaen Playing and Mawlum Singing in Northeast Thailand* (Westport, Conn.: Greenwood Press, 1985).

gious chanting, generally in unison or organum-like forms. The majority of these chants are, like most liturgical music, *centric melodies;* that is, they center on one tone and use other tones to surround it. The styles of Southeast Asian religious musics usually reflect the cultural origin of the faith (Chinese Buddhism, Indian Hinduism, Near Eastern Islam, and Western Christianity), although there are many interesting mixtures, such as the *caodai* of Vietnam.[11] The most accessible indigenous religious music of Southeast Asia is perhaps the dream songs of village clairvoyants: After personal problems of life and love are presented to these seers, they go into a trance and then through song relate the advice of the supernatural. With such music we touch on our next topic—folk music.

FOLK AND TRIBAL MUSIC

The dream songs just mentioned are found throughout Southeast Asia. The need for extraterrestrial help in health and happiness is not limited to the rice fields and jungles as rural populations migrate to urban centers, nor are temples or churches the major sources. Vitality remains in the animistic shaman and trance traditions of Southeast Asia as they adopt and adapt to outside influences. For example, a *put(e)ri* spiritualists of northern Malaysia villagers may use instruments and tune names of *mak yong* drama while dancing with Thai-inspired movements before whirling his or her head in a Near Eastern style in order to go into trance and become the spirit of the illness.

The functionality of Southeast Asian folk and tribal music is still guided by the yearly cycle of wet rice agriculture[12] through genres like love, death, and lullaby songs that follow personal clocks. The functions of such musics need not be singular. For example, among the Pwo Karen people of North Thailand, funeral songs are actually considered primarily social because they offer the best opportunities for young men and women to meet and flirt.[13] The soft sounds of a bamboo jaws harp in a northern Thailand village often contain a whispered text of love to be heard by the young girl for whom it is intended through the thin flooring of a raised hut. A duet of village *khaen*-like mouth organs may be an abstraction of Buddhist chant.[14] Near many a Southeast Asian rice paddy, sets of tuned bamboo tubes may be found hung from trees or activated by water wheel into tunes for the entertainment of the spirits of the gods and the

[11] Religious music in Southeast Asia is discussed in Volume 1 of *Encyclopédie des Musiques Sacrées* (Paris: Labergerie, 1968).

[12] For a study of music and the agricultural cycle in Laos see Kristina Lindell and others, *The Kammu Year* (London & Malmo: Curzon Press, 1982).

[13] See Judith Becker, "Music of the Pwo Karen of Northern Thailand," *Ethnomusicology*, 13/1 (1969).

[14] Examples of all the music mentioned were heard in the field recordings of Uchida Yuriko in the recording *Music of Minorities in the* [sic] *Northwestern Thailand,* Nippon Victor SJ 1010, 1960. The University of Michigan Library has a copy.

workers. The live presence and immediacy of such music is especially meaningful in the modern industrial and mass communication world, for so much of our urban music is *schizophonic;* the listener is seldom the participant and is cut off electronically from the maker of the sounds who, in turn, may have used a computer and synthesizer to "perform" the music.[15]

The relation of ecology to musical instruments is strong in either a Western city filled with plastic and electronics or a Southeast Asian village. The latter also will have its industrial products and military leftovers (artillery shells make instant gongs). However, bamboo and cane dominate its traditional organology. Stamping tubes, trumpets, panpipes, and flutes (including nose flutes) are as common in continental Southeast Asia as they are in other humid areas like New Guinea (see p. 22). This does not mean they are all the same. A tropical forest or jungle culture has different materials to create instruments than one based on rice paddies and water buffalo. Although tacked and glued-on drum heads exist, Southeast Asian drums may use buffalo hide laced with rattan rather than rawhide (which is susceptible to rot). The heads are tightened to the desired sound by wooden wedges driven under the rattan laces or by rattan rings that pull two laces closer together.

Southeast Asian jungle drums most often have single laced heads and hourglass-form or extended pot-shaped bodies, although there are two-headed barrel drums that seem related to the Indonesian *gendang.* Perhaps the most intriguing item of diffusionist potential is the knobbed bronze gong, which is as equally prized in tribal Southeast Asia as it is in the Indonesian archipelago (see p. 40). The origin of such an instrument is controversial, as is that of the Southeast Asian flat-surfaced gong with wide, slightly concave sides. Sometimes the latter has frog figurines or other animals etched into its surface or attached to its rim. It is played like a drum or suspended like a gong and seems related to a very ancient Chinese bronze drum. It may, however, be either a survival of that tradition or a predecessor of it, for later tenth-century Chinese military expeditions into Southeast Asia found such instruments quite "exotic" with their magical sounds of the bullfrog.[16] The *khaen* kind of mouth organ has already been mentioned as another historical mystery. Many plucked lutes in the northern tribes of Southeast Asia, by contrast, seem clearly derived from China. Obviously there is much to learn from Southeast Asian tribal music beyond its melodies and social functions. Some of its oral history and literature has been passed on to theater traditions.

[15] The author derives the term and thought from R. Murray Schafer, *The New Soundscape: A Handbook for the Modern Music Teacher* (Ontario, Canada: BMI. 1969).

[16] See Edward Schafer, *The Vermilion Bird* (Berkeley: University of California Press, 1967), 254.

Similar ensembles can be found accompanying Malaysian *ronggeng* and *joget* social dances. Such dances are often in quadrille or line form like those of the Philippines or rural Euro-America. The dances themselves differ from their Western counterparts in several ways. As in most Southeast Asian couple dances, the partners never touch, a preference adopted in Euro-American culture only since the 1950s. Unlike the Western preference for hip movements, the Malaysian and other Southeast Asian emphases are on movements of the feet and torso and on delicate hand gestures derived from classical Southeast Asian dance traditions. Urban dance halls, however, reflect whatever the latest Euro-American fad may be. Although national pride has sometimes aided regional traditions, it usually results in military bands and Western orchestras and choruses, along with an urban interest in jazz. Urban comic theater is dominated by Western and Chinese instruments, and the latest pentatonic popular tune may be played by saxophones and trumpets with chordal accompaniment. All this apparent potpourri reinforces the maxim that musical culture is never completely static. When one hears a piano played in the manner of a native xylophone (*Burmese Folk*, Smithsonian/Folkways, 4436, side 2, track 9), there is hope that all the foreign importations have not yet deadened the natives to the charms of their own indigenous styles.

BIBLIOGRAPHICAL AND AUDIOVISUAL NOTES

To accommodate researchers in the use of these reference notes, the written and media sources are placed together under common geographical names in alphabetical order. Articles from *Traditional Drama and Music of Southeast Asia*, ed. Mohd. Taib Osman (Kuala Lumpur: Dewan Bahasa Dan Pustaka, 1974) are listed as TDMSA and *Asian Music in an Asian Perspective*, eds. Koizumi and others (Tokyo: The Japan Foundation, 1977) as AMAP. General research material includes Jose Maceda, *A Manual of Field Music Research with Special Reference to Southeast Asia* (Quezon City, Philippines: University of the Philippines College of Music, 1981), and Judith Becker, "Percussion Patterns in the Music of Mainland Southeast Asia," *Ethnomusicology*, 12/2 (1968).

Burma (Myanmar)

Becker, A.L. "The Journey Through the Night: Some Reflections on Burmese Traditional Theater," TDMSA.

Becker, Judith. "The Anatomy of a Mode," *Ethnomusicology*, 8/2 (1969).

Garfias, Robert. "Preliminary Thoughts on Burmese Modes," *Asian Music*, 7/1 (1975).

Garfias, Robert. "The Development of the Modern Burmese Hsaing Ensemble," *Asian Music*, 16/1 (1985).

Garfias, Robert. "A Musical Visit to Burma," *The World of Music*, 17/1 (1975).

Okell, John. "The Burmese Double-Reed Nhai," *Asian Music*, 2/1 (1971).

OO, U. Mya. "The Music of Burma," *Musical Voices of Asia* (Tokyo: The Japan Foundation, 1980), 7.

THEATRICAL, RURAL, AND POPULAR MUSIC

Theatrical music in Southeast Asia has a long tradition goin dance-dramas depicted in ancient stone reliefs such as those of Angk Cambodia (Plate XIX). We have already shown that the *pi phat* and *ma* sembles can be used to accompany modern versions of these old classic mas. Rural and urban theatricals such as the *lakon* or masked dance (tradition of Thailand deal with a variety of folkloric or topical events anc more modest accompaniments. Characteristic *lakon* ensembles include dru gongs, and clacking bamboo sticks, the tunes being carried by an oboe, xy phone, gong circle, or bowed lute, alone or in combination. *Lakon* are oft performed at temples, for their function is semireligious, although their action may become very secular and comic. The drama of northern Malaysia also seems to have been based on religious needs but became thoroughly secular. Its musical style, mentioned earlier, may imply a Muslim influence in this border area of Buddhism.

The sounds of theatricals supported by Chinese and Indian populations in Southeast Asia[17] are very different, as are the musics of the various indigenous puppet theaters. The latter differ from their Indonesian colleagues in preferring a quadruple reed as their major melodic instrument. The Buddhist countries may include idiophones like those of Plate XX; Malaysia only shares with them a tendency for a drum leader and knobbed gongs as time markers.[18] The rise of conservative Islam in Malaysia and wars in many other areas of Southeast Asia have seriously damaged these fine traditions.[19] We can only hope that twenty-first-century Southeast Asian people may enjoy the special pleasures of an all-night puppet play live rather than old TV reruns.

As we have noted throughout this book, mass communications plus the recording and tourist industries tend to create regional pop music traditions as much as imitations of the international styles. They occasionally enhance the national dissemination of local folk and courtly art musics, although their general effect is negative. In the former Portuguese port of Malacca in Malaysia the tourist industry has taken a novel direction, importing "authentic" music and dance from Portugal! At the same time they may use a genre called in Malaysia *dodang sayang*, which is said to have been derived from old Portuguese popular music. Its Malaysian version, like Indonesian *kroncong*, is very localized. It is sung melismatically to the accompaniment of a Western violin (or a *rebab*), an Arab tambourine, a pot drum (see Plate IX, p. 76), and Southeast Asian knobbed gongs.

[17] See Sooi-beng Tan, "From Popular to Traditional Theater: The Dynamics of Change in Bangsawan of Malaysia," *Ethnomusicology*, 33/3 (1989).

[18] For details and photographs see Patricia Matusky, *Malaysian Shadow Play and Music* (Oxford: Oxford University Press, 1993).

[19] See *Asian Music*, 21/1 (1989) for five articles on the topic. Our earlier discussion of *mak yong* was written in the past tense, for the Malaysian government forbade performances as of 1994.

Otake, Tomoyoshi. "Aspects of Burmese Musical Structure," *Musical Voices of Asia*, 68.
Picken, Laurence. "Instruments in an Orchestra from Pyu . . . in 802," *Musica Asiatica*, 4 (1984).
Williamson, Muriel. "Aspects of Traditional Style Maintained in Burma's First 13 Kyo Songs," *Selected Reports in Ethnomusicology*, UCLA, 2/2 (1975). See also her Burmese harp study in same issue and in 1/2 (1968).
Zaw, K U Khin. Director of Broadcasting (Rtd.), *Burmese Culture: General and Particular* (Rangoon: Sarpay Beikman, Printing Publishing Corporation, Ministry of Information, 1981), 80, 81, 83.

Cambodia (Kampuchea)

Brunet, Jacques. Eight articles in TDMSA.
Cravath, Paul. "The Ritual Origins of the Classical Dance Drama of Cambodia," *Asian Theatre Journal*, Vol. 3/2 (1986).

Laos

Catlin, Amy. "Harmonizing the Generations of Hmong Musical Performance," *Selected Reports in Ethnomusicology*, UCLA, 9 (1985); in the same issue see Miller, Terry. "The Survival of Lao Traditional Music in America."
See also footnotes 10 and 12 (pp. 158, 159).

Malaysia

Chopyak, James. "The Role of Music in Mass Media, Public Education and the Formation of a Malaysian National Culture," *Ethnomusicology*, 31/3 (1987). See also footnote 17.
Malm, William. "Malaysian Ma'yong [sic] Theater," *The Drama Review*, 15/3 (1971). See also TDMSA.
Malm, William. "Music in Kelantan, Malaysia, and Some of Its Cultural Implications," *Studies in Malaysian Oral and Musical Traditions*, Michigan Papers on South and Southeast Asia, no. 8 (1974).
Matusky, Pat. "An Introduction to the Major Instruments and Forms of Traditional Malay Music," *Asian Music*, 16/2 (1985).
Matusky, Pat. *Malaysian Shadow Play and Music Continuity of an Oral Tradition* (Kuala Lumpur: Oxford University Press, 1993).
Nor, Mohd. Anis Mo. *Zapin Folk Dance of the Malay World* (Oxford: Oxford University Press, 1993).
Tan, Sooi Beng. "The Performing Arts in Malaysia: State and Society," *Asian Music*, 21/1 (1990).
Roseman, Marina. "The Temiar of Pennisular Malaysia," *Ethnomusicology*, 28/3 (1984).
Roseman, Marina. *Healing Sounds: Music and Medicine in the Malaysian Rain Forest* (Berkeley: University of California Press, 1991).
Sheppard, Tansri Dato Mubin. "Traditional Musical Instruments of Malaysia," *Selected Reports in Ethnomusicology*, UCLA 2/2 (1975). In the same issue Gerald P. Dyck wrote a paean, "the vanishing phia," plus an article on the making of Thai drums.
Sheppard, M. Two articles in TDMSA.
Sheppard, M. *Taman Indera: Malay Decorative Arts and Pastimes* (Kuala Lumpur: Oxford University Press, 1972).

Thailand

Duriyangi, Phra Chen. "Siamese Music in Theory and Practice (1948)," *Asian Music,* 13/2 (1982).
La-iad, Herabat. "Development of Thai Music," AMAP.
Wong, Deborah. "Thai Cassettes and Their Covers," *Asian Music,* 21/1 (1990).
Yupho, Dhanit. *Thai Musical Instruments* (Bangkok: Department of Fine Art, 1960), translated by David Morton.
See also footnotes 9 and 13 (pp. 157, 159).

Vietnam

Pham Duy. *Musics of Vietnam* (Carbondale: Southern Illinois University, 1975).
Tran-Van Khe. *La Musique Vietnamienne Traditionelle* (Paris: Presses Universitaires de France, 1962).

Audiovisual Materials

The *JVC Anthology* videotapes are as follows: 6, Vietnam and Cambodia; 7, Thailand and Burma; and 8, a poor selection from Malaysia. The original UNESCO Musicaphon records included *Laos* (BM 30 L 2001), *Cambodia* (BM 30 L 2002), *Vietnam* (BM 30 L 2022 and 2023), and *Malaysia* (BM 30 L 2026). Their newer series has *Hat Cheo Vietnamese Traditional Folk Theater* (6586 035, CD D 8035), *South Vietnamese Entertainment Music* (6586 028), *Traditional Music of Southern Laos* (6586 012), *Royal Music of Cambodia* (6586 002, CD 8011), and *Thailand* (D 8007). The Hugh Masters Series of Celestial Harmonies has a CD set of Cambodian music (19902) plus separate issues (13074-75). The Smithsonian/Folkways series contains *Folk and Traditional Music of Burma* (4436), *Music from South Asia* (4447), *Music of Thailand* (4463), and from Malaysia, *Temiar Dream Music* (4460). Lyrichord has *Traditional Music of Vietnam* (LLCT 7396). The King Records World Music Library includes *Vietnam* (KICC 5121-22 and 5160-61) and *Thailand* (KICC 5123-25).

A SONIC GLOSSARY INDEX FOR CHAPTER 5

Burmese
(Speaker: Sai Khai Mong)

Cambodian

(Speaker: Dorasy Paul)

Loatian

(Speaker: Dorasy Paul)

Malayasian

(Speaker: Rizwal Zakaria)

Thai

(Speaker: Montatip Krishnamra Brown)

Vietnamese
(Speaker: Nguyen Thi Nga)

*not on language cassette

SIX
EAST ASIA

Geographically, East Asia in this survey is restricted to the Asian mainland area from Tibet in the south to Mongolia and Manchuria in the north, with all of China proper in the center. The many ethnic peoples of the western portion of this vast area share common bonds from two directions; the nomadic, pastoral traditions of Central Asia (see Chapter 4) and Chinese culture. Korea and Japan are equally influenced by China but we treat them separately along with arctic cultures in Chapter 7.

TIBET

Locked in its mountain fastness, Tibet has often seemed to Westerners to be the very symbol of an ancient, unchanging, Shangri-la world. Historically, however, the culture of Tibet has been altered periodically by influences from India, China, Mongolia, and even the West. Before the introduction to Tibet of Indian Buddhism in the seventh century, there existed an indigenous religion called *bon,* whose music influenced the newer tradition and still survives in Tibet as a distinct religion and in various "shamanistic" religious practices.

Although Buddhist writings may have existed in Tibet by the third century A.D., it was only after the seventh century that Buddhism began to have an impact on Tibetan rulers. Monasteries were established in the eleventh and twelfth centuries that later had populations ranging into the tens of thousands. By the thirteenth century, Lamaistic Buddhism became a politico-religious force so dominant that Tibet's unique theocracy was able to remain intact until the Chinese invasion of 1950.

Like any large religious tradition, Buddhism has various sects, and within such sects in Tibet and among exiled Tibetan communities around the world there are different schools. The core of Tibetan religious music is vocal *dbyyangs,* normally sung on a very low pitch. To the Westerner, the most astounding form is one used by some schools of the Gelugpa sect; in this chant the monks not only produce a fundamental tone some two octaves below middle C but at the same time reinforce the partials above, so the tone is extremely "rich," and a note like E above middle C seems actually to be sounding at the same time.[1] Such a "throat" tone or "split" tone gives the impression that a single person is singing a chord. (We note related phenomena in Mongolia and Siberia later.) The function of this unusual musical phenomena is religious. In most world music cultures we find that humans do not communicate with God in the same voice they use for their fellow beings. In Tibet, these seemingly nonmelodic chants not only are intended to communicate with the Buddha and his followers but to offer the performer a possible path out of the objective world toward inner transformation and eventual enlightenment. The challeng-

EXAMPLE 6–1. Tibetan chant notation derived from Walter Kaufmann, *Tibetan Buddhist Chant* (Bloomington: Indiana University Press, 1975). Performed by Lama Senge Norbu for Terence Beech in 1966 at the Padung Lamasery in Katmandu, Nepal. Tape used by permission of Indiana University Library and notation by permission of Indiana University Press.[2] Book cassette, track 22.

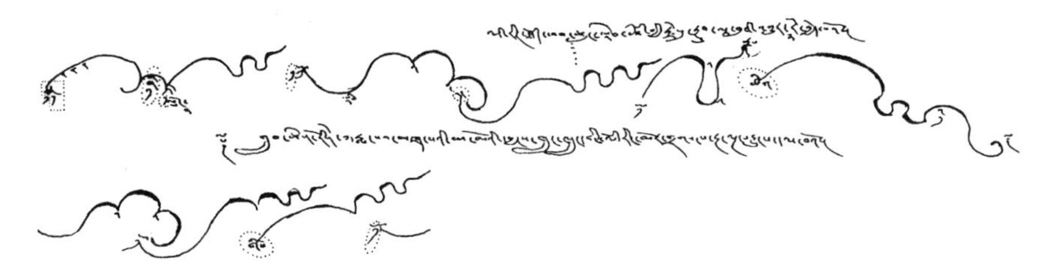

[1] This can be heard on the CD *Tibetan Buddhism* (Nonesuch 9 79198-2).

[2] There are ten notation units seen and heard in this example. The two Tibetan script lines are instructions on how to perform the music (see Kaufmann's book, pp. 38–40). The sung text is the last five syllables of a standard opening passage for many ceremonies: *dad pa dang ni dam tshig gis* ("By reason of my faith and pledge"). These syllables are imbedded in vocables (*ah, ra, ai,* etc.). The text *da* sounds as *de* to Western ears. Like Catholic mass settings, the meaning of words is well known, and following the spirit of the sounds is often more important than hearing the text as such. Special thanks to reference librarian David Lasocki for locating the original recording among the Kaufmann papers deposited at the Indiana University library.

ing low pitch and the frequent clouding of the sung text with extra syllables serve as protection for these goals. The proper and safe use of such ritual material must be limited, in the Tibetan view, to those who truly understand its meaning and its power.

To ensure the accuracy of such important chant, notated songbooks (*dbyangs-yig*)[3] were created that are, as is suggested in Example 6–1, as handsome in calligraphy as in the sounds they represent.[4] Because the definition of a *neume* in Western music is any sign that represents more than one pitch, this notation has been called *neumatic.* However, one could equally call it by the Western notation term *graphic*—that is, a system that indicates pitch heights (like Western staff notation)—for the contour of the notation applies just as well to the upward and downward motion of the melody.[5]

Tibetan ritual may include a variety of musical instruments. The most common section marker is a *dril-bu* hand bell. This bell is found in all Buddhist countries, its shape remaining amazingly consistent from Sri Lanka and Bali to China and Japan. The most striking idiophonic color surrounding Tibetan chant is the use of cymbals. The term *rol-mo* has been used to mean the music of percussive interludes that occur during chant or the cymbals that dominate this music.[6] Their rhythms are often notated, for accurate performances are spiritually significant.[7] Such notation shows not only tempos and dynamics but also performance styles on the cymbals. In that context the notation could be called a *tablature,* a notation that shows finger positions or playing methods on an instrument. Most Tibetan instruments have a notation specific to their performance practice, for we are dealing with set pieces, often with known composers.

A quite different idiophone is found in some monasteries to signal events of the day. It is a wooden board (*gandi*) that is balanced on the left shoulder and struck with a wooden beater.[8] Although wooden "gongs" (*semantron*) have been found in European Christian communities, and hanging wooden signaling devices are common in Buddhist temples of East and Northeast Asia, this portable form (with spiritual as well as functional connotations) seems unique to South Asian and Tibetan Buddhism.

[3] The romanization and pronunciation of Tibetan terms depends on one's choice between the standardized spelling of written Tibetan and the many different dialect pronunciations. The most standard spellings are attempted in this chapter.

[4] See Walter Kaufmann, *Tibetan Buddhist Chant.* See also Ter Ellingson, "Buddhist Musical Notation," in *The Oral and the Literate in Music,* ed. Tokumaru and Yamaguti (Tokyo: Academia Music Ltd., 1986).

[5] For other classifications such as contour notation see Ter Ellingson, "Buddhist Musical Notation," and Example 6–8 in this chapter.

[6] The monastic terms for the smaller cymbal is *sil-snyan* and larger, *shub 'chal.*

[7] See Ter Ellingson, "The Mathematics of Tibetan Rol Mo," *Ethnomusicology,* 23/2 (1979).

[8] See Ivan Vandor, "The Gandi . . .," *The World of Music,* 17/1 (1975), or Mireille Heiffer, "Le Gandi," *Yearbook for Traditional Music,* 15 (1983).

Membranophones are another part of Tibetan religious sonic color. One is the *chos-rnga*, a large two-headed tacked barrel drum set on the end of a pole that players grip as they beat on one head with a curved stick. A smaller, more portable form of this drum is the *lag-rnga.* The Hindi word *damaru* is the usual name for a small hourglass-shaped drum as it is found in India as well. If, in Tibet, the two attached hemispheres that form the body are made of the tops of human skulls, the drum may be called the *thod-dam.* The instrument is sounded by knobs or knots at the end of two strips of cloth that are attached to the waist of the drum so the knobs strike alternate heads when the drum is twisted back and forth in the hand. This instrument is heard in many contexts including itinerant monks in public and non-Buddhist trance rituals.

The most spectacular Tibetan ritual instruments are long copper trumpet (*dung-chen*, "long trumpet," or *rag-dung*, "brass trumpet"). These straight conical-bore natural horns vary in length from some 1.5 to 7 meters. Many are made in sections that can be telescoped for portability. Each horn has a fairly shallow cup mouthpiece and, like the Western bugle, is capable of producing different tones. The basic use of these horns is not to play fanfares, but to be part of the instrumentation of ritual music. Smaller hand trumpets have dragon heads at the bell end; the players of these tend to concentrate on one note, from which they slide up and down. The shamans of Tibet use short trumpets made of human leg bones. The conch-shell trumpet is also found in Tibet.

The only melodic instrument in Tibetan religious orchestras is the double-reed *zurna,* called *rgya-gling* in the monasteries. It plays preludes and interludes to the chants, but not the chants themselves.

The best opportunity to hear Tibetan music in all of its splendor is during the annual *cham* festival. For three days, actors in gorgeous costumes and fearsome papier-mâché heads perform an involved religious dance-drama to the accompaniment of a variety of instrumental combinations chosen from the instruments just listed. Whether a festival event is held in public or within the confines of a monastery, the music structure is generally percussion-accompanied singing alternating with instrumental interludes. The secular dances and historical plays of Tibet tend to use drums and cymbals for accompaniment. The influence of Tibetan culture on neighboring countries such as Sikkim and Nepal and the increase in expatriate Tibetan refugee communities since the middle of the twentieth century have naturally led to many variants on the traditions mentioned here; it may be, however, that through marginal survival many of the older forms of Tibetan religious music and Tibetan dance-drama can still be found in communities as distant as Switzerland.

So far, we have not mentioned any Tibetan string instruments because they are not used in Tibetan religious music. In secular music, one finds a variety of bowed lutes similar to the Mongolian or Chinese fiddles (see Figures 57 and 62). Example 6–2 shows excerpts from two songs accompanied by the *sgra-synan* plucked lute. It has five or six strings, some in double courses, often tuned in a second and a fourth. It varies in size and playing methods in villages throughout the Himalayan countries. In Tibet it usually duplicates the melody[9] but in our example the instrument is used more like a percussion accompaniment, playing an ostinato on open strings without regard to the tonality of the singers. Such "bitonality" is found in other countries, particularly in dance music, when the accompanying instrument performs a rhythmic rather than a melodic function.

Although most Tibetan folk songs use the whole-step pentatonic scale, the two excerpts in Example 6–2 were chosen not only because the accompaniment illustrates an ostinato but because the melodic tonal systems are unusual. Example 6–2A makes a striking use of the tritone (G to D flat) and exploits harmony in seconds at each cadence. Example 6–2B shows a so-called chain melody[10] built in thirds (G to B flat to D to F).

MONGOLIA

If we move down from the mountains of Tibet and out onto the steppes and deserts along China's western border, we find the tribal remnants of the Mongol Empire. In ancient times, these hardy horsemen made their fame in the art of war rather than music; but even in war, drums and bugles were used for signaling. In the thirteenth century Marco Polo mentions a battle before which both sides sang. The signal for the start of the battle was given on a large kettledrum with the familiar name of *nagarah* (see *naqqara,* p. 78).

Although the Mongolian nomadic people were strong militarily, they were always susceptible to outside cultural influences. Today their western tribes are influenced by Islamic culture; Lamaistic Buddhism and Chinese culture dominate in the East. An indigenous shamanistic tradition survives in a few songs found in present collections, although the shamans and their drums can best be found further north in Manchuria and Siberia, as well as across the Bering Straits in Alaska and Canada (see p. 249).

The musical legacy of the Mongols is found today primarily in their folk music, known generically as *duun.* This music can be divided into several types of songs according to subject matter, such as spiritual songs, songs about the heroic deeds of the days of the great khans, contemporary political songs, and epic narratives (*uliger*). Whereas the political songs tend to be sung by unison chorus, the most common Mongolian performance practice is for one person to

[9] A comment by Ter Ellingson to the author.

[10] For a discussion of melody building with various interval chains, see Curt Sachs. *The Wellsprings of Music* (The Hague: Nijhoff, 1962), 143–67.

EXAMPLE 6–2. Two Tibetan folk dance excerpts from the recording *Songs and Music of Tibet* (Smithsonian/Folkways 4486, side 1, bands 5 and 2 [fourth entrance]; book cassette, track 23). Transcription and sound used by permission.[11]

sing while playing the *khil-khuur* bowed lute.[12] This fiddle has a flat trapezoid body with sheepskin covering both the front and back. It has two strings tuned in fifths. The pegbox is often topped with the carving of a horse's head in a manner similar to the carving on the *gusle* fiddles of the Yugoslavian epic singers. As seen in Figure 57, the strings are so far above the neck that pitches may be set by either the tip or the nail of a finger. Ornamentation can be added by striking the string with the finger from the side.

[11] In the record notes, the first song text is "In spring there are five rainbows. As the sun shines upon them they grow with brilliant colors and the sky is filled with beauty. The second song says, "Oh yonder mountain. Let us not dare to build our homes on top for we would block out the sun's warm rays that heat the valley below. Let us not build a bridge on yonder river."

[12] On *JVC Video* no. 5 a professional singer is separate from the accompanist.

There seem to be two common styles of folk singing in Mongolia. One is in an even *tempo giusto,* usually isometric; the other is in a *parlando-rubato* style. In both styles, the relation of the voice to the accompaniment tends to be heterophonic. The *parlando-rubato* pieces make extensive use of melismatic improvisations in both the vocal and instrumental parts. Thus, although the songs tend to be strophic, there is considerable variation between each strophe. In the study of such variant strophic music it is often useful to construct a comparative score[13] in this way one can quickly see the areas of similarity and difference. No notation, however, can successfully symbolize the low yodel (ululation) that is characteristic of the Mongolian manner of singing these songs.

In Mongolia one finds another version of the split-tone (biphonic) singing we noted earlier in Tibet. Since this fascinating tradition is found also among other Central Asian and Siberian groups such as the Tuvinian, Oirats, and Bashkirs, we discuss it for all of them at this time.[14] The use in the secular music of these peoples of a fundamental tone plus various partials tends to follow two methods. In Mongolian *xoomij* style, a low rough-toned drone is "split" so that arpeggios can be performed by reinforcing such partials as the sixth through tenth and the twelfth. This would mean that, if the fundamental were C two octaves below middle C, the arpeggio could use G above middle C plus B flat, C, D, E, and G above that.[15] The second method seems to concentrate on melodies growing directly out of the overtones, which can be enriched by moving the fundamental to a different pitch. Although some twentieth-century European composers have tried this kind of sound production, it is only in Central and North Asia that it has been established as a popular musical style.

Returning to Mongolia, we find a few Central Asian plucked lutes, plus Chinese-style violins and flutes. With the increase of government controls in both China and Outer Mongolia during the mid-twentieth century, there was a tendency to form state folk ensembles whose music seemed more reminiscent of Rimsky-Korsakov than of the great khans. However, there are still Mongolian bards practicing their solo art. Although they may now sing about the new ponies on the collective farm, there is much of the Asian steppes tradition left in their performance style.

[13] Mongolian songs in comparative scores are found in Ernst Emsheimer, *The Music of the Mongols,* Publication 21, VIII, Part 4 of *The Sino-Swedish Expedition,* Sven Hedin, director (Stockholm: Thule, 1943), 22–35.

[14] For more detail see A.N. Aksenov, "Tuvin Folk Music," *Asian Music,* 4/2 (1973), translated by Mark Slobin.

[15] Although neither a Mongolian nor a Tuvinian, I find that placing the tone in the throat, curling the tongue against the roof of the mouth, and shaping the mouth cavity and lips correctly seems to generate most of the pitches described. See further two research articles on *xoomji* in *Musical Voices of Asia,* eds. Koizumi, Tokumaru, and Yamaguchi (Tokyo: The Japan Foundation, 1980). It can be heard on the accompanying record and seen and heard on *JCV Video* 3.

PLATE XXIII. Mongolia and ancient China

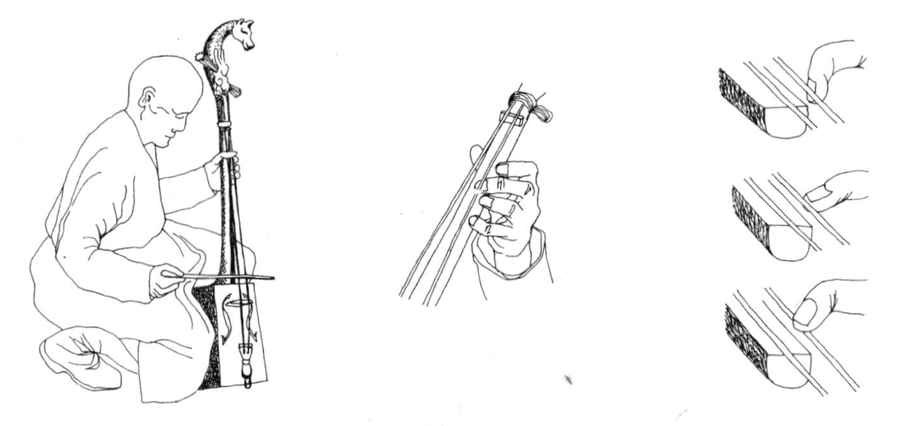

FIGURE 57. A Mongolian *khil-khuur* and its fingering method.

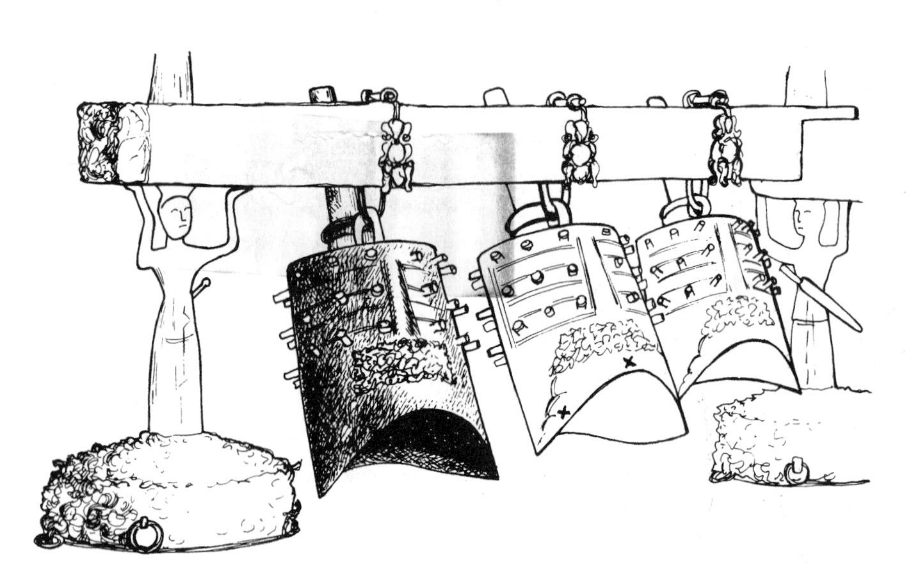

FIGURE 58. Two-pitched Chinese chime bells *(bianzhong)*. The figurine is approximately 32 inches tall and the bell is 140 pounds.

CHINA

Organized civilizations of Mongoloid peoples have occupied the Chinese mainland continuously since at least 3000 B.C. By the time of their first verified dynasty, the Shang (1766–1122 B.C.), they were already using a writing system that, unlike the ancient scripts of the Egyptians and the Sumerians, related directly to the system used by their modern descendants. Thus we find in China a tradition of amazing age and continuity which, with a great interest in history and respect for the written word, has left a vast legacy of information about the ways of Chinese civilization over a period of some three thousand years of actual history, plus another two or three thousand years of legend and pseudo-history. Within the thousands of volumes of ancient Chinese history, philosophy, and literature that have survived to the present day, there are many scattered references to music. A composite of these sources gives us many details concerning the history, theory, instrumentation, and uses of music throughout the ages. Unfortunately, it tells us nothing about the sound of ancient Chinese music. Thus both Western and Oriental scholars tend to concentrate on the history of Chinese music to the neglect and often the disparagement of its living tradition. Our survey, reflecting the historical orientation of available material, is organized into four general periods: the formative (third millennium B.C. through the fourth century A.D.; the international (fifth century to the tenth); the national (the tenth through the nineteenth centuries); and the period of world music (the twentieth century). The first section deals primarily with the theoretical foundations of Chinese music; sections of the second and most of the third periods concentrate on history; only in materials since the seventeenth century do we begin to say something about the actual music. Compared to the scope of Chinese history, this last section is a tiny period, although in relation to the history of Western music it covers the time from J.S. Bach (1685–1750) to the present. An overview of Chinese music is obviously a study for a lifetime, but perhaps some of the grandeur of its history and the richness of its surviving traditions can be discerned in the discussions that follow.

The Formative Period (Third Millennium B.C. to Fourth Century A.D.)

The earliest musical artifacts in China date from around 1000 B.C.; they consist of rounded clay ocarinas and stone chimes. Instruments of less durable material no doubt existed before this time, but the oldest Chinese writings list only a few of the instruments of the early Jiou period (1122–221 B.C.). These writings also mention folk festivals, for ancient China seemed always interested in ceremonies, particularly those dealing with divination and the honoring of ancestors. Thus it is not surprising that one of the first extensive discussions of music is found in the second-century B.C. *Book of Rites* (*Ligi*). The other famous Chinese classics of this period that deal with history and court activities also contain scattered references to music; the poetry collection, the *Book of Odes* (*Shinjing*), has many texts that seem, originally, to have been sung. The teachings of Confucius (551–479 B.C.) likewise make frequent mention of music, primarily because, like the philosophers of other ancient civilizations, Confucius considered the performance of music to be an ethical as well as pleasurable experience. From all these sources four basic kinds of information emerge: (1) the mythological origins of music; (2) the theoretical basis of Chinese music; (3) the instruments of the court; and (4) the relation of music to court life and ritual in the Jiou and later the Han (third century B.C. to A.D. 220) dynasties. These four areas form the basis of our discussions of the foundations of Chinese music.

The most famous legend concerning the origin of Chinese music says that around 2697 B.C. a certain Ling Lun was sent by an emperor, Huang-di, to the western mountains to cut bamboo pipes (*lu*'s) from which the fundamental pitches of music could be derived. The legend is interesting in three respects. First, it places the origins of music at the western borders, where so many other new ideas have crossed over into China. Secondly, the concern of the emperor to secure proper fundamental pitches reflects indirectly the close relationship of early Chinese music to ritual and to the extramusical, for, in China, setting a proper pitch meant literally putting music in tune with the various forces of the universe. Further proof of this relationship is seen in the fact that a new emperor traditionally ordered his musicians and astrologers to work together on recalculating the length of the imperial pitch pipes so his reign would harmonize with all the elements of nature and supernature. This reflection of the natural order of the universe in the arts remained fundamental to Chinese music speculations until very recent times.

The third point of interest that stems from the legend of *lu*'s is that Jiou and Han dynasty writers used these pipes as the basis for an elaborate tone system that still strongly influences Chinese music. The Near Eastern and Indian tone systems studied earlier were *divisive,* that is, they were based on the divisions of a vibrating string (on the *'ud* and *vina,* respectively).

Chinese theorists at some time may also have used the divisive method, but the traditional explanation of Chinese music was *cyclic.* It was created from a cycle of tones generated by blowing across the tops of a set of tubes closed at one end (like a bottle), whose lengths were arranged in a set of mathematical proportions.

The pitch produced by the first tube was called Yellow Bell (*huangzhong, huang chung*).[16] This does not mean it was played on a bell; it was merely a name for that pitch—as, for example, the pitch vibrating 440

[16] The two common romanization methods for Chinese are the twentieth-century mainland *pinyin* system and the Wade-Giles system based on a nineteenth-century English/Chinese dictionary. The *pinyin* system will be used. Since both are found in other music studies, a comparative list of most terms is found at the end of this chapter.

times a second is called in the West "A." For the sake of comparison with other material in this book, we shall call the Yellow Bell pitch middle C, although traditionally it is placed on the F above that. Additional tones are produced by constructing tubes that are alternately ⅔ and 4/3 the length of their previous tube. The acoustical basis for this method is the principle of the *overblown fifth*[17]—that is, by blowing hard on the first tube, a tone one fifth higher (G in our series) is produced. A tube ⅓ shorter than the first one will produce this G without overblowing. If this second tube is overblown, the note D appears in an upper register, as shown in Example 6–3. The note D is played more easily an octave lower on a pipe ⅓ longer than the second pipe. A pipe ⅓ shorter than the D pipe produces an A, and a pipe ⅓ longer than the A pipe produces an E at the lower octave.

Because the pipe length is concerned with thirds, this system is sometimes called a trisectional method rather than the overblown-fifth method. When the tones are written in the manner in which they are generated, we see they follow a pitch pattern of going up a fifth and down a fourth, as shown in Example 6–3B. Chinese music theorists carried this process through twelve tubes to produce the same twelve pitches found in the chromatic scale of the ancient Greeks that, in turn, was the foundation of Western music. This neat theoretical system was challenged by the 1977 discovery in Hubei, Suixian, of the fifth-century B.C. tomb of the Marquis Yi of Zeng. In it were found sets of sixty-four Chinese chime bells[18] dating no later than 433 B.C. As seen in Plate XXIII, Figure 58, each bell in one of the sets was inscribed in two places with the names of different pitches, generally a major third apart.[19] This inspired a new theory of building the Chinese tone system shown in Example 6–4. One starts with five tones using the cycle of fifths (Example 6–3A) and generates the remaining seven from major thirds above and below the first four fundamental pitches.

EXAMPLE 6–3. The Chinese *lu* system.

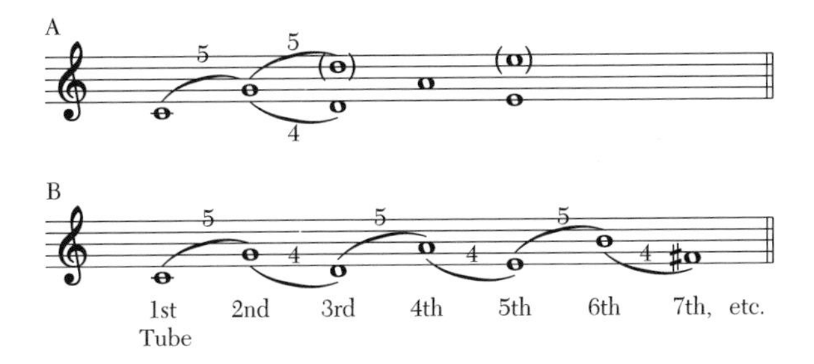

[17] See the term in the index for other references to it in this book.

[18] It is called a chime bell or bell chime because it has no clapper. The bells are struck from the outside. They are arranged in several separate sets, varying in size from giant to small. Each set is hung in pitch order from low to high.

[19] The striking points are marked with an *x* on the center bell in Figure 58. See further a study of Chinese bells: Lothar von Falkenhausen, *Suspended Music* (Berkeley: University of California Press, 1993).

EXAMPLE 6–4. Generating 12 pitches by the Chinese 5th and major 3rd method.

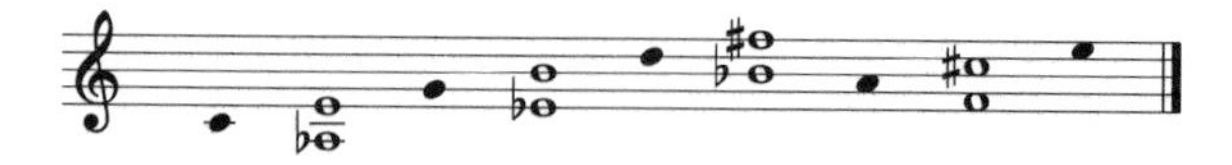

These pitches allow for the practical use of more scales than do the pitches of the overblown fifth system because in both the Greek and Chinese systems the thirteenth pitch is not quite the same as the original first pitch. This so-called Pythagorian *comma*[20] problem was solved in the sixteenth century by a mathematical solution when a complete tempered tuning appeared both in the West (Werckmeister, 1691)[21] and in the writings of Prince Zhu Zaiyu (circa 1596). However, it was not really significant in Chinese music until the twentieth century, when indigenous and Western instruments needed to play together "in tune."

The names of the twelve Chinese pitches are more exotic than those of the West; rather than A, B, or C sharp we find terms like Yellow Bell, Forest Bell, and Lush Vegetation. However, many of the names, such as Old Purifier and Equalizer, hint at scientific observations. The sweet frustration of ancient music studies is that there are always more questions than answers.[22]

Whatever theoretical system we choose, it is evident the fundamental Chinese orientation is toward a basic pentatonic scale (the *wusheng*). Example 6–5 shows such a scale plus its sixth and seventh *lu* tones (F sharp and B from Example 6–3). The latter are called "changing" (*bian*) tones and seem to be used as passing tones or as a means of modal change within a basic five-tone framework. The pentatonic core can be built from any pitch, just as in the West we can have various major scales (for example, C major or A flat major). The words below the pitches in Example 6–5 are like the Western *do re mi.* They are not specific pitches (such as middle C or *huangzhong*) but rather indicate position in a scale. As with Western scales one can also create modes by using a different note in a scale as the pitch center (for example, using the note D as the tonic in the context of a C major scale or D as the pitch center in Example 6–5).

EXAMPLE 6–5. The basic Chinese scale system and its changing tones.

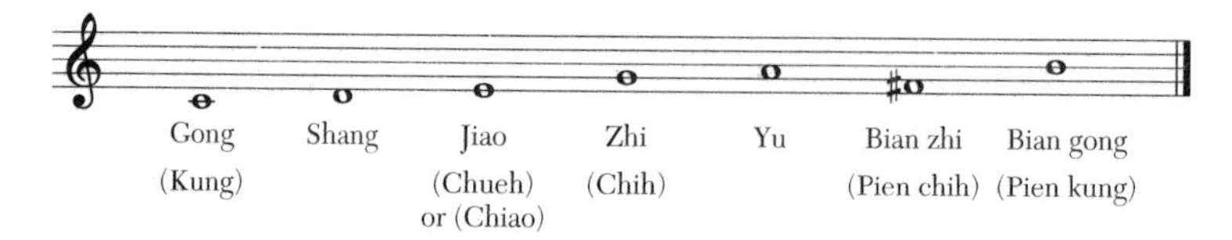

[20] See page 87 of Chapter 3.

[21] See Murray Barbour, *Tuning and Temperament* 2nd ed. (East Lansing: Michigan State University Press, 1953).

[22] See Fritz Kuttner, "A Musicological Interpretation of the Twelve Lus in China's Traditional Tone System," *Ethnomusicology*, 9/1 (1965).

Chinese theoretical speculations share with the ancient writings of other urban cultures (including the West) an interest in extramusical ideas. For example, the twelve chromatic *lu* tones have been divided into two six-tone series according to whether they are generated by going up a fifth or down a fourth (see Example 6–3). The main function of such a listing is to organize the tones of Chinese music along the lines of the female-male (*yin* and *yang*) principles of Chinese metaphysics. Thus the legends explain that the notes of the upper series are those sung by the male phoenix bird, the lower series those of the female. The influence of such symbolic structures is seen in some of the imperial panpipes (*piaxiao*) in which the male and female pipes are arranged separately, outward from the middle of the instrument rather than in ascending order. *Yin* and *yang* tones also tended to be arranged separately in the racks of sixteen bronze bells (*bianzhong*) and similar sets of stone chimes (*bianqing*) so popular in Jiou court orchestras.

The twelve tones themselves were supposedly created in order to provide a cosmologically correct tone for the proper scale to be used in each of the twelve months or the twelve hours. The five tones, in turn, were connected with the five directions, the five elements, and many other qualities in a manner that reminds us of the other great musico-philosophical constructs of Asia and the Near East.

The importance of music as a reflection of the natural philosophy and orderly penchants of Chinese thought has been much emphasized in the writings on ancient Chinese music. This plethora of legendary analogies, however, has combined with the pictographic nature of the Chinese language to cloud the fact that the ancient Chinese were skilled, knowledgeable acousticians. Many of the fanciful legends and terms are actually ancient ways of reporting important scientific and musical findings derived from controlled, empirical experiments. At least two thousand years ago, Chinese scientists knew as much about soundproof research laboratories, the laws of vibrations, and tuning as did Western scientists at the turn of the twentieth century.

Like the Greek theoretical foundations of Western music, many of the early Chinese concepts concerning music have faded away; others remain as the subliminal heritage of modern musicians. Besides the usual pentatonic scale, many of the structural principles of Chinese music today can be traced to the grand syntheses created in an age that parallels the era of Aristotle and Pythagoras but predates Al Farabi or Pope Gregory by several centuries. Thanks to the literacy of Chinese and Greek civilizations, we can still savor some of the wonders of the ancient theoretical foundations of music, although the concomitant practical musics of both the East and West are lost. However, there are descriptions of musical instruments which, in China, give us tantalizing hints of the flavor of a musical cuisine as exotic as even the most romantic Westerner could imagine.

The Chinese genius for orderly systems appears again when we study musical instruments. These were classified under the so-called "eight sounds" (*bayin*) system, which differentiated instruments by the main material from which they were made—earth (pottery), stone, metal, skin, wood, bamboo, gourds, and silk. This system often relates to the design of the Chinese characters used to write the names of Chinese instruments. For example, the character for the clay ocarina (*xun* 壎) has the symbol for earth at the left; the stone chime's character (*qing* 磬) has the stone symbol on the bottom; and the idiogram for metal appears in the word for the bronze bells so often seen in books on Jiou dynasty art.

The ancient lists contain wonderful legends about instruments as well as much accurate information. For example, the same Huang-di who "ordered" the invention of music is said to have had a drum made from the skin of a one-legged monster which, when struck with a huge bone, could be heard for hundreds of miles. This fabulous drum is listed under the "skin" category along with several types of drums we know to have existed in ancient times. An exotic entry in the "wood" category is the *yu*, a model of a crouching tiger with a serrated ridge or a set of wooden slats along its backbone; it is seen in its surviving Korean form in Plate XXVII, Figure 70. A split bamboo whisk is swept along its back to indicate the end of a piece in Confucian ritual music. Another ancient Chinese instrument surviving in Korea is a box (*zhu*) that is thumped with a pole stuck through a hole in the top.

Under the "bamboo" category one finds the *lu* pipes bound together as a panpipe (*paixiao*). Both the vertical notched *xiao* flute and the horizontal *di* flute are in this category. The *sheng* mouth organ (Plate XXIV, Figure 61), although using seventeen bamboo pipes, is classified as a gourd instrument because of the gourd-like windchest in which the pipes are set. We explained earlier how chords may be played on the Southeast Asian relatives of this instrument by closing the hole on the side of each pipe, thus activating the free reed that is placed at the windchest end of each pipe. The *sheng* uses the same system, although the pipes are much shorter (compare Figure 53 and Figure 61). The placement of the pipes in a circle around the edge of the windchest facilitates the performance of chords as well as melodies. The ancients say the *sheng* sound is an imitation of the cry of the phoenix bird and its shape is that of a phoenix with folded wings. The facts of history say it is the oldest known instrument in the world based on the organ principle and that it was apparently responsible for the introduction of the reed organ into Europe in the seventeenth century. We meet it again in modern Chinese music and in the court ensemble of Japan.

The "silk" category contains a surprisingly large number of multiple-stringed zithers with movable bridges, such as the thirteen-stringed *zheng*. The most famous of the "silk" instruments, however, is the seven-stringed *qin* (Plate XXIV, Figure 59). This instrument and its music have long been associated with Confucius and the life of the intellectual in China. A look through any collection of Chinese landscape paintings as they survive from later periods will inevitably reveal a bearded scholar either seated behind his *qin* while viewing the

PLATE XXIV. China

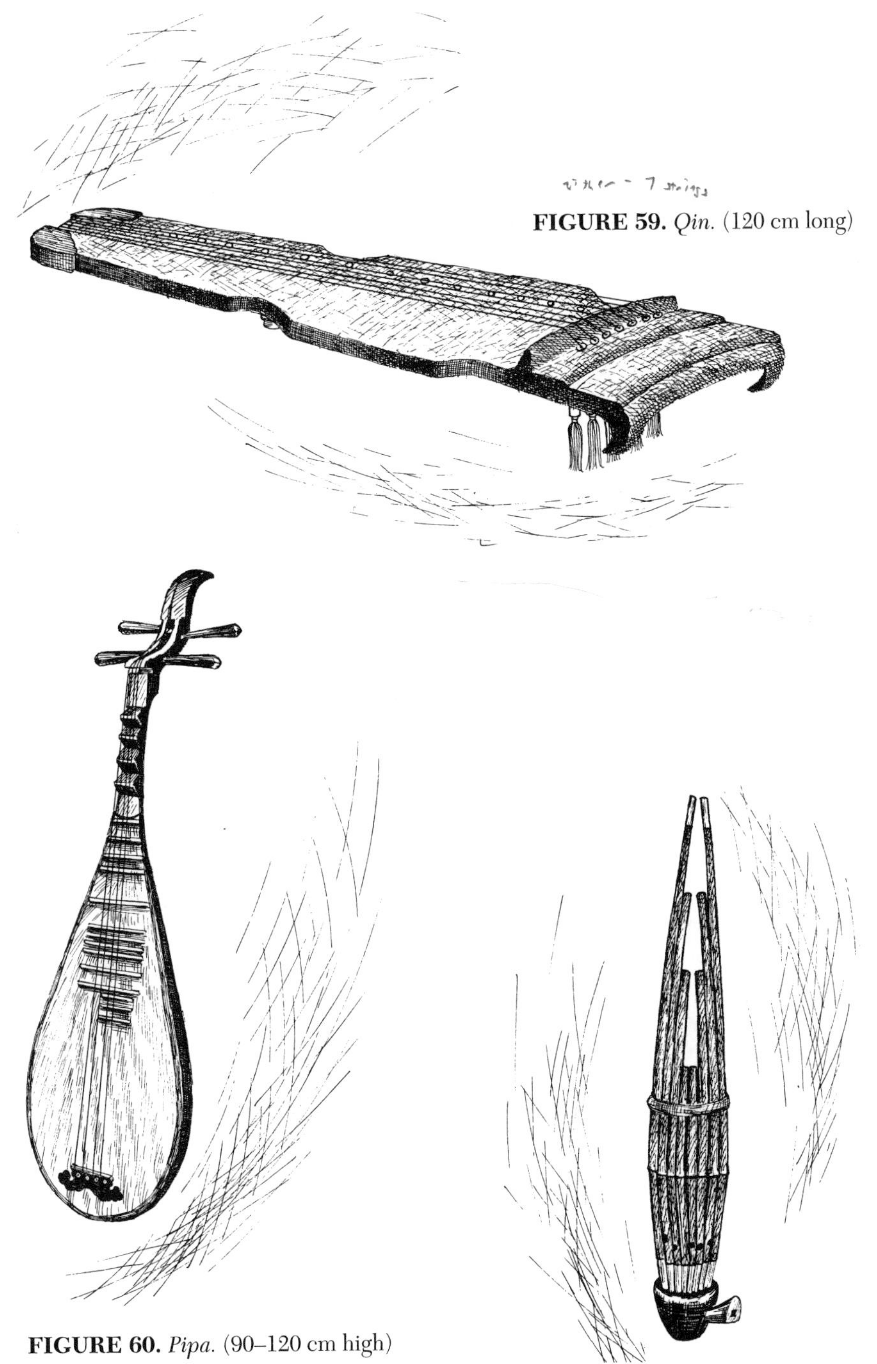

FIGURE 59. *Qin.* (120 cm long)

FIGURE 60. *Pipa.* (90–120 cm high)

FIGURE 61. *Sheng.* (46–56 cm high)

scene or followed by an apprentice carrying this lovely instrument. Unlike the other zithers of China, the *qin* has no bridges. Rather, it is played by touching the strings along and between thirteen positions marked by ivory dots inlaid on the side of the instrument. Although the *qin* is played in this divisive manner, its seven strings are tuned according to the cyclic principles (C, D, E, G, A, c, d). Some scholars claim that the many sliding effects, harmonics, and other special strokes used by both hands were derived in the international period from the *gamaka* ornamentations of India.

Although no *qin* music survives from Confucian times, the notation used during the Sung dynasty (960–1279) shows a system of symbols that look like Chinese characters but actually are artificial constructs that indicate simultaneously the note, the fingering, and the stroke to be used.

Since the classics were written by scholars in Confucian-oriented courts, they do not give a complete picture of the musical life of ancient China. For example, outside of the few folk festivals already mentioned, the music of the peasants went unnoticed, although it is said that many ancient poems were court versions of folk songs. Nevertheless, by at least the third century B.C. the basic categories of court music were codified. The two principal divisions were ritual music (*yayue*) and banquet music (*yenyue*). Within the Confucian ritual were found six dances, divided into military (*wuwu*) and civil (*wenwu*) forms. Over the centuries there were changes in the precise meanings and contents of common and court music, ritual and banquet music, and the civil and military dances, but the distinctions themselves survived until the twentieth century. We discuss them first as they were systematized during the Han dynasty (202 B.C.–120 A.D.).

Because of the destruction of many books and instruments under Qin-shi-huangdi in the short Qin dynasty (221-206 B.C.), the court music of the Jiou period disappeared; but the idea of court music was far from dead in the great intellectual revival under the Han ruler Wu-di (140–87 B.C.). A governmental office of music (*yuefu*) was established, the job of which was to set the correct pitch of the *lu*'s, supervise of all ceremonies, and also collect regional popular and folk music as well as poetry for court songs. The basic *lu* pipe preserved in this office was also used as a standard measure for length and weight. Thus the music office was a bureau of the Office of Weights and Measurements and remained so through many dynasties even though, in the later Han period, bronze bells were used as a standard for pitch in place of the *lu*'s.

The orchestras used in the Han official court rituals and banquets were quite large and, somewhat like Western symphony orchestras, consisted of large numbers of string and wind players plus a backing of percussionists. (The instruments, of course, were of the types mentioned earlier; thus their sound was totally different from their modern Western counterparts.) The ritual dance troupe was also generally large. In both cases the number of participants was governed by Confucian numerology.

Non-Confucian musics were found in certain warrior dances (not the *wuwu* already mentioned) whose accompaniment relied heavily on stone and metal instruments, and in the banquet music of the women's quarters. In the latter the sound of strings and winds prevailed. The ladies sang songs based on folk texts to create a lighthearted mood. Theatricals had already been known in the Jiou dynasty and continued to find a place in the court, although the great flourishing of Chinese drama was centuries ahead.

By the end of the Han period, the Chinese Empire had reached its maximum size and surpassed its contemporary giant, the Roman Empire, in territory, population, and power. As Chinese armies and foreign traders returned from Central Asia and Northern India, they brought with them many exotic items, including "barbarian" instruments such as a crooked-neck relative of the *pipa* lute (Plate XXIV, Figure 60) around the second century B.C. and, in the first century A.D., a new religion, Buddhism. When the Han dynasty began to break up and the barbarians themselves invaded the borderlands of China with renewed vigor, the effects of this new religion and the new musics began to change the surface of Chinese music. It was the Six Dynasties period (220–589 A.D.) that saw the struggle of the old ways against an ever-increasing influx of new ideas. In music, however, as in many other basic Chinese attitudes, the foundations laid in the more insular formative period remained essentially the same during the international period that followed.

The International Period (Fifth Century to Tenth Century)

The two major areas of cultural and political vulnerability in China were its western and northern borders. During the Six Dynasties period the Chinese heartland was no longer unified; hence we find the North China kingdoms were heavily influenced by music from both border areas; the southern kingdoms held as best they could to the old court and popular traditions, although they also were affected by the flood of new ideas coming over the Western trade routes. The influences from the north consisted primarily of militaristic drum, trumpet, and oboe music, including Tartar cavalry bands. The Western influences included Indian music theory, particularly as it related to Buddhist chanting. The main streams of Western music came from the Central Asian Gandharan, Iranian, and Tokharian cultures. These traditions came into China by three main routes: via the trade cities of Khotan (now Hotien) to the south (third to fifth centuries), Kuche (Kucha) in the center (fourth through eighth century), and Turpan (Turfan) to the north (fifth through ninth centuries). Although all these towns are now only dust mounds in the deserts, their artifacts and cave paintings, along with the larger Buddhist cave paintings such as Dunhuang in China proper, reveal a host of new instruments, including cymbals, the Assyrian angle harp (*konghou*), and a variety of plucked lutes, some of which have been traced back as far as ancient Egypt.

It was the short Sui dynasty (589–618) that began to reunify China. In the process, court music was revived, this time with many of the new instruments added or with entirely new music ensembles imported from outside China. All these national musics were organized by the government into seven (and later nine) kinds of music. The codification and flourishing of international music in China, however, occurred in the brilliant Tang dynasty (618–907) that followed.

Some idea of the international scope of the Tang musical world may be gleaned from a listing of the ten kinds of music (*shibuji*) found in the government music bureau at the time of the famous ruler Xuan Zong (712–756). The most distant musics were those of a band of five instruments from Samarkand, beyond the Pamir mountains, and of another group from Bokhara, still farther west. Kashi (Kashgar), at the doorway of the Western world, sent yet another music. The trade centers of Kuche and Turpan each had orchestras at the court (Khotan by this time was destroyed). A sixth music came from India to the southwest; another came from Korea to the northeast. One group of musicians specialized in a music that combined Chinese and Kuche styles. Indigenous Chinese folk music from earlier periods was yet another category, and finally, a large orchestra using 25 different kinds of instruments was dedicated to performing Chinese court music. In addition to these ten official kinds of music, there are records of musical tribute coming from Tibet and the kingdoms of Southeast Asia. Each of these groups maintained its own repertoire, instruments, performers, and dancers. Even the color of their costumes varied. Truly this was an international period, and the fads for various "Western" musics and manners that ran through the populace were the subject of many essays and reproving poems by classical scholars of the time.

This host of foreign and native musicians resided primarily in the capital city of Changan, supported out of tax funds as government slaves. But even slavery had its ranks, and many musicians rose to comfortable positions by way of their musical or political talents. In addition, there were a great many musicians and dancers dedicated to purely secular entertainment. In the days of Xuan Zong, the section of Changan called the Pear Garden (*Liyuan*) was a huge school for the training of such personnel. Its music was a synthesis of foreign and Chinese secular styles, and it is said that the emperor himself taught there.

Since the days of Gaozi (618–626), selected girls (*gungnu*) had been taught music in a special school inside the court (the *neijiaofang*). One of the earliest extant pictures of Chinese secular music shows a group of these ladies entertaining the emperor.[23] In another school outside the court (the *waijiaofang*), professional female musicians were trained; these became a source for the teahouse girls in the later Tang dynasty and are distant ancestors of the famous Japanese geisha.

[23] See Shigeo Kishibe, "A Chinese Painting of the T'ang Court Women's Orchestra," in *The Commonwealth of Music*, ed. Gustave Reese and Rose Brandel (New York: The Free Press of Glencoe, 1965), 104–17.

To the basic distinction between court music (*yayue*) and common music (*suyue*) of previous eras, the Tang dynasty added the category of foreign music (*huyue*). While we can see each of these as a separate style in some of the musics listed here, the important characteristic of the period was the manner in which the three musics exchanged idioms and instruments. This adventuresome spirit resulted in new instruments as well, such as a set of sixteen iron slabs (*fangxiang*) used in imitation of the bell and stone chime sets of before. The greatest changes instrumentally, however, came in the chordophones.

We have mentioned the appearance of harps and plucked lutes. The former are the only harps to play any significant role in Chinese music. Among the lutes, the *srga-snyan*—still used in Tibet (see Example 6–2)—is of interest not only because it is mentioned in Tang documents but also because it may have led to the better known three-stringed lute tradition of later Chinese and Japanese times (see Figure 63 and Figure 72). The four-stringed pear-shaped *pipa* (Plate XXIV, Figure 60) was the dominant lute of Tang times and was used extensively in ensembles. It also had a repertoire of descriptive solo pieces and was used to accompany songs. In Tang sources we begin to learn the names of pieces, their composers, and the events for which specific pieces were written. In the repertoire of the court ritual music, for example, there are titles and descriptions of eight pieces played without strings as "standing music," probably outside in the courtyard, and six pieces played as "sitting music" inside the palace halls. Famous emperors and empresses are credited with the composition of such popular pieces as "The Lion Dance of the Five Directions" or "The Battleline–Smashing Music." The choreography of the dances required from 4 to 180 dancers. The larger groups sometimes formed letters in a manner familiar to viewers of American football half-time extravaganzas.

A few Tang documents give general descriptions of the manner in which pieces were performed. Useful detail about performance practice, however, is lacking except as it is implied by the imitations of Tang music found in the surviving court orchestras of Korea and Japan. There have been attempts in China to revive certain Tang popular melodies primarily as they appear in collections of later dynasties. At present the closest we can come to the spirit of such Tang dance pieces as "A Night of Flowers and Moonlight by the Spring River" is to read the poetry of Li Po or gaze at Tang clay figurines with their flying sleeves, curved bodies, and aristocratic heads encased in haute coiffure.

Since the huge and complicated art-music establishment of the Tang period was supported by tax funds, it declined rapidly as soon as the imperial fortunes began to wane. The singing girls of the court (*jinu*) became teahouse singing girls (*jiguan*); male musicians from the court found themselves at liberty to starve or to find new audiences. Theaters and brothels, both of which had always been present in some form in China, began to absorb more of the governmental musicians and dancers, and the center of Chinese musical interest shifted from Confucian rites and courtly life to the demands of the public stage or the homes of wealthy merchants.

PLATE XXV. China

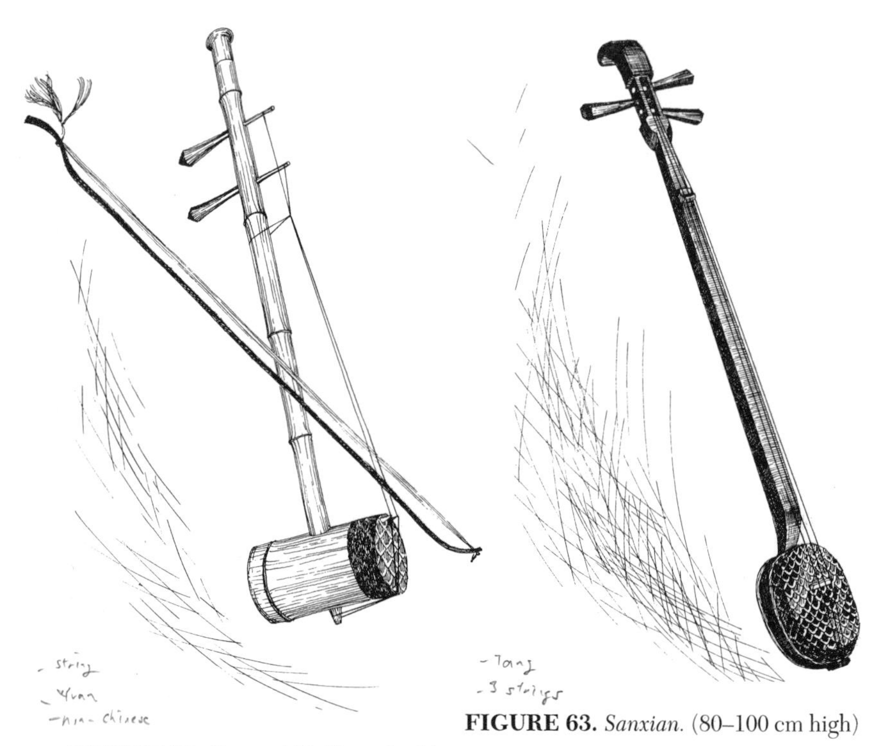

FIGURE 62. *Huqin.* (63–70 cm high)

FIGURE 63. *Sanxian.* (80–100 cm high)

FIGURE 64. *Yueqin.* (62 cm high)

FIGURE 65. *Bangu.* (25 cm diameter)

During the chaotic Five Dynasties and Ten Kingdoms period (907–979), a few more "barbarian" instruments such as the two-stringed Mongolian fiddle were adopted in China (the *huqin,* Plate XXV, Figure 62), but this time such additions are first noted in the theater rather than in the court. China had passed its peak as a land of cosmopolitan taste and as a pacesetter for the Asian world. Out of the new Chinese society, however, came the standard practices of a national style that are still in effect today.

The National Period (Tenth through Nineteenth Centuries)

The Sung dynasty (960–1279) brought to China a new stability and prosperity that were based primarily on military and mercantile activity. The court periodically refurbished Confucian music, although its main musical contributions came through new theoretical studies and indirectly through its support of huge encyclopedic and historical compilations and the fostering of new poetry forms. The latter developed along two lines, each of which reflected important factors in the further development of Chinese music. One form was chanted in such a way as to exploit the basic tone levels of the Chinese language. This form was called *shi,* a term applied to many earlier poetry styles as well as to this late Tang and early Sung development. Some feel the relation of speech tones to melodic structure has been fundamental to Chinese music since at least this era. The other form of poetry, *ci,* also uses the tone system, but it originated in songs sung in the entertainment districts of the cities and reflected a new emphasis on urban secular music. The freer meters and colloquial language of the *ci* were important factors in the theatrical music that was soon to dominate the Chinese scene. The use of standard melodies for the singing of different poems in both the *shi* and *ci* traditions also became idiomatic of Chinese vocal music, particularly as it appeared in drama.

Sung dynasty writers distinguished between two kinds of drama, the southern (*nanqu*) and northern (*beiqu* or *zaqu*) styles. Although both used the *ci* poetical forms, the southern school of favored the pentatonic scale and emphasized flute accompaniment, whereas the northern one used a seven-tone scale and the *pipa.* In addition to these two kinds of theaters, there were lute-accompanied storytellers and a variety of street and restaurant entertainments. In all, the Sung cities were as lusty and gay as eighteenth-century London.

When the Mongols under Jenghiz Khan, and later Kublai Khan, put an end to Sung glories, they by no means stopped the growth of Chinese opera. The infusion of Mongol lutes and percussion instruments, in fact, was an important contribution to opera in the succeeding Yuan dynasty (1279–1368). Yuan drama (*Yuan qu*) continued the distinction of northern (*zaqu*) and southern (*xiwen* or *nanxi*) styles. A freer *sanqu* poetry form was used for texts sung to *qupai* tunes that had specific emotional or situational connotations and thus operated as repertoire-wide clues to the meanings of aria—an important function, since the dialect of the text was not necessarily that of the audience. The acrobats and pantomimists of the street found their place in the opera, with a concomitant brightening of the productions.

Although the emphasis of this period was on vocal music, instrumental forms existed as well. For example, the *pipa* lute and *qin* zither, although used for vocal accompaniment, developed extensive repertoires. During the Sung dynasty, both manuscripts and the first printed music included instrumental pieces, some of which claimed to have been copied from Tang sources.[24] Many collections survive from the succeeding Ming dynasty (1368–1628). The composite form of *qin* notation used in these works has already been discussed (see p. 182). Other instrumental notation used a symbol for each note in a five- or seven-note scale and named at the start of the piece the type of scale or mode desired. Tempo and meter markings also appeared, but rhythmic details of the melodies were lacking, leading to a variety of interpretations over the centuries. Nevertheless, the two basic types of instrumental solo music found in the Sung and Ming times have remained dominant to the present day. The first type is the descriptive or impressionist piece. The *pipa* is particularly famous for its battle pieces, in which the clash of armor, zinging of arrows, and cries of the wounded are all depicted; the *qin* tends more toward impressionistic scenes like "The Drunken Fisherman." The second type of solo instrumental music is the abstract piece, best known in a kind of variation form played on the *qin*. The social context of instrumental music was originally the court, but the merchant class also enjoyed such music. This led in the Ming and Qing (1644–1911) periods to a kind of bourgeois chamber music[25] using *pipa* plus newer theater instruments such as the two-stringed fiddles (the *erhu* and *huqin*, Figure 62), the three-stringed plucked lute (*sanxian*, Figure 63), and the "moon" guitar, with four strings in double courses (*yueqin*, Figure 64). Flutes included the end-blown *xiao* with six finger holes. The *xiao* is noted for its three extraneous holes: The two at the end of the instrument are used to tie a long silk tassel, which adds a decorative touch to the performance; the third, just below the mouth hole, is covered with thin rice paper, which adds a gentle buzzing quality to the instrument's tone. Some of the chamber music using these various instruments is purely instrumental; other pieces have a vocal part. In either case, much of the chamber music repertoire is derived from the all-pervading style of Chinese opera.

The generic term for Chinese opera is *xiqu*. A survey of its history since the fading of Yuan drama reveals some 300 regional popular theatricals that go under the generic term *difangxi*. Most of these are small theatricals amounting to folk dramas; others are urban professional theatricals. Many of these forms

[24] See further Rulan Chiao Pian, *Song* [sic] *Dynasty Musical Sources and Their Interpretation* (Cambridge, Mass.: Harvard University Press, 1967).

[25] See Lawrence Witzleben, "Jiangnam Sizhu Music Clubs in Shanghai," *Ethnomusicology*, 31/2 (1987), and Hai-Hsung Yao, "Music in Ming Daily Life," *Asian Music*, 23/2 (1992).

survive today and are generally known by the name of the location of their origin. Since Beijing opera (*jingxi* or *jingju*) is the best known form in the West and the dominant form in China today, both our historical and musical discussions concentrate on that genre.[26]

Four major regional theatricals set the state for the rise of Beijing opera: *kunqu, yiyangqiang, bangziqiang,* and *pihuang.*

Kunqu was a form of theater popular with the aristocracy in the sixteenth century and derived its name from the city in which it is said to have begun, Kunshan in the northeast coastal province of Jiangxi (Kiangsu).[27] Its texts and musical style reflect the preferences of the class of its patrons. Delicate falsetto voices are usually accompanied by a flute of the horizontal (*dizi*) or end-blown (*xiao*) type, although the *pipa* plucked lute, *sheng* mouth organ, and even the plebian *sanxian* plucked lute can be found in regional forms of the genre. The term *guan,* which usually refers to a double-reed aerophone of the type surviving in Korean and Japanese court music, is used for a free-reed pipe that sometimes accompanies *kunqu.*[28] Since a *kunqu* text is in classical Chinese and thus is (and was) not understood by many listeners, the vocal line often treats one syllable melismatically (like the coloratura tradition of Italian opera) without concern for communicating the meaning of the words.

In the early sixteenth century *yiyangqiang* opera appeared in Yiyang, a city in Jiangxi province. It attempted to clarify its classical text by inserted passages call *gundao,* which were in colloquial local languages. The singing was in a more syllabic style in order to communicate better with general audiences. *Yiyangqiang* orchestras were bombastic and more filled with percussion instruments than those of *kunqu,* and a unison chorus (*bangqiang*) was added, a tradition that still survives in some regional operas of Jiangxi, Hunan, and Sichuan (Szechwan). Perhaps the Ming period theatrical that was most influential on a later development of Chinese opera was the so-called clapper opera (*bangziqiang*), which seems to have originated in the northwest province of Shensi. Its name relates to wooden clappers that are part of the accompanying ensemble. The *yueqin* plucked lute (Figure 64) is basic to the string section.

By the middle of the Qing (Ch'ing) dynasty period (1644–1911) some regional theatricals, particularly those from Guangdong (Canton), included in their ensembles a "western zither" (*yangqin*). Some writers call it a "butterfly harp" because of its shape, but note that it is not a harp but a hammered dulcimer—a Chinese version of a Near Eastern *santur* (Plate XIII, Figure 33) that

[26] The author is particularly grateful for the historical information concerning this topic found in the works of the Australian scholar Colin P. Mackerras, such as his *The Rise of the Peking Opera* (Oxford: Clarendon Press, 1972) and "The Growth of the Chinese Regional Drama in the Ming and Ch'ing," *Journal of Oriental Studies,* 9/1 (1971).

[27] The student of European opera history will recognize such a tradition of nomenclature, for we speak of Venetian or Neapolitan opera for the same reason. The parallels between Chinese and European opera history becomes more evident as one delves deeper into both fields.

[28] The closest relative to the single-reed form of the *kuan* is the *pi saw* mentioned in Chapter 5.

was imported into China in the eighteenth century. In that same period many regional theatricals became classified not as clapper operas but rather as *pihuang,* an abbreviation of the two terms *xipi* and *erhuang.* These terms refer to two styles of singing that we discuss later. The origin of the terms is unknown and a direct translation of their meaning is of little help (*xipi,* 西 皮, means "western skin" and *erhuang,* 二 黃, is "two yellows"). Interpretations vary from opinions that they may be regional musical jargon to other views that see them as shorthand references to various cities or as attempts to reproduce in Chinese character form the sounds of pronunciations in local dialects. Whatever their historical origin, they did become basic nomenclature in Chinese opera, and the *pihuang* musical syndrome joined a host of other theatrical traditions in a migration to the more lucrative metropolitan world of the capital. There, all styles combined in the eighteenth and nineteenth centuries into *jingxi,* Beijing (Peking) opera.

If our historical introduction has seemed full of names of places and genres, you must realize we are dealing with a tradition that developed in a period longer than that of the entire history of European opera and involved the regional preferences over some 500 years of peoples from many Chinese provinces, most of which contained larger populations than that of Europe. In that context our introductory remarks have been brief indeed. They must serve our goal, however, which is to prepare us for a discussion of the musical aspects of this vast tradition.

Although Chinese opera includes instrumental music for dances, pantomimes, and interludes as well as vocal recitatives, its characteristic musical styles are found in arias. There are two general approaches to the settings of arias. The first, called *lianqu,* selects from a body of standard pieces a set of works that are appropriate to the moods of a given drama. This kind of structure is only possible when the text uses a rather rigid poetical form. Hence the *lianqu* were used in the oldest opera forms, like those of the Sung dynasty around the twelfth century and the *kunqu* Ming opera form we mentioned earlier. Although this standard-piece approach is linked to the court poetry tradition, it has a basis as well in the structure of folk theatricals.

The second approach, called *banqiang,* uses stereotyped melodies rather than complete pieces. These melodies are subject to extensive variation, depending on the dramatic situation. Rhythm plays a very important role in determining how these tunes are used. This approach began in the Ming dynasty but prevailed most strongly during the Qing, when the clapper opera tradition flourished. A unique and extreme example of rhythmic emphasis is found in the *gaoqiang* opera of the Sichuan and Hunan provinces, which originally used only gongs and drums as accompaniment. (Modern productions of such operas have added complete songs in the *lianqu* style accompanied by winds and strings.) In truth, both basic approaches, the complete-song and the stereotyped-tune-and-rhythm methods are found within one opera genre today. It is the mixture of these approaches, along with various features of the northern and southern styles, that make traditional opera interesting. Beijing opera, as the cumulative tradition in the capital of the country, offers the greatest variety of sights and sounds—from deafening preludes of crashing cymbals and stages filled with sword-swinging acrobats to pathetic arias sung by a comely girls or a female impersonator standing before a set consisting of only two chairs and a cloth-covered table. In discussing its music, we start with the orchestra.

Two basic kinds of instrumentation are used in Beijing opera. The first is used for battles or military entrances and consists of a battery of gongs, cymbals, and drums, plus the double-reed *suona,* already familiar to us from the Near East and South Asia (see Plate X, Figure 25). The other ensemble is used for all civil and domestic scenes and, therefore, is heard more often. Its instrumentation varies with each number according to the mood; however, two kinds of instruments are basic: a time beater and a bowed lute.

The most common time beater is a *bangu* (*danpigu,* Plate XXV, Figure 65). It consists of a skin stretched over a set of wooden wedges bound in a circle and so hollowed out that only a small part of the skin covers a cavity at the center of the drum. The sharp, dry, cracking sound produced by this instrument penetrates nicely through the other instrumental sounds—as it should, since the *bangu* player is the leader of the orchestra. The rhythm the musician plays (see Example 6–6) often determines the nature of a piece. Additional time beaters used in conjunction with or in substitution for the *bangu* include wooden blocks, thick wooden sticks, or various sets of wooden clappers often played in the manner of castanets. The generic term for most of the clappers is *ban* 板 (a term using a different Chinese character from that of the *ban* in *bangu* 班 鼓).

One common bowed lute in Chinese music is the *huqin* (Plate XXV, Figure 62), the barbarian fiddle borrowed from the Mongols around the Yuan dynasty. Its pegs are in the back of its neck so the two strings, tuned in fifths, are aligned vertically over the snakeskin soundboard. This position allowed the bow to pass between them rather than over them in the manner of Near Eastern and Western bowed lutes. The *huqin* is played with the finger along the strings like the *rebab* (see p. 44), rather than pressed against a fingerboard like the Western violin. A smaller *junghu* version of this instrument is used in Beijing opera. Such an instrument leads the ensemble in performing the stereotyped melodies as set in the matrix of the time beaters. It is often doubled by a larger two-stringed *erhu,* which sounds an octave lower and is similar to the *huqin* in appearance, except its body may be either hexagonal or round. There are further variants in shape, size, and number of strings.

The plucked lutes most commonly found in opera orchestras are the *pipa* (Figure 60), the *yueqin* (Figure 64), and the *sanxian* (Figure 63). The *yueqin* has a thin metal plate suspended inside its wooden body to add resonance. A similar metal strip is suspended inside the neck of the larger northern form of

EXAMPLE 6–6. A *xipi* aria from Scene 12 of *The Ruse of the Empty City [Kongchengji]* (Smithsonian/Folkways 8882, side 2, track 1; book cassette, track 24). Transcription and sounds used by permission.[29]

[29] Bell Yung's translation of the line by General Ssu Mai-i is "Here is this general on horseback watching the situation. He sees Chu Ko Liang playing the *qin* with only two boy attendants and decides to enter the city." The sound "sa.sa" is the army calling to kill but Ssu Ma-i calls for restraint. The notation is one whole tone higher than the recording used in order to conform with the traditional Chinese uses of Western notation and with Example 6–7. The modern Chinese convention of writing music in a 2/4 time signature (see Example 6–7) is derived from a nineteenth-century adoption of the French Chevé system (see *The New Grove Dictionary of Music and Musicians*, Vol. 7, p. 99). It is convenient but reflects poorly the indigenous concept of rhythm. Example 6–6 is set in 2/2 time in order to make the rhythm of the percussion part easier to follow. Traditionally the time beaters mark the first beat of each "measure" as seen in the clapper part of Example 6–7. The Example 6–6 transcription is what the author actually hears happening in the recording.

the *sanxian,* although this is not found in the smaller southern version. Either style may appear in the opera accompaniment.

The double-reed *suona* has already been mentioned as the aerophone used in ensembles accompanying military scenes. In other types of scenes the only melodic aerophone is the *di* or *dizi* flute mentioned earlier. Besides its use in the older *kunqu* style, it can still occasionally be heard in other opera traditions in a solo or duet backing for an aria. Normally, like all other melodic instruments listed so far, it plays a heterophonic version of the main melody. The *sheng* mouth organ is also occasionally used melodically in opera, although it usually adds harmony in fourths or fifths.

Various sizes of cymbals (*bo*) and thin knobless gongs (*luo*) appear in most Chinese opera ensembles. Their most important uses are in the long percussion overtures that begin most scenes, or as accompaniment for recitatives. At the end of each phrase in a recitative, the time beater will signal it with short clashes on cymbals and gongs. These sounds are functionally rather like the chords played on the harpsichord in eighteenth-century Western opera recitatives.

The voice quality and range used in a Beijing opera depend on the character portrayed. Heroines may use a high thin tone derived from the stylizations of the female impersonators who dominated the feminine roles until the mid-twentieth century. Military heroes, by contrast, may emphasize a powerful voice quality that would damage the vocal cords of a Western singer. Such vocal styles are like those of Western opera in one important respect: They are artificial; that is, they are the result of deliberate training. They require years of rigorous practice and, when brought to perfection, they are capable of portraying a wide range of emotions. In this the singers of Chinese opera are aided by the specific connotations of the stereotyped melodies they perform.

In terms of vocal music, traditional Chinese opera consists of recitatives with percussion interjections followed by appropriate arias. In Beijing opera there are some 30 different standard aria melodies, of different moods, to which the text of a given opera situation can be attached. Poetically, the texts of almost all arias are based on a series of rhymed couplets with seven or ten syllables in each line, although they may be divided between two singers or split into dialogue, which can even leave the first line of a couplet in one aria and the second in the aria that follows with poetically unrelated dialogue in between. Melodically, arias are usually classified under the two basic types mentioned earlier, the *xipi* and *erhuang.* In musical analysis these two types can be distinguished by their tonal emphases and certain melodic or rhythmic conventions. (Similar criteria could be applied to eighteenth-century Italian opera, although the specific results would certainly be different.) The average Chinese opera enthusiasts are not scholars, however; they learn the distinctive characteristics of an aria subliminally by hearing it used in fairly consistent conventional dramatic situations. (Just as, even without knowing musical theory, let alone the language, one can recognize a love duet or a vengeance aria in traditional Italian opera.)

The dramatic function of an aria is most directly implied by its style and the tempo of its rhythmic accompaniment.

Example 6–6 illustrates a typical *xipi* melody with its tonal emphasis on G sharp and C sharp. It is pentatonic except for the ornamental *"bian"* tone A in the final phrase.[30] A mild heterophony between the singer and accompaniment is common in such aharmonic linear traditions as Chinese opera. The density of the rhythmic accompaniment makes a strong cadence with the cymbals before starting the next verse. Example 6–7 is clearly an *erhuang* aria in

EXAMPLE 6–7. An *erhuang* aria from *Entering the Palace Twice [Erjingong]* (Transcription, text, and recording courtesy of Nancy A. Guy. Recorded in 1988 during a performance in Taiwan; book cassette, track 25). Used by permission of Guy.[31]

[30] It is marked as B in Chinese notation of the aria.

[31] Guy's text translation is "It is not that I am grieving over personal matters. It is because within my court there is no peace." The text mood is somber because the Empress Dowager is realizing her father has tricked her and is planning to usurp the throne by dethroning her infant son.

the ears of Chinese opera fans, although they may not know the major sonic clue is its modal emphasis on B and E. The style of the rhythmic accompaniment often reflects the nature of the text and dramatic situation. Both our examples use *yuanban*, "steady" or "level clapper," rhythm. This is common to narrative arias. More dramatic areas might use *yaoban*, "unsteady" or "wavering clappers." An aria indicated in a libretto as *xipi manban* ("slow clappers") would be lyrical; a highly animated aria would have its rhythm marked as *liushui* ("flowing clappers") or *guaiban* ("rapid clappers"); and, if there is to be a sung interjection on a different topic in the middle of one aria or between two arias, the interjection would be accompanied by *daopan* ("guiding or inverted clapper [rhythms]"). One can double the variety of choices in the Chinese opera tradition by applying such rhythmic accompaniments to *erhuang* melodies instead. There are, of course, further arias and rhythmic patterns that are used in special dramatic situations.[32] On the level of this brief overview of the tradition, however, we need realize only that all these aria forms are not specific melodies but rather combinations of tonal, melodic, and rhythmic conventions that make distinctions possible in the ears of Chinese opera fans. Because of this, individual performers can sing a well-known aria in a way that

[32] For rhythmic examples see Rulan C. Pian, "The Function of Rhythm in the Peking Opera," in *The Musics of Asia*, ed. Joe Maceda (Manila: National Music Council of the Philippines, 1971).

may differ not only from renditions of other performers but also from previous performances by the same artist.[33]

Our preliminary remarks and the two short excerpts from two arias can give us only an inkling of the organization of Beijing opera's music, but we may now know enough to be able to recognize the musical and theatrical validity of the tradition. The use of connotative melodies is of great importance in the appreciation of a given situation; and the use of rhythm to demarcate melodies and give them a sense of progression is as valid here as it is, in different forms, in the time cycles of Indonesian *gamelan* music and the *tala* of India. Add to these elements the gorgeous costumes and a troupe of acrobats, and you have good theater by any standards. It is our contention that it is also good music.

The Chinese narrative tradition does not always require such an elaborate setting. In addition to many kinds of small regional theatricals, there are hand and shadow puppet plays that use small ensembles of opera instruments backstage to accompany the narrator-manipulator. There are also at least two major traditions of solo narrators. The first, sometimes called *tanci,* is that of one performer who accompanies his or her songs, which are usually strophic, with a *pipa* lute that plays a steady stream of melody heterophonically related to the narrator's own short melodic phrases. The other narrative tradition is called *daguci* after the name of a small flat drum (*dagu*) that is usually used as accompaniment. The singer often plays a castanet with the left hand and the drum with the right. A *sanxian* may also accompany the strophic songs. Although both these traditions have their professional performers, musical storytelling as such, since at least the Sung dynasty, has belonged to the itinerant street musicians whose appeal was to the peasant and the passerby. The roles of both singers and their audience have changed in the contemporary scene.

The World Music Period (Twentieth Century)

After dashing through thousands of years of one culture's music, the topic of a single century may contain detail of little long-range historical value. Still, this book is written at the end of the twentieth century. Its summaries may prove useful to those of us who have lived through it and those of future generations who may wonder what it was like.

In 1911 the last of the Chinese dynasties fell and a republic was declared. The stormy years that followed witnessed sporadic attempts at Westernization that were compromised by internal strife and external pressure. Western music, which had appeared in China as early as the Ming period, still found little favor with the general public, but the Chinese elite accepted it along with men's suits and automobiles as symbols of Western culture. Western

[33] Variations in a melody sung by the same singer at different times can be seen in Liu T'ien-hua, *Selections from the Repertoire of Operatic and Terpsichorean Melodies of Mei Lan-fang* (Peiping, 1929). See also Rulan Pian, "Aria Structural Patterns in the Peking Opera," in *Chinese and Japanese Music-Dramas,* Michigan Papers in Chinese Studies, no. 19 (1975).

music teachers began to appear in the cities of China, and Chinese students went to Western conservatories. Orchestras were formed, musicales were given, and talk of a synthesis of Chinese and Western music was heard from both Asian and Western writers and musicians.

The search for a new East/West art was not particularly successful in either world. On the peasant level in China, however, a new tradition of unison singing arose as greater numbers of Chinese became involved in civil construction, civil wars, and the struggle against the Japanese. At the same time, the harmonic tradition of Christian hymns became part of the learning of a new rising educated class. Perhaps the most famous and most appropriate symbol of the musical spirit and style of the times is the patriotic march shown in Example 6–8. It was composed in 1934 by Nieh Erh to a text by Tian Han, a modern

EXAMPLE 6–8. The national anthem of People's Republic of China.[34] Track 26

[34] The mainland English version of the text is "Arise you that refuse to be slaves! With our own flesh and blood build us a new Great Wall. The Chinese nation is facing the most crucial hour, everyone feels impelled to let out a final cry of defiance. Arise! Arise! Arise! Millions of us, with a single purpose, braving the enemy's gunfire, advance! Braving the enemy's gunfire. Advance! Advance! Advance!

Chinese playwright. The piece was motivated by increasing confrontations between China and Japan (much as "The Star Spangled Banner" was one result of British intervention in the United States), and in 1949 it became the national anthem for the People's Republic of China on the mainland. In the example, the first line of the melody has had added to the Western five-line notation the standard modern Chinese form of number notation, which was derived from the French Chevé system. The style of this first line seems quite Western, with its four-bar phrases, major-mode implication, and a leading tone, G sharp. Thereafter, however, the melody becomes intriguingly Chinese, with a pentatonic scale, varying phrase lengths, and different rhythmic patterns.

The communist victory on mainland China in 1949 is of special interest to us because it made a Marxist-Leninist doctrine of music the national policy for a country that contains one third of the world's population. Chairman Mao Tse-tung (or Zedong) of the Chinese Communist party explained the function of the arts is to serve the whole mass of the nation's people and to reflect the class struggle as well as the triumphs of socialism.[35] The musical results of this admonition are most easily noted in modern operas. Many of the arias are quite traditional in their melodic and rhythmic names, but now the characters who are to sing them are workers or soldiers rather than members of the nobility or mythological characters.[36] At the same time, larger orchestras are used, including Western instruments and new families of traditional stringed instruments that have been constructed to reflect the communal spirit of Chinese society. Large choruses now appear frequently and sing spirited unison or harmonized pieces that grew out of the protest tradition of previous decades mentioned earlier. Acrobats remain popular in Chinese opera, although their costumes are modern peasant or military clothes, and the influence of Russian ballet is frequently evident. In a word, Chinese opera on the mainland has continued in its tradition of creative adoption and adaptation of topics and materials that are socioeconomically viable in the period in which they were created. To see and hear traditional Chinese opera, one must follow the marginal survival principle and seek out performances in Taiwan, Hong Kong, Singapore, or New York.

In the midst of this musical reconstruction period we should note the position of the composer, whose duties now are to serve the people in a new society. A study of earlier Chinese (or even Italian Neapolitan) opera traditions shows that the composer was seldom given special attention as compared with the prestige of the singer. (One could also make this comparison in most popular music in the world.) In modern communist communities such as China's, one often finds that the creation of an opera or some other large work is assigned to a composition committee rather than to an individual. Thus the person employed to create the music (known in the West in the singular as *the*

[35] See Mao Tse-tung, *On Literature and the Arts* (Peking: Foreign Language Press, 1960).

[36] For librettos and polemics concerning the new Chinese operas, see *The Drama Review*, 15/3 (1971). See also the controversy over reconstructed Beijing opera in *A Great Revolution on the Cultural Front* (Peking: Foreign Language Press, 1965).

composer) is placed in the position of other skillful artisans in other trades, whose rewards are judged according to their talent for serving, together with others, the needs of the people, rather than by demonstrating special "genius" or "originality." Such a position for a composer returns him or her to a role not unlike the one noted in our earlier studies of tribal or village musicians in Oceania and thus gives the composer a strong sense of sociological function in an ever-changing world, although it also places external restraints on the idioms in which he or she may work. Indeed, the individual sometimes was absorbed into a composition committee whose job it was to create a symphony or opera filled with socialist realistic meaning but devoid of the cult of personality.

The nature of compositions themselves in contemporary mainland China reflects the goals of the new system, as suggested by the titles of such works as "The Sacred War Symphony," "The Yellow River Concerto," and "The Ming Tombs Reservoir Cantata," or of the opera "Raid on the White Tiger Regiment" and the ballet "The Red Detachment of Women." Ballet has become particularly useful as a new idiom because it easily communicates social messages without the operatic problems of the many dialects of China. The challenge of so many languages and minority peoples in mainland China was met musically with energetic attempts to reconstruct or newly compose the idioms of the peoples involved. The soloistic and traditional instrumental traditions of various areas in China were reconstructed through a new emphasis on communal choral training and the creation of folk orchestras. The new families of different sizes of traditional instruments we noted earlier not only reflect the communal spirit but allow the composition committee to create vertically balanced sounds with materials which grew in earlier times out of a basically horizontally oriented line. Given the potentially rich sources of musical materials found in the many ethnic groups of China, it has been possible for some composer-arrangers to create quite original compositions by combining basically Western-style pieces with the sound ideals and tone qualities of indigenous musics. Because of the rather tonally conservative dogma of national policy and the importation of music teachers from neighboring Russia, much modern Chinese music at this stage sounds somewhat like Russian choral music—Rimsky-Korsakov in his "Oriental" moments—or light opera with loud sounds. However, functional music that serves the people need not be "great" music, and the cult of compositional personality and total originality, which is still found in some Western traditions, remains anathema in mainland China. One must always remember when hearing new Chinese music that its goal is to sell or reinforce national or regional ideas. In the West such music is used only to sell material goods, although there have been a growing number of popular singers who have become concerned with communicating with the masses on important social issues. It is in context of the Chinese national goals that such songs as "I'm So Happy on the Collective Farm" and "Red Is the East" make sense.[37]

[37] For tune and text, see *Songs of New China* (Peking: The Music Publishing House, 1955).

Some of these seemingly trite songs may be as valuable to their singers as are athletic team "fight songs" in Western schools or as are "We Shall Overcome," "Stand Up, Stand Up for Jesus," and "Hare Krishna" to other groups of involved people. In all these situations the functional value of the music must be considered more important than the sonic event itself. The song "Socialism Is Good" often was used to open meetings and study session of the writings of Chairman Mao.[38] During the so-called Social Revolution (1966–1976) songs in praise of Mao and of the Communist party became ever stronger.[39] At that time, eight "models" were created on which all new "art" compositions were to be based.[40] Traditional musics and performers suffered grievously.[41] After the fall of the Maoist leadership (1976) an "open door" policy developed. The West learned more about the surviving music traditions and about research centers on the many minority musics of China. At the same time Chinese were given access to modern Western music and a flood of pirated popular music tapes from Taiwan, Hong Kong, and the West filled the ears of young mainlanders.[42] The ebb and flow of governments have encouraged or suppressed musics in China for over two thousand years. In the modern world of mass communication the sounds of music cannot be stopped. For better or worse mainland China is part of the action in the pop music industry.

Overseas Chinese communities have shown special interest in furthering native Chinese traditions in the light of idioms from other parts of the world of music. There has been a tendency to emphasize music for ensembles that often include Western instruments, thus allowing tempered tuning to make strong inroads into Chinese idioms. The traditional arts of opera and solo instrumental music are still patronized, and Confucian rituals have occasionally been revived on Taiwan, somewhat in the spirit of Western collegium musicum revivals of old European traditions. In all expatriate Chinese communities forms of popular and film music combine foursquare strophic forms and international social dance rhythms with singers using hybrid vocal qualities and a mixed orchestra playing harmonized accompaniments. At the same time, composers in major Chinese communities have nurtured contemporary music in both a regional and international sense.[43]

Some say Chinese music will never return to its former greatness until its theoretical-philosophical base is restored. The same has been said, of

[38] Tune and text can be seen in Mao Yu Run, "Music under Mao," in *Asian Music,* 22/2, (1991), 114.

[39] For examples see *Songs of New China* 117–19.

[40] Five operas, one ballet, one concerto, and one orchestral work. For detail see Bell Yung's study in *Popular Chinese Literature and Performing Arts in the People's Republic of China, 1949–1979.* ed. B. McDougall (Berkeley: University of California Press, 1984).

[41] A *qin* player told me that he buried his instruments so Red Guard youths would not find them as they searched to destroy "old ideas, old culture, old customs, and old habits."

[42] See articles in *Asian Music,* 22/2 (1991).

[43] For composers from the Chinese mainland, Taiwan, Singapore, and Hong Kong, see Harrison Ryker, *New Music in the Orient* (Buren: Fritz Knuf, 1991).

course, of Western music. It seems unlikely that the *lu*'s and their cosmological significance will ever return to China, any more than the ethical power of the ancient Greek modes will ever affect the European scene again. Nevertheless, the overwhelming past and brilliant present of Chinese traditional music provide ample material for an appreciation of the musical genius of the Chinese people. Their impact on world music has been strong; and it is still evident in our last remaining area of study: the music of Manchuria, Korea, and the Asian islands.

BIBLIOGRAPHICAL AND AUDIOVISUAL NOTES

Peter Crossley-Holland provided an annotated bibliography of Western studies of Tibetan music in *Ethnomusicology,* 11/21 (1967). *Asian Music,* 10/2 (1979), is a Tibetan issue. Other articles in that journal are Lobsang P. Lhalungpa, "Tibetan Music: Secular and Sacred," 1/2 (1969), and Brian Perti, "Some Observations on the Dung Chen of the Nechung Monastery," 23/2 (1992). Other articles are Atsuko Tsukamoto, "Tibetan Buddhism in Ladakh," *Yearbook for Traditional Music,"* Vol. 15 (1983), and Dya Nasa, "Newar God of Music," *Selected Reports in Ethnomusicology,* UCLA, 8 (1990). Ter Ellingson wrote on "Music and Religion and Drums" in the *Encyclopedia of Religion* (New York: Macmillan, 1986), and his book on Tibetan music is in progress. *The Voices of Asia* (Tokyo: The Japan Foundation, 1980) has detailed studies of Mongolian split-tone singing plus photos; the sounds are heard on the CD *Folk Songs of Asia and the Pacific, Asian Cultural Centre for Unesco* (Tokyo: UFSCD 100).

Fredric Lieberman's annotated bibliography *Chinese Music* (New York: Society for Asian Music, 1970) lists 1,483 items in Chinese and European languages. Historical documents are found in Rulan Chiao Pian, *Song Dynasty Musical Sources and Their Interpretation* (Cambridge, Mass.: Harvard University Press, 1967), and Chinese sources are produced in *Chung-kuo ku-tai yin-yueh shih-liao chi-yao* (Beijing: Chung-kao, 1962). J.A. Van Aalst's *Chinese Music* (1884) was reprinted (New York: Paragon, 1964). A newer general book is Mingyue Liang, *Music of the Billion* (New York: Heinrichshofen, 1985). *A Pictorial Guide to the History of Chinese Music* (Beijing: Research Institute of Music, 1988) has an English table of contents and good pictures.

Ancient music is the topic for such series as the Lawrence Picken et al., *Music from the Tang Court* (London: Oxford Press, 1981–), and the monographs *Musica Asiatica* (London: Cambridge University Press, 1981–). See also Fritz Kuttner, *The Archaeology of Music in Ancient China* (New York: Paragon, 1990), and Kenneth J. DeWoskin, *A Song for One or Two,* no. 42, Michigan Papers in Chinese Studies (Ann Arbor: Center for Chinese Studies, 1982). R.H. Van Gulik's *The Lore of the Chinese Lute* (Tokyo: Sophia University, 1940) remains a classic, as do Edward Schafer's *The Golden Peaches of Samarkand* and *The Vermillion Bird* (Berkeley: University of California Press, 1963 and 1971). Details of *qin* performance are given in articles by Tsun-yuen Lui in *Selected Reports in Ethnomusicology,* UCLA, 1/1 and 2 (1968), and David Liang's *Music of the Chinese Ch'in*

(Taiwan: Chinese National Music Association, 1972). See also John Myers, *The Way of the Pipa* (Kent, Ohio: Kent State University, 1992), and Lawrence Witzleben, "Jiangnam Sizhu Music Clubs in Shanghai," *Ethnomusicology*, 31/2 (1987). The *Chinoperl Papers* (Ithaca: China-Japan Program, Cornell University, 1969–) carry materials on opera and other oral traditions. For Chinese opera, see Bell Yung, *Cantonese Opera* (Cambridge: Cambridge University Press, 1989), and *Ethnomusicology*, 26/2 (1983). Modern times are seen in Colin P. Mackerras, *The Performing Arts in Contemporary China* (London: Routledge & Kegan Paul, 1981); Richard C. Krause, *Piano and Politics in China* (New York: Oxford University Press, 1989); *Asian Music*, 22/2 (1991), Views of Music in China Issue; and Isabel K.F.V. Wong, "From Reaction to Synthesis: Chinese Musicology in the Twentieth Century," in *Comparative Musicology and Anthropology*, eds. B. Nettl and P. Bohlman (Chicago: University of Chicago Press, 1991).

Audiovisual Materials

JVC Video has material in Vols. 3, 4, and 5. Tibetan records in the UNESCO series are BM 30 L 2009-2011 and 6586 007 and, via Harmonia Mundi Inc., CD 8035. The Nonesuch Explorer series includes *Tibet,* M 72000. Smithsonian/Folkways has *Songs and Music of Tibet* (4486) and *Tuva* (CD SF 40017). The King Records World Music Library contains Mongolia on CDs 5133-36 and Harmonia Mundi D 8207. More Chinese opera is on Smithsonian/Folkways, *Beating the Dragon Robe* (8883). Lyrichord records are *Chinese Classical Masterpieces for the Pipa and Chin* (LL 82), *China's Instrumental Heritage* (LL 92), *Chinese Drums and Gongs* (LL 102), *Shantung Music of Confucius' Homeland* (LL 112), and *Chinese Classical Music* (LL 72). The *zheng* zither is featured on Nonesuch 72089 and *pipa* on 72085. The Hugo Masters Series of Celestial Harmonies Chinese CDs are in the 13000 numbers and Harmonia Mundi in D 8031 and 8209.

A SONIC GLOSSARY INDEX FOR CHAPTER 6

Tibetan and Mongolian

(Speakers: Nima Dorjee, Tanya Frank)

Chinese
(speaker: Qian Ning)

律 or 呂
lu (lu)
a bamboo pitch pipe, 176, 178, 179, 180, 182, 201

鑼
luo (lo)
knobless gong, 193

慢 板
manban (man pan)
opera rhythm style, 195

南 管
nanguan (nan kuan)
southern ensemble, 216

南 曲
nanqu (nan ch'u)
southern drama, 187

南 戲
nanxi (nan hai)
southern drama genre, 187

內 教(房 or 坊)
neijiaofang (nei chiao fang)
court music school, 184

排 簫
paixiao (p'ai hsiao)
official panpipes, 179, 180

皮 黃
pihuang (p'i huang)
regional opera style, 189, 190

琵 琶
pipa (p'ip'a)
a plucked lute, 154, 181 (Fig. 60), 183, 185, 187, 188, 189, 191, 196

琴
qin (ch'in)
a board zither, 180, 181 (Fig. 59), 182, 188

磬
qing (ch'ing)
stone chimes, 180

曲 牌
qupai (ch'u p'ai)
melodies for poetry, 187

散 曲
sanqu (san ch'u')
a poetry form, 187

三 絃
sanxian (san hsien)
a plucked lute, 186 (Fig. 63), 188, 189, 191, 193, 196, 216

商
shang (shang)
a pitch in a tone system, 178 (Ex. 6–5)

笙
sheng (sheng)
a mouth organ, 42, 156, 180, 181 (Fig. 61), 189, 193, 231

詩
shi (shih)
a poetry form, 187

十部伎
shibuji (shih pu chi)
a music classification system, 184

哨 吶
suona (sona)
a double-reed aerophone, 191, 193

俗 楽
suyue (su yueh)
common music, 185

弾 詞
tanci* (t'an tz'u)
a narrator, 196

外 教(房 or 坊)
waijiaofang (wai chiao fang)
ancient female music school, 184

文 舞
wenwu (wen wu)
civil music, 182

*not on language cassette

SEVEN
NORTHEAST ASIA AND THE ISLAND COUNTRIES

We noted in Chapter 6 the influence of China on all the areas surrounding it. This chapter deals with northern countries of the Sinicized belt (Manchuria, Korea) and the island cultures off the continental shore (Japan, including the Ryukyu island chain). It ends with a view of indigenous cultures from Siberia to northern Japan and arctic North America, implying continental connections along the Arctic Circle. This is independent of the traditional views of East/West cultural relations along the trade routes of the old continent.

MANCHURIA AND KOREA

The nomadic tribes of Manchuria have at various times been vassals of Chinese or Mongolian dynasties as well as the conquerors and rulers of China itself. Russian and Siberian influences have also been felt. The resulting musical culture displays features of each external area. Both Lamaistic and Chinese Buddhism exist in Manchuria, as do Mongolian- and Siberian-style shamans with their pan drums. Russian-style folk choruses, in which a rhythmically free, melismatic solo is sung over a sustained chordal background, can also be heard.

At the same time, Chinese puppet plays and operas are a main source of entertainment. Finally, one can find, in late-twentieth-century Manchuria, remnants of court orchestras playing music derived from the lost court traditions of China, now preserved primarily as Manchurian Confucian ritual music. While the names of many of the pieces played can be found in very ancient Chinese sources as well as in the repertoire of the Tang dynasty-inspired orchestra remaining in Japan, the instruments used in Manchuria derive from around the time of the Manchu conquest of China (1644). Moreover, the storerooms of Chengde (Jehol) and other Manchurian centers of culture have produced several unique instruments of great importance in the tracing of the movement of musical ideas and materials over Asia.

Although Korea was also subject to long periods of Chinese domination and Mongolian intrusion, it maintained its own kingdoms which, though based on Chinese models, developed many indigenous characteristics. The same is true for the music genres that have survived from these Korean courts. Confucian ritual music (*a-ak*) has obvious Sino-historical roots, and its two surviving pieces seem ancient and Chinese in their stately performance style and orchestration. In the contemporary sense they are authentic, for they present to Koreans what they think such music should sound like. Throughout this book we have observed this irrepressible need for each generation to "improve" on older traditions and over time to respect the last improved version as the original ancient tradition. The Korean changes were part of the great improvements in courtly cultural life that occurred during the reign of Sejong (1418–1450) of the Yi (Choson) dynasty (1392–1910). Confucian music was recreated from fourteenth-century Chinese writings that, in turn, had recreated earlier Chinese sources.[1] National pride continues to support twentieth-century versions of such ancient court traditions.

The Chinese characters for the Korean word *a-ak* (雅 樂) are the same as that of Chinese *yayue* and Japanese *gagaku*. All three terms came to mean courtly music in general. In Korean, the term *tangak* was used to imply other Chinese-derived music, literally Tang dynasty music, although no works from that period are found in the repertory. Korean-composed court pieces were called *hyangak*. However, centuries of Korean creativity have made these distinctions historical rather than musical. The term *habak* meant mixed orchestrations. The instruments used in each genre continue to change. What intrigues the general listener are the instruments themselves.

The court music *taegum* flute is of particular interest for its considerable length (74 cm) and its membrane-covered "buzzing hole," which pro-

[1] See Robert C. Provine, "The Nature and Extent of Surviving Chinese Musical Influence on Korea," *The World of Music,* 29/2 (1987). Provine notes that Taiwan recreated the same tradition with one of the same notations in 1960.

duces a tone of unusual richness. The major Korean aerophone for both classical and folk musics is some form of a double-reed *p'iri*. In lively folk traditions its large reed and small bamboo body produce a sound like that of a soprano saxophone.

The basic zither for all kinds of Korean music is the *kayagum* (*kayakum*), seen in Plate XXVI, Figure 66 (with its court music player). Its twelve movable bridges allow the pitch of each string to be changed. Pushing on the string beyond the bridge with the left hand while plucking the notes with the right hand (as seen in Figure 66) gives further tonal variety to each string. The instrument's body is relatively thin in comparison with the resonance chamber of the Japanese *koto* (See Plate XIX, Figure 73). This thinness helps to produce percussive sounds when a player flicks a finger outward so the fingernail strikes the string. The sound adds greatly to the dynamic contrasts in *kayagum* music. The *kayagum* is claimed as an indigenous instrument, as is the *komun' go* (Plate XXVI, Figure 67). The latter, credited to the seventh-century court musician Wang San-ak, is unique in its stringing. While three of its outer strings are run over bridges, the middle three pass over sixteen high frets. The strings are plucked by a wooden stick (seen lying on the strings in Figure 67) that is clenched in the right hand with the thumb stretched along the top of it. An equally unusual Korean court zither is the *ajaeng;* its seven strings pass over movable bridges like those of the *kayagum,* but it is played by bowing the strings with a resined wooden dowel.

The Korean *haegum* bowed lute (Plate XXVII, Figure 69) also seems "exotic" when compared with its Chinese relatives such as the *huqin* (Plate XXV, Figure 62) or other bowed lutes like the *kamanche* (Plate XII, Figure 30). Compare the opposite curve of the *haegum*'s pole, the inside placement of the larger part of the pegs, and the attachment of the strings to that part so that one has to tune the strings with one's hand forward of the pole. An added special aspect of this instrument is that, when played in court music, a cloth is hung from the top so the movements of the fingers on the strings are hidden.

The main Korean percussion instrument is the *changgo,* shown in Plate XXVI, Figure 68. In classical music the right-hand skin is played with a stick and the left-hand skin with the hand. In many folk dances, a heavier bamboo stick is used on the right and a mallet with a wooden ball on the left.

Among the more exotic marginal survivals of ancient Chinese idiophones found in Korea[2] are the rack of sixteen tuned bells (in Korean, the *p'yonjong*) and stone chimes (*p'yon'gyong*). A musical curiosity of old China survives in Korea in the form of the *o,* the crouched wooden tiger in Plate

[2] They are found also in Vietnam and in twentieth-century Taiwan and mainland revivals of old traditions.

PLATE XXVI. Korea

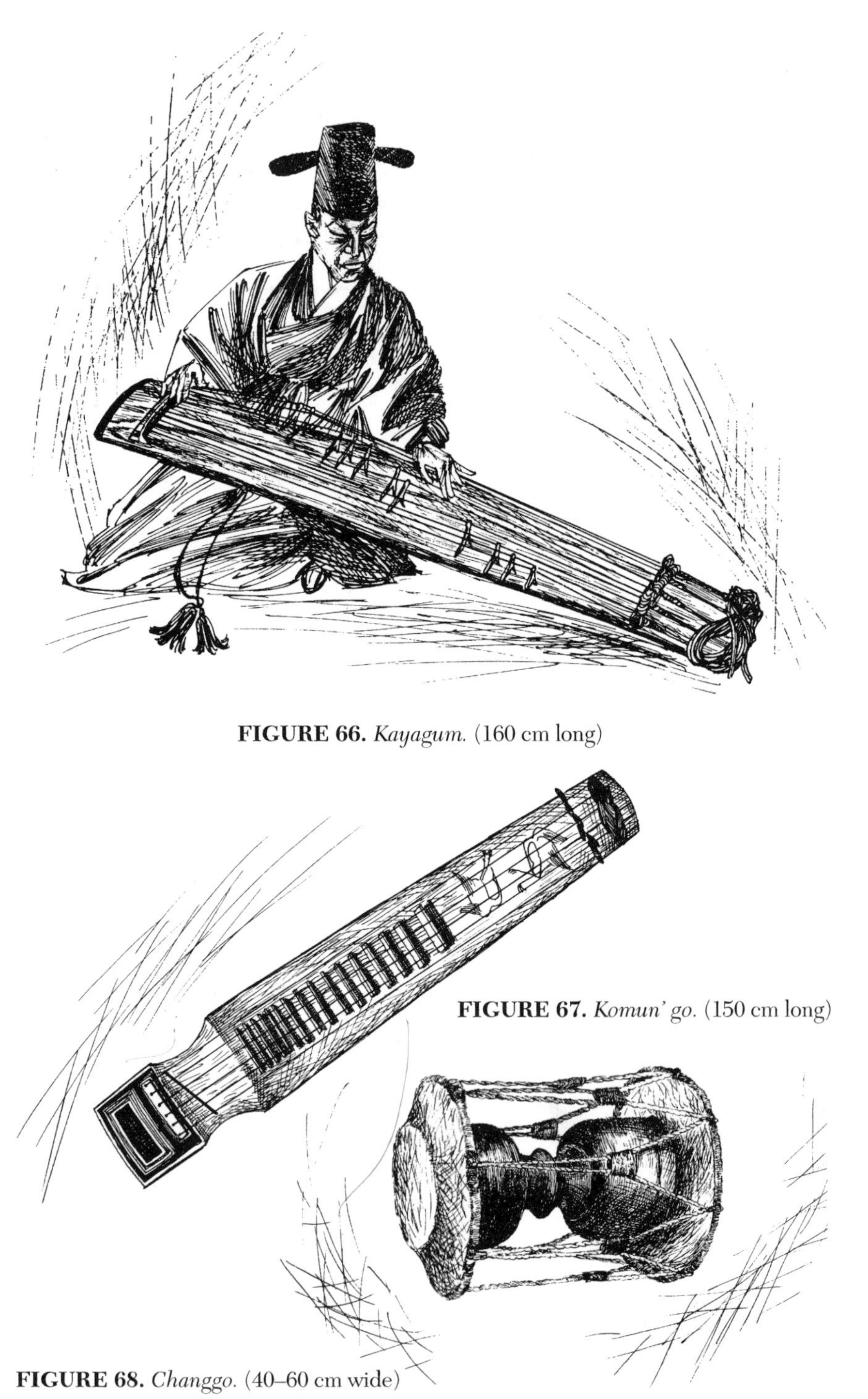

FIGURE 66. *Kayagum.* (160 cm long)

FIGURE 67. *Komun' go.* (150 cm long)

FIGURE 68. *Changgo.* (40–60 cm wide)

PLATE XXVII. Korea

FIGURE 69. *Haegum.*

FIGURE 70. *O.*

XXVII, Figure 70. Its serrated backbone is scratched with a split bamboo whisk at the end of Confucian ritual pieces. Another Chinese survival is the *pak,* a clapper made of six slats of wood held together at the end like a folded fan. The director of the orchestra begins and ends each piece with the sound of this idiophone. Chinese-derived globular clay flutes (in Korean, *hoon*) can be heard in Korea (as well as in Taiwan and China) at academic demonstrations, but the Chinese mouth organ (in Korean, *saing*) is now obsolete in Korea. As performed today, Korean court music is played in a slow tempo, often beginning in a free rhythm. There is heterophony between the melodic instruments except in the bell or chime parts.

Classical chamber music (*p'ungnyu*) and vocal forms have also been preserved from the dynastic periods of Korean history. *Norae* is a general term for vocal music. In the classical tradition cycles of *kagok,* songs are accompanied and enriched with instrumental interludes by an ensemble of winds, strings, and the *changgo* drum. Lyrical *shijo* songs may be accompanied by only the *changgo* or include the flute, fiddle, and double reed. The same is true of the surviving narrative *kaso* songs that reflect Korean indigenous styles more than their courtly roots. New versions of all these courtly music traditions were created primarily through the efforts of the Korean Traditional Performing Arts Centre in Seoul. In attempting to restore some of the old traditions, the Centre has been aided not only by oral tradition but also by early notation books and historical sources. While early Chinese-derived notations show only a solfège or pitches, the earliest surviving Korean notations of mid-fifteenth-century *hyangak* and *tangak* imply rhythms as well as melody.[3] It is called "square notation" (*chongganbo*) because it uses columns in which squares represent beats. Like the Korean phonetic writing system (*han'gul*) that was invented at the same time, Korean notation was one of the clearest methods known. Still, much is lost or becomes conjectural once the actual performance tradition is forgotten. The "correct" interpretation of old notation in modern times is as challenging in Korean classical music as it is in old Western traditions. Fortunately, the oral traditions of both worlds today are stored for a while on recordings, so genres like early jazz and the interpretations of classical musics may be revived with help from such clearer performance practice data. If history is any judge, however, styles will change despite all struggles for authenticity.

The most famous Korean historical document on music is the *Akhak kwebon* ("Handbook of Music"), which first appeared in 1493.[4] It is a compendium of instrumental tunings and fingerings, theoretical tone systems,

[3] In both Chinese and Korean notations for some zithers, fingerings and playing methods also appear.

[4] For a discussion of an even earlier work see Robert C. Provine, Jr., "The Treatise on Ceremonial Music (1430) in the Annals of the Korean King Sejong," *Ethnomusicology,* 18/1 (1974). See also his "Early Sources for Korean Ritual Music" in *Essays on Sino-Korean Musicology* (Seoul: Il Ji Sa, 1988). He is preparing an English translation of the *Akhak kwebon.*

EXAMPLE 7–1. One interpretation of the Korean mode system.

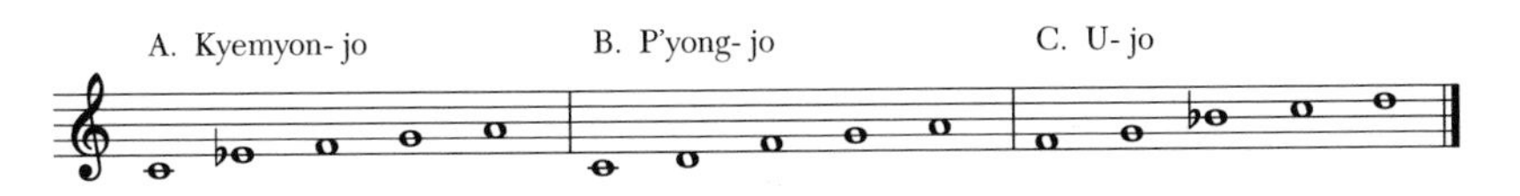

choreographic patterns and orchestral seating arrangements, and ceremonial costumes and paraphernalia. Ancient Korean music theory was based on the Chinese pentatonic system we discussed earlier (p. 176), although it varied greatly over the centuries and within the genres themselves.

Example 7–1 shows one interpretation of classical Korean tone systems today.[5] Note that the major difference between the pentatonic scales of *kyemyon-jo* and *p'yong-jo* are their second pitches. *U-jo* is a variant on *p'yong-jo* on a higher pitch. By now, our discussions of various mode systems of other cultures have made it clear that the tonal vocabulary of any mode is only a small part of its real musical meaning. This is certainly true for Korean music. Although we can compare its pentatonic core with basic Chinese (Example 6–3) or Japanese (Example 7–7), the sonic results are very different.

As in other literate societies, East or West, the ancient music history and theories of Korea are found not only in courtly writings but also in religious texts. Korean solemn ritual Buddhist chant (*pomp'ae*) can be traced to the first century in China; the simplier *yombul* chant text is a Chinese version of Sanskrit sutra and is, in fact, sometimes called *sutra* in Korean. Continuing the analogy with other great religions, we can find in Korean Buddhism a form of chant called *hwach'ong* that is in the vernacular and folk song style. Christian missionary work made Western hymns another common sound in twentieth-century Korea, but more exotic materials are found in Buddhist ritual *chakpop* dances and their accompaniment of drums, cymbals, and winds. To this one can add the rich folk tradition of shamanism. Rural ceremonies (*kut*) and personal needs are often enhanced by a female shaman (*mudang*) whose dance accompaniments (*muga*) include strong *changgo* rhythmic cycles, colorful small gong or cymbal sounds, and lively heterophonic instrumental melodies. The triple meters (6/8, 12/8, etc.), pentatonic tunes, and syncopated rhythms give such music a characteristic Korean sound. These are heard in Example 7–2, a farmer's song being performed in concert style with *kayagum* zither, *haegum* fiddle, a *tanso* end-blown flute accompaniment plus the *changgo* drum. Remember that in the linear, aharmonic world that has dominated almost all the cultures, we have studied here, the relation between the singer and all melodic instruments tends to be heterophonic.

These same qualities are heard in the solo instrumental variation form called *sanjo*. It begins slowly, usually to the accompaniment of a *changgo* drum,

[5] The interpretation of the terms continues to vary, particularly as applied to folk music.

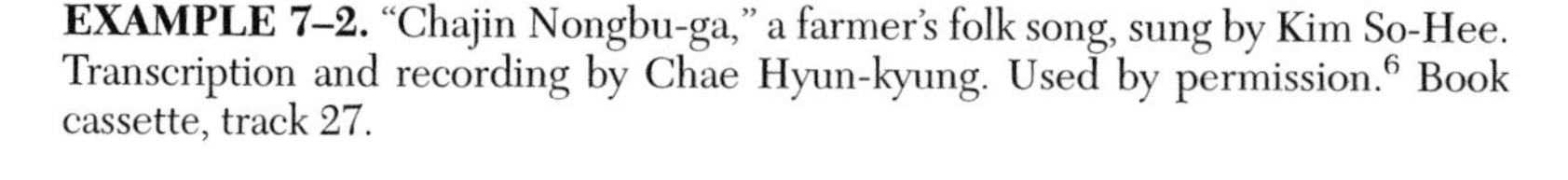

EXAMPLE 7–2. "Chajin Nongbu-ga," a farmer's folk song, sung by Kim So-Hee. Transcription and recording by Chae Hyun-kyung. Used by permission.[6] Book cassette, track 27.

and builds to a high-speed and rhythmically exciting finale.[7] Professional singers or *kisaeng* (*gishang*) entertainment girls keep the *chapka* ballads equally popular, but the most powerful narrative genre is *p'ansori*. To the accompaniment of a small *puk* barrel drum, a single man or woman speaks, sings, and acts out a long story with only a fan as a prop. Performers in either genre produce startling effects through sudden changes in style, from intense throaty renditions of low tone-centered lines to high steel-edged tones that may turn into dynamic vibratos seldom heard elsewhere in the world's vocal traditions. The notational outline of Example 7–3 is only a pale reflection of the true sounds heard on the book cassette, track 28. The narrator continues for hours to complete the story.

Like Korean food, these two vocal examples seem spicy and rather un-Oriental. The singing style and combinations of *parlando* and compelling rhythmic accompaniment almost seem closer to the Spanish flamenco or pan-Islamic music than to the surrounding Oriental traditions. Perhaps further music studies will shed light on the possible continuities between East and West caused by the constant moves of ancient Asian hordes. We know that ancient Chinese traditions were lively and the swinging sleeves of modern Korean

[6] The text is "Ah be happy. Listen, farmers. Ah listen, farmers." It goes on to speak of the beauty of the scenery. The text romanization uses the Yale system.

[7] Recordings of *kayagum sanjo* are common in the West (for example, East-West EWM 1001).

EXAMPLE 7–3. A *p'ansori* excerpt from the story "Hungbu-ga," sung by Kim So-Hee. Transcription and recording by Chae Hyun-kyung. Used by permission.[8] Book cassette, track 28.

dancers are seen in Tang dynasty Chinese clay figurines. Third-century Chinese sources note Korean masked theatricals and folk festivals (*nongak*). Such events still occur in Korea to enhance the vitality of its music.

TAIWAN AND THE RYUKYU ISLANDS

Within the various musical cultures of the islands off the East Asiatic shore, we can find reflections of traditions we have already surveyed here as well as unique regional solutions to the standard musical problems of function

[8] The story concerns a poor couple who opens a melon to find it filled with money. The plot then thickens. The text at this moment speaks of being saved from hunger as they are about to cut open the melon, not knowing its content. *JVC Video* no. 32 shows this part being sung on stage. The opening text says, "Go away smaller ones. Come near me, bigger ones. Let's open the gourd. We will eat inside of the gourd, will sell the gourd to the rich, so we will not go hungry." One hears the gourd being cut at the end of the excerpt.

and structure. On Taiwan (Formosa), for example, one is first struck by the predominately Chinese styles of music heard in the cities. Japanese and Western occupations of the island have also left their musical marks. Tribal traditions reminiscent of Borneo and Indonesia are more evident in the jungle. Harmonic singing, like we noted in Oceania and Borneo, and instruments like the musical bow point to a very different world from that of the urban Chinese-dominated society. The latter maintains traditions from many areas of China. Thus, in addition to various Chinese opera styles, one can see hand and stick puppet shows on the street or attend concerts of the southern Chinese *nanguan* ensemble music. Refugees from the mainland communist victory in 1949 added a new elite that not only provided further examples of marginal survivals of mainland genres but also created reconstructed versions of such ancient traditions as Confucian rituals with their stone chimes and tuned bells. Thus the musics on Taiwan historically and stylistically face in two directions: The Chinese traditions look toward the mainland; the indigenous arts imply more Oceanic and Indonesian influences. When we turned in Chapter 2 from the Philippines south and westward toward Indonesia and the African-West Asian world, the choice was arbitrary. We could have continued instead north through the aboriginals of Taiwan and beyond to the chain of the Ryukyu (Loochoo, Luchu) Islands that lie between Taiwan and Japan off the coast of China. There the cultures of East and Southeast Asia seem to make their last significant mix.

An independent Ryukyuan kingdom existed as early as the fourteenth century.[9] Trade with cultures to the south, southeast, and east brought other Asian traditions and populations to its shores. It became a Japanese colony in the seventeenth century and was absorbed into that country in the late twentieth century. Its earlier courtly style is slightly reflected in a few dances, and indigenous traditions survive in some religious chants (*umui*). Japanese *koto* (Plate XIX, Figure 73) music was imported by at least the eighteenth century. Some surviving Okinawan *koto* pieces have provided data for the study of earlier Japanese repertory. Since the mid-twentieth century there has been a revival of the tradition, and *koto* may appear in the accompaniment of indigenous music. However, when Okinawans sought cultural self-expression in the late twentieth century their best vehicles were songs (*bushi*) and ballads (*yunta*) accompanied by the *sanshin* or *jamisen*. The latter is a three-stringed lute with a snakeskin head, derived from the Chinese *sanxian* (Plate XXV, Figure 63) in the fifteenth century. It developed its own shape and playing style. Tuned by a

[9] The Ryuku chain is presently divided into three groups (*gunto*)—the Sakishima in the south, Okinawa (central) and Amami (north)—and are called by Japanese the Okinawa prefecture. We use the word *Okinawan* hereafter in the prefectural sense.

EXAMPLE 7–6. A comparative score of four versions of the Japanese folk song "Hakone Hachi ri." Book cassette, tracks 31 and 32.

fourth and a fifth or fifth and a fourth, the *sanshin* is plucked by a talonlike buffalo-horn pick attached to the right forefinger. Restoring older court pieces was aided by an eighteenth-century form of *shansin* notation (*kukushi*). It uses Chinese characters, for pitches like *ku* (工) and *shi* (四). They were later set in columns so that rhythm could be notated and further improved as other songs and vocal parts were added.

Okinawan songs usually begin and end with an instrumental section like the one shown in Example 7–4 and heard on book cassette, track 29. The jogging rhythm and cadence pattern (measure 5) of this *sanshin* style are typical Okinawan musical conventions. Note the addition of a neutral pitch (E) to the pentatonic core. Is that related to Southeast Asian traditions?[10] When the singers enter (on book cassette, track 29), the response to the first line with interjections (*hayashi kotoba*) by singers from the other sex reflects a style found all along the island chain into Japan (compare with book cassette, track 33).

Example 7–5 illustrates yet another characteristic of music from the Ryukyus and many other areas of Japan. The rhythm patterns (like much jazz) fall between a duple and a triple meter. Both may appear at the same time if percussion accompaniment is used. Note that the drum pattern is not a simple ostinato. Cadences are clearly marked (measures 4, 13, and 15) by a pattern that includes a different drum. Although Japanese folk music is generally in duple meter, this Okinawan example is extended in measures 10 and 14 because of text. Always remember that a transcription of an oral tradition does not necessarily reflect the manner in which the indigenous performer

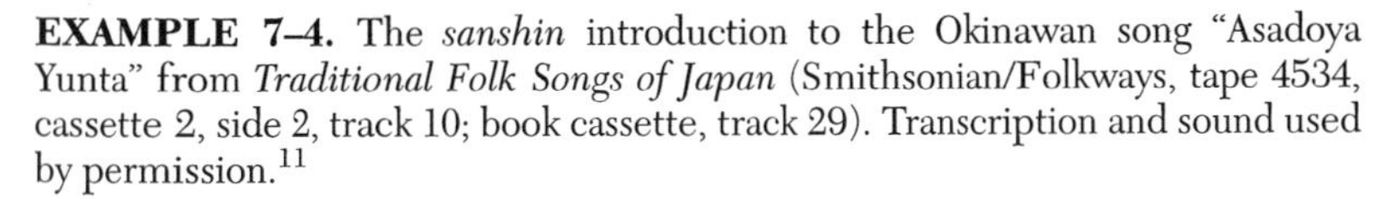

EXAMPLE 7–4. The *sanshin* introduction to the Okinawan song "Asadoya Yunta" from *Traditional Folk Songs of Japan* (Smithsonian/Folkways, tape 4534, cassette 2, side 2, track 10; book cassette, track 29). Transcription and sound used by permission.[11]

[10] Japanese scholars recognize this as unique to Rukyuan traditions. See Example 7–8.

[11] The text of the first verse of this love song says, "You are the wild rose, Blooming in the field; You take a hold of me, going home at sundown."

EXAMPLE 7–5. The Ryukyu song "Hatoma Bushi" from *Traditional Folk Songs of Japan* (Smithsonian/Folkways, tape 4534, cassette 2, side 2, track 9; book cassette, track 30). Transcription and sound used by permission.[12]

conceives the music.[13] The vocal calls (*kakegoe*) of the drummer are really part of the drum pattern as are the arm motions which, unfortunately, cannot appear in a transcription. Such choreographic drum performance style is

[12] The text says, "Climb the hill on Hototoi, And cast your eyes over there, You will see the kuba trees, Growing ever stately on the summit." The romanization of the transcription is based on the dialect of the recording in which, among other changes, the Japanese sound "u" is pronounced as "o." For a Japanese romanization of the text and a different notation, see *Ryukyu no Minyo,* ed. Yoshinoko Kinii (Tokyo: Ongaku no Tomosha, 1954), no. 63.

[13] See Kinii, *Ryukyu no Minyo,* in which the melody is notated as starting on beat 2 and there is one bar of 3/4 time. As a folk song, the total number of beats in the tune differ. Bar lines are pedagogically useful but often misleading in early Western and most non-Western music.

found throughout Japan. However, the hand gestures of the Okinawan dan and their quick-stepping feet seem more Indonesian and the courtly d costumes looks Chinese. All together the music and dance are someti quite Ryukyuan.

JAPAN

Folk Music

Japan is a country of many islands. This geographical fact has bined with a long history of feudalism to create strong regional folk tions. We have already studied the special features of Okinawan musi main islands of Japan exhibit similar but different characteristics. Ja folk song tends to be sung in a high, tight-throated, melismatic f Much of it tends toward the *parlando-rubato* style, although dance sc in regular rhythm.

Many of these characteristics are evident on the book cassette, rendition of the prescriptive (emic) transcription of a horse-pack song ple 7–6A.[14] The pentatonic core is clear in the notation version;[15] pitched ornamented *parlando* style dominates the recording. Ho must remember that the notation of a folk song is not *the* tune. It i version of a constantly flowing tradition. In this context three other versions have been put in what is called a *comparative score.* Versio on variants found in a folk song book.[16] Although the melodic conto placements of A and B are similar, the tunes start on a different pentatonic and generally stay a 6th apart. Example 7–6B does mak of the A flat and one ornamental D (measure 10), thus comple toned *yo* scale (see Example 7–8). Version C comes from a Japan book.[17] Again the tune starts and ends on different pitches fro though many of the long notes of A and C correspond. It is twelv perhaps to conform with the choreography of some folk d adapted the tune to its need for new material. Version D (book turns the piece to its function as a horse-pack song but now as lude to a *kabuki* theater scene that takes place on the Tokaido

[14] From the recording *Traditional Folk Songs of Japan* (Smithsoni sette 1, side 2, track 6). Transcription and sound are used by permission. Th the first verse as "One may go riding for eight ri on the Hakone pass, Bu across Oi, the river that lies beyond."

[15] Hence there is no need for an A flat in the key signature of ve

[16] Kinbu Ishitaka, ed., *Nihon Minyo Taizenshu* (Tokyo: Kyoei also *Nihon Minyo Taikan* (Tokyo: NHK, 1954), Kanto volume, p. 358. All in the same general tonal area for comparison purposes.

[17] *Nihon Minyo Kyoku shu* (Tokyo: Kyodo ongaku shuppan sh

EXAMPLE 7–6. *(continued)*

to Hakone.[18] The first phrase resembles A but the long melismatic phrases are missing and the tonality of its second phrase (from measure 9 of the score) uses the very different *in* scale (Example 7–8). Vocables (*na, a, yo*) are used for cadencing ornaments. To declare authenticity in such a folk song situation, it is best to follow one of our common aphorisms: Form follows function. What is correct relates to what it is being used for. Still, in contemporary society authenticity can take on new meanings. Even the Japanese term *minyo* (folk song) is new. It was created in the late nineteenth century as Japanese scholars became aware of Western terminology. With the twentieth-century rise of mass communications, regional traditions became known nationally (see Egypt, p. 97), and folk song contests arose. A unique aspect of this movement in Japan was the creation of folk song preservation clubs (*hozonkai*). Their function is

[18] The transcription and track of the book cassette tape are from the opening of the play "Suzugamori" as heard on a King record KC 1029. Sound and transcription used by permission. The tune can be used in other plays that require the same general geographic setting.

to practice only *one* song! They then compete with other such clubs that practice the same song to become national champions at the singing of one song perfectly.

Example 7–7 is different from the horse-pack song (Example 7–6) in rhythm, ornamentation, and style. It shares the *in* tone system of our *kabuki* example (7–6D). Its transcription demonstrates one Japanese solution to the problem of notating the duple/triple rhythmic ambiguity mentioned earlier.[19] All these characteristics do not confirm this tune as a folk song, for the text is a hot springs advertisement and the scale and tune style resemble that of geisha music. The classification of its several versions can be called popular (*ryukoka*) or folk song. It depends on the view and age of the classifier.[20]

The two basic scales of Japanese folk music, as well as most other music after the appearance of the *shamisen,* are the *yo* and *in* (A and B in Example 7–8). While they both reveal a pentatonic core with two possible additional tones (shown as black notes in Example 7–8), they differ particularly in their use of half steps. The *yo* scale is basically an anhemitonic pentatonic, relating to the ancient scales of the Japanese court (C and D in Example 7–8); the *in* scale produces a more obvious Japanese-like sound by its frequent use of half steps above the root and fifth of the scale (Example 7–7 uses the *in* scale).

EXAMPLE 7–7. The Japanese song "Kusatsu yumomi uta" from the recording *Traditional Folk Songs of Japan* (Smithsonian/Folkways 4534, cassette 1, side 2, track 2; book cassette, track 33). Transcription and sound used by permission.[21]

[19] See various volumes of the *Nihon Minyo Taikan* mentioned in footnote 16.

[20] See *Nihon Minyo Taikan,* Kanto volume, 135–36.

[21] The words say, "Kusatsu is a nice place. You may take home with you the fragrance of hot springs on your sleeves."

fourth and a fifth or fifth and a fourth, the *sanshin* is plucked by a talonlike buffalo-horn pick attached to the right forefinger. Restoring older court pieces was aided by an eighteenth-century form of *shansin* notation (*kukushi*). It uses Chinese characters, for pitches like *ku* (工) and *shi* (四). They were later set in columns so that rhythm could be notated and further improved as other songs and vocal parts were added.

Okinawan songs usually begin and end with an instrumental section like the one shown in Example 7–4 and heard on book cassette, track 29. The jogging rhythm and cadence pattern (measure 5) of this *sanshin* style are typical Okinawan musical conventions. Note the addition of a neutral pitch (E) to the pentatonic core. Is that related to Southeast Asian traditions?[10] When the singers enter (on book cassette, track 29), the response to the first line with interjections (*hayashi kotoba*) by singers from the other sex reflects a style found all along the island chain into Japan (compare with book cassette, track 33).

Example 7–5 illustrates yet another characteristic of music from the Ryukyus and many other areas of Japan. The rhythm patterns (like much jazz) fall between a duple ♪. ♬ and a triple meter ♩ ♪ (triplet). Both may appear at the same time if percussion accompaniment is used. Note that the drum pattern is not a simple ostinato. Cadences are clearly marked (measures 4, 13, and 15) by a pattern that includes a different drum. Although Japanese folk music is generally in duple meter, this Okinawan example is extended in measures 10 and 14 because of text. Always remember that a transcription of an oral tradition does not necessarily reflect the manner in which the indigenous performer

EXAMPLE 7–4. The *sanshin* introduction to the Okinawan song "Asadoya Yunta" from *Traditional Folk Songs of Japan* (Smithsonian/Folkways, tape 4534, cassette 2, side 2, track 10; book cassette, track 29). Transcription and sound used by permission.[11]

[10] Japanese scholars recognize this as unique to Rukyuan traditions. See Example 7–8.

[11] The text of the first verse of this love song says, "You are the wild rose, Blooming in the field; You take a hold of me, going home at sundown."

EXAMPLE 7–5. The Ryukyu song "Hatoma Bushi" from *Traditional Folk Songs of Japan* (Smithsonian/Folkways, tape 4534, cassette 2, side 2, track 9; book cassette, track 30). Transcription and sound used by permission.[12]

conceives the music.[13] The vocal calls (*kakegoe*) of the drummer are really part of the drum pattern as are the arm motions which, unfortunately, cannot appear in a transcription. Such choreographic drum performance style is

[12] The text says, "Climb the hill on Hototoi, And cast your eyes over there, You will see the kuba trees, Growing ever stately on the summit." The romanization of the transcription is based on the dialect of the recording in which, among other changes, the Japanese sound "u" is pronounced as "o." For a Japanese romanization of the text and a different notation, see *Ryukyu no Minyo,* ed. Yoshinoko Kinii (Tokyo: Ongaku no Tomosha, 1954), no. 63.

[13] See Kinii, *Ryukyu no Minyo,* in which the melody is notated as starting on beat 2 and there is one bar of 3/4 time. As a folk song, the total number of beats in the tune differ. Bar lines are pedagogically useful but often misleading in early Western and most non-Western music.

found throughout Japan. However, the hand gestures of the Okinawan dancers and their quick-stepping feet seem more Indonesian and the courtly dance costumes looks Chinese. All together the music and dance are sometimes quite Ryukyuan.

JAPAN

Folk Music

Japan is a country of many islands. This geographical fact has combined with a long history of feudalism to create strong regional folk traditions. We have already studied the special features of Okinawan music. The main islands of Japan exhibit similar but different characteristics. Japanese folk song tends to be sung in a high, tight-throated, melismatic fashion. Much of it tends toward the *parlando-rubato* style, although dance songs are in regular rhythm.

Many of these characteristics are evident on the book cassette, track 31, rendition of the prescriptive (emic) transcription of a horse-pack song in Example 7–6A.[14] The pentatonic core is clear in the notation version;[15] the high-pitched ornamented *parlando* style dominates the recording. However, we must remember that the notation of a folk song is not *the* tune. It is only one version of a constantly flowing tradition. In this context three other "authentic" versions have been put in what is called a *comparative score*. Version B is based on variants found in a folk song book.[16] Although the melodic contours and text placements of A and B are similar, the tunes start on a different pitch in the pentatonic and generally stay a 6th apart. Example 7–6B does make clearer use of the A flat and one ornamental D (measure 10), thus completing a seven-toned *yo* scale (see Example 7–8). Version C comes from a Japanese folk dance book.[17] Again the tune starts and ends on different pitches from the rest although many of the long notes of A and C correspond. It is twelve beats shorter, perhaps to conform with the choreography of some folk dance club that adapted the tune to its need for new material. Version D (book cassette 32) returns the piece to its function as a horse-pack song but now as an offstage prelude to a *kabuki* theater scene that takes place on the Tokaido road on the way

[14] From the recording *Traditional Folk Songs of Japan* (Smithsonian/Folkways 4534, cassette 1, side 2, track 6). Transcription and sound are used by permission. The record notes translate the first verse as "One may go riding for eight ri on the Hakone pass, But [it is] impossible to go across Oi, the river that lies beyond."

[15] Hence there is no need for an A flat in the key signature of version A of this score.

[16] Kinbu Ishitaka, ed., *Nihon Minyo Taizenshu* (Tokyo: Kyoei shobo, 1984), p. 177. See also *Nihon Minyo Taikan* (Tokyo: NHK, 1954), Kanto volume, p. 358. All versions have been placed in the same general tonal area for comparison purposes.

[17] *Nihon Minyo Kyoku shu* (Tokyo: Kyodo ongaku shuppan sha, circa 1960), p. 74.

EXAMPLE 7–6. A comparative score of four versions of the Japanese folk song "Hakone Hachi ri." Book cassette, tracks 31 and 32.

EXAMPLE 7–6. *(continued)*

to Hakone.[18] The first phrase resembles A but the long melismatic phrases are missing and the tonality of its second phrase (from measure 9 of the score) uses the very different *in* scale (Example 7–8). Vocables (*na, a, yo*) are used for cadencing ornaments. To declare authenticity in such a folk song situation, it is best to follow one of our common aphorisms: Form follows function. What is correct relates to what it is being used for. Still, in contemporary society authenticity can take on new meanings. Even the Japanese term *minyo* (folk song) is new. It was created in the late nineteenth century as Japanese scholars became aware of Western terminology. With the twentieth-century rise of mass communications, regional traditions became known nationally (see Egypt, p. 97), and folk song contests arose. A unique aspect of this movement in Japan was the creation of folk song preservation clubs (*hozonkai*). Their function is

[18] The transcription and track of the book cassette tape are from the opening of the play "Suzugamori" as heard on a King record KC 1029. Sound and transcription used by permission. The tune can be used in other plays that require the same general geographic setting.

to practice only *one* song! They then compete with other such clubs that practice the same song to become national champions at the singing of one song perfectly.

Example 7–7 is different from the horse-pack song (Example 7–6) in rhythm, ornamentation, and style. It shares the *in* tone system of our *kabuki* example (7–6D). Its transcription demonstrates one Japanese solution to the problem of notating the duple/triple rhythmic ambiguity mentioned earlier.[19] All these characteristics do not confirm this tune as a folk song, for the text is a hot springs advertisement and the scale and tune style resemble that of geisha music. The classification of its several versions can be called popular (*ryukoka*) or folk song. It depends on the view and age of the classifier.[20]

The two basic scales of Japanese folk music, as well as most other music after the appearance of the *shamisen,* are the *yo* and *in* (A and B in Example 7–8). While they both reveal a pentatonic core with two possible additional tones (shown as black notes in Example 7–8), they differ particularly in their use of half steps. The *yo* scale is basically an anhemitonic pentatonic, relating to the ancient scales of the Japanese court (C and D in Example 7–8); the *in* scale produces a more obvious Japanese-like sound by its frequent use of half steps above the root and fifth of the scale (Example 7–7 uses the *in* scale).

EXAMPLE 7–7. The Japanese song "Kusatsu yumomi uta" from the recording *Traditional Folk Songs of Japan* (Smithsonian/Folkways 4534, cassette 1, side 2, track 2; book cassette, track 33). Transcription and sound used by permission.[21]

[19] See various volumes of the *Nihon Minyo Taikan* mentioned in footnote 16.

[20] See *Nihon Minyo Taikan,* Kanto volume, 135–36.

[21] The words say, "Kusatsu is a nice place. You may take home with you the fragrance of hot springs on your sleeves."

EXAMPLE 7–8. Japanese tonal theory.

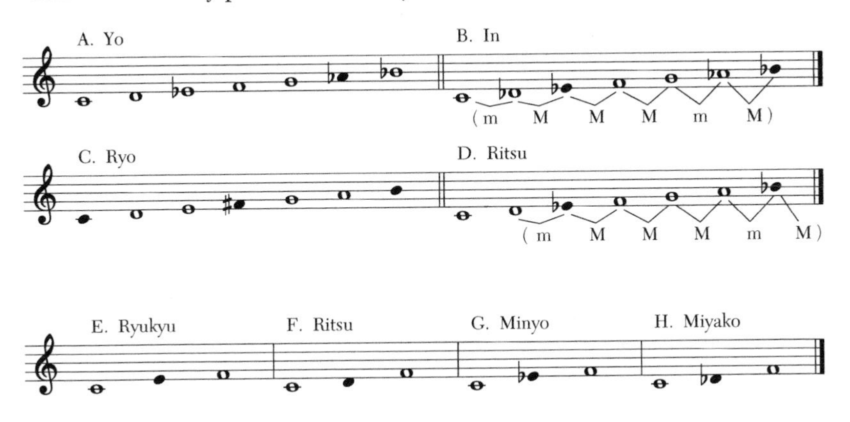

Japanese researchers often deal with the three-note units shown in Examples 7–8E through H rather than scales. This reduction of research data is meaningful in Japanese music for, like most of the music we have already studied, it is aharmonic and linear. It depends largely on subtle shifts of melodic tension and release for its sense of forward motion. The distinction of the Okinawan tradition is seen in the term *ryukyu* attached to one set.[22] The term *ritsu* is derived from Chinese-derived court terminology. The *minyo* unit is certainly common to folk song (Example 7–6); the term *miyako* (meaning Kyoto area) seems appropriate for that half-step interval which evokes the music of the pleasure quarters and theaters since the seventeenth century (Example 7–7).

For all its modernization Japan still maintains a large number of festivals (*matsuri*) and folk theatricals (*minzoku geino*). The sponsor may be the local Shinto shrine, Buddhist temple, or chamber of commerce, but the primary drive seems to be regional pride and sense of togetherness. The summer *bon odori* dance can be found in overseas Japanese communities far from home.[23] Modern adaptations of festival drumming, folk music, and pantomimes have captured a world entertainment market and thus some of Japan's fad-oriented youth.[24] The local folk theatricals events include a variety of animal dances, from Chinese-inspired lions to fearsome bands of deer with large horns, and bamboo strips projected high in the air. Elaborate flowered hats and grotesque

[22] The Japanese apply the term *tetrachord* to such units, meaning the distance of a fourth rather than four tones. See Fumio Koizumi, "Musical Scales in Japanese Music," *Asian Musics in an Asian Perspective* (Tokyo: The Japan Foundation, 1977), 73–79.

[23] The University of Michigan ensemble has played in Detroit for Japanese automobile company gatherings of *bon* dancers in the parking lot of a sushi restaurant. Visiting Japanese dancers from Indiana often join the event as do non-Japanese employees of the companies. See also Judy Van Zile, *The Japanese Bon Dance in Hawaii* (Kailua, Hawaii: Press Pacifica, 1982).

[24] In the 1990s the Kodo drummers' base on Sado Island became a veritable mecca for world folk-oriented drummers, and Caucasian Japanese-style drum groups flourished in the West. Young Japanese took up Tsugaru folk *shamisen* playing because it was as flashy as a banjo while still being native.

masks can also be seen. Many of the pantomimes and ritual dances are related to the ancient theatricals of the court or to the surviving professional traditions such as *noh*.[25] The generic term for Shinto-related theatricals is *kagura* and the regional forms are called *sato kagura*. Such events share common features such as purification ceremonies with salt, often a pot of boiling water, and ritual dances done in magic number repetitions or sets (often 3 or 3 × 3).[26] They also share the accompaniment of the *hayashi,* a generic term of any combination of percussion with or without a melodic instrument.[27] A Tokyo festival ensemble (*matsuri bayashi*) illustrates the basic principles of such music.

EXAMPLE 7–9. An excerpt from the student version of the *matsuri bayashi* piece "Yatai." Book cassette, track 34. Recordings used by permission.[28]

[25] See P.G. O'Neil, *Early No Drama* (London: Humphreys, 1958).

[26] See a summary of Yasuji Honda's theories in Frank Hoff, "Shinto and the Performing Arts," in *Song, Dance, Storytelling: Aspects of the Performing Arts in Japan,* ed. Frank Hoff (Ithaca: Cornell University, 1978), East Asia Papers, no. 15.

[27] Throughout this chapter we use the standard Hepburn system of romanization of Japanese. The *kunrei* system changes all *sh* to *sy, chi* to *ti,* and *chu* to *tyu*. For example, *shakuhachi* would be syakuhati.

[28] The transcription is based on oral lessons given the author by Taneo Wakayama, director of the Edo bayashi troupe in Tokyo. The book cassette performance of the beginning of the piece is performed by students of St. Andrews College, Lauringberg, North Carolina, under the direction of David Fish. The advanced version is by Wakayama musicians in Tokyo from the University of Oklahoma Early Music Series videotape *Shinto Festival Music.* Note that the author's version of the hand gong part is silent on the last beat, unlike the tape example learned by Fish from the same teacher decades later.

Festival ensembles tend to be in magic numbers (3 or 5). The bamboo flute (*takebue* or *shinobue*) provides the melody. The general term for drums hit with sticks is *taiko*. A standard ensemble has two of regular size (similar to Plate XXX, Figure 77) and a larger one (*odaiko*). The fifth member plays a small brass gong (*kane*). These ensembles play sets of pieces in varying tempos and moods, rather like Western dance suites. Although improvisation hardly exists in Japanese music, the festival music often seems improvisatory because of the ornamentation (*ashirai*) of the melody by the flute and because different groups seem to play the same piece in a very different manner. Actually, each group plays the piece with little internal variation from performance to performance, but the version of each may differ from those of the others among the guilds (*ryu*) of players, to distinguish it from the others and keep it "secret" from them. Although the flourishing of recordings in Japan now makes this sonic control impossible, the attitude reflects well the guild tradition that is typical of Japanese music in its older forms and, at least in principle, in modern idioms as well.

Book cassette, track 34, provides both the beginner and secret versions of a piece called "Yatai," a word meaning the carts in which ensembles are pulled in a festival procession. The music produces a strong sense of driving forward through the time continuum by frequently exploiting what is known in Japanese as a rhythmic "gap" (*zure*).[29] A Westerner might understand this concept more quickly by calling it a *sliding door effect.* In an ensemble piece the length of phrases for each part might be the same but at some point, like sliding doors on two tracks, they may be moved so they don't begin at the same place. Example 7–9 shows the section in which the drums' eight-beat pattern is one beat out of syncronization with the eight-beat pattern of the flute and hand gong. A shift in the drum pattern lengths brings them together at the cadence. Since all such music is learned orally by mnemonics, the conflict that might be revealed by a written score does not exist for a traditionally trained student or professional performer. The importance of orality is equally powerful in Japan's art music.

Japanese Art Music: Ancient Traditions

Artifacts and Chinese references inform us of indigenous Japanese musics as far back as the third century B.C., but historical information does not surface until much later, when Japan gradually adopted and adapted the Chinese writing system (from the fourth century A.D. on). The first major importation of continental court musicians is traditionally dated as A.D. 453, when eighty Korean musicians were sent to perform at the funeral of a Japanese ruler. In the sixth century, Chinese Buddhism joined the indigenous Shintoism

[29] See Japanese article by Toshijiro Oka comparing Western and Japanese rhythm in the magazine *Chuo Koron* (August 1989).

as an official religion in Japan. Thus Buddhist chant (*shomyo*) and continent-derived court music (*gagaku*) became the two foundations of Japanese classical music.

The nomenclature and tone systems of Buddhism bear the same relation to Japanese art-music traditions as the Catholic Gregorian chant theories do to the growth of Western musical styles. Selected Japanese converts were sent to the international centers for Buddhist studies in China. They returned with treasures of enlightenment and information, including music theory and practice. The major surviving source for the Japanese interpretation of such material in the Tendai sect of Buddhism is the *Shomyo yojinshu* by Tanchi (1163–1237). It is paralleled in the Shingon sect by *The Great Collection from Fish Mountain* (*Gyosan taikaishu,* 1496), which takes its name (*gyosan*) from the Japanese equivalent of the name of the center in China where so much of such information was taught. The notations of Buddhist chant, like those of Tibet discussed in Chapter 6, are generally neumatic. However, since Sino-Japanese writing is ordered in vertical columns rather than horizontal lines, the shapes and styles of Japanese neumes are quite different from those of Tibet. Perhaps the most interesting (and historically controversial) system is the *go-in hakase,* said to have been invented by Kakui (b. 1236) of the Shingon sect. In this system the five notes of each set of three octaves of pentatonic scales are indicated by short angled lines (like the hands of a clock). Starting with the fourth note of the lowest pentatonic as G, the pitches G, A, C, D, E, G would be notated o—, o\, ϙ, ρ, —o, \o. This system contrasts with most Western neumatic notations, especially in that the graphic direction of the line has no necessary relation with upward or downward motion from one pitch to the next (for example, low G up to C is o—, ϙ). An interesting comparison has been made between this system and the ritual hand gestures (*mudras*) and oracle stick placements of earlier Indian Buddhism.[30] Whatever its origin, it provides for professional singers an equally logical but different memory-aid system, as well as a means of preserving the "secret" traditions of their sect. Within the traditions of each sect are found not only different notation systems but also the names of stereotyped melodic patterns that require aural memory rather than notation for their performance. This principle of named stereotyped patterns is characteristic of many of the Japanese musics that developed in later historical periods. Of equal influence was the tone system of early Buddhism and music of the court.

Example 7–8C and 7–8D are the two basic scales of ancient Japanese court music, the *ryo* and *ritsu,* here built on the note C for convenience in comparing them with Example 6–3. The *ryo* scale conforms to the traditional view of East Asian pentatonicism, but the *ritsu* seems to imply something that may be indigenous: the greater use of half steps. It is possible to think of *ritsu* as

[30] See Walter Kaufmann, "The Mudras in Samavedic Chant . . . ," *Ethnomusicology,* 11/2 (1967).

some ancient theoretical attempt to explain the *in* scale of folk song (Example 7–8B) in terms of a more "classical" Chinese system. In this view, the *in* scale is seen as a "hidden" mode in the *ritsu* scale; such a relationship is shown in Example 7–8 by the parenthetical listing of major and minor seconds beneath the *ritsu* scale (starting from its D instead of C) and beneath the *in* scale. Such an interpretation is conjectural, however, and is not part of the traditional Japanese music theory.

In traditional theory the two scales may be constructed on three pitches each. These tone systems (*cho*) are normally listed in modern writings on the following Western pitches: D (*ichikotsu*), G (*sojo*), and E (*taishiki*) for *ryo;* E (*hyojo*), A (*oshiki*), and B (*banshiki*) for *ritsu,* the two names of E appearing in order to distinguish between the two *cho* that can begin on that pitch. Note that the five different pitch centers put together would create an anhemitonic pentatonic scale, which is the core of so many East Asian scale systems.

The scales and transpositions mentioned here represent only a small part of the essential differences that actually distinguish one *cho* from another. As in Near Eastern *maqamat,* Indian *raga,* Catholic chants, or African American blues, there are melodic units, ranges, and, in the case of *cho,* even accompaniment figures that may play equally important roles in the aural definitions of the sonic whole. Modes as such are not discussed in the writings on *cho,* although *cho* is often mistranslated as "mode." There are, however, a few compositions that appear in two *cho.*

The comparative (emic) score in Example 7–10 shows the basic melodies for the *hichiriki* of one of the few pieces found in two *cho.* Both it and book cassette, track 35, demonstrate that such a "crossing over" (*watashimono*) is not merely a transposition. The melodic line is redesigned to fit more easily in the range of the instruments and to use ornamentation characteristic to that *cho.* Book cassette, track 35, contains the opening two periods of the *hyojo* version and the complete performance of the *banshiki* composition.[31] In addition to the variant melodies, note the form. Sections are repeated and the form is closed (ABA). These formal features are common in Western music. In *gagaku* they support its historical origins for they are equally frequent in continental East Asia although rarely found in other Japanese traditions such as *noh, kabuki,* or *koto* music.

Although the modal aspect of *gagaku* may not be clearly stated, there is no lack of documentation concerning the general tradition. In 735 a Japanese ambassador, Mabi Kibi, brought back from China a ten-volume *Digest of Music Matters* (in Japanese, *Gakusho yoroku*) which still survives. A Japanese court dancer, Chikazane Koma, produced a similar ten-volume set, the *Kyokunsho,* in 1233, and extensive *Taigensho* was written by a court musician, Sumiaki Toyohara, in 1512. But perhaps the most powerful source of information about and

[31] Complete *hyojo* versions of "Etenraku" are heard on most Western commercial recordings such as the Lyrichord CD *Gagaku* (LYRCD 7126).

EXAMPLE 7–10. Modal versions of "Etenraku"; *hyojo* from *Gagaku,* University of Oklahoma educational videotape directed by Eugene Enrico, and *banshiki* from CD *1,000 Years of Japanese Classical Music* (Tokyo: Kodansha/Victor, 1982, record 1, side 2, band 1; book cassette, track 35). Used by permission of Victor JVC and of University of Oklahoma.

symbol of the *gagaku* tradition and its performance practice is the Shoso-in storehouse, built in 756 as a repository for objects from the Todai-ji temple and the household goods of the late Emperor Shomu. When it was opened in 1872, among its thousands of items was found a marvelous set of 45 musical instruments plus one fragment of lute notation and sets of dance masks and accessories, as well as a catalog of most of the contents of the storehouse listing the origins of many items.[32] Inlays, etchings, and masks show lions, Bactrian

[32] Photographs, measurements, and an English summary of these objects in the collection are found in two handsome Japanese volumes, *Shosoin no gakki* and *Shosoin no men* (Tokyo: Nihon keizai shimbun sha, 1967).

EXAMPLE 7–10. *(continued)*

camels, and palm trees as well as Chinese acrobats and bearded, big-nosed Westerners—that is, traders from Central Asia and the Near East. Plate XXVIII, Figure 71, taken from a *biwa* lute in the Shoso-in, shows a scene appearing on the cover (*bachikawa*) of the *biwa,* which protects part of its face from the strokes of a plectrum (*bachi*). End-blown and side-blown Chinese flutes are seen joining an hourglass-shaped drum played by a big-nosed "foreigner" in the accompaniment of a dancer who cavorts on the back of a white elephant. We show this one scene from one instrument to suggest some small part of the excitement of the historical and musical treasures of ancient Japan in general and of the Shoso-in collection in particular.

Perhaps Figure 36 in Plate XIV (p. 99) is an even more powerful example. It shows a *kugo,* the best preserved example of the kind of angle harp that is seen elsewhere only in bas-reliefs in Babylon or in painting and statuary from Egypt, Persia, Central Asia, and China. Although the *kugo* has not been played in Japan for centuries, it is still, thanks to the Shoso-in storehouse, our most striking example of marginal survival. It is an excellent and beautiful symbol of Japan's cultural-historical position as a kind of cul-de-sac into which a rich stream of ancient Asian traditions flowed. Some of the sonic remnants of their musics are heard in *gagaku* performances today.

The term *gagaku* ("elegant music") is actually a Japanese reading of the characters (雅 樂) that are pronounced *yenyueh* in China and *a-ak* in Korea. *Gagaku* flourished in Japan during the Nara (710–784) and Heian (794–1185)

PLATE XXVIII. A Japanese Shoso-in treasure

FIGURE 71. Figures on the face of a *biwa*.

periods, which correspond with China's "international period" (see p. 183). Japan's musical imports at that time were quite exotic: In addition to China, Korea was always an important source, and there is some evidence of South and Southeast Asian materials as well. Official court music was administered through a music bureau (*gagaku-ryo*) established in 702, and by the early ninth century a "Big Sound Hall" (*outadokoro*) was added to handle Japanese compositions. *Gagaku* is called *kangen* if it is an instrumental performance and *bugaku* if it accompanies dance. Historically, the many types of *gagaku* were organized, in the best Confucian style, into two categories: the music of the right and of the left. Music of the right was called *komagaku.* It contained Korean- and Manchurian-based music, and the costumes of its dancers emphasized green. Music of the left was called *togaku;* it contained music from China and India and featured red costumes. Japanese compositions are said to have appeared in *komagaku,* although it is possible they occurred in both categories, since composers are not listed nor are the repertoires further differentiated. The titles of compositions, however, often at least reveal continental origins: for example, "The Barbarians Drinking Wine" (*Konju* or *Koinju*) is obviously a Chinese composition; the dance of *Genjoraku* can be traced to an old Indian Veda story about the exorcising of a snake.

The major means of differentiating *togaku* and *komagaku* today is through their instrumentation. The basic *gagaku* and melodic instrument, in both categories, is a short double-reed aerophone called the *hichiriki.* It is joined in performance by different side-blown flutes, the *ryuteki* in *togaku* and the *komabue* in *komagaku.* In either case, the melodic instruments play heterophonically. (These differences in interpretations of a melody may have been part of the ancient tradition, but also may reflect unyielding discrepancies that occurred when musicians from separate ensembles were merged as part of the modernization of Japan during the late nineteenth century.) Contemporary performance practice on the 17-pipe *sho* mouth organ, derived from the ancient Chinese *sheng* (Figure 61), is also a puzzle. At present the *sho* provides a handsome harmonic matrix for *gagaku* melodies by playing chords (generally tone clusters) built on basic pitches of the melody. Such a performance style has never been found in any of the related instruments of East or Southeast Asia, although tone clusters are effectively interjected into some melodies of the *khaen* (Figure 53). Surviving *sho* notation usually contains only one pitch name for about every four beats, like a guitar lead sheet in Western popular music; in both notations there is little except tradition to tell us how it actually is to be performed. Whatever the original sound of the *sho* may have been, modern versions of its music have provided a special texture in *gagaku* that has captivated many a Western listener.

The center of the percussion section of a *gagaku* ensemble is a large hanging barrel drum (*gaku-daiko*) with two tacked heads, one of which is played with two beaters, and a small hanging gong (*shoko*). Their entrances are so spaced that they seem to function in a manner suggesting the time-marking concept originally noted in Indonesian music by Jaap Kunst (see p. 52). For example, in an eight-beat phrase the gong marks off the second and sixth beats while the *gaku-daiko* sounds on beats 4 and 8. The leader of the ensemble performs more actively, on a small barrel drum (*kakko*) in *togaku* or on a larger hourglass-shaped drum (*san no tsuzumi*) in *komagaku*.

Today, stringed instruments are not used in *komagaku*, nor are they used in *togaku* when it serves as dance music (*bugaku*). Concert *togaku*, however, uses the 13-stringed *koto* zither (Plate XXIX, Figure 73) and a pear-shaped *biwa* lute similar to the one shown in Plate XXIX, Figure 74. As used today, these instruments do not play the melody but, rather, short stereotyped melodic phrases or arpeggios which, while influenced by the melody and its tone system, function as time markers through the regular spaces that exist between their entrances. This performance practice is based on a literal translation of traditional notations, which originally may have been merely "lead sheets" from a much richer tradition. From the novels and memoirs of the Heian period (794–1185) we know that both the *koto* and *biwa* were frequently used in accompanying courtly songs or in instrumental solos. Today all that survives of this tradition is the poetry and some descriptions of romantic performances, plus a small repertoire of vocal music performed with great solemnity by musicians of the court or of large Shinto shrines.

From the few surviving genres of vocal music sung today, we can gain insights into the spirit of the past. *Roei* songs show an inspiration from Chinese poems. *Saibara* seem to be derived from songs of pack-train drivers.[33] *Imayo* are of particular interest because they were apparently derived from popular songs and texts of the day, often set to well-known courtly tunes.

The Shinto vocal music performed in the palace or in a large temple falls into two types, songs of praise or petition for aid (*torimono*) and songs to entertain the gods (*saibari*). These songs are sung by a unison chorus usually accompanied by a *hichiriki*, a *kagurabue* flute, a *sho*, and a six-stringed board zither (*wagon*) that resembles the Korean *kayagum* (Figure 66). The leader may mark the start and finish of a piece or its verses with the sound of a pair of long thin *shakubyoshi* clappers (see the *pak* of Korean Confucian music, p. 212). Shinto music and dance for the palace is called *mi-kagura*, that for the large shrines *o-kagura;* the local shrine events mentioned earlier are *sato-kagura*. Together, they reflect an ancient agricultural sense of time that remains as fundamental in modern Japan as it does for most of the West.

The vocal and instrumental traditions of Japanese ancient music have all been preserved not in scores but in part books. In instrumental music these combine fingering indications with mnemonics that (unlike Western and Indian systems) do not necessarily represent pitches in a scale but, rather, help the reader recall the melody with its contour and ornamental nuances. Rhythmic aspects of the melody are not indicated, although beside each column of

[33] See Example 7–6 or listen to its book cassette track 31 and 32.

PLATE XXIX. Japanese chordophones

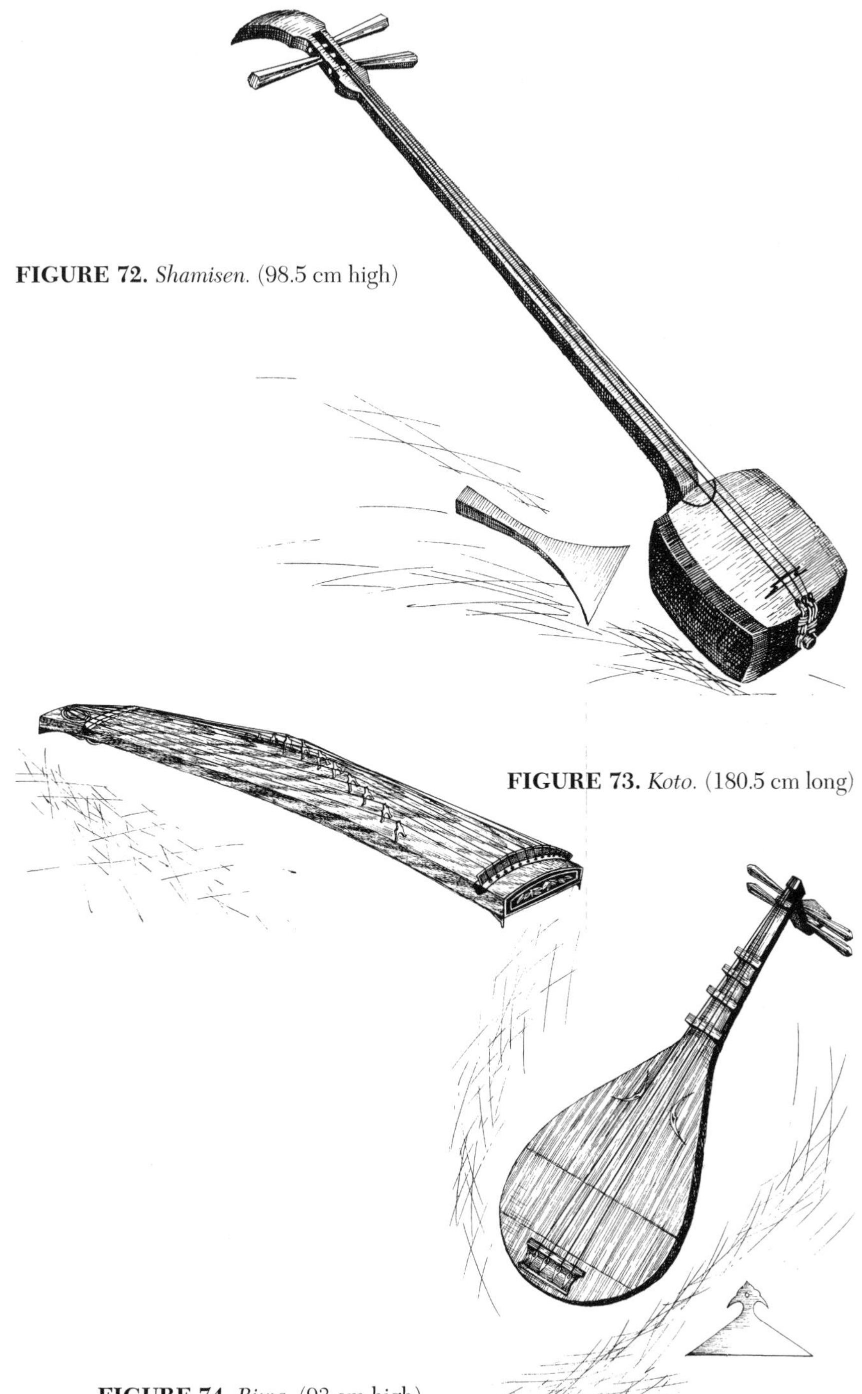

FIGURE 72. *Shamisen.* (98.5 cm high)

FIGURE 73. *Koto.* (180.5 cm long)

FIGURE 74. *Biwa.* (93 cm high)

notation dots appear; these correspond to the moments when each time-marking instrument plays. Although pieces are arranged in such books according to their *cho,* the various pitches available from a single fingering on the main melodic instruments make it difficult to determine what the actual tune is. Originally this was no problem, since the music was first taught orally—by singing the mnemonics while beating out the rhythmic divisions—and then learned on the instrument. Whatever the relation of modern practice may be to the original product, however, Japanese *gagaku* is still one of the rarest and oldest orchestral musics in the world.

We have intimated that many of the principles found in these ancient musics are basic to Japanese music in general. One of these is the concept of getting the maximum effect from a deliberately restricted amount of material. For example, the many techniques possible on various *gagaku* instruments are generally not all exploited. Rather, there is a concentration on only a few basic sounds in order to enhance their effectiveness. At the same time, one can observe in *gagaku* performance the Japanese principle that instruments are to be played in a graceful manner, so that the music provides an aesthetically pleasing sight as well as sound.

Both *gagaku* and Buddhist chanting make use of a common Japanese principle of *elastic* or *breath rhythm.* There are, of course, many steady, metronomic beats in Japanese music, but one also finds sections—like the opening of any *gagaku* piece (the *netori*)—in which the beat simply cannot be conducted. The melody moves from beat to beat in a rhythm more akin to that of a breath taken deeply, held for an instant, and then expelled. In ensembles, such a rhythm can only be coordinated when the performers listen to each other and feel the music together. This is the kind of attitude Westerners associate with chamber music, and much Japanese music has this chamber music quality regardless of the size of the ensemble. It also is chamberlike in the sense that the individual instrumental lines are designed to be heard separately, rather than merged as they are in the Western orchestral sound ideal.

We have noted—in the string parts of *gagaku* as well as in Buddhist music—the important principle in Japanese music of using stereotyped patterns that are aurally perceptible. This will become even more evident as we look at later theatrical traditions.

Early Japanese Narrative and Theatrical Traditions

During the twelfth and thirteenth centuries a tradition arose called *Heike biwa,* in which a famous war narration was sung to the accompaniment of a *biwa* lute. The music consisted of lines of poetry chanted to named, stereotyped melodies separated by pitch-giving notes or stereotyped interludes played on the lute. Many of the names of both the vocal and instrumental patterns were derived from Buddhist chant nomenclature. This style of narration became very popular and, although *Heike biwa* itself is rare today, its tradition is carried on in a similar if more flamboyant style by modern *biwa* and *shamisen* narrators. The *Satsuma biwa* shown in Figure 74 is only one of several styles of *biwa* used today, but the music of all tends to continue the tradition of alternating vocal and instrumental sections. In such a tradition, the notation need only show the text plus the name of the particular pattern to be played or sung. The individual performer must interpret these patterns according to the requirements of the particular piece, as well as those of the style of the specific guild of performers to which he or she belongs. This does not mean the performer improvises. As we mentioned earlier, in Japan there is variation but not improvisation. Whatever the version of a piece, it must be played as accurately as a Mozart sonata, despite the existence of other versions of the same composition.

Our earlier references to festivals and to dance materials in court imply that theatricals have been a part of Japanese music for a long time. Continental theatricals are believed to have been brought into Japan in 612 by a Korean musician, Mimashi. Throughout the subsequent centuries there are many records of street entertainments, folk festivals, and pantomime plays in Shinto shrines and Buddhist temples. Through a skillful combination of such materials, Kiyotsugu Kanami (1333–1384) and his son, Motokiyo Zeami (1363–1443), created a major theatrical genre that became known as *noh* (or *no*, "accomplishment"). *Noh* combines music, dance, poetry, design, and a Buddhist worldview in a manner that remains meaningful to this day. The music of *noh* consists of singing, known generally as *yokyoku* or *utai*, by the main actors or a unison chorus with or without instrumental accompaniment. In *noh* the term *hayashi* is used for an ensemble of four instruments: a flute (*nokan*), a shoulder drum (*ko tsuzumi*, Plate XXX, Figure 75), a side drum (*o tsuzumi*, Plate XXX, Figure 76), and a floor drum played with sticks (*taiko*, Plate XXX, Figure 77). The *taiko* is included only in some dance sections of a play.

The flute may mark off sections in a play or enhance a mood. It often is unrelated to the tonality of vocal parts. In dances accompanied by the *hayashi*, the flute uses sets of named, eight-beat melodic patterns.[34] Similarly, the music of all three drums consists of named patterns, usually in eight-beat units (*yatsubyoshi*). In dance accompaniment the patterns fall into conventional order so they can be anticipated and followed to predictable cadence points.[35] Similar stereotyped patterns appear in Western music in the form of harmony. For example, after a C major, F major, and G major chord, there is a strong possibility that the next chord will be a cadential C major chord (a tonic chord). Of course, other chords are possible—just as other rhythm patterns are possible in our Japanese example. The important point is that both systems involve sets of aurally identifiable, stereotyped patterns that tend to move in predictable

[34] For flute pattern explanations see William P. Malm, *Six Hidden Views of Japanese Music* (Berkeley: University of California Press, 1986), Chapter 3.

[35] These pattern progressions are studied in Malm, "The Rhythmic Orientation of Two Drums in the Japanese No Drama," and "An Introduction to Taiko Music in the Japanese No Drama," *Ethnomusicology*, 2/3 (1958), 4/2 (1960).

PLATE XXX. Japanese membranophones

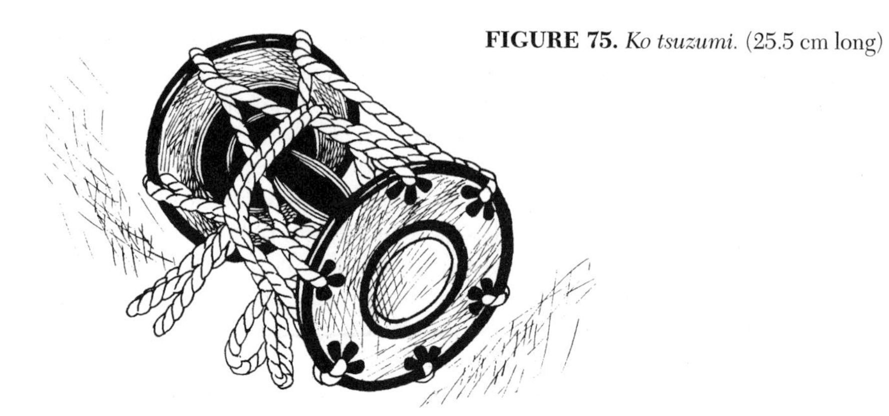

FIGURE 75. *Ko tsuzumi.* (25.5 cm long)

FIGURE 76. *O tsuzumi.* (28.4 cm long)

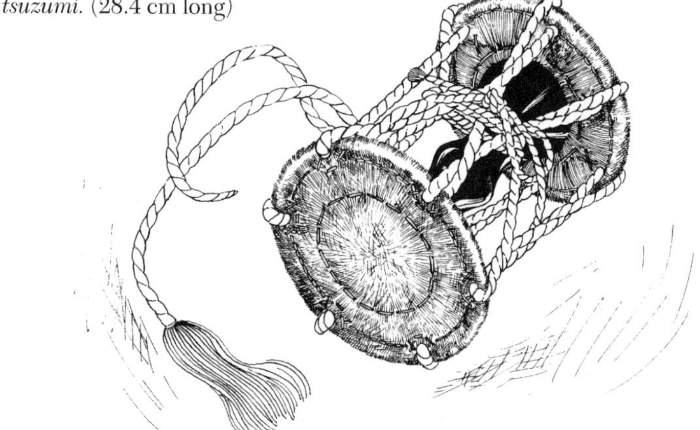

FIGURE 77. *Taiko.* (35.1 cm diameter)

succession so the forward motion of the music is enhanced. The only significant difference between the Western and the Japanese system is that one involves vertical stereotyped sonorities called chords whereas the other involves horizontal rhythmic patterns. Here is one answer to the lack of harmony in much non-Western music; it is not needed, for its forward-moving function is served by a different concept of rhythm. How many times in this survey have we seen similar "strange" uses of rhythm that put a third dimension into the music beyond those of melody and rhythm as they are understood in the West? The lack of the development of an involved concept of harmony in non-Western music may be because its functions had already been supplanted by special uses of rhythm. The Japanese *noh* drama certainly illustrates one such use very clearly.

The relation between the *tsuzumi* drum patterns and the sung text demonstrates yet another different approach to rhythm in *noh* music. The texts are influenced by the Japanese poetry convention of five- or seven-syllable units although other sizes are used. The music is influenced by a general use of the eight-beat units although other binary-length units are possible. Text can be sung with one syllable per beat *(onori)* or two per beat *(chunori),* but the most interesting and common unit is called *hiranori* in which twelve syllables (5 + 7 = 12) are placed in an eight-beat framework.[36] Specific, named drum patterns often guide the singer in the displacement of syllables within the eight beats. The determining factor is whether the music is text-oriented or music-oriented.

Example 7–11A shows the theoretical basic rhythm *(jibyoshi)* setting of a text of twelve syllables in the *hiranori* style. Note there are no syllables on beats 3 and 5. Such divisions relate to a fundamental *noh* drama tripartite structural concept that can be applied to all levels of a play. It is called *jo-ha-kyu:* the introduction, the scattering, and the rushing toward the end. The drum pattern *mitsuji* (three points) has a similar division when played alone, with accents on beats 3 and 5. However, Example 7–11B shows that, in a word-oriented performance, the beats are not equally spaced between the singing and the accompaniment, although beats 3 and 5 do match. Another approach to a rhythmic "sliding door" has occurred. In the last phrase of the example, the drums play the pattern *tsuzuke* (continuous) and the passage is more music-oriented, the two parts sharing all the same beats.

For Western listeners the most puzzling sounds in *noh* music are often the drummers' calls. It is possible they were originally teaching aids in drum lessons, although there are no historical data to support this theory. As used today, however, they have several truly musical functions. Since the principle of elastic rhythm is very prevalent in *noh,* drummers' calls are an important means of controlling and signaling the progression from one beat to another in a manner that all participants and listeners can understand. They also function as an aid in identifying aurally a named pattern, for the calls are specific for each

[36] See Richard Emmert, "Hiranori—A Unique Rhythm Form in Japanese No Music," in *Musical Voices of Asia,* ed. F. Koizumi and others (Tokyo: The Japan Foundation, 1980), 100–7.

EXAMPLE 7–11. Singing and drum patterns for text from the *noh* play "Hagoromo." Performed by Richard Emmert (vocal, Kita school), Umeno Noriyoshi (*ko tsuzumi*, Ko school), and Kama Mitsuo (*o tsuzumi*, Kadono school). Used by permission.[37] Book cassette, track 36.

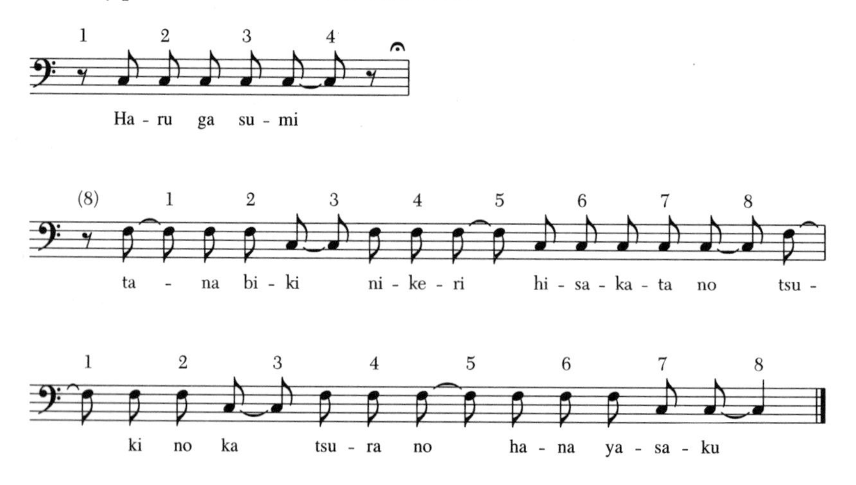

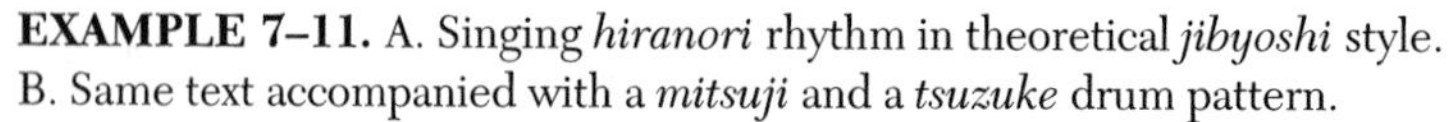

EXAMPLE 7–11. A. Singing *hiranori* rhythm in theoretical *jibyoshi* style. B. Same text accompanied with a *mitsuji* and a *tsuzuke* drum pattern.

[37] The texts say, "Mists of spring trailing through never-ending skies. Moontree laurel flowers blossom forth." The first line uses only four beats but traditional notation shows the four beats "taken out" (*tori*) of the eight-beat unit. The recording is pedagogical and the actual performance of this opening of the *kuse* section of the play differs.

pattern and often specific to the guild of the drummers who are performing it. Thus the particular arrangements of the drummers' calls and drum sounds in Example 7–11B are "correct" for the drum patterns shown as performed by members of one guild of drummers in the context of this one phrase of one *noh* play; the calls will never appear in quite the same manner in another pattern of a different name, although renditions of patterns seen in Example 7–11 may be the same or very similar when played by drummers from a different guild.

Although the melody of Example 7–11 uses the distance of a fourth, it can be said to be in the lyrical soft style (*yowagin*) of *noh* drama singing. The stronger style (*tsuyogin*) remains in the narrow range of a third. *Noh*-drama vocal music notation grew out of the Buddhist chant methods we mentioned earlier (p. 226), and drum and flute notations are specific to the instrument. Since there are such strong named rhythmic conventions, drum music publications often consist of only pattern names, rather like the continuo parts of European harpsichord accompaniment or the lead sheets of jazz pianists. With such a strong, published theoretical base, *noh* drama music has continued to flourish from subsequent Japanese eras ahead to the modern international theater world.

Music during Japan's Edo Period (1615–1868)

In Japan, as in the West, the major kinds of traditional music heard today arose in the period from the seventeenth through the nineteenth centuries. This is called the Edo or Tokugawa period in Japan because the Tokugawa clan controlled the country and moved the government to a new center called Edo, known today as Tokyo. It was during this period that Japan became isolated from outside contact and thus was able to develop its own artistic resources without extensive foreign influence. It was a period marked by the rise of a merchant class and an emphasis on city life. Music reacted to the needs of this new audience.

One of the first theatricals to flourish in the new society was the puppet theater (*bunraku*), which found its greatest audience in the business town of Osaka. The three-string plucked *samisen* (in the Tokyo dialect *shamisen*, Figure 72), adapted from the Ryukyuan *sanshin* in the sixteenth century, was used to accompany a singer-narrator. This music became known as *gidayu-bushi* after the name of its most famous singer, Gidayu Takemoto (1651–1714). It was one of many such *shamisen*-accompanied narratives, known generically as *joruri*, that flourished during the Edo period.

The musical style of *gidayu* developed from the previous *biwa* lute narratives with extensive use of stereotyped patterns and interludes. As these were connected with a theatrical art aimed at a bourgeois rather than a courtly audience, their style became more flamboyant and intricate. Specific melodic phrases took on dramaturgical meaning in much the way that emotions and situations could be portrayed in Western baroque music and in Wagnerian operas through the use of special tunes. As performed today, *gidayu* music has all the melodrama and pathos of Italian opera, although the narrator-singer (*tayu*) must be as great an actor as singer, since he (or in some concert performances, she) not only sings all the music and provides comments and narrations in the story but also speaks the dialogue for *all* the roles: masculine, feminine, hero, and villain.

The excerpt on book cassette, track 37, gives you some sense of the power and talent needed to perform *gidayu*.[38] In this scene from "Imoseyama," a princess is trying to contact her beloved across a river. The text is as follows:

Narrator: Her pain—all greater knowing he cannot hear.
Maid: How vexing! Things just won't go right. Hey! Look this way over here!
Narrator: Both maids wave widely, stirring Hinadori, who gets an idea.
Princess: That's it! Spoken words can't express my heart.
Narrator: Tender love flows through the deer-hair brush into a missive, strong as the stone she ties it to. With all her heart, she hurls the rock; tumbling, splashing, it falls into the rapids. It is caught in a whirlpool, carried away by rushing waves.
Princess: How irritating! No matter if my heart will fly to him, my arm hasn't the strength. Unrequited love. Doomed to wait—could I but become Princess Matsurasayo and turn to stone pining for my husband's return! As fruitless as Mount Hirefusuyama, which lay down and wept, tears bring no results.

The voice of a maid and the princess are clearly different and one can hear the stone drop in the river with a snap from the *shamisen*. More important, note the constant flow between speech (*kotoba*), *parlando* style (*ji iro*), and lyrical music (*ji*). This is the special art of *gidayu*.

Since the Edo period the basic human theatrical has been *kabuki*. Traditionally an all-male troupe (although it began as all-female), *kabuki* continues to please Japanese and foreign audiences with its combination of melodrama, stage effects, and colorful dancing. The musical accompaniment of these theatrical events are of three types: narrative music, onstage music, and offstage music.

Kabuki narrative (*joruri*) music is usually derived from the *gidayu* tradition we mentioned earlier in the puppet theater. In *kabuki* the performers (*chobo*) are usually placed downstage left in the puppet-theater manner.

[38] The source of the recording is the book cassette tape from a study and complete text translation of this scene by C. Andrew Gerstle, Kiyoshi Inobe, and William P. Malm, *Theater as Music* (Ann Arbor: University of Michigan Press, 1991). The entire scene is 112 minutes long.

Other *kabuki* narrative music may relate more to our next topic, onstage music.

Onstage (*debayashi*) ensembles in *kabuki* may be a mixture of genres or one, depending on the play and stage setting. The traditional dance accompaniment consists of the three-drums-and-flute *hayashi* group derived from the *noh* plus *shamisen* and singers. The major lyrical genre used in this manner is *nagauta*, the long songs.[39]

An excerpt from *nagauta* is seen in Example 7–12.[40] The drums may use *noh*-derived patterns, but they also employ new units created for *kabuki* dance accompaniment like the ones seen in this example. In *tsuzumi* music such patterns are categorized as *chiri-kara*, a term derived from the mnemonic with which they are learned. These patterns tend to support the rhythm of the *shamisen* line. The *taiko* is playing a named *kabuki* drum pattern (*wataribyoshi*). The *noh* flute follows the rhythm of this *taiko* pattern. Note that the *taiko*/flute unit seems to start on a different first beat than that of the *tsuzumi* and *shamisen*. This is yet another example of the sliding-door effect like that seen in Example 7–7.

A major tension-building device for most Japanese melodic instruments is the use of upper or lower "leading" tones around basic tone centers. It is evident in the *shamisen* line of Example 7–12B. The tone centers (E, F sharp, or B) do not appear at pauses. The tension does not resolve until measure 11. Another characteristic of *shamisen* music seen in Example 12B is the tendency to sing "off beat" or, perhaps more accurately, with a different first beat. Besides adding another sense of forward motion to the music through rhythmic tension, this style of singing places the syllables between the percussive sounds of the *shamisen* so the text can be understood.[41]

The form of *nagauta* is influenced by its text. Rather like Renaissance choral music, when the text mood or topic changes, the music follows suit. Thus the music is through composed—it is not based on the development of specific melodic themes but rather moves through sections of new music related to the words. The Western analogy ends here, for *nagauta* uses orchestrational conventions as well to distinguish sections. The flute player may change to a bamboo flute (*takebue*) in order to enhance a lyrical section or reflect a plebian rather than courtly setting. Drum patterns likewise may be chosen to

[39] The others commonly heard are *kiyomoto* and *tokiwazu*. Each genre has a different style of *shamisen* and voice quality.

[40] The piece was composed in 1841 by Kineya Rokuzaemon X (1800–1859). For a complete Western score of the piece see William P. Malm, *Nagauta: The Heart of Kabuki Music* (Tokyo: Tuttle, 1963; reprint Greenwood Press, 1982).

[41] The same style can be seen in the *kabuki* song in Example 7–6D. Notated in a common meter it looks like a mass of syncopation although the sound is more fluid. It is notated in that Western manner in William P. Malm, *Nagauta: The Heart of Kabuki Music* (Tokyo: Tuttle, 1963), 305.

EXAMPLE 7–12. Excerpts from the *nagauta* piece. "Goro Tokimune"[42] (Victor Cassette VCK-30179, side 2, track 3. Book cassette, track 38.) Used by permission.

[42] Example A is the *michiyuki* entrance section and B is the lyric *kudoki.* For further details see Malm, *Nagauta.* The text of 12B says, "He is easily ensnared by the affairs of the pleasure quarters. A letter comes from someone." The sudden short modulation in the next passage relates to his rude reply.

EXAMPLE 7–12. *(continued)*

reflect the context of a text (a festival, a geisha house, a temple).[43] Of course, another factor in form is that this music functions as dance accompaniment. Example 7–12A is purely instrumental because it is entrance music for a dancer. When the singer begins, the offstage music enters in.

Behind a bamboo curtain on the stage-right flat of the scenery in *kabuki* productions is a small room for offstage (*geza*) music. The music's basic purpose is to provide mood, set scenes, and give musical clues as to action or location.[44] For example, behind the singer's entrance heard on the book cassette, track 38, after Example 12A, one hears a large drum and later a gong. The drum is playing a pattern called "the sound of rain" because the text says that even on rainy nights[45] and snowy days the lovers meet. The gong is often heard in night, winter, or secret meeting scenes so it is equally appropriate to the text.

The dotted rhythm of the *shamisen* part at the end of the excerpt imitates the drunken steps of the dancer for the word "sake." Other *geza* music

[43] For specific examples see William P. Malm, "Four Seasons of the Old Mountain Women," *Journal of the American Musicological Society*, 31/1 (1978), 81–117.

[44] For specific examples see Chapter 3 of James Brandon, D. Shively, and W. Malm, *Studies in Kabuki* (Honolulu: University of Hawaii Press, 1978).

[45] The dancer enters with an umbrella and high wooden rain shoes.

functions are heard in the book cassette, track 32, recording of Example 7–6D; the horse-pack song implies the scene is on the Tokaido road and the drums, playing the "sound of the waves" pattern, tell you that you are near the sea. A different pattern would have placed you in the mountains. In *geza* music, singers, *shamisen*, flutes, drums, and a battery of special gongs and bells are used singly and in combination. They blend with onstage ensembles (*debayashi*) to provide a varicolored accompaniment for yet another of the Orient's many enjoyable theatricals.

Not all the music of the Edo period is theatrical. In addition to many kinds of intimate *shamisen*-vocal forms, there developed other vocal instrumental traditions, such as those using the 13-string *koto* (Figure 73). Movable bridges allow for several different tunings; three picks attached to fingers of the right hand and varying pressures on the strings with the left hand provide a variety of timbres and pitches. While much *koto* music is vocal, there is an important genre of variation solos (*danmono*) that is very popular. In addition, the *koto* may be combined with a singer, a *shamisen*, and a five-hole end-blown flute (*shakuhachi*)[46] to form chamber music (*sankyoku*) ensemble. The particularly soft sound of the *shamisen* in this ensemble is caused by the use of a heavy bridge, a thin plectrum, and strings of a special weight. Actually, each kind of *shamisen* music requires an instrument of different size as well as different accessories in order to produce a particular tone color. The *shakuhachi* also comes in various sizes; however, the choice of length is determined not by tone color but by the tuning of the other instruments in the ensemble, since Japanese music is played heterophonically. The *shakuhachi* is best heard when performing its solo literature, for a good player can produce a beautiful variety of tone colors and ornaments on this deceptively simple-looking bamboo tube.

Edo-period music is usually not anonymous. The composers of most basic *koto* pieces (*honkyoku*) are known, as are writers of a continuing line of new compositions. In theater music the date, location, and players of first performances also can be identified. In the puppet theater the playwrights and musicians were equally famous. Programs of *kabuki* or classical (*buyo*) dance recitals or music concerts can list composers, but in the Western sense the term is misleading. In *kabuki* productions, actors and playwrights will contact the head *shamisen* and singer, who will work in conjunction with a poet to create a dance piece to which the director of the *hayashi* and offstage music will add percussion and flute materials. The result is a communal composition, so well integrated it is hard for a Westerner to think of it as not being the work of one mind.

[46] Instead of the *shakuhachi*, a three-stringed bowed *kokyu* fiddle may be used. Its origin may be more Portuguese than East Asian. See David Waterhouse, "An Early Illustration of the Four-Stringed Kokyu, with a Disquisition on the History of Japan's Only Bowed Musical Instrument," *Oriental Art*, 16/1 (1970), 162–68.

In the early nineteenth century the popularity of theater music led to the growth of *shamisen* compositions not meant to accompany dance.[47] The creation of this music concert tradition fed well into needs of the century ahead.

Music in Modern Japan

The modernization of Japan, begun in 1868 under the Emperor Meiji, has drawn special interest from the West because of the swiftness with which it proceeded. Actually, Western materials (including music) were known in Japan as early as the sixteenth century through merchants and Catholic missionaries,[48] but the suppression of Christianity and foreign trade in the Edo period left only one trade center as a source of what became known as "Dutch learning." In the Meiji era (1868–1912), Western music developed in Japan primarily through two channels, the military and the educational. Through them Western music was introduced, at first not out of any special interest in the music itself but rather as part of a desire to reproduce various foreign systems accurately. Thus bands were formed because they were included in the standard table of organization for military services; and music was made part of the newly formed public schools because it was included in the foreign models. Foreigners were brought to Japan as instructors, among them Luther Whiting Mason (1828–1896) who, along with Shuji Izawa (1851–1917), helped found a music teachers' college and form a curriculum for the public schools that was to affect Japanese musical life for generations. Their original intent was to combine the best of East and West, and both Western and Japanese instruments were taught at the college; similarly, songbooks for schools tried to include the best of the Boston public school tradition plus harmonized Japanese tunes. Unfortunately, only the Western-style instrumentalists from the college went into public school teaching, the Japanese-style players returning to their own traditional world. At the same time, the children found the new military songs composed for the Chinese and Russian confrontations to be of greater interest than the old Japanese tunes. To capture the children's interest, many of these songs were reworked with suitable words. The net result of these various factors was that a child in school heard only Western instruments, Western children's songs, or heavily Westernized Japanese military-style music. Indeed, not until the late 1950s was Japanese traditional music to be found on music appreciation records issued for public school use, and Japanese music as part of music education was not required until the 1990s. Today the songs of Stephen Foster can be claimed as part of the Japanese musical tradition, since they have been sung by at least three generations.

[47] See William P. Malm, "The Rise of Concert Shamisen Music in Nineteenth Century Japan," in *Recovering the Orient,* ed. Andrew Gerstle (London: Harwood Academic Press, 1994).

[48] A survey of the first Christian music in Japan is found in Eta Harich-Schneider, *A History of Japanese Music* (London: Oxford University Press, 1972), Chapter 14.

Another interesting result of Japan's American-based public school music system has been that young people are trained to sing in harmonized choruses, unlike the monophonic style of traditional music. Various political and religious groups have taken advantage of this training and have organized workers, students, or co-religionists into choral societies.[49] These have proven to be very useful in recruiting new members as well as in unifying large bodies of people in public demonstrations.

You probably will assume—correctly—that throughout its history Japan, like other parts of the world, has always had some form of popular music. Thus the so-called *hayari uta* of the Edo period became the *ryukoka* of the Meiji era simply by giving a different reading to the characters used for the term "popular" and changing the character for "song": (流 行 歌 became 流 行 唄). In some ways, popular music of the early modernization period was more creative than its military, educational, and religious competitors because it had no firm dogma. Its major rule was (and probably always will be) that it had to sell. Thus bugle songs *(rappa-bushi)* were all the rage during the time of military events in the Meiji era; patter songs *(oppekepe-bushi)* in music halls became well-known outlets for commentary on Japanese developments and problems.[50] During the subsequent years in Japanese popular music exhibited the characteristics of the genre we noted before under the TIPEE acronym (see Chapter 3, p. 96). With the burgeoning Japanese mass communication industry, the computerized pop-song-minus-one singing (*karaoke*) became the fad of the 1990s.

If we turn our attention to "serious" music in Japan over the past 100 years, we see that traditional Japanese music (*hogaku*) and Western music (*yogaku*) have continued to develop, but along basically separate if parallel lines. We discuss traditional music first.

During the Meiji restoration, the monopolies of Japanese guilds were declared illegal, and traditional musicians thus lost control over an important source of income. One positive result of this action, along with the growth of concerts we mentioned earlier, was the increase in music lessons for amateurs and therefore an increase in appreciation and support for traditional music. Many traditional composers naturally became concerned with and curious about the strange sounds of Western music. From a Japanese standpoint it seemed that Western music, when first heard, differed from indigenous idioms in the following ways: It used "exotic" tone systems (the major and minor); it preferred large ensembles; it was louder; it seemed based on the idea that playing faster meant playing better; and it was thicker, its melodies clouded by chords, although undernourished rhythmically. On the basis of these insights "new" traditional music (*shin-hogaku*) was attempted. The establishment of

[49] See William P. Malm, "A Century of Proletarian Music in Japan," *The Journal of Musicological Research*, 6/3 (1986), 185–206.

[50] Examples are found in the author's "The Modern Music of the Meiji Era," Chapter 7 of *Modernization and Japan in the Humanities*, ed. D. Shively (Princeton: Princeton University Press, 1971). See also his "Layers of Modern Music and Japan," *Asian Music*, 4/2 (1973).

orchestras of traditional instruments was matched by new works with virtuoso parts and much plunking of chords. Perhaps the most successful of all such compositions were those of a *koto* musician, Michio Miyagi (1894–1956) of the Ikuta guild. His modern pieces, written before World War II, are now part of the standard repertoire.

In the field of Western classical music in Japan we find several pioneers who had no experience in Japanese traditional music at all and who sought their training abroad, particularly in Germany. Among them is Koscak (né Kosaku) Yamada (1886–1965), who founded Japan's first major orchestra and opera organizations and who composed many works in a European style, usually based on Japanese ideas. For example, his 1940 opera *The Black Ships* (*Kurobune*), which deals with the first visit of the American fleet to Japan in 1853,[51] is composed in a style reminiscent of Richard Wagner's *The Flying Dutchman* and the late operas of Giacomo Puccini. In general, we find interesting parallels between the solutions by composers in Japan and those in developing countries (and in America in the 1930s–1940s) to the problems of using national materials in Western-style concert idioms. Regional folk songs and folktales are the standard source for such attempts.[52]

Japan's international reputation is even greater for the efficiency with which it has produced both performers of Western music and, in addition, instruments and a teaching-method industry. The last is exemplified by Shinichi Suzuki (b. 1898), whose violin method combines some elements of the Japanese traditional rote-learning system with a business organizational acumen.

The many efforts by traditional and Westernized Japanese musicians and by foreign composers of "Oriental" taste are sometimes quite pleasant, but they seldom accomplish any real meeting of East and West. The problem is not any lack of talent; rather it has been that no composer has really understood both musics on an equally deep level. It was not until the second half of the twentieth century that the "anational," transcendental idioms of the times—and talent along with supranational understanding—could be combined to provide musical abstractions that were international in appeal but still evocative of indigenous music. In Japan of the 1990s, the most frequently successful composer in this manner seems to be Toru Takemitsu (b. 1930).

It should be obvious from our discussion that almost any kind of music is available in Japan today. In the modern world of mass communications, this is somewhat true for any part of the world if one is willing to find the right radio band or search out the special music store. Under the international pressure of a unicultural world, Japanese youth has joined that of other countries in seeking national roots, even though it may accompany its folk songs with guitar and accordion rather than *shamisen*. We mentioned a late-twentieth-century fad for

[51] A very different approach to the same topic was made in America in 1976 in a musical titled *Pacific Overtures*.

[52] The record *Tokyo: 1918–1942* (Victor VX-116–8) provides an excellent selection of such materials.

EXAMPLE 7–13. Ainu canonic singing from the sound sheet in *Ainu Dento Ongaku,* ed. Y. Tanimoto (Tokyo: NHK, 1965). Transcription and sound used by permission.[53]

Japanese folk drummers that influenced youth both nationally and internationally. Other classical Japanese genres such as *koto* or *shakuhachi* music are also found worldwide. It seems that we can listen to the best of several musical traditions both in and out of Japan. After all, we can hear Beethoven just as often in Tokyo.

THE NORTHERN ISLANDS AND BEYOND

On Hokkaido, Japan's most northerly island, and the Russian-occupied Shakalins beyond that, we find the remnants of several ethnic groups quite unrelated to the general East Asiatic traditions. The best known of these are the Ainu, a Caucasoid group, possibly with some racial affinity to the Australian aborigines. Much of the Ainu's music seems equally remote from its surroundings. The Ainu two- to five-string *tonkori* plucked zither, for example, has few parallels outside of Africa; we have not mentioned the canonic style of singing seen in Example 7–13 since we left Melanesia. Although none of these facts necessarily has any historical connections, some things do imply more logical and possible relations between the Ainu and other parts of the world. Ainu shamanism and, more specifically, its bear cult have relatives in Korea and in many cultures of North Asia.[54] The Ainu jaws harp (*mukkuri*), which is sounded by jerking a string as seen in Plate II, Figure 3, from Papua New Guinea, also is common in Siberia.[55] Similarly, we are tempted to compare the quavering, half-spoken voice quality and short iterative melodies of Ainu narratives (*yukar*) with style heard in Siberia and among the Lapps of Sweden. More intriguing and tempting in terms of comparative musicology is the Ainu *rekkukara,* a quick, iterative sound created by two women who use each other's mouths for resonance (book cassette track 40). Is it music or play? The book

[53] The text is of a woman concerned for the safety of her husband.

[54] The Jungian approach of Joseph Campbell would trace it all the way to prehistoric Europe in his *The Masks of God* (New York: Viking, 1954), 341–43.

[55] The Osaka Museum of Ethnology now has a newsletter devoted exclusively to jaws harp research.

cassette track 40 contains examples of similar sounds from the Chukchee (Cheknyk) in Siberia and from Canadian children panting into oil drums.[56] For the Inuits of northern Canada such sounds are considered throat games;[57] an interweaving of shared sounds rather like their cats cradle two person string figures. Intellectually we have returned to the definition of music question discussed in Chapter 1. Sonically we have discovered another interesting non-Western experience.

Research has only just begun; but it would seem that we could learn much about possible human cultural relations or about ecology and culture if we studied *circumboreal* music, that is, music produced by cultures that live around the arctic world in regions that view most closely the aurora borealis. Plate XXXI, Figure 78, shows a style of performance from the North American area of that region. The type of pan drum shown is often made of bone and sealskin because these are basic raw materials in the circumboreal world.[58] Of greater cultural interest is the position in which the drum is used. If one traverses the circumboreal region from Alaska, Canada, and Greenland to Siberia other positions will, of course, be found, but this "backward" stroke on the drum is in the majority. The way in which the drum is held and struck from the "outside" is the opposite of the method that most Euro-Americans would use "naturally." It begins to make sense only when we note that the drummer is also singing into the face of the drum. This enhances the drummer's tone in an acoustical world often muffled by snow and ice blocks or animal skins.

Slowly but surely we begin to find in the seemingly barren tundra world (as in other areas we have surveyed) a logical (if different) system of music enriching human life. The circumboreal chants themselves, with their short texts surrounded by meaningless syllables, may seem "primitive" outside their cultural context. To correct this error in understanding, we must place the chants in a world where survival depends on sensitivity to minute differences (for example, in one dialect there are a dozen words for the various kinds of snow) and a patient view of time. Only then can we realize that the Inuit with their drums in Figure 78 may be communicating with their audience as powerfully as Mozart and his symphony or Art Tatum and his jazz piano do with theirs. And all three musicians would be evaluated as critically by their listeners as the *dijeridu* player in Figure 1. Our first drawing, from Australia, along with the last one, from Alaska, have been used to enclose the text of this book partly as symbols of the fact that a musical event is most meaningful when it is heard in its own cultural context. Because music is *not* an international language, such meaning and functionality can seldom be enjoyed more than vicariously by an outsider. If this were not true, lecturers would not have to explain Beethoven to

[56] The example is from Smithsonian/Folkways *Eskimo songs from Hudson Bay and Alaska* (4444). Use by permission.

[57] Listen to *Inuit Games and Songs* (Phillips 6586 036).

[58] Other terms are *circumpolar* and *circumarctic*, but the word *circumboreal* seems to best represent the geographical area where humans live.

PLATE XXXI. Arctic membranophones

FIGURE 78. Inuit pan drums.

modern Western music lovers, nor would uninformed persons speak of the "tuneless ditties of the natives." Fortunately, music *does* seem to be a universal *need.* Thus there has been much to study and appreciate musically in our journey from Australia to the myriad cultures of Asia and finally across the northern frontiers of human society.

BIBLIOGRAPHICAL AND AUDIOVISUAL NOTES

Korea

Bang-Song Song's *Korean Music* (Providence: Asian Music Publications, 1971) is an annotated bibliography of 1,319 items, mostly in Asian languages. A supplement is found along with English research articles in the Korean issue of *Asian Music,* 9/2 (1978). Song's *Source Readings in Korean Music* (Seoul: KNC. for UNESCO, 1980) is in English, as is his *The Sanjo Tradition of Korean Komungo Music* (Seoul: KNC for UNESCO, 1986). Lee Hye-ku's *Topics in Korean Music* (Seoul: Korean Musicological Society, 1967) has English summaries. A good general source is *Survey of Korean Arts: Traditional Music* (Seoul: National Academy of Arts, 1973). *Kagok* (Providence: Asian Music Publications, 1972) by Coralie Rockwell studies classical vocal music, and Jonathan Condit's *Music of the Korean Renaissance* (Cambridge: Cambridge University Press, 1984) contains vocal music transcribed with text into Western notation. Robert Provine has specialized in historical studies as well as drum music. His definitive essays on Korean music is in *The Grove Handbook of World Music* (London: Macmillan, 1994).

The Korean Traditional Performing Arts Centre has produced eleven cassettes of traditional music since 1985. The Korean Broadcasting Corporation (KBC) and the Korean Cultural Service (New York) have brought out other excellent large sets. Lyrichord has *Korean Social and Folk Music* (LLST 7211) and *Korean Court Music* (LLST 7206). The UNESCO series includes *Korean Music* (6586 011). Nonesuch has *Pansori* (H-72049) and *Samul-Norii: Drums and Voices of Korea* (72093-1). King Records World Music Library includes two Korean CDs, KICC 5144 and 5163, and Okinawa, 2025. Jan LaRue has published two Okinawan music studies, "Native Music on Okinawa," *Musical Quarterly,* 32 (April, 1946) and "Okinawan Notation System," *Journal of the American Musicological Society* (Spring, 1951). Music and dance are mentioned in Douglas Haring's *Okinawan Customs: Yesterday and Today* (Tokyo: C. Tuttle Co., 1969). Several unpublished studies on Okinawan music or dance can be found in the University Microfilm Library.

Japan

An early general introduction to Japanese music was Francis T. Piggott, *The Music and Musical Instruments of Japan* (1909; reprint, New York: Johnson Reprints, 1971). Later was William P. Malm, *Japanese Music and Musical Instruments* (Tokyo: Tuttle, 1959); *Practical Approaches to Japanese Music* (1965), reproduced in Kay Kaufmann Shelemay, ed., *The Garland Library of Readings in Ethnomusicology* (New York: Garland, 1990), Volume 2; and "Interlude" in *Six Hidden Views of Japanese Music* (Berkeley: University of California Press, 1986). Genichi Tsuge edited *Japanese Music: An Annotated Bibliography* (New York: Garland, 1986). Eta Harich-Schneider's *A History of Japanese Music* (London: Oxford, 1972) is an excellent source for Buddhist and court music studies. A fine court orchestra study is Robert Garfias, *The Music of a Thousand Autumns* (Berkeley: University of California Press, 1975), and vocal music is considered in Elizabeth Markham's *Saibara* (New York: Cambridge University Press, 1983).

The *Musica Asiatica* monograph series (Cambridge: Cambridge University Press, 1980–) contains major studies of old Japanese and Korean music notation in relation to mainland East Asia.

An interesting general book on *noh* is Kunio Komparu, *The Noh Theater* (Tokyo: Weatherhill, 1983). Richard Emmert has written the most musical studies, such as "The Maigoto of No," *Yearbook for Traditional Music,* Vol. 1. 15 (1983). He and Monica Bethe produced the most musical *noh* text translations (Tokyo, National Noh Theatre, 1992–). Monica Bethe and Karen Brazell produced excellent books on *noh* along with videotapes in East Asia Papers nos. 19 and 29, 3 vols. (Ithaca: Cornell China-Japan Program, 1978–82). Mario Yokomichi's valuable work has been translated by Frank Hoff and Willi Flindt in *The Life Structure of Noh* (Tokyo: Nogaku shorin, n.d.). A French approach is seen in Akira Tamba, *The Musical Structure of No* (Tokyo: Tokai University Press, 1974). See also James Crump and W. Malm, eds., *Chinese and Japanese Music-Drama* (Ann Arbor: Michigan Papers in Chinese Studies, 1975), no. 19.

Koto studies include Willem Adriaansz, *The Danmono of Japanese Koto Music* (Berkeley: University of California Press, 1973), and Bonnie Wade, *Tegotomono* (London: Greenwood Press, 1976). Excellent text translations are found in Gen'ichi Tsuge, *Anthology of Sokyoku and Jiuta Song Texts* (Tokyo: Academia Music, 1983). The Tokyo Ongaku Company started an *Encyclopedia of Musical Instruments* series with *Shakuachi,* Ko Tanimura, ed. (Tokyo: Ongakusha, 1990). Other *shakuhachi* studies are Donald Berger in *Asian Music,* 1/2 (1969) and Elliot Weisgarber, *Ethnomusicology,* 12/3 (1968). See also Andrea Gutzwiller, *Die Shakuhachi der Kinko-Schule* (Kassel: Barenreiter, 1983). For *kabuki* materials see James Brandon, William Malm, and Donald Shively's *Studies in Kabuki* (Honolulu: University of Hawaii Press, 1978). Bunraku music is part of *Theater as Music* by C.A. Gerstle, K. Inobe, and W. Malm (Ann Arbor: Center for Japanese Studies, 1990).

Japan has produced impressive sets of recordings and videotapes concerning music and theater but usually without English text or romanization of titles. For example, Nippon Victor has twelve CDs, *Taikei nihon no dento ongaku* ("An Outline of Traditional Japanese Music," KCDK-1110–), which contains every major genre as well as a separate series of videotapes (Victor PVTK-1013). Another video series is *Nihon koten geino taikei* ("A Japanese Classical Theatricals Outline," Victor VTMV-121). Like the previous series, it is totally without romanization as is a fourteen-volume video set, *Nihon rekishi to geino* ("Japanese History and Theatricals" [Tokyo: Heibonsha, 1990–92]). The twelve-volume set of LPs

1,000 Years of Classical Japanese Music (Tokyo: Kodansha, 1982) had separate English-language books in each album but is out of print. Shigeo Kishibe's *Traditional Japanese Music* (Victor JL 52-54) may still be available. The Japan Society in New York carries NHK films on music or theater, some of which have English narration. The National Theater in Tokyo sells an English-language videotape, *The Tradition of Performing Arts in Japan* (VHS NTSC), and the University of Oklahoma Early Music Series has four videotapes in English on Japanese music (*gagaku, gidayu, nagauta,* and Shinto music). The UNESCO record series includes *Japan* (BM 30 L 2011-2016), *O-Suwa Daiko Japanese Drums* (65586 029), and *Shomyo-Buddhist Ceremony* (6586-021). Modern drumming is *Heartbeat Drumming in Japan* (Sheffield Lab CD-Kodo). Lyrichord has *Japanese Koto Music* (LL 131), and Nonesuch, *The Koto Music of Japan* (72005) plus *Shakuhachi* (72076-1) and *A Bell Ringing in the Empty Sky* (*shakuhachi* H-720225-4). The King Records CD World Music Library contains Japanese folk and art music with English titles in the KICD 2000–2030 series.

Circumboreal

Circumboreal comparisons occur in Thomas Johnston's article on Alaskan dance in *Dance Research Journal* (CORD), 7/2 (1975). Beverly Cavanagh's annotated bibliography on Eskimo music is in *Ethnomusicology,* 16/3 (1972). An Inuit recording is *Inuit Games and Songs* (Philips 6586 036) and for other groups there are Smithsonian/Folkways, *Eskimo Songs from Alaska* (4069) and *The Eskimo of Hudson Bay and Alaska* (4444).

A SONIC GLOSSARY INDEX FOR CHAPTER 7

Korean
(Speaker: H.K. Chae)

Japanese plus Okinawan and Ainu terms
(Speaker: Obata, Yuri)

EPILOGUE

In a survey that covers such a vast number of musical cultures for pedagogical purposes, materials have had to be categorized and dealt with as separate units. As you read these sections, keep in mind the ever-present flow of sounds and aesthetics within and between musics, particularly in this modern mass communication world.[1] Still it is appropriate that we make some attempt at generalizations. The search for musical categorizations can begin by turning to literate societies where specific theoretical explanations are found for many tonal and compositional principles. These principles cluster around three of the four major written music theory systems of the modern world: the Arab-Persian, Indian, and Chinese. The fourth, the European, shares with the Near Eastern traditions certain historical roots in the Greco-Roman world. National music systems such as those of, for example, Uzbekistan, Japan, Sri Lanka, and the United States can be considered as satellite variations on the "big four." A fifth large unit may be the knobbed-gong culture of Southeast Asia, since it represents distinctive musical styles and instruments, although it did not possess

[1] A handsome discussion of the concepts of musical subculture, interculture, and superculture in a Euro-American context is found in Mark Slobin, "Micromusics of the West," *Ethnomusicology*, 36/1 (1992).

extensive theoretical and historical written materials before the twentieth century. (Its early influences from the Buddhist, Hindu, and Muslim traditions also complicate the picture.)

Over the centuries, conflicting approaches to music theory can be found in literate cultures as well as in the later interpretations of older documents. The general opinion is that three of the four large music cultures base their tone systems on the divisive principle, whereas the Chinese refer most often to an overblown cycle of fifths.

On the basis of surviving sources from the four traditions, the Chinese and Indian systems contain more documentation concerning the ethical or extramusical implications of music. Such implications, of course, exist in the Arab-Persian and European systems and can be traced back not only to Greco-Roman roots but also to ancient Assyrian-Egyptian concepts. All four living traditions are closed theoretical systems; that is, they are complete in themselves and offer a thoroughly logical explanation of the particular characteristics of the music for which they were created. We have noted equally logical explanations of music in many non-literate cultures in which regional environments contribute to the terminology of such intellectual insights. Throughout this book it has emphasized that an appreciation of these logical but different systems is basic to an understanding of art music as a worldwide phenomenon.

Form seems to follow function in music as well as in architecture, as, for example, we have seen in the various religious musics studied. To attach extramusical values to specific instruments and elements of a tonal system is also a common tendency, and one important to the carriers of the culture that determined these values. One possible tool for those wishing to make comparative studies is musical cartography, in which maps are made of phenomena such as the locations of canonic singing, a gong culture, or pitch-center preferences, or of the presence of a given type of musical instrument such as the *rebab* spike fiddle.[2] Some of these studies give us historical information about such matters as the spread of Islam, whereas others may indicate more general technological or physical similarities in conditions—for instance, the prevalence of bamboo or bronze instruments or the ecology of arctic regions.

If we turn now to view the multitudinous variety of musics mentioned in this survey plus the equally large number from other parts of the world, a fundamental question arises: Are there any universal principles in music? Speaking always in the broadest terms, a few can be suggested. There does seem to be a basic need for musical tension and release, with all their melodic or rhythmic implications. Equally widespread are a need to mark off temporal lengths of music with distinct cadence sound, a tendency to find a tonal orientation or center in melodic music, an interest in creating a sense of forward progression by melodic, harmonic, or rhythmic conventions, and a principle of unity along

[2] Examples of such maps are seen in *The Historical Atlas of Music,* ed. Paul Collaer and Albert Linden (Cleveland: World Publishing Company, 1968). See also the many musical maps in *Cultural Atlas of Islam,* ed. Ismaeil and Lois Al-Faruqi (New York: Macmillan, 1986).

with variety. Such things are necessary if music is to be perceived as moving logically and inexorably in a time continuum toward a recognizable ending. The use of some semiredundant patterns and progressions allows knowledgeable listeners to engage in prediction and anticipation (which is another way of saying they are really participating in or listening to the music).[3]

There are some musics in highly spiritual or functional situations and in parts of contemporary Western society that do not consider the generalizations stated here as logical necessities. Their composers are sometimes able to create viable sonic events that seem to lie outside the neat concepts of the equally logical but different systems on which most of this book is based. Ethnomusicologically speaking, however, they also fall within our generalizations. The logic of their "alogic" is found in their relation to the specific worldview or function in which such sonic events occur. Their "value" is likewise seen in a cultural context. Thus an answer to such a question as "Is it good music?" can only be made after a reply is given to yet a further question—"Good for what?" An instrumental variation piece played by a professional musician on the Korean *kayagum* zither or on a Burmese harp and a song about water buffalo herds sung by a blind street musician playing a monochord in a Thailand village market are, in this sense, incomparable. They can really be evaluated best by members of the society that inspired them. They are of potentially equal value for a foreign listener only to the degree that he or she can understand their original cultural context, or, perhaps, relate them to some aspect of one's own cultural or personal aesthetics.

Music is obviously as much a part of culture as a hoe or a potsherd. More than some aspects of culture, however, it has the ability to be emotionally moving and aesthetically pleasing. We have tried to show that when carriers of a given culture become aware subliminally or consciously of the specific ways in which "their" music moves them, through some of the principles listed here, culture carriers begin to anticipate the events of a given piece. With this anticipation comes aesthetic pleasure. On occasions we have been able to give clues as to what to listen for in a given music, so you might enjoy such musical experiences as well. However, our knowledge of world music is still rather narrow, and in many cases we can offer only the exotic surfaces of non-Western music—the sensuous titillation of a recording with a strange label and curious sounds. Intellectually, our message remains the same: These sounds, whatever they seem to a given listener, are *music* to someone, and as music they contain an inner logic that can be understood and admired—but only if one is inclined to listen to them on their own terms. It is not necessary to enjoy the music of every land, although understanding and exposure may certainly broaden our musical tastes. What is necessary is that we recognize the value and tolerate the existence of these many systems of music.

[3] See further discussions of this principle in Leonard Meyer, *Emotion and Meaning in Music* (Chicago: Phoenix Press, 1956).

Hedonistically speaking, new musical pleasures may have been gained from our study. Intellectually, many curious new facts may have been learned. These gains, however, are for naught without a new or reinforced sense of respect for humans' musical inventiveness. The world is filled with logical but different systems in many other fields of human endeavor besides music. Perhaps a bit more understanding in music may contribute in a small way toward the great general need for better communication in other areas of international contact.

INDEX

Note: All non-Western musical terms are found in the index of the chapter to which they relate.